The **DISCOVERY** of the **SECRET** of **LaSalette**

RENÉ LAURENTIN & MICHEL CORTEVILLE

OFFICIAL ENGLISH TRANSLATION OF THE THEOTOKANS

The Discovery of the Secret of LaSalette

Copyright © 2024 Mary K. Farran ("Sister Anne of Yahweh"), Holy Water Books

ISBN-13 (paperback): 978-1-950782-64-2
ISBN-13 (ebook): 978-1-950782-65-9

All rights reserved. Holy Water Books (Publisher)

Cover design by Holy Water Books

No part of this book may be reproduced, or stored in a retrieval system, or transmitted in any form or by any means, electronic, mechanical, photocopying, recording, or otherwise, without the express written permission of the author(s) and/or editor(s).

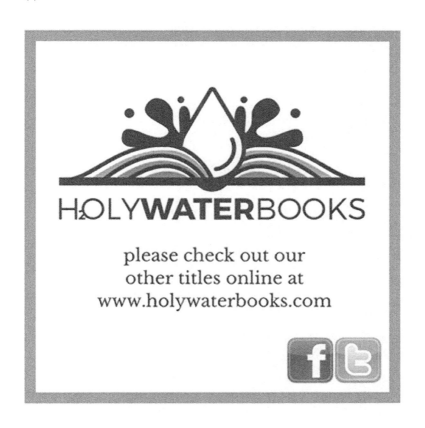

TO THE READERS OF THIS FIRST ENGLISH EDITION

Theotokans are pleased to offer you this English translation of the original French book published by Fayard (Paris 2002) under the title *Découverte du la secret a La Salette*. We offer very special thanks to Mary Muller, a trilingual Dutchwoman who did the first phase. Since English is her third language, we promised that we would refine her grammar, which was actually quite good. Brian Murphy, PhD, and Chairman of God's Plan For Life, performed this editorial service. Using his knowledge of French, he was able to cross-check the English for accuracy, while making only minor changes to Mrs. Muller's English grammar. Mary Farran ["Sister Anne of Yahweh"] coordinated the information with other works on LaSalette and was able to clarify ecclesiastical and convent terminology. She was particularly interested in gathering information on the persons whom Melanie had encountered, either to assist her in her mission of making known "the Secret" or to inhibit her efforts. This English edition offers the reader a bonus over the French edition, in its more detailed Chronological Table. The Theotokans have done extensive research on the many 19th century personalities mentioned in the LaSalette saga. Readers are welcome to access their alphabetized synopses at https://houseofmaryomd.org

If you are a lifelong Catholic, there is no need to feel embarrassed if the Marian Apparition of LaSalette is unfamiliar. The initial Apparition captivated Europe in the 1840s, but the subsequent release of the "Secret," led to endless controversy. Very briefly, on September 19, 1846, two shepherds, ages 14 and 11, experienced a direct visitation by the Blessed Virgin Mary on the mountain of LaSalette in the Alps of southeast France. She spoke to them kindly but had words of severe warning about tribulations to come to France and Europe because of the sins and godlessness of the people. She asked that certain particularly dire warnings be kept Secret for twelve years. For the rest of their heroic lives the two "seers" gave abundant testimony of Mary's message at LaSalette. Their testimony is substantiated by its consistency, direct fulfillment of numerous prophetic elements, and the holy lives of the seers themselves.

The Secret of LaSalette has a long line of ardent supporters and writers. However, controversy was ignited due to lack of access to the official texts of the Secret related by the two seers. After the recent opening of the archives of the Holy Office [January 1998], Michel Corteville, author of a monumental thesis on the topic, discovered the Secrets and many other documents hidden in Rome and elsewhere. He continues his report here with Father René Laurentin, an eminent specialist in Marian Apparitions.

This book will address many aspects of the Secret of LaSalette: an attack on the Pope expressed in more precise terms than at Fatima, the collapse of the Faith in France on the threshold of the year 2000, despoliations and peace, subsequent worldwide conversion, the Antichrist and the Apocalypse. It will consider to what extent are these predictions being fulfilled, or will be fulfilled.

The visionaries will be presented as upright and trustworthy witnesses of the Marian Apparition, indeed an example of the holiness of the poor.

The book will explore the respectful and significant place that should be given to LaSalette and was given in the numerous early pilgrimages. There is a proper place for pilgrimages in an authentic life in God, at a time when faith is suffocating in a world that is materialistic, secularized, and marked with a double atheism, both ideological and socio-economic.

TABLE OF CONTENTS

HOW DID THIS BOOK COME ABOUT?   1
THE ESSENCE OF THE UNIQUE APPARITION   5
THIS BOOK OFFERS OPEN ACCESS TO HIDDEN SOURCES   7
THE CANDID CONTRIBUTION OF THIS BOOK   9
FORWARD   10

CHAPTER 1 | The Apparition of September 19, 1846   17
    I. The Oldest Account (September 20th, 1846)   17
    II. The Detailed Account of Maximin (1866)   18
    III. The Investigation and Recognition of the Apparition   24
       1. The First Step   24
       2. Official Investigation   24
       3. Continuation of Events   26

CHAPTER 2 | The Discovery   29
    Rene Laurentin interviews Michel Corteville   29

CHAPTER 3 | Is the Message of LaSalette Strange or Particularly Different?   47
    I. A Deeply Incarnate Word   47
    II. A Letter Dropped from the Sky?   49
    III. The Language of Tears   53

CHAPTER 4 | The Eight Preserved Versions of the Secret   59
    Versions and Sources   59
    How the Seers Perceive the Message   60
    Words to Express the Heavenly Images   61

I. The Two 1851 Versions presented to Pope Pius IX (July 3-6, 1851)	64
1. The Written Text of the Secret by Maximin, July 3, 1851	64
2. The Written Text of the Secret by Melanie	67
3. Maximin's Text Written for Benjamin Dausse, August 11th, 1851	69
II. New Versions made at the Request of Bishop Ginoulhiac	70
4. Maximin, August 5th, 1853	71
5. & 6. Melanie, August 12 and 14, 1853	73
III. Melanie's Expanded Versions (1858-1878)	76
[7] In 1858, Melanie sends the Pope the Complete Secret: the Lost Version	76
7. The First Known Manuscript (Marseille, circa 1860: 5 pages)	77
8. The Definitive Version of Lecce (1878 to 1879)	77
IV. Disclosures about the Last Times: "the Other Secret" of Melanie?	100

CHAPTER 5 | What to Think About the Seers?   105

I. Are the Seers Uneducated and Witless?	106
II. Were They Unstable?	111
III. Were They Coherent?	118
IV. What About their Mental Equilibrium?	118
Natural Reactions	122
Their Spiritual Trials	123
A. The Mystical Dimension	123
B. Abuse by Satan	124
C. The Stigmata of the Passion	128
Should we accept the Mystical Experiences of Melanie's Childhood as Factual?	130
Was Melanie a Masochist?	132
Was Melanie Self-Centered?	138

| | | Was Melanie an Anti-Semite? | 139 |
| | | Were the Seers Corrupted by Political Influences? | 141 |

    V. Are they saints?   141
        Melanie   141
        Maximin   150
    A Program for the Rehabilitation of their Reputations   153

ADDITIONAL TESTIMONIES   158

    1. The Stigmata of Melanie: An Overview of the Testimonies   158

        A. Childhood in Corps and its Vicinity, 1835-1846   160
        B. Her Youth at Corps, Corenc and LaSalette: 1847-1854   163
        C. Melanie as an Adult in Darlington, England (1854-1860)   165
        D. Marseille, 1860-1867   166
        E. Castellammare-di-Stabia, Italy: (1868-1882)   168
        F. Cannes, 1885   168
        G. Messina, Italy (1897-1898)   168
        H. Melanie in her Seventies: Diou, Argoeuves (1899-1904)   171

    2. Why were the Seers Rejected?   172

        A. Tension between Institutions and Personal Charisms   172
        B. The Pastoral Factor   173
        C. The Political Factor   173
        D. Pseudo-Mystical Incidents   174
        E. The Cultural and Philosophical Factor   175

CHAPTER 6 | Important Unexpected Testimonies   181

    I. Writers   181
    II. Spiritual Persons   194
    III. The Saints   198
    IV. Bishops   206
    V. Popes   211

CHAPTER 7 | The Secrets — 221
- I. The Short and the Complete Versions — 221
  - A. The Short Versions — 221
  - B. The Complete Version — 222
- II. Norms for Interpretation — 222
- III. Royalist and Apocalyptic Influences? — 224
- IV. What Do the Secrets Say? — 226
  1. France — 227
  2. The World — 233
  3. The Church, the Pope, and Rome — 234
     - A. Conversion of the Nation(s) — 234
     - B. The Pope and Persecution — 234
     - C. Unworthy Priests or "Cesspools of Impurity" — 236
  4. The Antichrist and the End Times — 239
     - A. Antichrist? — 239
     - B. Last Times? — 241

The Importance of the Secrets — 241

CHAPTER 8 | The Rule of the Order of the Mother of God, a Practical Complement to the Secrets — 247
- I. A Final Secret is Reserved for Melanie — 247
  1. How the "Missionaries of LaSalette" were established — 248
  2. How Melanie Received and Revealed the Rule — 250
     - A. The Initial Confiding of the Rule — 252
     - B. Resistance to the Growth of an English Foundation — 253
     - C. The "Sight": a Prophetic Vision of the Apostles of the Last Times — 256
     - D. Encouragement in Rome, Opposition in France — 264
- II. Spirit and Character of the Rule — 275
  - A. The Inspiration — 275

	B. Revival of the Gospel, and of the Primitive Church	277
	C. Simplicity	278
	D. The Order of the Mother of God and its Development	278
III.	The Authentic Text of the Rule	280

CONCLUSION — 285

I.	Insight on the Secrets	285
II.	New Insights on the Seers	286
	A. Melanie	286
	B. Maximin	288
III.	The Universal Dimension of Holiness	289
IV.	The Holiness of the Poor	291

DOCUMENTS — 295

I. Maximin — 295

1. Letter to Bishop DeBruillard — 295
2. Maximin to Henry LeChauf of Kerguenec, Best Friend in the Papal Zouaves — 296
3. Letter to Felicie Berot of Aire-sur-Adour — 298
4. Letter to Mrs. Jourdain, his Adoptive Mother — 300

   The Apparition — 301
   The First Disclosures — 303
   The Conversion of the Wheelwright, Giraud — 307
   More Disclosures — 317

5. Excerpts from Letters to his Adoptive Parents: — 320

   August 1, 1869 — 320
   August 10, 1869 — 321
   August 20th, 1869 — 321
   September 18, 1869 — 322
   October 26, 1869 — 323

II.	Melanie	324
	1. Letter to "Mother Carron" at Ablandins	324
	2. Letter to Maximin	325
	3. Letter to her Parents	327
	4. Description of the Virgin, Written during her Novitiate	328
	5. Autographed Prayer by Melanie (unpublished)	330
	6. Letter to her Mother and the Inhabitants of Corps	330
	7. Letters from Melanie to Father Felicien Bliard	333
	8. Litanies of Love of the Blessed Virgin Mary composed by Melanie	335
	9. Prayer to Our Lord Jesus Christ in a Time of Sorrow	336
III.	Jacques Maritain	337
	1. Letter to Dom Paul Delatte, Abbot of Solesmes	337
	2. Is Melanie's Secret Inspired?	345
IV.	Reputation for holiness	348
	1. Letter from Father Garrigou-Lagrange to Fernand Corteville	348
	2. Letter from Bishop Paciello of Altamura to Father Ciro Quaranta	348
	3. Letter from Father Georges Nalin	349
	4. Circular of the Postulator for the Sacred Congregation for the Causes of Saints	350
	5. Prayer for the Beatification of Melanie	351

CHRONOLOGY	353
BIBLIOGRAPHY	401
ABBREVIATED REFERENCES	405
ENDNOTES	411
TABLE OF CHARACTERS	415
ABOUT THE PUBLISHER	436

HOW DID THIS BOOK COME ABOUT?

Father Michel Corteville discovered the official Secret of LaSalette, and many other documents that augment our knowledge of the Apparition. A quarter of the documents that he is currently publishing with Téqui were heretofore unpublished, notably concerning Melanie's stigmata and the Rule of Life given to Melanie. Father Laurentin, who followed the development of this monumental thesis (1104 pages), conceived this new book to answer, in due order, the questions of the public regarding this controversial Apparition, because the answers, with the new information, are also reconciliatory, moving the discussion in a positive direction past polemics.

The book was developed in continuous collaboration over the course of a year. Father Rene Laurentin organized the format according to key questions. Michel Corteville furnished the heretofore unpublished documents. The two authors produced this book while in constant and stimulating dialogue using their complementary expertise in theology, spirituality and the history of Apparitions. Each of the authors expresses his point of view and offers conclusions in the areas involving his particular competence.

From the Secret of Maximin

At the latest in the 2000s the Faith will die out in France...

A pontiff whom no one expects...

We'll shoot him, we'll want to put him to death, but there's nothing we can do to him.

From the Secret of Melanie

The Church will experience a frightful crisis.

Nihil obstat:
Abbaye Notre-Dame de Tournay
February 13, 2002
(anniversary of the death of Marguerite Aron in Auschwitz, devoted research assistant on Melanie)
Dom Bernard Billet, OSB

Imprimatur:
Evry-Corbeil-Essonnes, France Solemnity of the Resurrection, March 31, 2002
+ Bishop Michel Dubost, CIM (Congregation of Jesus and Mary)
On April 19, 2018 the Bishop emeritus was appointed National Director of the Pontifical Mission Societies in France for a five-year term.

Early Publishers of the Secret

A) Venerable Sixtus Riario Sforza, Cardinal-Archbishop of Naples
B) Venerable Francis Xavier Petagna, Bishop of Castellammare, Italy
C) Servant of God Xavier Aloysius Zola, Bishop of Lecce, Italy
D) Father Gilbert Joseph Emile Combe, parish priest of Diou, France
Image not available) Mr. Amedee Nicolas, French attorney, author

The Great Bishop DeBruillard

A) Bishop Philibert DeBruillard, ca. 1860, age 95
B) Consecrated Bishop of Grenoble, 1826 age 60
C) LaSalette was located near Corps in the Diocese of Grenoble

THE ESSENCE OF THE UNIQUE APPARITION

On September 19, 1846, Melanie Calvat (14 years old) and Maximin Giraud (11 years old), two shepherds from Corps, go up together to the mountain pastures of the village of LaSalette. They gather flowers, build a stone house, share a lunch "of bread and cheese," then fall asleep... contrary to their usual custom.

Around 3 pm, Melanie wakes up with a start: where is the herd? Climbing up the valley, they see their cows resting higher up the slope; then they head back to their place. Then Melanie sees a bright light and calls Maximin. He comes close to her and sees the light also. They both gradually discern a lady. She is sitting with her head in her hands, but She straightens her head, all in tears, and looks at them:

"Come forward," She says, "do not be afraid! I am here to tell you great news."

She stands up. Her clothing is unusual. A Crucifix shines on her chest. Then the message of which this is the essential:

"You, peasants, you work on Sundays; you, carters, you swear by the name of God. And you, the others, during Lent, you go to the butcher's shop like dogs. Your sin will result in the loss of your crops. Already the wheat is spoiling. The potatoes are rotting. I warn you as your Mother. Do not sow your wheat this year. It will be lost and you will have nothing left. Famine is coming, along with disease. It will cause deaths among your children. Hence my tears."

"I have been suffering through you people for so long [...] and you don't care [...] his is what weighs so much on my Son's arm."

"What happens next depends on men." The Lady says this in a graphic way: *"If they convert, stones and rocks will turn into wheat, and potatoes will be sown."*

In the midst of this message to the 'public,' She entrusts to the children the 'Secret,' the subject of this book. The children are to keep the Secret until further notice.

She concludes: *"Well, my children, you will pass this on to all my people."*

That same evening, the children tell their employers about the Apparition. The very next day, they send the children to speak to the parish priest, Father Jacques Perrin, who announces it immediately in his Sunday homily. The pilgrimage begins in the afternoon. The Apparition becomes the subject of discussion. Bishop DeBruillard of Grenoble waits cautiously. His metropolitan, Cardinal DeBonald, Archbishop of Lyon, is against it. After sending the Secret to Pius IX, who welcomes it, Bishop DeBruillard acknowledges the Apparition in November 1851.

THIS BOOK OFFERS OPEN ACCESS TO HIDDEN SOURCES

This book brings to light several versions of the Secret:
- the version recently discovered and opened in Rome
- other unpublished versions

Altogether, the eight versions of the Secret and the authors' evaluation feature prominently in this book. However, the emphasis is placed on the importance of the fundamental message of the Apparition, which was disseminated immediately (1846). The Secret(s) came afterward. As with Fatima, the Secret of LaSalette emphasizes the grave need for conversion, and the risk of ignoring the requested conversion. The seers prayed for a long time how to communicate it. Although, the Secret was not the essential message, we can no longer regard it as a delayed postscript of the seers' subjective predictions because we can now verify that it was in the original official versions.

While it is surprising to see the considerable variations between these versions, there are reasonable explanations: each, except the last (1878), was penned without the seers having access to what had previously been written. Moreover, only the core of the Secret was imparted verbally, being accompanied by a vision of complex images, subject to interpretation. The visionaries were overwhelmed by what they beheld and it was difficult for them to put it into words. Melanie expressed what she saw with finesse (p.216).

In each draft therefore they courageously take a fresh plunge, sometimes unfurling, sometimes concealing, depending on the circumstances and the recipient. The two official drafts of 1851 are paramount, while discussion remains open for the subsequent versions. Over time, Melanie clarifies what was definitely affirmed for her. She subtracts dates that she had previously inserted (p.29). Finally, when the time comes, she publishes the full text of the Secret (1879).

What is clearest beyond dispute is the fidelity of the seers to the message received, and the concern to fulfill their mission well: *"You will pass this on to all my people!"* They kept passing it on until their death. We investigate them to probe what may have influenced them, but we encounter more resistance to outside influence than we expected. We will attempt a closer look at these influences, but only with a precise analysis of the texts taken in due order, not on amalgamations or assumptions.

This book is attentive to the human substrate of the seers: their authentic mountain culture, and the limpid wealth of the poor, taught by the Gospel and recognized by all the servants of the poor, from Vincent DePaul to Mother Teresa or Sister Emmanuel. They are left to instruct those they help out.

The divine predilection for the children of the "proletariat" constitutes of the lesson of LaSalette, twelve years before Lourdes. Rejected and driven out on so many occasions, they were not dissolute wanderers. Their tenacity on the essentials was unwavering. Their contrasting temperaments, which kept them separated, provides a stereoscopic relief to their testimony. Melanie's existence was characterized by constant and generous service to the message and to her neighbor, in deep contemplation and the totally sacrificial gift of herself, but not by any sickly withdrawal. How to put an end to the suggestions of clairvoyant and psychic powers, or postulations borrowed from incompetent attempts at psychoanalysis!

THE CANDID CONTRIBUTION OF THIS BOOK

Since the invention of photography, history has taken on a new dimension. The faces of Socrates or Seneca, Jesus Christ, and the Apostles were left only to our imagination. Since the 19th century, historical figures have had a face, and locations can be observed in their primitive state.

The seers of LaSalette were photographed very early, in their youth, and the Apparition sites were fixed by stereotypes, at different stages of its development. It is very instructive. That is why in this historical book it is good to form an initial pictorial concept of the event. In our generation, we assess a great deal with our eyes. Many readers will be gratified to form an initial concept that will familiarize them with the characters, whose names they will see appearing in the course of this volume. Our journey proceeds from the original site and the seers, throughout their lives, to the popes, bishops, and various characters or writers who knew them, or supported them, during the strongly conflicting historical debates to which this book endeavors to generate a solution, beyond polemics and passions.

We will conclude with an "areopagus" of prestigious writers, the record of victory of LaSalette, and then the last resting place and tomb of Melanie.

FORWARD

THE UNVEILING OF THE SECRET OF LASALETTE IS THIS AN EVENT, AND WHAT EVENT?

After the third part of the Secret of Fatima is revealed by Pope John Paul II on May 13, 2000, the Secret of LaSalette is revealed, in turn, along with many other unknown documents.

The very first written descriptions by the two shepherds, addressed to Pope Pius IX, were presumed lost, according to the response of the *Sacred Congregation of the Doctrine of the Faith* to Father Jean Stern, then archivist of the Missionaries of LaSalette. He had spared no effort to uncover this official version, collected in 1851 by Bishop DeBruillard and handed-over to Pope Pius IX by two canons of his diocese.

Subsequently, in 1998, Cardinal Bertone, Secretary of the Sacred Congregation, opened to researchers the archives prior to the death of Leo XIII (Nov. 20, 1903). Father Michel Corteville, who was working on his thesis in Rome, was the first to consult this file, and he discovered the lost Secret.

To find it, it was necessary to be prepared for the task. Father Corteville had been familiar with this much-discussed Apparition since his childhood. His father, Fernand Corteville, had been interested in it since the foundation, in 1958, of a research group in the wake of Jacques Maritain, whose monumental work on LaSalette has yet to be published. Father Corteville had thus been thoroughly saturated in an education on LaSalette. After having completed his licentiate in Spanish, and studying theology in Rome, he became passionate about LaSalette. He devoted his licentiate thesis, and then his doctoral dissertation, to LaSalette. After 4 years of ministry in Africa and 9 years in Mexico, he successfully defended his thesis at the Faculty of the Angelicum in Rome. It is more than a thousand pages long. The publication was begun by Téqui [France] under the title: *La Grande Nouvelle des Bergers de la Salette [The Great News of the Shepherds of LaSalette]* The first volume was published in May 2001. The second, devoted to the life of Melanie and the Rule revealed to her, will be published later. It highlights the interest of this little-known text, which has subsequently inspired several religious foundations.

This thesis is a treasure trove of documents; the non-specialist can be overwhelmed. Hence, this shorter book is to respond to the animated questions that have been raised since the discovery. I advised Father Corteville regarding his work, because I feared that his discovery, in October 1999, might be stolen from him by a media company. As soon as possible, I published a special issue of *Chrétians Magazine [Christian Magazine]* to publicly ensure him the authorship of his discovery. Too many researchers are surreptitiously stripped by others of their original discoveries because priority of publication prevails.

The fragmentary knowledge of the documents left room for multiple questions. The numerous texts discovered, renews the question so much discussed. Critics highlighted the rustic side, the limitations and weaknesses of the seers (especially Maximin). But a wide range of renowned Christian authors: Léon Bloy, Maritain, Claudel, Massignon and others, discerned and admired the sincerity, or even the holiness, of the two shepherds, (especially Melanie). The debate was opened by the hierarchy itself. For, unlike Bishop DeBruillard who recognized the Apparition, and held the two seers in esteem, his successor, Bishop Ginoulhiac, who was obliged to continue [the promotion of] LaSalette, nevertheless compromised the seers. *"The mission of the shepherds is finished, that of the Church is beginning,"* he declared tersely on September 19, 1855.

This critical dictum was therefore imposed on the LaSalette Fathers as well as on the clergy of the diocese, and it was in this spirit that they stressed the negative side of the life of the seers. There was no shortage of material at a time when psychology was unilaterally revolutionizing spirituality. Those who thought they could discern the profound value of the two shepherds were then seen as outsiders. So, Maritain did not dare plead the cause of Melanie before Dom Paul Delatte, Abbot of Solesmes (1890-1921), without characterizing himself as *"an ignorant layman, unworthy Christian, poor philosopher"* (Letter of March 2, 1912, below Letter n° 10).

According to the dominant theory, the seers were "since 1847" under the influence of sophisticated and plotting royalists. According to the discovered documents, the influences, on the contrary, put politics into perspective. Maximin dissuaded the Count of Chambord ("Henri V") from seeking royalty, and Melanie accepted the principle of the Rally of Catholics to the Republic advocated by Leo XIII. These examples suggest the extent to which stereotypical clichés and hasty generalizations need to be revised.

But the crux of the problem or the object of the conclusion, is, the holiness of the poor of which the Gospel speaks. It is often disconcerting and unrecognized, in spite of recent successful efforts to bring about change, to see many canonizations of popes, bishops, doctors, founders, kings or national heroes, rather than the beggar, Saint Benedict Labre, and others like him, such as humble mothers of families, laymen of the lower classes, and children, according to the desires expressed by Daniel Ange.

This volume will therefore attempt to provide brief answers to the burning and controversial issues at all levels, according to the following plan:

1. First, the indispensable account of the Apparition.
2. Father Michel Corteville will be heard recounting his discovery and his principal conclusions in response to the questions of Father Laurentin (interview in *Chrétians Magazine* of

March 15, 2002 which broke the news of the "discovery").

3. We will then examine the problems raised by the fundamental message of Fatima: the apparent disservice which it has caused.

4. The full text of the "Secrets" of LaSalette will then be presented in the six successive forms that have been preserved. In addition, we will hear what the principal interlocutors of the seers have to say about them.

   Then, we will respond to the great questions discussed for a century and a half:

5. What should we think of the "recognition" of the Apparition which aroused so much enthusiasm: J. Joris, Karl Huysmans, Léon Bloy, Claudel, Maritain, Massignon, but also critics...? What do the popes say about it?

6. What to think of the *seers*, who were constantly subjected to terrible contradictory assaults: indiscreet fervor, contradictions, and defamations? Are the seers stupid, or intelligent? Balanced or not? Unstable or steady? Confused or coherent? Average people or holy?

7. What does one think of the Secrets and a dozen predictions so diversely judged? Do their variants stem from a confusion of mind, or from the diversity of circumstances in which they expressed anew the memory of what they beheld, something richer in images than in words? Is the long form, unique to Melanie, a late and subjective extrapolation of the years 1860-1879: "LaSalette II," after "LaSalette I"? Could it be a heterogeneous extrapolation? Is it, on the contrary, a testimony of her fidelity in gradually disclosing it according to Our Lady's instructions, as happened with Fatima and elsewhere?

8. Finally, it is indispensable to present the *Rule of LaSalette,* a charter received from the Virgin by Melanie on September 19, 1846, but written only in 1853 in brief form, and completely

in 1876. It is, in a way, a completion to the Secret in its practical and eschatological dimensions: its positive, constructive, evangelical side.

We find in the Rule (topics and terminology) the prophecy of Saint Louis Grignion DeMontfort about the *Apostles of the Last Times* (this expression being explicit only in the text of 1876). To Melanie, not having been able to found the Order she desired according to the Rule revealed to her, it seemed a utopia without benefit or fruit. But Leo XIII took it into consideration in 1878, and since then it has inspired, to varying degrees, several religious congregations: those of Blessed Giagomo [Jacques, James] Cusmano and [Saint] Annibale Di Francia. More recently, the Brothers of Saint John have taken their first steps in its spirit. A Mexican community was founded at Merida according to this clear and contemplative, apostolic and eschatological, evangelical Rule. Father Gaston Hurtubise, a Canadian, had begun a foundation in the same direction where vocations were pouring in, but his impressive death (1992), in the midst of preaching to 2,000 people, stopped his nascent project in 1990. It is currently arousing interest in Colombia, Haiti, and even France.

Friends of LaSalette and specialists in the Apparitions in the history of the Church will be grateful to Father Corteville for having renewed the history and problems of LaSalette through his discoveries. It is not a question of evading its particular, even particularistic aspects, nor the influences suffered by the seers, nor the hesitations in the transmission of a message whose richness in words and images surpassed them. These unlearned children of peasant stock, faithfully, without consulting previous writings, had received everything in a single Apparition, in less than two hours. They wrote it down over thirty years, under very diverse conditions, for various recipients and requesters, drawing from their memories according to the letter, and even more according to the spirit. Their successive drafts are more or less explicit, depending on time and circumstances. One will have to ask whether the variations arise from their interpretations or extrapolations, but the substance is more constant than was presumed in the earlier documentation.

The fulfilment of prophecies (always symbolic and polyvalent in the unfolding of Biblical prophecies, insists Cardinal Ratzinger) is more precise in LaSalette than in the third part of the Secret of Fatima, and the second part of [the Secret of Fatima] which was more important and more adequate. The earliest redactions of that Secret contain several themes that were attributed to latter extrapolations ("Fatima II").

The works of Father Corteville confirm the value, the coherence and even the current topicality of LaSalette's message, and the all-too-little-known value of the seers, quickly sacrificed on the altar of political, and then rational or rationalist, criticism.

René Laurentin

Apparition (Seated) of BVM to Max. and Mel. Sept. 19, 1846
Conversation (Standing) "How I suffer for you! The blasphemies, etc."
Assumption (Rising) "Well, my children, pass this on to all my people!"

CHAPTER 1

THE APPARITION OF SEPTEMBER 19, 1846

The Oldest Account (September 20th, 1846)

The very day after the Apparition, the evening of Sunday September 20th, the employers of the two shepherds, Baptiste Pra and Pierre Selme, received the message of Maximin and Melanie[1]. We are holding to their rough style, supplying only some rare missing words and minimally correcting spelling, grammar and punctuation.

Message dictated by the Holy Virgin to the Two Children on the Mountain of LaSalette-Falavaux

> *Come near, my children. Do not be afraid. I am here to tell you an important message. If my people do not want to submit themselves (to God), I am forced to let go of the hand of my Son. His hand (of justice) is so strong and so heavy that I can no longer hold it back. For so long I am suffering for you! If I wish my Son not to abandon you (to yourselves), I am compelled to intercede for you unceasingly; but you are oblivious to this. Never will you be able to recompense the pains I have undertaken for you.*
>
> *I gave you six days in which to work. The seventh is reserved for God. But you don't want to observe it (the Lord's Day). This is what makes the hand of my Son so heavy. And also, those who are pushing their carts are swearing and abusing the Name of my Son. These are the two things weighing down so much the hand of my Son.*
>
> *If the harvest spoils, as you were made to see in the potatoes last year, you do not turn to God but rather swear and take his Name in vain.*

The ruined harvests will continue, even this year until Christmas.

Do you not understand, my children? I will explain it to you another way.

If you have wheat fields, all that you sow will be eaten by creatures. Anything that remains uneaten, this coming year, will be stricken and fall to dust.

A great famine is coming. Before the famine arrives, the children under seven years old will quiver and die in the arms of their caregivers.

The others will be punished by the famine. The nuts will be bad and the grapes rotten. If many are converted, the rocks and stones will become piles of wheat, and the potatoes will be sown for the next year.

In the summer, there are only a few old women at Sunday Mass. The others are working. And in winter, the young men who are aimless only go to Mass to scoff and mock at religion. The people are not observing Lent. They go to the butcher shop like dogs.

Do you say your prayers well my children?

Not very much, Madame.

You must say them well morning and night, and pray at least a Pater Noster and an Ave Maria when you are not able to do more. Have you not seen spoiled wheat, my children?

No, Madame.

But my child, you must have seen it once when you went with your father to a neighbor's... there was a man who told your father to come and see his spoiled wheat. So, your father went and took some stalks in his hands, rubbed them and they fell as dust. Then while returning, your father gave you a piece of bread and told you: Take, my child, eat some of this year's bread, as we do not know who will be able to eat in the coming year, if this continues.

Go, my children, make this known to all my people.

THE DETAILED ACCOUNT OF MAXIMIN (1866)

On February 2, 1866, having matured through trials, Maximin (35 years old) writes and publishes his own account of the Apparition.[2] He introduces his account with a prayer:

Most Holy and Immaculate Virgin Mary, Our Lady of LaSalette,

Permit me to come place at your feet these few pages produced today. Now I have become a man, my voice being just as pure and true as on September 19, 1846 when I came down from the Holy Mountain to announce to all your people the important message which you had entrusted to me. I would never have written this, good and most excellent Mother, if my witness had not been doubted, or if it was not being turned against you, and if false words had not been attributed to me while I was keeping strict silence.

I pray and supplicate thee, O most holy Virgin Mary, imploring you under the title of Our Lady of LaSalette, to grant me, as long as I live, the grace to witness to your appearing, just as the witnesses (Saints) of the Church have done in witnessing to the divinity of Our Lord Jesus Christ.

It was noon, not yet at the hour of shadowiness so conducive to illusions. The sky was clear and calm. The clouds in their odd forms did not make us see any ghost or mirage. The sun was shining its brightest. It's easy for the two seers to compare its splendor and brightness with that of the most Holy Virgin. I say all these things, because such things and anything that could discount us was fabricated by doubters.

Sitting at the height of the Holy Mountain, on the stones piled on top of each other (forming a kind of bank), near a dried-up spring which would flow that very day and which flows ever since and bears the name "miraculous spring," Melanie and I were having our simple meal. The cows were drinking and wandering about. Since I was tired, I stretched out on the grass and slept. A few moments later I heard Melanie's voice calling to me:

Memin *(a diminutive of Maximin)*, Memin, come quickly, we need to go see where the cows have gone.

I awoke, jumped up, grabbed my staff and followed Melanie who was guiding me. We crossed over the Sezia, quickly climbed up the slope of a hill and perceived on the other side our animals resting tranquilly. We were coming back toward the stone bank where we had left our bread boxes a few moments before, when suddenly Melanie froze. Her staff fell from her hands. Startled, she turned to me and said,

Do you see that bright light over there?

Yes, I see it, I responded to her, but pick up your staff.

And I brandished my staff threateningly saying, *if it tries to touch us, I'll hit!*

The light, beside which the sun would seem dim, seemed to open to us and we could distinguish within it the form of a lady even more luminous. She had the appearance of a person profoundly afflicted. She was sitting on one of the stones of the small bank, her elbows leaning on her knees and her face hidden in her hands.

At a distance of about twenty meters away, we heard a soft voice as though it came from closer to our ears, saying,

"Come near, my children. Don't be afraid. I am here to announce to you an important message."

The reverent fear we had vanished and we ran to her as to a good and excellent mother. The beautiful Lady also advanced toward us and, suspended about ten centimeters off the ground, facing us, began again to speak.

"Come near, my children. Don't be afraid. I am here to share an important message with you. If the people do not want to submit to God, I will be forced to let go of the arm of my Son. It is so heavy that I am no longer able to hold it back.

For a long time, I have been suffering for you. If I want my Son not to abandon you, I must pray unceasingly; and you are paying no heed to this.

I gave you six days to work. The seventh is reserved for God, and one doesn't want to observe it. This is what is weighing down so much the arm of my Son.

Also, those pushing the carts don't know how to speak without swearing and profaning the Name of my Son. These are the two things which are weighing down his arm so much.

If the harvest spoils, it is nothing for you. You were made to see this last year with the potatoes. There were none and when you find some that were spoiled, you swore and profaned the Name of my Son. It will continue until Christmas until there will be no more."

Melanie did not understand the meaning of the word *"pommes de terre"* (potatoes). The beautiful Lady perceived this and said,

Ah! You don't understand French, my children, wait I will speak to you another way.

And so, She continued speaking to us, rewording the message in our native patois.

Oh! No, Madame, it's not true!

Yes, my child, you will see it.

She continued her discourse:

Those who sow wheat, should not sow it, the insects will eat it, and if a few plants come up, when it is threshed, it will fall to dust.

There is a great famine coming. Before the famine comes, the little children under seven will tremble and die in the arms of their caregivers and the older ones will do penance by their hunger. The grapes will spoil and the nuts will go bad.

It was at this point that the beautiful Lady gave us each a Secret. Speaking in the same tone of voice as She spoke to Melanie, I could hear nothing. And when She confided to me my Secret, Melanie was completely deaf to it. Then this temporary deafness disappeared, and She continued to speak to us:

If they are converted, the rocks and stones will turn into wheat and potatoes will be found sown in the soil.

Then She asked us,

Do you say well your prayers my children?

Both of us responded,

No, Madame, not very much.

Ah! My children, you must pray well morning and night. When you don't have the time, say a Pater Noster and an Ave Maria, and when you have time, you must pray more.

There are only a few old women at Mass. The others are working all summer. Then in winter they go to Mass only to mock religion. They go to the butcher shop like dogs, during Lent.

Then She asked us:

Have you seen spoiled wheat, my children?

I answered,

No, Madame, I haven't seen any.

So, the beautiful Lady continued:

But you, my child, you must have seen it once near Coin with your father. A man said to your father, come see my wheat that is spoiled. You went, and your father took two or three stalks in his hands, rubbed them, and they fell to dust. When you weren't but a half hour from Corps, your father gave you a piece of bread, saying,

Take, my child. Eat this year, because I don't know who will be able to eat next year if the wheat spoils again.

I answered,

That's true, Madame, but I had forgotten about it.

She finished her message in French with these words:

Well! My children, you must share the message with everyone.

The beautiful Lady crossed the Sezia, lightly brushing against my right side, continuing her passage without turning back toward us, and as a final "adieu," She repeated again the words,

Well! My children, you must share the message with all my people.

Once we had come back to ourselves, Melanie and I looked at each other speechless, at times raising our eyes to the sky, sometimes looking down to our feet and around us, sometimes looking questioningly at everything around us. We seemed to be looking for the resplendent individual whom I was no longer seeing.

My companion was first to break the silence and said,

Memin, that must have been the good God or the Holy Virgin of my father, or perhaps a great saint.

Ah! I answered her, *if I had known it, I would have asked her to take me with her to heaven!*

When I must speak of the beautiful Lady who appeared to me on the Holy Mountain, I experience an awkward difficulty like Saint Paul must have experienced after coming down from the third heaven. No indeed, *"the eye of man has not seen, nor ear heard ever that which was given to me to see and to hear."* [1Cor 2:9]

It was a light, but light much different from all others. She went directly into my heart without passing through my ears, and nevertheless with a harmony that the most beautiful concerts could never reproduce. What can I say? A beauty not of this world.

The sun was beginning to set. Melanie and I gathered up the cows which had barely moved. Walking alongside my animals, which were moving single file along a straight path, I became dreamy and thoughtful about the villagers of the Ablandins. I spoke first of the beautiful Lady to Melanie's employer.

The words of the Lady, brilliant as the sun, must have made her believe I had lost my mind. She pleaded with me to tell her that which I had seen and heard on the Holy Mountain, and she was amazed. I myself was astonished that she had not seen this bright light at the top of the mountain (and thus visible from a great distance). I couldn't imagine that I had received a special grace.

The next day, I went to my father's home in Corps, while Melanie continued keeping guard of her herd. We were providentially separated then, about three months, telling (each of us, from our experience) of that which we had seen and heard, responding to all the challenges presented to us, and in French! We hardly understood it on the very morning of September 19, 1846. Such was our memorable experience.

Later one will see the definitive account of Melanie, including the complete Secret confided to her.

THE INVESTIGATION AND RECOGNITION OF THE APPARITION

1. THE FIRST STEP

The day after the Apparition, Sunday September 20, Baptiste Pra brought Maximin and Melanie to the rectory. The pastor, Father Jacques Perrin, was impressed by their recital. He spoke of the Apparition in his homily. That evening, Pra summarized the account under the title *"Letter Dictated by the Holy Virgin to Two Children on the Mountain of LaSalette"* which we have read. It was only on Sunday October 4 that Father Melin, Archpriest of Corps relayed the message to the Bishop.

2. OFFICIAL INVESTIGATION

While warning his clergy against any hasty publication of the account, Bishop DeBruillard discreetly began the investigation. On July 15, 1847, he appointed two diocesan priests to this work: Canon Orcel, who had a critical spirit, and Canon Pierre-Joseph Rousselot, the seminary superior, and one of its professors, who was to have an important and positive role in the proceedings. On November 4, the report of the two canons was submitted to a commission of 16 priests. On November 22, the occasion of their fifth session, twelve pronounced their approval. Meanwhile, private devotion was growing. The Commission convened up to December 1847 and recorded two healings which took place on April 16 and August 15, 1847.

The Bishop had announced that he would recognize the Apparition if the Commission concluded in its favor. But they held back. Why?

It was because Cardinal DeBonald, Archbishop of Lyon (his city) was supporting two opponents in the Commission.

On September 19, 1850, Maximin was brought to Father John Vianney (the Curé d'Ars) by his Vicar, Father Raymond, under difficult circumstances. Maximin came to consult with the Saint about his plan to join the Marists, but Father Vianney referred him back to his bishop. At the second meeting, the brusque and aggressive manner of Maximin brought about a misunderstanding: Father Vianney passed from believing (considering the account credible) to doubt in the matter.

Father Raymond announced the news [of the Saint's hesitation] Cardinal DeBonald felt confirmed in his opposition. He had a bad notion of the Secrets because the seers did not want to reveal them. In favor of the new opposition, he asked Bishop DeBruillard to insist that the two children write down the Secrets to have them communicated to the Pope.

Under obedience to the Bishop, Maximin recorded his Secret on July 3, 1851, and Melanie recorded hers on the 6th. The same evening, the two canons, Gerin and Rousselot, were sent by Bishop DeBruillard to Rome. On July 18, they placed the recorded Secrets in the very hand of Pope Pius IX. Cardinal Lambruschini, Prefect of the Sacred Congregation of Rites, read the Secrets, as well as Msgr. [Andrea Maria] Frattini the Devil's Advocate [Promotor of the Faith], who gave a favorable opinion of the Apparition. Bishop DeBruillard outlined his account in 1848. He communicated it to the Prefect of Rites. The Cardinal [Lambruschini] responded that the document "left nothing to be desired," the examination of the event "had proceeded with edifying and completely trustworthy rigor."

The Bishop had Maximin interrogated once again by two bishops, and the Prior General of Chartreuse. Then, he signed the document, dating it (significantly) on the 19th of September 1851, the fifth anniversary of the Apparition. He ordered it read in all the parishes: on November 9th in Grenoble, then on the 16th, in the rest of the diocese. The spontaneous and massive pilgrimages of the faithful to the site of the Apparition, and the marvels associated with it, brought a new degree of certainty, he concluded. "The Apparition of the Holy Virgin... is clothed in all the characteristics of truth... the faithful are well-founded in believing in it with confidence."

3. CONTINUATION OF EVENTS

On the first of May, 1852, the Bishop announced that the laying of the first stone of the sanctuary would be on the 25th. He formed a group of missionaries to be ministers of reconciliation according to the message of the Apparition. Thus, the Missionaries of LaSalette were founded, although some were opposed to the Apparition. The Bishop was aware of this, but did not impose his own discernment. He admitted leniency, allowing that his decision was not dogma, but a proposed authorized judgement and not to be imposed (forced) upon Christian liberty.

On July 2, 1852, at the age of 86, Bishop DeBruillard submitted his resignation to the nuncio Garibaldi. On the advice of Cardinal Mathieu of Besancon, animator of the Gallican clan, he ordered as his successor Bishop Ginoulhiac, Vicar General of Aix en Provence, well appreciated by the new regime. The Secretary of State Antonelli rejected this Gallican candidate, but the nuncio, alerted, could not impede his nomination by the government and his installation at Grenoble in May 1853. Bishop DeBruillard assured himself that his successor would confirm his judgement on LaSalette, but Bishop Ginoulhiac dreaded opposition from Napoleon III and his government, which had recommended him for the episcopate.

In July 1854, Father Jean Pierre Cartellier, pastor of Saint-Joseph of Grenoble, submitted to Cardinal DeBonald, for the Pope, an infamous memoir against LaSalette and Bishop DeBruillard. Pius IX had not finished reading it when Cartellier's memoir appeared in the press, without ecclesiastical authorization. Compelled to intervene, Bishop Ginoulhiac, the new bishop, sent to the Pope a letter expressing himself in favor of the Apparition and denouncing the claims of Father Cartellier, calling for the priest to be held accountable for his conduct. Pius IX referred the claims to canon law, while at the same time inviting the Bishop to confirm the, already recognized, Apparition.

On November 4, 1854, in his letter to the clergy on LaSalette, Bishop Ginoulhiac condemned the book. Father Cartellier formally resigned on February 26, 1855.

The two seers, Maximin and Melanie continued independently their difficult life, trapped by both the admiration and solicitations of some, and by the contradictions and bullying of others. Our Chronology at the end of this book traces their trials. Likeable and carefree, Maximin was vulnerable due to his being an orphaned child, naive and generous. Melanie's vulnerable point was her gravity. Her heroic sacrifices, her determination, and her witnessing in season and out of season were misunderstood and criticized.

Maximin, courageous lay witness in an era when the Church would only respect priests and religious, was often calumniated. He died before the age of 40, in the poverty in which he was born.

Melanie was welcomed by the Sisters of Corenc, who provided her formation. But Bishop Ginoulhiac caused her to be exiled to England. Subsequently she went to Marseille, Greece, France and finally, Italy, where she passed some happy years and where she would die, single and poor, at age 72. Maximin was also rejected by several seminaries. One can follow the vicissitudes of the life of the seers in the Chronology.

Throughout their journeys, their fidelity was undeniable. They felt naturally overwhelmed by the message from the Virgin, which caused them to be received by the Pope, through several bishops and cardinals, in three successive steps (1851, 1858 and 1878). On the last occasion, Leo XIII met with Melanie in a private audience. The witness of the shepherds of LaSalette are more coherent and more in agreement with each other than the systematic critiques of their adversaries make it appear.

The Unveilers of the Secret

A) Msgr. Rene Laurentin: International Mariologist. Died 1997, aged 99.
B) Fr. Michel Corteville: LaSalette authority. Born in France 1956.
C) Fr. Corteville ordained for the Ivory Coast, defended his doctoral dissertation, on LaSalette in Rome. Our English translation is nearly complete.

CHAPTER 2

THE DISCOVERY

RENE LAURENTIN INTERVIEWS MICHEL CORTEVILLE

I have before me, this Thursday February 8, 2001, Father Michel Corteville, a priest hailing from Beaupréau *(courtyard)*, pronounced "Bopro" in spite of the accent. He turned 40 in May 1996. After studies at the Dominican University of the Angelicum, he was ordained a priest in Rome on June 11, 1985 and served in the Ivory Coast (1986-1990). He came back to Rome to defend his thesis for a licentiate in spirituality on the Rule received by Melanie for the foundation of the Missionaries of the Mother of God, also called, by Saint Louis-Marie DeMontfort *Apostles of the Last Times*. After eight years in Mexico (as parish pastor and teacher at the seminary), he came to Rome for two years (1998-2000) to complete his degree in theology, successfully defending his thesis on October 26, 1999, at the Angelicum. Over the course of his exploration of about ten archival documents he discovered, in the Sacred Congregation for the Doctrine of the Faith recently opened by Cardinal Bertone, the written text that the seers had sent to Pope Pius IX. I interviewed Father Corteville just before his latest departure to Central America. Here are his responses:

RL: (René Laurentin): Your father, Fernand, was a devotee of LaSalette and a diligent researcher for a long time. He came to speak to me around 1953. You weren't yet born. Under his guidance, and with my encouragements, you set aside two years for your monumental dissertation on LaSalette (800 pages). Upon arriving in Rome, did you think of discovering the written Secrets sent to Pope Pius IX by the Bishop of Grenoble?

MC: (Michel Corteville): No, because the archivist of the Sacred Congregation had already responded ten years ago to Father Jean Stern, the eminent archivist of the Missionaries of LaSalette, that those items were not to be found among the documents. Each of us had done our mourning over that. My proposal was a group thesis on the seers of LaSalette so much discussed, and on Melanie in particular. The discovery of those texts, nearly at the end of my research obliged me to revise my work.

RL: This discovery puts an end to vain and obscure discussions for the lack of knowledge of the first and most important parts of the document. When and how did you discover the Secrets?

MC: I learned that at the Vatican Archives certain items I was researching had been transferred to the Sacred Congregation for the Doctrine of the Faith. These archives were open as far back as the end of the Pontificate of Leo XIII (1903). I asked what steps to follow. That was in July, and they told me to return in September. A letter from my thesis advisor justified my research to Cardinal Ratzinger. The additional support of a Roman theologian opened the doors for me of the consultation room, but only after waiting three weeks in one place. In the meantime, an Italian religious, skeptical of Melanie, removed any mistrust about my endeavor by declaring "If you find the famous Secrets, we would see things more clearly!"

It took me about ten days to explore the depths of the archives of the Sacred Congregation of the Doctrine of the Faith (formerly Sacred Congregation of the Index, of the Inquisition, etc.) about questions relating to the Apparition and I made some discoveries.

But the principal file of LaSalette wasn't appearing, and for a reason. The catalog of that section no longer existed! Finally, the archivist indicated, from memory, the location of the document, providentially classified in the years 1879-1883, and I began to dust off some bundles which hadn't been touched for ten or twenty years. The documentation was interesting. On Saturday October 2, 1999, Feast of the Guardian Angels, travel being less congested on the weekend, I arrived promptly at the Vatican. The idea came to me to go and pray before the place of the Confession of Saint Peter, under the main altar of the basilica, and to promise something, if I should by chance find a trace of the Secrets. I leafed through stacks of papers all morning. The edges of some folders were falling to pieces.

Right in the middle of the last bundle, at the moment the closing bell was sounding, I perceived, on a paper with blue lettering, what seemed to me to be the handwriting of Melanie. I only had time to read, under the date July 6, 1851, several prophetic statements. The date and the subject made me think of the Secret, and especially the packaging that accompanied it, with the mark of the seal and the signatures of the witnesses from the Diocese of Grenoble. A text of another writing and a second folder convinced me that I had in my hands the precious writings of the seers, brought to Pius IX by the envoys of Bishop DeBruillard, the Vicar General [Canon] Rousselot and Blessed John-Baptiste Guerin, the holy canon of the Grenoble Cathedral, but I did not have time to read them. As I was leaving, I shared the news with the archivist and research assistants and I phoned the Italian nun, who no longer agreed with any importance of the Secrets: "You called me for that!?" she said.

RL: What is the importance of the file on LaSalette, preserved in the archives of the Holy Office, comprised of articles which remained for a long time in the hands of the Pope?

MC: It is comprised of about ten large extendible fastened files, from 10 to 20 cm. thick, essentially manuscripts. But the Secrets, subsequently transferred from the private collection of Pope Pius IX in 1946, are in a separate folder of several millimeters thick.

RL: To discover the Secret, it's therefore like searching for a needle in a haystack? And it was, on that morning, that your wish was fulfilled.

(Father Corteville was not eager to respond, but as we had eaten together afterwards and he refused the wine I offered to him, drinking only water: "Is it a promise you made?" I said to him with a smile. "It would seem so," he answered. It reminded me of an old archbishop in his eighties from China, with whom I travelled by night. He didn't have breakfast in the morning because he had made the vow to fast every morning if the diocesan clergy were saved from the fire [of persecution] threatening them.)

MC: The seers hesitated for a long time to communicate the Secret. "Even to the Pope" responded Maximin to Father Auvergne who expressed to him the directives of Cardinal DeBonald: "The Holy Virgin forbade me to tell."[1] Before 1851, she (Melanie) was worried: "It's not the Pope who demands the Secret; it's others who have told him to ask for it." Previous to the decisive visit of Father [Canon] Rousselot, she was not about to change her mind: "I cannot tell him something other than what I told you."

She stated further: "I do not have permission to tell any person, and the Pope is a person." She did not change her mind until the last moment, "between evening and morning," doubtless upon a fresh intervention of the Holy Virgin. "You will not tell any person; you will not tell it. If you are forced to tell it one day, you will not tell what it regards, and you will say nothing until I tell you." Such were the last words of Mary in the second discovered Secret. When a teacher from Nantes asked the seer if she had seen the Virgin again, she responded with silence, admitting however that she now knew that she could reveal it to the Pope. Melanie had no way of knowing how the Pope was asking for her Secret. Yet she was correct in affirming that he did not do so of his own accord. The one who heard her, who didn't know her, was amazed. Who had given her this certainty?

RL: What were the final motives for the reserve of the seers at the moment they surrendered their Secret?

MC: According to a letter from 1855 and the topics noted when she wrote this Secret, Melanie feared to cause too much pain to the Pope, as Bishop DeBruillard, who read it first, shed tears, evocative of the weeping Apparition. That's why Melanie only wrote a small portion of the Secret. The moment of the full revelation would not come until 1858.

> [† Editor: It is true that Engineer Dausse discreetly gave Bishop DeBruillard an unexpected and unsought opportunity to read the Secret. Melanie was distraught in trying to convey to the pope, in words, what she had seen in vision. She was concerned also about her spelling and grammar. She had sought the assistance of her Mother Superior on July 3rd in Corenc, and traveled to Grenoble on July 6th to add something to the text. Dausse, a witness, suggested that she might feel better if Bishop DeBruillard looked it over. Melanie handed him the text. "*As you wish*, said Melanie, and offered her writing to the Bishop. He did not need to be told twice. He took it on the spot and went to read it in his room. He came back red-faced, in tears, *gripped*, returned it to seal it, without saying anything." English translation in preparation: *The Great News, by M. Corteville*, Vol. 1 Ch 4 "Notes of Benjamin Dausse]

RL: After having revealed the Secret to the Pope in 1851, the seers would confide more to him. These confidences, oral and written, are of various lengths. The Secret, written and published in 1879 by Melanie with the Imprimatur of an Italian prelate, Bishop Zola, is much longer. How do you explain these differences?

MC: Contrary to Maximin, who wrote to the Pope all he knew of the Secret, the careful account given by Melanie for Pius IX is an abridged version. In 1858, from England where she was residing, she sent, under seal, through the intermediary of the Bishop of Exham, a new text, lost, certainly close to that which she rewrote after her arrival in Marseille in 1860 and which she progressively revealed around that time.

RL: What were the feelings of Pius IX about this Secret which he desired to know, but did not publish?

MC: He took a position of extreme prudence, like the predecessors of John Paul II regarding the Third Secret of Fatima. His words, pronounced in 1851 at the time when he read them and carefully recorded by the emissaries of Bishop DeBruillard, demonstrated his faith in the Secrets of the Shepherds. If the text of Maximin had reassured him, the text of Melanie had profoundly moved him. Whereas the Bishop of Grenoble had shed tears, the Pope blanched. Then he recalled to what extent the Church is militant: "I am her captain... Christian indifference is more damaging to her than open persecution" he specified significantly. Faced with the retreat of the Faith, prophesied of France for the twentieth century, a prediction today verified, and to the subversive forces against the Church having enormous consequences for the peace of Europe, the Pope advocated for spiritual warfare. After the study of the Secrets and the diocesan recognition of the Apparition, he confirmed his conviction in accord with the liturgical privileges of her sanctuary. In 1860, his intentions were in agreement with the complete Secret of Melanie, which caused him be cautious, from 1858, of the hypocrisy of Napoleon III.

RL: What was the position of Bishop DeBruillard, of Grenoble, who approved the Apparition in spite of opposition?

MC: With the priests of LaSalette and Corps and the chief members of his clergy united with the commission, he believed in LaSalette. He held Melanie in high regard, but before engaging with her, he patiently verified the beneficial (and even miraculous) fruits of the Apparition. After having read and transmitted her Secrets and consulting Rome, he officially recognized it, on November 9, 1851. However, the decree bears the date September 19, 1851.

Being aware, then, of the Secrets, he presented LaSalette as a rally cry for believers, a "serpent of bronze" in the midst of the European crises, a providential help for the Church and for France. For this bishop, who had exercised the sacerdotal ministry in Paris under the

Reign of Terror, the grace of LaSalette was not limited to a private or local devotion. It had important social repercussions.

The principal objection made against LaSalette was the initial negative judgement of the Curé d'Ars. It had to do with an exchange he experienced with Maximin, which investigators were able to clarify. Saint Jean-Marie Vianney himself came back to faith in the Apparition. The misunderstanding was exploited by the Archbishop of Lyon, Cardinal DeBonald. Jealous of his Marian sanctuary of Fourvière, as was Bishop Depéry of Laus, DeBonald supported two opponents from the Diocese of Grenoble, Fathers Cartellier and Father Déléon, who were against the Apparition of LaSalette, of which he knew very little. For example, he called Maximin "Marcellin," and mistook Melanie for Maximin's sister.

RL: What was the position of Bishop Ginoulhiac, the successor of Bishop DeBruillard? Opposed to the dogma of infallibility at the First Vatican Council, Bishop Ginoulhiac was among those who refused to assist with its promulgation by adherence to the opinion of the Council, but later submitted himself. He seemed to have been less favorable (to the Apparition) than his predecessor.

MC: Installed under Napoleon III, in May 1853, the new bishop had been proposed to Bishop DeBruillard by Cardinal Mathieu, leader of the Gallican group of the time. Ginoulhiac had a strong theological mind. Bishop DeBruillard was confident that such a successor would safeguard recognition of the Apparition, but Bishop Ginoulhiac kept a low profile from the start.

He did not so much support the authenticity of the Apparition as he did the legitimacy of the Marian devotion that resulted from it, and the good fruits that its warnings brought about in the people. He observed, however, the aversion of the seers for the so-called protector of the Church, Napoleon III, and this prince himself was disturbed by it. Friend of the Minister of Worship and thurifer of the government, Bishop Ginoulhiac wanted to bring things into the light. He demanded of the two shepherds a fresh written account of their Secret. An authentic copy of this version recorded by Maximin, which had been unknown, was revealed to me (Corteville) by the Sacred Congregation of the Doctrine of the Faith. The censure of Napoleon indisposed him to the Apparition and, as Ordinary, Bishop Ginoulhiac formed a severe opinion of the seers: "day dreaming" by Maximin, an orphan deprived of affection, and the mystical overflow of Melanie incurred his disapproval of her. He defended theologically the devotion of LaSalette in accord with Pius IX, even while letting his doubts show.

In addition, he would cover up his violation of the correspondence of Melanie while she was in England, threatening her former confessor with loss of faculties if he refused to turn over her correspondence, and that he, Ginoulhiac, would prevent the exiled seer from returning. He had never understood her profound spiritual life, nor the nature of certain trials she underwent. He rejected her stigmatization, soon attested to by some credible witnesses. Poorly counselled, he listened to one of the false mystics who was against the seers, the Countess DeNicolay. This sentence which summarizes the Bishop's position: *"The mission of the seers is over, that of the Church is beginning."* Leading a grand lifestyle, he wasn't concerned about the poverty of Maximin, reduced to begging after his departure from the seminary. The Archbishop of Lyon, in 1870, did not excel in the virtue of poverty either, according to the Nuncio.

RL: The most cumbersome part of this business is the subsequent multiple rewritings and variations. How to manage this plethora?

MC: To break things down, in total Maximin wrote his Secret three times and Melanie five times.

The very first transcripts were given to Pius IX in 1851

1. Maximin, on July 3
2. Melanie, on July 6

Maximin rewrote it on two other occasions

3. On August 12, 1851 he shared his Secret with a close friend, Benjamin Dausse, but not without error. Saint Peter Julien Eymard was familiar with this copy.

4. On Friday August 5, 1853, at the request of Bishop Ginoulhiac, he wrote a longer text. He presumed to connect the pitiable departure predicted of Napoleon III with the image of an eagle: "a young eagle soars [...] higher [...] then he will fall on some daggers. Chaos will happen after his death" (the Communist Revolution after his fall but before his death).

Melanie, for her part, left four additional rewritings

5. On August 14, 1853 at Corenc, she rewrote it for Bishop Ginoulhiac. She prudently expurgated it of any of Maximin's political allusions.

6. She wrote a new version at Darlington, in 1858, under seals for Pius IX, of which the manuscript disappeared.

7. At Marseille, from the end of 1860 through 1861 (before her departure for Greece), she did a complete rewriting of the Secret (five pages). It was published in France beginning in 1870, notably in Grenoble, by the canon lawyer Father Regis Girard who disseminated it with the blessing of Pius IX. [See entry "1871—1874" in the Chronological Table.]

8. The final writing, dated November 21, 1878, filled the gaps left by the "*et ceteras*" of the previous writing. Melanie was granted permission for its publication in 1879 at Lecce, with the Imprimatur of Bishop Zola. She would defend until her death its scrupulous authenticity. To these texts were added some of Melanie's private oral statements about the "Last Times of the world." They were noted in 1904 by Father Émile Combe, pastor of Diou, village of Allier, where she lived at the beginning of the twentieth century. They recount the "Second Secret of the Last Times" mentioned in the August 1853 (#5) version ordered by Bishop Ginoulhiac.

RL: More than one reader has become disoriented in all these versions in which the visionaries endeavored to re-express what they had seen. What does the discovery of the two texts, written for Pius IX by Maximin and Melanie, bring to bear?

MC: The official texts of 1851, closer to the events, more sober, written for the Pope with great and exacting care, are the official texts, appraised by the Pope and the Bishop [of Grenoble] for judging the Apparition. These texts establish the essential themes of the prophecy of LaSalette, including some points that were regarded until now as apocrypha: the ruin of Paris and Marseille, the Antichrist, persecutions against the Faith, and finally the reform of the Church after a great infidelity of priests and consecrated souls.

To his writing of 1851, Maximin added, from 1853, the description of the vision that had accompanied the words of the Secret (the image of the eaglet, etc.) and his subjective understanding of the events. Literally speaking, for Maximin, the pure text is that of July 3, 1851, received by Pius IX. With Melanie, conversely, the complete formulation of the Secret (published in 1879) is more convincing than those of 1851 or of 1853. Thus, the final expression "there will not pass two times 50 years (or 40 years)" occurring in the early texts, disappears in the definitive version. The seer admitted in 1870 that she had inserted the expression, doubtless according to something she had seen during the apparition. The Secrets of LaSalette are disconcerting in their concrete (and at the same time theological, symbolic and apocalyptic) character.

RL: What are the principal additions or omissions that differentiate the texts?

MC: The text of Maximin for Bishop Ginoulhiac shows the progression of the downfall of Napoleon III, his support of Garibaldi, and his conquest of the Papal States, which the seer will defend as a pontifical "Zouave" in 1865. Melanie said the same in her final writing: "God withdrew from him [Napoleon]" And she put the Pope on high alert. In 1853, she writes a Rule of apostolic life for the *"Apostles of the Last Times"* (having received the Rule during the Apparition).

RL: What are the main points common to all the versions of the Secrets?

MC: The various writings of the Secret by Melanie, quite unequal in length, agree in content with the writings of Maximin, even in their "ups and downs": troubles, peace, apostasy, persecutions and conversion, with the same conclusion, namely, the victory of God because grace overcomes sin. Where Maximin speaks generally of France, Melanie mentions particular cities (Paris, Marseille, later Rome). As for the "beast" spoken of by Maximin, Melanie calls it "the Antichrist" like Saint Paul.

RL: What called attention to the Secret of LaSalette? Was it due to the support given by Leon Bloy, his godson Jacques Maritain, as well as Massignon, Huysmans and Claudel?

MC: The writers you cited were clear-sighted with regard to the good bourgeois (middle class) conscience which was inherited from the Revolution. They recognized that the clergy was more brilliant in the salons than close to the poor. For example, Cardinal Perraud, a scholar hostile to Melanie, fought against social Christianity in the name of "the alliance of Presbyters and Castles." The historians of the nineteenth century deplored the lack of profound evangelization in France. The Rule of Melanie instilled the deep engagement of spiritual battle, free from old leaven.

RL: What did the message of LaSalette mean for you personally? Did it play a role in your priestly vocation?

MC: It seems to me that LaSalette, of which the affiliated missionaries speak better than myself, is an invitation to humility before God, to poverty, to the action of grace, and the assurance of the merciful wedding of heaven and earth. It's also a call to compassion, that of Christ, which is expressed in the tears of Mary for his suffering members, and finally of Christian unity and solidarity; a new actualization of the divine light and love addressed to the world as a prophetic challenge.

RL: Before your birth, your father lived the mystery of LaSalette. He reflected, worked and published about it. Was it his influence that determined your research?

MC: During my adolescence, I was steeped in, and even wearied by, my father's immersion in it, but my interest came back in responding to the call of Christ (to become a priest). From my time in seminary, I shared with my father several journeys to Rome, including some meetings with John Paul II where we discussed the Apparition: "I pray to her every day... " "We are living these prophecies," the Pope told us.

RL: How many collections of archives have you consulted?

MC: Aside from numerous Vatican archives, I benefited from an unparalleled invitation to the study group of Jacques and Raïssa Maritain (*Cercles d'etudes J. et R. Maritain*) the friendship of some LaSalette Fathers and some Rogationist Fathers in Rome, as well as some Benedictines from Solesmes [Dom Philippe Dupont, Abbot since 1992] where I consulted the collections of Father Paul Gouin, and Maritain's correspondence with Dom Paul Delatte. The Servants of the Poor of Palermo, the Sisters of the Sacred Hearts (of Jesus and Mary) from Castellammare-di-Stabia and the Dioceses of Altamura and Grenoble also opened their doors to me with a great solicitude. And of course, I made use of the archives of *l'Association des Enfants de N. D de La Salette et de Saint Louis-Marie Grignion de Montfort,* [The Association of the Children of Our Lady of LaSalette and Saint Louis-Marie Grignion DeMontfort, founded by his father, Fernand]

RL: Do I understand correctly that the Gouin Collection [Solesmes *fund P. Gouin,* MYC] is the one which was in the possession of your father?

MC: It was indeed the collection of Father Paul Gouin, friend of Maritain and Our Lady of LaSalette. My father worked to publish that collection in the three first volumes of *Documents pour à servir l'histoire réelle de La Salette* [Documents to Serve the True Story of LaSalette] After the death of this priest, my father published three other collections of documents and Father Gouin's biography of Melanie:

- *Sœur Marie de la Croix, Bergère de La Salette* [Sister Melanie of the Cross, Shepherdess of LaSalette], completed in 1954, posthumously published in 1970, then translated into five languages. The Association also re-edited:
- La vie de Mélanie écrite par elle-même [The Life of Melanie Written by Herself], released by Leon Bloy, and the journal of Father Émile Combe, entitled:
- *Dernières années de Sœur Marie de la Croix* [Last Years of Sister Melanie of the Cross.] My father wrote three other books: on Pius IX and the Secrets, on Melanie and Bishop Zola, on Father Semenenko...

RL: The Secret of LaSalette lends itself to criticism; Paris was not destroyed.

MC: The prophecy of Melanie about Paris may be compared with that of Jonah; Nineveh wasn't destroyed after forty days because it converted. Cardinal Ratzinger also avoids the weak points of the Third Secret of Fatima; the Pope is not dead, he wasn't on a mountain, nor in the midst of a hostile crowd. A prophecy is not the pronouncement of a death sentence. It's a warning that invites to prayer and conversion in order to avert danger. Adherence to the message could change the course of events. Paris wasn't destroyed in 1870 but besieged, devastated by famine, suffering and finally, a revolution.

In the 1850s, Melanie had carved "Prussians 1870" on a table, with the formula "P S B 1871." Her religious Sisters understood effortlessly: "Paris will burn in 1871." Contrary to other mystics, the shepherdess from LaSalette had not spoken of an absolute destruction of the capital, as she perceived the limits of the disaster. In his vision of *The Epiphany* (1870), Saint John Bosco announced three successive chastisements on Paris, and four on Rome. Melanie spoke of the destruction of several other cities. In September 1870, she wrote to a priest: "Our prayers must be unceasing. If not, I'm beside myself in seeing these great cities torn up by the roots." In 1944,

Hitler asked "Is Paris burning?" The great atomic threat has receded these last few years, but the bomb has been popularizing itself little by little. Other countries have been threatening each other. India and Pakistan are examples. As the saying goes, "One cannot stop progress."

Where Don Bosco noted in his vision: "the events will unfold inexorably." Melanie said "Paris will be destroyed infallibly." Did the prophecies make such bold claims for nothing? I fear that the tears of Mary at LaSalette could not resemble more closely those of Christ in Jerusalem. Christian thinkers have already made the connection.

"Paris is worth a Mass," Henry IV would have said. All the stones of the capital, all the beautiful houses and monuments of the world are not worth the body and soul of a man, white or black, Palestinian or Jew, rich or poor. God "infallibly" reminds us of this. Melanie was reproached for her words about the negligence/apostasy of priests.

MC: The hyperbolic terms of the Secret resemble those of the [Biblical] Prophets. Mary compares unfaithful Christians to dogs. This echoes well the formulations of the Scriptures found in the New Testament: "Do not give to the dogs that which is holy" (Mt 7:6). "Look out for the dogs" (Phil 3:2) and the maximum severity regarding "the dog that returns to its vomit" (Prv 26:2; 2Pt 2:22).

RL: Permit me to come back to some difficulties. At the beginning of the very first recording of the Secret in 1851, Maximin said, "I don't know if it's the Blessed Virgin." She didn't tell them?

MC: No. Bernadette didn't receive, until after more than a month and a half, the revelation: "I am the Immaculate Conception." At LaSalette, only Melanie had certainty that it was "God [...] he Blessed Virgin [...] or some great saint." It's through Melanie (14 years old), that Maximin (11 years old) entered into the vision. She called him to come and see, up close, the stunning clarity that he was not seeing. He did not perceive it until he was close to her, at the moment when she shook him by the shoulder. It transpired for Maximin somewhat like it happened at Fatima for Francisco. Now, it's our turn to approach the Blessed Mother after them... in humility and sincerity. Maximin was careful not to anticipate the judgement of the Church.

RL: At the beginning of the twentieth century, Cardinal Mercier had begun a very advanced dialogue with Lord Halifax and the Church of England. He urged Rome to work toward reconciliation. There was perhaps, at that time, a possibility. But Rome officially declared the invalidity of the Anglican ordinations. This caused a severe and lasting rift. But this led to a happy consequence: the Anglicans took care to validate their ordinations by the presence of Old-Catholic Bishops or of confessions which kept the Apostolic succession. Other facts were positive in this way. Catholicism became the most common "denomination" in the United States. The Anglican movement and German Protestantism have experienced a similar evolution.

MC: Saint Dominic Savio, in the years 1850-60 had prophesied more explicitly the conversion of England. Saint John Bosco took up his pilgrim's staff to go and reveal this prophecy to Pius IX, who undertook to reinforce the Catholic hierarchy on the island.

RL: On July 6, 1851, Melanie wrote: "The Pope will be persecuted on all sides. From all sides he will be fired at." That formula was confirmed for John Paul II in more literal terms than the Third Secret of Fatima which related that the Pope would be killed. The Secret of LaSalette is not therefore less accurate than that of Fatima. Melanie speaks of a Pope who will be shot at, but who will triumph, and Maximin of a Pope "whom no one will expect" and who "will not be Roman" according to the Secret related to Mr. Dausse. Such was the election of John Paul II. No newspaper had prepared the biography of Cardinal Wojtyla among the expected group of papal contenders of which the white smoke of election would announce. Lucia of Fatima declared the deficiencies of the clergy of her time, and exhorted the Spanish and Portuguese Bishops to undertake its reform. She emphasized the sorrow of Mary about the crisis in the clergy. The prophecies of LaSalette and Fatima (from at least the third part of the Secret, visibly illustrated yet less exact) do not have the stunning precision of the Predictions of *Yvonne Aimée of Malestroit* to which I devoted a special volume.

MC: The prophecy of Melanie about the Vicar of Christ connects at least two popes. Gunshots were fired against the Quirinal Palace where Pius IX resided as Head of State, and John Paul II collapsed in Saint Peter's Square.

When in 1851 Maximin spoke of a pope to come who would not be Roman, the Engineer Dausse understood that he would be "foreign" to that part of Italy comprising the Pontifical States. But all the "images" of the Secrets are not to be taken literally. The styles must be distinguished. The apocalyptic "hail," the dreadful creatures of which Melanie speaks, may signify the discreet but powerful unchaining of Satan under various forms in our time. Reiterating his prophetic vision, Maximin distinguished, theologically and historically, the advent of (first) a collective, then a personal Antichrist. "Surfing" the waves from the depths of atheistic philosophies, the satanic dictators (Hitler, Stalin, Pol Pot, etc.) had, in effect, carried forward these ideas in their collective ideologies. Maritain noted again that the term "king" (who will reign for some years in France, according to Melanie) is primarily to be understood as one who takes leadership in the generic and Biblical sense.

As for Mother Yvonne, it's perhaps she who unites them. She believed in the Secret of Melanie, the Shepherdess of LaSalette, whom she declared to be "a great unrecognized mystic." Like Thérèse of Lisieux, Mother Yvonne offered herself for the sanctification of priests. She also suffered for them. There, where a Eucharistic miracle was produced, she prophesied a source of purification for priests. Certainly, LaSalette is Marian, but primarily ecclesial and sacerdotal. The living Crucifix is essential, worn by the Blessed Mother at LaSalette, and held in her hands at Pontmain.

RL: Your book comprises considerable research. It contains hundreds of references to unpublished texts. It extends and complements the "Authentic Documents" of Father Jean Stern, which stopped at November 4, 1854. Yours is a veritable treasure trove of documents. It permits a new evaluation of the scope of the Secrets.

Thank you for your discovery. It puts an end to a century and a half of uncertainties and controversies. It permits one to distill the meaning and importance of the message of LaSalette, an active call always to conversion and Christian solidarity, extended since then by other messages. The tears of Our Lady at Syracuse, Akita, Naju and elsewhere are always of relevance. These are the tears of love for a world preparing its own destruction by sinking into sin.

A) Fr. Pierre Archier, MS: First Superior General. Died at LaSalette
B) Bishop Bernard Bernard, MS: Founder in Norway
C) Fr. Henri Berthier, MS: Died repenting of his persecution of Melanie
D) Venerable Jean-Baptiste Berthier, MS: Founder in the Netherlands

CHAPTER 3

IS THE MESSAGE OF LASALETTE STRANGE OR PARTICULARLY DIFFERENT?

A Deeply Incarnate Word

The message of LaSalette has amazed, surprised and shocked many intellectuals. "Absurd, ridiculous, impossible!" exclaimed Lacordaire, the famous Dominican preacher, leader, and great intellectual.[1]

At Lourdes, where he made his last pilgrimage, Cardinal Saliège (1870-1955), a formidable defender of the Jews during the war, "killed" me [Corteville] with his gaze during our meal at the House of Chaplains. He repeated over and over again a question that I could not understand, because he was paralyzed up to, just above, his jaw. He was employing an expressive gesture that meant: "Saliège, up to here!" His active mind, his look, and an inarticulate groaning were his only means of oral expression. His secretaries, who were accustomed to his mumbling elocution, finally succeeded in transcribing his words to me, while dessert was served: "So what about the potatoes of LaSalette? What do you think of that?" One could discern the irony in the Cardinal's attitude.

In point of fact, the Virgin was speaking to the peasants of that time in a down-to-earth language, addressing their main concerns. At face value her message seemed to stoop to a low bar, for the rough and uncultivated. In France, there was general contempt for the peasant culture, for its very earthiness. However, this culture was more human, and in many ways superior, to the culture of the literate. Peasantry has long been a matrix for heroes and great minds. Even today, children from the countryside hold a certain superiority in school, until university level studies begin. Peasants are more balanced, better connected to reality, without technically being inferior.

Our Lady of LaSalette addresses the daily and vital concerns of the farmers of the Isère. She talks about a vineyard and fruits of the earth, just like the Bible describes the happiness of the wise man "in his vineyard and under his fig tree" (Mic 4:4) which means: in peace. She motivates them by the threat of disastrous crops and with promises of prosperity.

This language was proven to be true the next year. In 1847 potatoes and grapes rotted away. This sign induced a large conversion movement.

At a time when theology was mere abstract scholasticism, when some preachers learned the sermons of Bossuet or Massillon by heart, the patois of Our Lady of LaSalette took on the language of the Bible: prophetic, concrete, symbolic, and closely related to man's earthly life, including politics.

The seers were blamed for predicting the surrender of the Second Empire to the Prussians, and the revolution of the Communists. (Melanie gave exact dates). And after that, in a faraway future, the coming of a great king, or leader, who would guarantee peace. The prophets of Israel did the same thing. They admonished kings and even touched upon politics, without however getting involved in the government (just as the Polish bishops conducted themselves under Communist rule). The prophets of old reminded the powerful of the foundation of morals. God must be first in everything. Negotiations with great dominating empires leads to ruin: the forgetfulness of

God, their only daily and future hope.

Rousing the peasants of that time, Our Lady of LaSalette reminded them of the priority of God, whom they offend with their stupid blasphemies, their negligence of Mass, of the Sunday rest, of abstinence and fasting during Lent. She lays bare the conspiracies of Napoleon III against the Pope and, foremost, the collapse of Christian faith. But do we recognize the prophetic force, even in the Bible, so often reduced to mere history and anthropology?

Above all, the message of LaSalette reminds us that God is not indifferent to us. Consider Him, who has shared our life and given his life for us. Consider Him, who said: "There is no greater love than to give one's life for those whom He loves" (Jn 15:13).

A Letter Dropped from the Sky?

The improbability of any celestial communication has led to the search for a natural explanation, such as:

- a subjective invention of the imagination of the seer
- the influence of some text or a misleading person

It is not strange that at LaSalette, as elsewhere, this communication has been doubted. Some attribute the message to the imagination of the seers, especially regarding the Secrets. Others attribute it to the external influence of some person or text.

Father Delehaye, Dean of the Bollandists, those highly educated Jesuits who had the mission to clear the lives of the saints from legends and spurious miracles, took it upon himself to apply their critical method to LaSalette. Just as Father Dhanis, another Jesuit with a prominent reputation was involved in Fatima, so Father Delehaye searched for the key that could reduce the LaSalette phenomena to the natural level.

Father Delehaye was struck by the title given by the very first investigators (Ch 1:III) dating from September 20th, 1846: *Letter Dictated by the Blessed Virgin to Two Children on the Mountain of LaSalette*. This title resembles those of the leaflets which hawkers had distributed from the beginning of the 19th century.

Those "letters fallen from heaven" were divine threats because of the neglect of prayer and attendance at Sunday Mass, with the announcement of agricultural disasters, but promises of protection to whoever would take these messages seriously. In view of the fact that in good criticism, an earlier text is presumed to be the source of an analogous subsequent text, one would think that the message of LaSalette was only the echo of one of those, more or less, dramatic leaflets sought by keepers of public tranquility. However, before presuming such an influence, we have to take a closer look.

1. As to the existence of leaflets, according to Father Delehaye, and more precisely Father Jean Stern[2], the archives of the Isère have preserved three, "one, seized from a hawker in February 1818 in the north of the department," and the others in Gap, about forty kilometers from Corps, but nothing nearer to Corps. To the extent that we possess evidence of concurring investigations by which the constant testimony of the seers was established, to the same extent we lack the leaflets which would reveal the origin of the complete message, especially of the Secrets. Although the leaflet and other texts show a similar literary genre, they are far from including predictions of such content and scope.

   These differences are significant. The [early] letters "fallen from heaven" don't mention a precise location or date. At the most, a far and sacred place is named: "Miraculous letter found in Jerusalem by a priest" is how a document begins which was found by the police on the 23rd of January 1844[3], whereas the message of LaSalette is obtained from young shepherds with indubitable historical precision. The children's employers, who wanted to set the record straight for the investigators, used their authority, to note concisely the coherence of the oral testimony.

2. The title given to the account, Letter Dictated by the Blessed Virgin to Two Children... is obviously untrue. By no means does it reflect any quasi-judicial relationship, confirmed by subsequent, meticulous and concordant investigations. The title obviously does not come from the shepherds. It is given by the investigators. And that explains the connection to that of the well-chosen formula of the hawkers. The title is not a result of the inquiry, but is given because it is popular.

3. If there is a probable similarity, the editor felt the need to modify the usual title: 'Miraculous Letter Found' or 'Letter From Heaven" by the following more precise terms: Letter Dictated by the Blessed Virgin to Two Children. This was a dictation, and not a celestial document, like the Koran in Islamic tradition, or the Tablets of the Mosaic Law.

4. The message lacks the authoritarian and threatening character of the famed letters. It confirms, in line with the prophets, that abandonment of God will result in catastrophes, including material ones. The message of the shepherds is not even dictated from heaven, or an exhortation. It is a maternal call, a live conversation. Their mysterious interlocutor is pedagogic, like a mother helping her children grasp concepts that surpass, or like Jesus who taught his disciples who were sometimes slow to understand. She told them: "You don't understand, my children? I am going to tell you in a different way."[4]

She does not use an authoritarian manner. She uses a method of revealing things through questions, the maieutic method of Socrates and modern pedagogues. She does not say, like the leaflet "You must sanctify the Sunday."[5]

Rather She makes them become aware of what She means, starting out by asking questions that set them on the trail:

"Do you pray well, my children?" "Have you never seen spoiled wheat?"[6]

The Discovery of the Secret of LaSalette   51

Furthermore, it is not a formal notice. It is the language of a mother, suffering from the evil that her children are rushing towards. She asks them to have mercy on her:

"For all those times I suffer for you!"[7]

This deeply personal and maternal conversation with another world, is going to mark the two shepherds forever, and will become the major reference of their lives. The deep upheaval is the echo of Mary's tears. She wants to have this *made known* to all people. This is the essence of the message of LaSalette. It does not proceed from a mysterious writing, but from a person, in an unheard-of intimacy. Foremost, it is a cry from the heart. Everything starts from the silent tears, to instill upon the seers the importance of opening up to God, and to not let oneself be distracted by earthly preoccupations.

In spite of the similarities uncovered by Father Delehaye, and developed by C. Brunel and L.E. Halkin, the explanation of LaSalette is not literary, something acquired or abstracted from books. Its starting point is a profound solidarity, expressed in actions and words, by the messenger. The analogy and influence are located on the level of the laborious manner of expression by the seers. They search for words to convey the supernatural reality of the Apparition, in accordance with the limits of their intelligence and of their memory, which is mediocre and will cause them so many difficulties at catechism. They have a restricted religious vocabulary. They learned it from some relative who went to church more often than their parents. As to the themes of *warning, chastisement, conversion, and offer of protection*, these might correspond to an existing literary genre, but are well known to the common people.

With Father Stern, we can conclude: indeed there is a similarity, and perhaps an influence from popular prophecies of hawkers, and of the simple sermons of countryside priests, in the message of LaSalette which was conveyed by the children, who were dependent on the language styles of their time as noted by the two investigators, Stern and Dhanis. Regarding the common background that Maritain designates as "the unconscious of the spirit," see below. By the way, those styles explain in large part, the structure of formula itself: theophany, announcement of a birth (of Isaac, of Samson, of Jesus to the Virgin Mary). However, common vocabulary and the related literary genre fail to explain the originality of the message.

In the Bible it is impossible to explain the transcendent revelation of God and his Name (so often reduced to words and structures of the time), without relating the prologue of Saint John to the influence of the Platonic *logos*,[8] or the new precept of Christ, "Love your enemies!" (Mt 5:44) to the earlier precept of the Old Testament on *agape*, that is to say, love as it is in God. Here the message of Christ takes a step to a higher level in the Gospels.

It is legitimate to work as a scribe or expert on literary sources. However, one should be careful, out of concern for professional deformation, not to trivialize the text to preceding ideas, or miss the genuine newness of the divine revelation or even human genius, be it literary or scientific. It was Newton who renewed the physics of his time, before Einstein renewed it to a second degree.

THE LANGUAGE OF TEARS

The message of LaSalette, more so in images than in words, is at foundation a personal conversation, comparable to the first encounter between a man and a woman which would affect their entire lives. Those silent tears translate the maternal sorrow of the Virgin and the sorrow of God, intimately ashamed of our offenses. Those tears are a very strong expressive language, stronger than spoken language. Tears are the ultimate weapon of a mother when she has nothing else left to overcome ingratitude and to make the essential matter understood. And sometimes it happens that a great love is enkindled when one person finds consolation in another person who allows him to confide his distress.

In our world, where God is relegated, where sin is overabundant, where laws institutionalize murder and vice of all kinds, the Virgin took up this language of tears in an extremely expressive manner in Syracuse, Sicily, a magnificent popular sanctuary visited by popes beginning with Pius XII, and in the city of Akita, Japan, and elsewhere.

Better than any other supplication, a mother crying over her children touched the hardened hearts of the peasants of that time, people dependent on agricultural, manual labor. This language of the heart has touched mankind and induced a response.

Even more disconcerting is the peculiar clothing of Our Lady, foreign to traditional iconography, neither provincial, nor royal. Her headdress is neither a bonnet nor a crown. Her solemn demeanor evokes identification with the miter of the high priests of Israel. The sacerdotal interpretation of the Apparition's attire claims priority over its similarity to the clothing worn by the Dauphine province. The headdress also evokes that of Notre-Dame-du-Conseil [a statue in the 12th century cathedral near the Palace of the People] in Avignon.

The chains[9] hanging on her shoulders remind us of the precepts of Wisdom. This unusual symbol calls for the attention of Christians and theologians, like the proverbs of the Old Testament ["Cast not away wisdom's counsel. Put your feet into her fetters, and your neck into her chains" Sirach/Eccl 6:24-25] The most prominent attribute of the chain is the Cross. At the beginning of the Apparition, the Virgin weeps while seated, resting her head in her hands. When She stands up to speak to the shepherds, She displays the Cross, centered on her breast. The tears of Mary express the mysterious sorrow of God, related to the outpouring of his Blood at the Passion: the agony, the flagellation, the crowning with thorns, the piercing of the hands, the feet and his Heart, proof of his love "until the end" (Jn 13:1). It is the silent language of unrequited and wounded love.

The tears of the Virgin, glorious today, manifest to the world that the Passion of Christ (like every single moment of his earthly life) stays present to her, because his divine eternity encompasses an eternal duration. The Blood of Christ and the tears of Mary proclaim their eternal solidarity. Above all theological speculation, they instill the mystery of our intimate relationship with God.

This language, superficial and profound, simply extends the essential language of the Incarnation, "the Word became flesh" (Jn 1:14), to share our life. He has taken ours to give us his. However, Jesus says something later: "The flesh is useless" (Jn 6:53). So, the flesh in itself is nothing, and often the Bible mentions it in a negative way, when it symbolizes the sordid side and the concupiscence of a rational animal. Nevertheless, when the Creator makes himself creature, when the transcendent God assumes human flesh, the flesh is transfigured, purified, deified as much as He is humanized. "The Word became flesh" does not invite us to carnal materialism, but rather to live our fallen state and our inescapable vicissitudes in Godly love. This love, being the essence of God Himself, deifies and transfigures us so as to realize the last prayer of Christ to his Father before his death: "May they be one as We are one!" (Jn 17:21-22).

It is at this concrete and profound level, that the message of LaSalatte has moved not only peasants and simple people, but also great minds of the world: authors like Huysmans and , philosophers like Maritain, poets like Claudel, men with a heart, who were no strangers either to human love nor to love of God, and who were not imprisoned in rationalism. They had freed themselves from the narrow framework of their time, which made them prophets and great witnesses, extending beyond the boundaries of the Church.

God does not speak in the language of the wise and learned, as the apostle Paul asserts (cf 1Cor 1:25 & 3:18; Rom 1:14). He speaks the language of the Cross, a language at once both human and divine.

The seers will live this Way of the Cross, and speak its language throughout their lives, in spite of the belated education they received after the Apparition, beginning at the school of the Sisters in Corps. Later Maximin benefited from teachers at several minor and major seminaries, presbyteries, colleges and a university. Melanie did her novitiate at the Providence convent in Corenc and would adapt to several international situations that she encountered. Both retained a frank, concrete language, Maximin's being somewhat rude at times. Their formation did not alter their country roots, nor their natural behavior. They talk straight and clear, often poetically. In this respect as well, they have been faithful to the message of LaSalette.

Is this message only of regional interest: for a time in the past, for a restricted area? Or is it on the contrary "for *all* my people," as the Apparition repeatedly states?

Christ himself, the "Galilean," was depreciated by the establishment of his time. He was given this description as an epithet (Mt 26:69). High priests, scribes, and Pharisees despised his origins, made obvious by his regional and country-like accent. Of his marginal province, no prophet could come (Jn 7:41,52). From Nazareth, nothing good could come (Jn 1:46). However, his rustic origins, well incarnated, were the root of his universalism. That is also why He is the most universal of men. Let's not oppose the particular to the universal, the symbolic to the essential. They interpenetrate and condition one another, more strongly than it appears.

By its concrete and palpable content, the message of LaSalette stands out from the past. It shakes up hierarchy and classes. It shakes up social segregation, the elitism of money and educational degrees. It anticipates the preoccupations of today's generations: deceived by ideologies, preoccupied with real estate, the economy, society, and ecology.

The Virgin of LaSalette reminds us that God is interested in the daily life and labor of man, in which, and by which, we must realize our divine stature, through integral and real love.

A) Servant of God Canon J-B Gerin: bearer of the Secret to Pius IX
B) Canon Pierre-Joseph Rousselot: bearer of the Secret to Pius IX
C) Brothers Louis (& Michel) Perrin: priests who served the early pilgrims
D) Resemblance of Benjamin Dausse: devoted friend of Maximin

CHAPTER 4

THE EIGHT PRESERVED VERSIONS OF THE SECRET

Versions and Sources

Let us now read the eight versions of the Secret, of which the collection is finally complete. The ones officially recorded and delivered by a special embassy to Pope Pius IX (versions 1 and 2), are the first. So, they serve as the prototypes, the official norm and key to those that follow. In total there will be eleven possible versions. However:

- The first two versions were drafts, composed respectively by Maximin and Melanie. These papers were destroyed intentionally, after having been checked and finalized. In this process only one phrase was changed, by Melanie herself.
- The first long, handwritten version, sent by Melanie to Pope Pius IX in 1858, has been lost. However, Melanie, while staying in Marseille between the end of 1860 and September 1861, produced a fresh version (the seventh).
- The eighth version (1878) is a literal and complete copy of the seventh, with about one-third of the text presented in a slightly different order. This version was issued with the Imprimatur of Bishop Zola of the Diocese of Lecce.

The interpretation of those eight handwritten versions can be augmented by several "interviews" collected between 1848 and 1900, which converge upon one another.

The first, prior to the version of 1851, summarizes in four words, "Paris and the Pope," the whole Secret of LaSalette entrusted to the two children. It was translated by an eminent historian of LaSalette, Father Antoine Bossan, and was published by Miss Dastarac.

Today, July 8, 1871, Miss Dastarac tells me that around 1847, 1848 and in subsequent interviews with the two shepherds regarding their Secret, this is what they said:

1. Interview with Melanie:

   I don't want to know your Secret, but can't you tell me a little bit of it? No miss, I cannot say anything...

   Still, by the end she repeats to Miss Dastarac several times:

   Paris and the Pope! Paris and the Pope. Oh! unfortunate Paris!...

2. Interview with Maximin:

   Well, beginning in 1860, there will be revolution after revolution, wars and great conflicts. Religion will be persecuted. There will be religious wars. After that, all religions, Protestant and all the others, will converge into one single religion (evidently the Catholic religion)... and then it will be the end of the world.[1]

How the Seers Perceive the Message

The most recent of these interviews, regarding the latter days, is recalled by Father Combe in 1900. These private statements of the seers made to their intimate interviewers (B. Dausse, M. Prudhomme etc.), are an object of study in the thesis by Father Michel Corteville.[2] The diversity of the versions might surprise us. It has to do with the different kind of requests, influences, events, and the working of the memory. But these differences do not compromise their overall unity. The variation corresponds to the nature of the revelation received by the children, namely in two forms, word and image.

Words to Express the Heavenly Images

The seers not only transcribe the remembrance of words, but also the visions that accompanied the revelation of the Secret, a revelation more defined by images than by words. Melanie pointed this out to Father Felicien Bliard, in a letter written on December 26, 1870 (reproduced below, Letter no 7). The vision was in images, in a symbolic display, beyond "words":

A great veil lifted, and events unrolled before my eyes and my imagination. She [i.e., the Blessed Virgin] uttered all her words while a large space unfolded before me and I saw the events, and from this vista one sees a thousand, thousand times more things than what the ears hear.

So, there is more in the vision than in the words. And this compendium, of words and visions, the seers grasped in the light of God. They are referring to a light, this transcendent light, which is also mentioned by the seers of Fatima: Francisco, Jacinta and Lucia. As Lucia said in the third Secret of Fatima:

The light, that is, God.

Melanie described these things in her own fashion:

I saw the changes taking place on earth, while God, unchanging in his glory, looked at the Virgin who was lowering herself to speak to the two shepherds [...] one raises oneself to a level that is not heaven perhaps, without a physical change in position. "Was I in my body or outside my body?" ("Whether in the body, I cannot tell; or whether out of the body, I cannot tell" as Saint Paul said similarly in 2Cor 12:2.) However, one sees and hears everything. One understands without a word being uttered, and one forgets oneself completely.

Therefore, despite her lack of intellectual education, Melanie analyses very precisely the fundamental perception to which both she and Maximin constantly refer to, while being obliged to express in human language the symbols of the future that they had perceived in the intense light of God. The images themselves are quite concrete:

> *We see the kings of the earth taking action, making alliances and undoing alliances. We see the jealousy of some, the ambition of others, and all of this in one single word escaping from the lips of She who makes hell tremble, the Virgin Mary.*

To those who criticize her by saying: "The Virgin hasn't really said that much," Melanie responds in *substance*: [The following is not a direct quotation:]

Our depictions are at once, too detailed and too inadequate; it is impossible to say everything. I am very ignorant. However, even if I were highly educated, I would still be unable to write accurately about the things from above, because the articulations of the most learned scholars could not describe a shadow of the truth by employing the common expressions which we use to speak to one another. The language from above, intuitive and immediate, is a movement of the soul, of the longings of the soul, of the momentum of the soul, of animated eyes that communicate with one another.

Ultimately, this light where everything gets unified, is simply love, since "God is love." Melanie concludes with utmost precision and depth, that all this is ineffable, inexplicable in the language of humans:

> *And above all, myself, poor vile dust, I need to be reborn to be able to speak about these things. Let us love Our Lord with all our heart, He who bestows on us interior knowledge and existence. Oh! One has to be mad with love for the One who was the first to be mad with love for us!*

Like all true mystics, she identifies herself deeply with love, according to the deepest confidence of Christ: "May they be one as the Father and I are One" (Jn 17:21-22 and passim), because the love of the Three Persons, who are all love, grace and benevolence, is the personal, interpersonal and objective principle of all creation, its light and its meaning.

It is in this light, and therefore in this love, that Melanie's last words to Father Felicien Bliard should be understood:

> *I saw the whole world. I saw with the eye of the Lord; it was a picture in*

> *motion. I saw the blood of those put to death, and the blood of the martyrs (as did Lucia at Fatima); but the love of this sweet Virgin (identified with the love of God) enveloped me, and took the place of everything else (including myself), and it made me melt. I could not think anymore. I did not have the power to reflect or react. At the time, I certainly was conscious, but I did not speak with words. When the sweet Virgin started walking, She did not need to tell me to follow, definitely not! I was not aware that I existed. I did not think of having feet to walk with. I was simply attracted. I was attached to this delightful beauty, Mary!*

She perceived God through Mary, like the seers of Fatima perceived the depths of hell. The light and the absolute Love, who is God Himself, the Source, the meaning and the purpose of all things, is the One in whom we are called to become one, out of love, according to Saint John (Jn 17:21-22). That is why Melanie ends her letter with these words, which justify the limits of the language for the world beyond:

> *Although I would like to explain all of this, never ever could I succeed in expressing it completely.*

The profound quality of this text bears witness to a true mystic, and not the mythomaniac some wanted to make of her, which only augmented her difficulty. Melanie and Maximin, like the shepherds of Fatima, were seized by the glory of God. Locution and life, unity and love, pervade their vision and their way of expression. It constitutes an inexhaustible source of words that are inevitably symbolic, and remain inadequate, causing them to improvise with new expressions each time (except versions 7 and 8). Undoubtedly, the prophetic vision with all its historical ramifications remained enigmatic to themselves.

This explains both the validity and the limitations of their testimonies, as well as their different versions. The more so since they did not multiply long versions in which they would have lost themselves. According to their mission, and the inquiries they underwent over time, they tried to express what seemed to them the most important, without however being ever completely satisfied with it.

Among mystics and seers there are some who, at times, lose the memory, deeply and radically of those perceptions as well as that secondary state of being. Others relive these revelations with an extraordinary intensity that transforms them. (I have met several of them, like Jacqueline Aubry of Île Bouchard). It is through their concrete trials and the fruits of these trials, through their radiance and their transparency, and through the consistency of words that flowed from the "source," that delineate their authenticity. This divine origin was evident in a transcendent degree in Maximin and Melanie, who failing in human language with its limited possibilities, walked in the footsteps of the prophets of Israel testifying to how God sees and feels about the world of their time, in its true meaning, created out of love and completed by love, which is the measure of the work and judgment of God.

I. THE TWO 1851 VERSIONS PRESENTED TO POPE PIUS IX (JULY 3-6, 1851)

The two versions of July 1851 agree on the essentials, but differ in their development and even in their tone. The Secret of Maximin is shorter, simpler and less severe. Melanie is concerned with her audience: being understood well, not causing too much pain, as she put it. However, this could not prevent the tears shed by Bishop DeBruillard.

1. The Written Text of the Secret by Maximin, July 3, 1851[3]

Maximin wrote his Secret for the Bishop, in the presence of close collaborators of Bishop DeBruillard, in the evening of the 3rd of July displaying not the least concern. Indeed, he was obliged to start all over again because of the sloppy ink stains he had made. The spattered autograph was burned. Solemnly, Mr. Dausse handed the Secret to Bishop DeBruillard, so that Maximin would grasp its importance, as he beheld the Bishop place his seal upon it before sending it to the Pope. At 1300 hours [1:00 p.m.] the sealed envelope was also signed by two witnesses.

The handwritten Secrets, carried to Pius IX by two trusted envoys in 1851, were kept in the Pope's nightstand. Leo XIII enthusiastically studied them a few months after his election. He invited Melanie tomeet with him. In 1999 the documents were discovered among his papers.

In the thesis [of Father M. Corteville], the Secrets are edited meticulously, line by line, with the misspellings and the punctuation mistakes of the young shepherds, for whom writing in French was no small challenge. This present book, intended for a wider audience, presents the literal version, but with corrected spelling and punctuation to present a clear and intelligible text. Like all prophecies, this one is a call to vigilance. It is a warning about the future, but without satisfying curiosity. The seers do their best to interpret unfamiliar pictorial elements. They extrapolate. They confuse the logical sense with the temporal (like the apostle Paul in the Epistle to the Thessalonians). In Chapter 8 we will try to untangle the testimonies. Here we will reproduce them in chronological order.

On September 19, 1846, we saw a beautiful lady.

We never said that this lady was the Blessed Virgin,

but we always said that She was a beautiful lady.

I do not know if it is the Blessed Virgin or another person.

As for me, today I believe that it was the Blessed Virgin.

Here is what this lady said to me:

If my people continue, what I am going to tell you will happen sooner.

If they change a little, it will be sometime later.

France has corrupted the universe; one day she will be punished. The Faith will die out in France. Three quarters of France will not practice religion anymore, or almost none. The other part will practice it without really practicing it.

Then, after [that], nations will convert; the Faith will be rekindled everywhere.

A great nation, north of Europe, now Protestant, will be converted. By the support of this nation, all the other nations of the world will be converted.

Before all that happens, great troubles will arise in the Church, and everywhere.

Then, after, our Holy Father the Pope will be persecuted.

His successor will be a pontiff that nobody expects.

Then, after, a great peace will come, but it will not last long.

A beast will come to disturb her.

All that I am telling you here, will arrive in the other century, or later than the year two thousand.

signed Maximin Giraud[4]

(She[5] told me to make this known some time before.)

My most Holy Father, I ask your holy blessing to one of your sheep.

Grenoble, the 3rd of July, 1851

2. The Written Text of the Secret by Melanie[6]

Melanie made a record of the Secret for the first time, on the 3rd of July at Corenc at the convent of the Sisters of Providence. She sealed this version at 10:00 a.m., and someone brought it to the Bishop's house. The next day she declared that she had not expressed herself adequately about the trouble that would happen to two cities (Paris and Marseille). She made it seem that it happened simultaneously whereas it happened successively. Canon Rousselot made her rewrite her Secret on the 6th of July. Then Engineer Dausse led her to the Bishop's residence, where Bishop DeBruillard read the document before sealing it.

J.M.J.

The Secret that the Blessed Virgin gave to me on the mountain of LaSalette, on the 19th of September 1846.

Melanie, I am going to tell you something that you won't tell anyone:

The time of God's wrath has arrived!

If, after you have told the people what I just told you, and also what I am still going to tell you

if, after that, they don't repent,

(if they do not do penance,

and if they do not stop working on Sundays,

and if they continue to blaspheme the Holy Name of God),

in one word, if the face of the earth does not change,

God will take vengeance7 against those ungrateful people, slaves of the devil.

My Son will release his power!

Paris, this city soiled by all sorts of crimes, will infallibly perish.

Marseille will be destroyed in a short while.

When these things happen, chaos on earth will be complete,

The world will surrender to its impious passions.

The pope will be persecuted from all sides.

He will be shot at. They will want to kill him,

But they cannot do anything against him.

Once more the Vicar of God will be triumphant.

Priest and nuns, and the true servants of my Son will be persecuted,

and some will die for their faith in Jesus Christ.

At the same time, a famine will reign.

After all that has happened,

many people will recognize the hand of God acting on them.

They will convert and do penance for their sins.

A great king will ascend to the throne, and will reign for several years.

Religion will flourish again and will expand everywhere on earth and fecundity will be great. The world, happy not to lack anything, will start to go astray again, abandoning God, and giving in to its evil passions.

Among the ministers of God, and the spouses of Jesus Christ, there will be some who will surrender to disorder, and that will be the most horrific.

Finally, hell will reign on earth.

That will be the time when the Antichrist will be born from a religious;

but woe to her! Many people will believe in him,

because he will claim that he is the one coming from heaven.

Woe to those who will believe this!

The time is not far off. There won't be more than twice 50 years from now.

My child, you won't tell what I just told you.

(You won't tell it to anyone.

You won't say whether you have to tell it one day.

You won't say what it's about.)

Finally, you won't tell any of it until I tell you to do so!

I pray our Holy Father the Pope to grant me his holy blessing.

Melanie Mathieu, shepherdess of LaSalette,
Grenoble the 6th of July 1851.
J.M.J.+

3. Maximin's Text Written for Benjamin Dausse, August 11th, 1851

On that day Engineer Dausse asked Maximin:

"Do you remember it well?"

And Maximin, generous as always (he would give away even his clothes), writes it down and gives it to him in response. The autograph was found in the archives of the Sacred Congregation of the

Doctrine of the Faith. It was edited by Father Jean Stern[8] after a copy by Benjamin Dausse. It looks very much like the text of the 3rd of July, but with some variations; in our rendering we respect the spelling. [This cannot be maintained in an English translation, so everything has been corrected for clarity.]

"On September 19, 1846, I did see a Lady bright as the sun, which I believe to be the Blessed Virgin. But I never said it was the Blessed Virgin. I always said that I had seen a beautiful Lady, but never the Blessed Virgin. It is for the Church to judge if it really is the Blessed Virgin, or someone else, by what I am going to say now. She told it to me in the middle of her speech. After, the grapes will rot and the nuts will go bad. She started by telling me:

If my people don't convert, what I am saying will happen sooner. If they change, the following will happen later. Three quarters of France will lose their faith and the other quarter will practice it without fervor. Then after that, faith will revive in France.

A country in the north, now Protestant, will convert and by support of this country the other nations will convert. There will be peace, and after the peace has come, a beast will come disturbing this peace, and peace will come after all countries will be converted. The successor of the Pope will be someone nobody expects. "He won't be Roman."[9] The beast will come during the peace, and the peace and the beast will come in the 19th century or in the 20th at the latest.[10] You won't tell this to anyone. That is all She said to me."

Maximin Giraud, shepherd
11th August 1851 at Grenoble[11]

II. NEW VERSIONS MADE AT THE REQUEST OF BISHOP GINOULHIAC

Why did Bishop Ginoulhiac ask for this new version, in an authoritarian manner that distressed Melanie?[12]

He had to decide on serious questions.

1. His own inner conviction was utterly aloof regarding LaSalette, but bearing the responsibility of a bishop and the pastoral care of the flourishing pilgrimage [to the site], up until what point must he agree with the judgement of Bishop DeBruillard?
2. What credit and what position should he grant the seers, cherished by his predecessor, popular and sometimes revered (not without risk), although so poor and disconcerting?
3. Finally, how to reconcile the instructions of Bishop DeBruillard and those of Pope Pius IX in favor of the Apparition, and those, quite opposed, of the Empire, with whom he was on good terms?[13]
4. He thought it necessary to get to know the content of the message destined for the Pope, which was never passed on to him, so as to be able to monitor the ongoing discussions.

4. Maximin, August 5th, 1853

Under these circumstances, Maximin, anxious to reveal the whole Secret, speaks daringly of "the Eaglet." At the time, this symbolic name of the Duke of Reichstadt (died 1832) designated his half-brother, Napoleon III, whose reign was just beginning, and whose fall is predicted. The "viper" designates the next regime and the persecutors of the 3rd Republic in a symbolic way, but also the anarchistic and revolutionary movements of the Communists (1871). The Marxist regime will prove itself to be more Communist than during the Revolution of 1789.

We have divided this meandering version into three paragraphs:

1. The first paragraph contains new elements, mainly about the Emperor. The later versions of Melanie specify that he "would like to be pope and emperor at the same time." They point out that, like his father, he will force the Pope in favor of his politics, by helping Garibaldi and Victor Emmanuel to reduce the Head

of the Church, as Pope Pius IX puts it, to a "prisoner of the Vatican."

2. The second paragraph repeats the substance of what Maximin wrote to Pope Pius IX in 1851.

3. The third paragraph mingles one and the other by associating ideas, not in a synthetic but rather in an intuitive way. In this way his memory actualizes visions that are difficult to interpret within the context of actual events, as some royalist pilgrims would have liked to see him do. Whereas Melanie talks about a king to come, Maximin says "the son of Louis XVI"; but just after the Apparition he had not known anything about this king. The version therefore has been falsely interpolated, and because of that, the inventive Maximin placed his head in the mouth of the wolf. The autograph, lost today, is known by a copy in the dossier of the Sacred Congregation of the Doctrine of the Faith, and was heretofore unpublished. It is the last version of Maximin (we have harmonized the typography).

An eaglet will rise.

When he grows a bit,

he will turn on himself.

Then he will rise higher.

Then his feathers will fall off.

Finally, without feathers, he will fall on daggers.

After his death there will be chaos.

Then a viper will come, which is in the heart of France today. Then she will die.

Then the son of Louis XVI will arrive;

He will reign for a short while.

A great man will succeed him;

then, after having restored everything, he will withdraw.

The East will chastise the West.

There will be great misfortunes in France during this war. But she will bloom again...

And then in France: three quarters of the population will lose the Faith; the other quarter will have Faith, but very little.

Then two great nations will convert.

England will be the instrument through which all the nations of the world will convert.

This all will happen between 1850–1860.

The beast will pass over the year 60.

But wars, revolutions, etc. between 50 and 60.

France will regain the Faith; then a great king will come.

The pope will die; a French pope will succeed him,

and this pope and this king will be as one.

There will be only one religion and one kingdom.

Then there will come a beast, who will ravage this peace, and who will disrupt the Church.

Many people will be its victim.

5. & 6. Melanie, August 12 and 14, 1853

Melanie, being pressured the same way as Maximin, was more careful. She did not reveal the message she had received about the emperor (of whom she will speak so explicitly in the versions of 1860 and 1878). She just makes a vague allusion to the reprehensible regimes mentioned above:

"A bad man will reign over France."

The government of Napoleon III was not anticlerical. He added to his popularity by reopening the grotto of Lourdes, which had been closed by the prefect in the beginning of autumn, 1858. In the Pyrenees, Napoleon's reputation would be hailed as "friend of the Virgin," while the fact that he was an enemy of the Pope was downplayed. Melanie had a presentiment of the anticlericalism of the Communists and the government of the prosecutor Combes, who at the end of the 19th and the beginning of the 20th century, confiscated the assets of the Church of France and expedited the expulsion of the religious.

But the request of the Bishop - to reveal the Secret "entirely" - caused much difficulty for Melanie since, unlike Maximin, she was aware of her mission: to reveal more of the message only when the Virgin would instruct her (i.e., in 1858). In 1853, she alluded to it slightly more than in 1851, however without explicitly mentioning religious and political questions, nor wars or persecutions.

Therefore, her version mixes in everything she already had said, or suggested to the people in her surroundings, regarding the troubles due to impenitence. She mixes the chronological order, as often happens with prophecies. For example, in the attack on the Quirinal where Pius IX was residing, she sees part of the message come true, but of course she did not know about the more specific attack that would almost kill John Paul II.

Melanie had edited the Secret twice, on the 12th and the 14th of August (the first with lapses of dates). Father Stern has published the second text,[14] after a copy of Father Ginon that was kept in the Bishop's house at Grenoble. We will reproduce the first text while respecting its orthography. We will mark in italics the additional text that is absent in version 6.

>J.M.J.
>
> The Secret that the Blessed Virgin told me on the Mountain of LaSalette, the 19th of September 1846.[15]
>
> Melanie Mathieu[16] I am going to tell you something that you won't tell anyone until I tell you to do so.
>
> If, after you will have told the people everything I tell you, and everything I will tell you, after what I forbid you to tell; if after that the world does not convert, if, in short, the face of the earth does not change for the good, there will come great disasters. There will be a great famine and a war at the same time, all

over France in the first place, then in Russia and England. After those revolutions, there will be great famine in three parts of the world. In 1863 during that famine, there will be many crimes committed, notably in the cities. But woe to the clergy, to the religious, for they will be the target of the worse crimes happening on earth, and my Son will chastise them in a horrible way. After those wars and those famines, all the people, for a little while, will recognize the hand of the Almighty God who strikes them. They will return to their religious duties, and peace will be restored. But it won't last long.

Persons consecrated to God will forget the duties of their religion and will fall into a great relaxation, forgetting God almost completely. Finally, everyone will forget their Creator.[17] *That is when a great chastisement will begin again.* God, irritated towards everyone, will most certainly strike in the way that I am going to describe; *a bad person will reign over France. He will persecute religion. Churches will be closed.* They will be burnt. A great and long famine will come, together with pestilence and a civil war. At the same time Paris will be destroyed. Marseille will disappear under the torrent, and that will be the time when the true servants of God will receive the crown of martyrdom. The pope and the ministers will be persecuted. However, since they will have remained faithful, God will be with them, and the Head of the Church will obtain the palm of martyrdom, as well as the religious. May the Sovereign Pontiff have his weapons ready and may he be ready to march and to defend the religion of my Son. May he unceasingly ask for the strength of the Holy Spirit, and those consecrated to God do so also. Because religion will be persecuted everywhere, many priests and religious will give up the Faith, oh, how my Son will be offended by the ministers and the brides of Jesus Christ. *After this persecution there will be just one more before the end of the world.*

There will be three years of calm, then will come the birth and the reign of the Antichrist, which will be more than horrible, he will be born from a religious of a very strict Order. This religious will be considered as the holiest of his monastery, [the father of the Antichrist will be a bishop, etc. etc. Here the Blessed Virgin gave me the Rule, and She told me another Secret about the Last Times] And the religious of that same monastery will be blinded, not recognizing that hell is leading them.

The end of the world won't occur until after twice forty years.

Sister Mary of the Cross, born Melanie Mathieu[18]
Corenc, the 12th of August 1853

In those last short versions, the two seers insist on persecutions. Melanie enlarges the horizon.

III. MELANIE'S EXPANDED VERSIONS (1858-1878)

[7] In 1858, Melanie sends the Pope the Complete Secret: the Lost Version

It was in September 1858 that she sent this to Pius IX, supplementing everything that she had not been able to reveal to him in 1851.

On the 3rd of September 1858, the ordinary of Darlington, Bishop Hogarth, wrote to Bishop Talbot, superior of the English college:

> Sister Mary of the Cross has informed me that part of the Secret given to her by Our Lady of LaSalette, had to be kept until this year. She therefore wrote a letter to His Holiness, handing over to him the other parts of the Secret. She really does not want to send these documents by mail, so she humbly requests you to deliver them to His Holiness in person.[19]

A little later he added this note to Bishop Talbot:

> The letter to His Holiness which is being handed to you is a deep Secret of which Sister Mary of the Cross has told me that she received from Our Lady at LaSalette, *but which was not to be revealed to anyone before the year of Our Lord 1858*. No one had anything to do with this writing; no one has seen the contents of it, nor heard anything about it, except what has been said before. I

saw her seal the letter herself in the presence of Rev. Mother Prioress and of the Very Rev. Canon Brown, the confessor of the Carmelites.

Certainly, Pius IX took note of this letter before it disappeared inside the Vatican.

7. The First Known Manuscript (Marseille, circa 1860: 5 pages)

By the end of September 1860, Melanie had arrived at Marseille. There she rewrote the Secret for her superiors, but she did not receive permission to divulge it. Her original manuscript (subsequently lost) was copied at Castellammare-di-Stabia by Father Felicien Bliard sometime before the end of January 1870. Father Bliard passed this on to the canon lawyer Father Regis Girard, who published it in France with the blessing of Pius IX, in an informal manner through articles in a journal. [See entry "1871—1874" in the Chronological Table.] In 1873 this version of the Secret was published in Italy by Father Felicien Bliard with the *Imprimatur* of the Archdiocese of Naples. [†Editor: Cardinal-Archbishop of Naples, Sisto Sforza was the Metropolitan and friend of Bishop Petagna of Castellammare where Melanie was residing. Therefore, this Archdiocese was the proper authority for approval of this private revelation.] This edition of the Secret was rediscovered by Father Émile Combes in 1902. It was photographed by Father Gouin.

8. The Definitive Version of Lecce (1878 to 1879)

At Castellammare on the 21th November 1878, eleven years after the 1866 detailed account of Maximin (refer to Ch1 Sec II), Melanie recorded her personal version, taking great care to relate the Apparition in detail. In his 1866 account Maximin had not included anything about the Secret, but now, at the point of the story where the Virgin gives her the Secret, Melanie transcribes it in full, making the text of Marseille complete in its definitive form. Then in Lecce, with the Imprimatur of Bishop Zola on the 15th of November, she published this testimony. In 1904, the year of her death, before leaving France, she will republish this booklet.[20]

In France, this testimony, because of its polished style, would be denounced as a subjective extrapolation of Melanie: the fruit of a "Copernican, egocentric revolution."[21] But the major themes, reputedly novel, can already be found in the earlier versions. Like Maximin in his later years, the seer remains passionate about the vision which had delighted her, and which no one else would be able to express in her place.[22]

In addition to the sections of the text which are numbered by Melanie [roman numerals], we have added subtitles [centered in parentheses], and printed in italics the additional texts that do not appear in the Marseille version. (our n. 7) Here is the text, with the title given by the seer.

[NOTE FOR THE 2024 ENGLISH EDITION: *All the words of the Blessed Mother have been italicized, making no distinction between the Marseille and Lecce texts, or the French or the patois. The Holy Virgin began her discourse in French. When Melanie had difficulty understanding the French word for potatoes, Our Lady changed to the local patois, Dauphinois, a sub-dialect of the Occitan Alpine-Provencal dialect, more Italian than French. For the Secret and the Rule, Melanie states in the Lecce text that these were given in French although much of the Secret seems to have been transmitted more by an apocalyptic vision than by words. After this section, Our Lady resumed in patois until the very end when She admonished in French that the message be made known. Paragraph numbering had been introduced to the Lecce text by commentators before 1907, according to Leon Bloy, but not reproduced in the French edition of* Découverte. *Paragraph numbering has been inserted in the English edition to facilitate study.*]

THE APPARITION OF THE MOST HOLY VIRGIN ON THE MOUNTAIN OF LASALETTE ON SEPTEMBER 19, 1846[23]

I
The Two Shepherds Meet One Another

On the 18th of September [1846], the eve of the holy Apparition of the Blessed Virgin, I was alone, as usual, watching over my masters' cows. Towards eleven o'clock in the morning, I saw coming towards me, a little boy. I took fright at this, for it seemed to me that everyone ought to know that I avoided any sort of company. This child came up to me and said: "Little girl, I'm coming with you, I'm from Corps, too."

At these words, my unpleasant nature displayed itself, and taking a few steps backwards, I said to him: "I don't want anybody around. I want to be alone."

But this child followed me, saying, "Please, let me stay with you. My master told me to come and watch over my cows together with yours. I'm from Corps."

I walked away from him, gesturing to him that I didn't want anyone [near me], and, having gone away, I sat down on the grass. There, I talked with the little flowers of the Good God. A moment later, I looked behind me and found Maximin sitting next to me. He immediately said to me, "Keep me with you, I'll be good."

But my bad nature would not hear reason. I jumped to my feet, and ran away a little further off without saying anything to him, and again I started playing with the little flowers of the Good God. In an instant, Maximin was there again, telling me that he would be very good, that he wouldn't talk, that he would get bored all by himself, and that his master had sent him to be with me, etc. This time, I took pity. I gestured to him to sit down, and I kept on playing with the little flowers of the Good God. It wasn't long before Maximin broke the silence by bursting into laughter (I thought he was making fun of me). I looked at him and he said to me, "Let's have some fun, let's make up a game."

I said nothing in reply, for I was so ignorant I didn't understand what games with other people were, always having been alone. I continued playing with the flowers, alone, and Maximin came right up close to me, doing nothing but laughing, telling me that flowers didn't have ears to hear me and that we should play together instead. But I had no liking for the game he suggested that we play. Meanwhile I began to converse with him, and he told me that the ten days he was to spend with his master would soon be over and then he would go home to his father in Corps, etc. While he was talking, the bell of LaSalette, started ringing; it was the Angelus. I gestured to Maximin to raise his soul to God. He took off his hat and was silent for a moment. Then I said, "Do you want to eat lunch?" "Yes," he replied, "Let's start."

We sat down and I brought out of my bag the provisions my masters had given me and, as was my custom, before breaking into my little round loaf, I made a cross in the bread with the point of my knife, and a little hole in the middle, saying, "If the devil's in there, may he come out, and if the Good God is in there may He stay in!" and quickly, quickly, I covered the little hole. Maximin burst into loud laughter and kicked the loaf out of my hands. It rolled down the mountainside and was lost from sight. I had another piece of bread which we shared. Then we played a game. Then, realizing that Maximin was still hungry, I pointed out a place on the mountainside covered with all kinds of berries. I urged him to go and eat some and he went straight away. He ate some berries and brought back his hat filled with them. In the evening we walked back down the mountain together and we promised each other to come back to keep our cows together.

(The Second Meeting: The Day of the Apparition)

The next day, September 19th, I met Maximin on the way up. We climbed the mountain together. I thought that Maximin was very good, very straightforward, and would willingly talk about what I wanted to talk about. He was also very flexible and had no fixed opinions. He was just a bit curious, for, when I walked off away from him, as soon as he saw that I had stopped, he would run over quickly to me to see what I was doing and hear what I was saying to the flowers of the Good God. And if he arrived too late, he would ask me what I had said. Maximin asked me to teach him a game. It was already late morning. I told him to gather some flowers to make the "Paradise." We both set to work. Soon we had quite a few flowers of various colors. I could hear the village Angelus ringing, for the weather was fine without a cloud in the sky. Having said to the Good God what [prayers] we had learned, I said to Maximin that we ought to drive our cows on to a small plateau near the ravine, where there would be stones with which to build the "Paradise."

We led our cows to the designated spot and then we had our little meal. Next, we started collecting stones to build our little house, which comprised of a ground-floor which was, so to speak, our living room, and then a floor above which was to be, according to us, "Paradise." This floor was all decorated with flowers of different colors, made into wreathes held together with flower stems. This "Paradise" was covered by a single large stone on which we strew flowers. We had also hung wreaths all around it. Once the "Paradise" was finished, we gazed upon it. We became sleepy. We took a couple steps backwards from there, then fell asleep on the grass.

The beautiful Lady seated herself upon our Paradise and it did not break down.

II
Debut of the Apparition

Waking up and not seeing the cows, I called to Maximin as I walked up the little hill. From there I could see that our cows were grazing peacefully. I was on my way down, while Maximin was on his way up, when suddenly I saw a beautiful light shining more brightly than the sun, and I could only just manage to utter: "Maximin, do you see, over there? Oh! my God!" At the same moment I dropped the stick I was holding. I can't explain all the beautiful things that happened inside of me during that moment, but I felt drawn to the Lady with a tremendous respect, full of love, and my heart beat so quickly that I thought it would burst from within me.

I kept my eyes firmly fixed on this light, which was motionless, then as though it had opened up, I saw another light, much brighter and moving, and in this light, I saw a most beautiful Lady sitting on top of our "Paradise," with her head in her hands.

This beautiful Lady stood up. She partially crossed her arms while looking at us, and said to us:

"Come forward, my children. Do not be afraid! I am here to announce to you great news!"

These soft, sweet words made me fly to her, and my heart would have wished to attach itself to her forever. When we drew close to the beautiful Lady, standing in front of her to her right, She began to speak, and from her beautiful eyes tears also started to flow:

"If my people will not repent, I will be compelled to let go of the hand of my Son. It is so heavy and weighs me down so much I can no longer keep hold of it.

For how long a time I have suffered for the rest of you! If I do not want my Son to abandon you, I must take it upon myself to entreat Him incessantly. And the rest of you, you think little of this. No matter how much you pray, how much you do, you will never be able to repay the suffering I have taken on for you.

I gave you six days for work. I kept the seventh for myself, and no one wishes to grant it to me. This is what weighs down so much the arm of my Son.

Those who drive carts cannot speak without putting the name of my Son in the middle. These are the two things which weigh down so much the arm of my Son.

If the harvest is spoiled, it is because of the rest of you. I made you see this last year with the potatoes. You took little account of this. On the contrary, when you found spoiled potatoes, you cursed, and you included the name of my Son. They will continue to go bad; by Christmas there will be none left."

At this point I was trying to interpret the word "potatoes" (*pommes de terre* in French); I thought I understood it to be apples (*pommes*). The beautiful and good Lady, reading my thoughts, started again in this way:

"You do not understand, my children? I will tell it to you another way."

(Her discourse[24] in patois begins here.)

"If the harvest is spoiled, it is because of the rest of you. I made you see this last year with the potatoes. You took little account of this. On the contrary, when you found spoiled potatoes, you cursed, and you included the name of my Son. They will continue to go bad; by Christmas there will be none left.

If you have wheat, don't sow it. Whatever you sow, the creatures will eat it, and whatever comes up will fall to dust when you thresh it.

A great famine will come. Before the famine comes, children under the age of seven will begin to tremble, and will die in the arms of those who hold them. Others will do penance through hunger. The nuts will go bad; the grapes will rot."

At this point I was enthralled with the Lady's beauty. I ceased to hear her for a time: nevertheless, I saw that She continued to move her lovely lips, as though speaking. Maximin was receiving his Secret.

Then, turning to me again, the most holy Blessed Virgin spoke to me and gave me a Secret in French. This Secret, just as She gave it to me, follows in its entire form.

III
The Complete Version of the Secret

[1]   *"Melanie, what I am about to tell you now will not always be secret. You can publish it in [18]58."*

(The Underlying Cause of the Misfortunes: the Unworthiness of the Ministers)

[2] *"The priests, ministers of my Son, by their wicked manner of life, by their irreverence and impiety in celebrating the Holy Mysteries, by their love of money, honor and pleasures, priests have become cesspools of impurity. Yes, the sins of priests cry out for vengeance, and vengeance looms over their heads. Woe to those priests and persons consecrated to God, who by their infidelity and wicked lives, are crucifying my Son again! The sins of those consecrated to God scream to heaven and call for vengeance, and behold, vengeance is at their door, since there is no longer anyone to implore mercy and forgiveness for the people. There are no more generous souls, no one worthy anymore to offer the unblemished Victim to the Eternal on behalf of the world.*

[3] *God will strike in an unprecedented manner.*

[4] *Woe to the inhabitants of the earth! God will exhaust his wrath, and no one will be able to escape from so many transgressions!* [... Melanie's ellipses]

[5] *The heads, the leaders of God's people, have neglected prayer and penance, and the demon has obscured their minds. They have become those roving stars that the old devil will drag with his tail in order to cause them to perish. God will permit the old serpent to cause strife among the rulers, among all social bodies, and in every family. There will be physical and moral suffering. God will leave people to themselves and will send chastisements that will succeed one after another for more than thirty-five years.*

[6] *Society is on the threshold of the most terrible calamities and of the greatest events; each should prepare to be governed by an iron rod and to drink the chalice of the wrath of God."*

(A Warning for the Pope, Apostasy and War)

[7] *May the Vicar of my Son, the Supreme Pontiff Pius IX, remain in Rome after the year [18]59. May he be firm and generous. May he fight with the weapons of faith and love; I will be with him.*

[8] *Let him be wary of Napoleon. He is double-hearted as one who wishes to make himself pope as well as emperor. God will soon withdraw from him. He is like an eagle, who, always wanting to soar higher, will*

fall upon the sword that he was using to force the people to exalt him.

[9] *Italy will be punished for her ambition in wanting to shake off the yoke of the Lord of Lords. Hence, she will be handed over to war. Blood will flow on all sides. Churches will be closed or desecrated. Priests and religious will be driven out. They will be put to death, and to a cruel death. Some will abandon the Faith, and the number of priests and religious who will separate from the true religion will be enormous. Among these there will even be Bishops.*

[10] *Let the Pope beware of those who perform marvels, for the time will come when the most astounding prodigies will take place on the ground and in the air.*

[11] *In the year [18]64, Lucifer, with a great number of demons will be unleashed from hell. They will abolish faith little by little, even in those consecrated to God. They will blind them in such a way that, unless there is a special grace, these persons will take on the spirit of the fallen angels. Various religious institutions will lose the Faith altogether and will lose many souls.*

[12] *Bad books will abound on the earth, and the spirits of darkness will spread everywhere a universal laxity towards anything that concerns the service of God. They will have a very great power over nature. There will be churches to serve these spirits. These evil spirits will transport people from one place to another, and even priests, because they will not have cooperated with the good spirit of the Gospel which is a spirit of humility, charity, and zeal for the glory of God. They will raise up the dead.* [Melanie understood that these so-called resuscitates will assume the likeness of righteous souls who had once lived on earth, in order to better deceive people. These so-called resurrected dead, will be none other than demons or even the souls of the damned in the guise of those known to be righteous. They will preach another Gospel contrary to that of the true Christ Jesus, denying the existence of heaven. All these souls will appear to be united to their bodies.] *There will be extraordinary prodigies everywhere because the true Faith has been extinguished and the false*

light illuminates the world. Woe to the princes of the Church who will be busy only to pile riches upon riches, to preserve their authority and to dominate with pride.

[13] *The Vicar of my Son will have much to suffer, because for a time the Church will be severely persecuted. This will be the time of darkness. The Church will undergo a frightful crisis.*

[14] *The holy Faith of God will be forgotten. Each individual will want to be his own guide and to be above his fellow men. Civil and ecclesiastical powers will be abolished. All order and justice will be trodden under foot. Nothing will be seen but homicide, hatred, jealousy, lies and discord, without love for fatherland or for family.*

[15] *The Holy Father will suffer greatly. I will be with him until the end, to receive his sacrifice.*

[16] *The wicked will make several attempts on his life without being able to shorten his days; but neither he nor his successor… will see the triumph of the Church of God.* [Melanie's ellipses]

[17] *Civil rulers will all have the same design, which will be to abolish and eliminate all religious principles, so as to make room for materialism, atheism, spiritism, and all kinds of vices.*

[18] *In the year [18]65 the abomination will be seen in the holy places. In the convents the flowers of the Church will be putrefied and the demon will establish himself as the king of their hearts. May the heads of religious communities beware about the persons they admit, because the demon will apply all his malice to introduce into religious Orders persons given over to sin, because disorders and the love of carnal pleasures will be spread all over the earth.*

[19] *France, Italy, Spain and England will be at war. Blood will flow in the streets. The French will fight against the French, the Italians against the Italians. Then there will be a general war that will be appalling. For a time, God will remember neither France nor Italy, because the Gospel of Jesus Christ is no longer known. The wicked will deploy all their malice. There will be killing and mutual massacre even inside the houses.*

(The Opening Divine Intervention)

[20] *At the first stroke of his lightening sword, the mountains and all of nature will tremble with terror, because the lawlessness and the crimes of men will have pierced the vault of heaven. Paris will be burned and Marseilles engulfed. Several great cities will be shaken and engulfed by earthquakes. It will be believed that all is lost. Only homicides will be seen. Only the sound of weapons and blasphemy will be heard. The righteous will suffer much. Their prayers, their penance, and their tears will mount to heaven, and all the people of God will ask pardon and mercy, and will ask for my help and intercession. Then Jesus Christ by an act of his justice and his great mercy for the righteous, will command his Angels to put all his enemies to death. Suddenly, all the persecutors of the Church of Jesus Christ and all men given to sin will perish, and the earth will become like a desert. Then there will be peace, reconciliation between God and men. Jesus Christ will be served, adored and glorified. Charity will blossom everywhere. The new kings will be the right arm of the Holy Church, which will be strong, humble, pious, poor, zealous, imitating the virtues of Jesus Christ. The Gospel will be preached everywhere, and mankind will make great progress in the faith, because there will be unity among the workers of Jesus Christ, and men will live in the fear of God."*

[21] *This peace among men will not last long. Twenty-five years of abundant harvests will make them forget that the sins of men are the cause of all the pains that come upon the earth.*

[22] *A forerunner of the Antichrist, with his troops of several nations will fight against the true Christ, the only Savior of the world. He will shed much blood and will want to annihilate the worship of God in order to have himself considered as god.*

[23] *The earth will be stricken with all sorts of plagues (besides pestilence and famine which will be widespread). There will be wars, until the last war, led by the ten kings of the Antichrist, who all aim at the same goal and who will be the only ones ruling the world. Before this happens, there will be a kind of false peace in the world. Thought will be given only to entertainment. The wicked will indulge in all sorts of*

sins, but the children of the Holy Church, the children of Faith, my true imitators, will grow in the love of God and in the virtues which are dearest to me. Blessed are the humble souls guided by the Holy Spirit! I shall fight at their side until they reach the fullness of the age.

[24] *Nature demands vengeance for men, and it trembles with terror in anticipation of what will happen to the earth soiled with crimes.*

[25] *Tremble, earth! And you, who profess to serve Jesus Christ but, in your hearts only worship yourselves, tremble; since God will hand you over to his enemy, because the holy places are places of corruption. Many convents are no longer houses of God but pastures for Asmodeus and his own.*

[26] *During this time the Antichrist will be born of a Hebrew nun, a false virgin, who will have had communication with the old serpent, the master of impurity. His father will be a bishop. At his birth he will vomit blasphemies. He will have teeth; in a word, this will be the devil incarnate. He will let out frightful screams. He will perform prodigies. He will feed only on impurities. He will have brothers who, though they are not like him, demons incarnate, will be children of evil. At twelve years old, they will draw attention upon themselves by the brilliant victories they carry off. Soon each of them will be at the head of armies, helped by the legions of hell.*

[27] *The seasons will be changed. The earth will produce only bad fruit. The stars will lose their regular movement. The moon will reflect only a faint reddish light. Water and fire will give to the globe of the earth convulsive movements and horrible earthquakes, which engulf mountains, cities, et cetera...* [Melanie's ellipses]

[28] *Rome will lose the Faith and become the seat of the Antichrist.*

[29] *The demons of the air, together with the Antichrist, will perform great prodigies on the earth and in the air, and men will become more and more perverted. God will take care of his faithful servants and men of good will. The Gospel will be preached everywhere. All the peoples and all the nations will have knowledge of the truth!"*

(A Call to the Apostles of the Last Times, and a Declaration of the Victory of the Faith)

[30] *I address an urgent call to the earth;*

> *I call the true disciples of the living God who reigns in heaven;*
>
> *I call the true imitators of Christ made Man, the only and true Savior of men;*
>
> *I call my children, my true devotees, those who have offered themselves to me so that I may lead them to my divine Son, those whom I carry in my arms, so to speak, those who have lived by my spirit;*
>
> *Finally, I call the Apostles of the Last Times, the faithful disciples of Jesus Christ, who have lived in contempt for the world and of themselves, in poverty and humility, in contempt and in silence, in prayer and in mortification, in chastity and in union with God, in suffering and unknown to the world.*

It is time that they come forth and enlighten the earth. Go, and show yourselves as my beloved children. I am with you and in you, provided that the Faith be the light which enlightens you in these days of woe. Let your zeal make you as if starved for the glory and honor of Jesus Christ. Fight, children of the light, you few who see; for behold the time of times, the end of ends!

[31] *The Church will be eclipsed. The world will be in consternation. But behold Enoch and Elijah, filled with the Spirit of God. They will preach with the power of God, and men of good will shall believe in God, and many souls will be comforted. They will make great progress by the power of the Holy Spirit and will condemn the diabolical errors of the Antichrist.*

[32] *Woe to the inhabitants of the earth! There will be bloody wars and famine, plagues and contagious diseases. There will be downpours of an appalling hail of pests; thunders which shake cities; and earthquakes which will swallow up countries. Voices will be heard in the air. Men will beat their heads against the walls. They will call for death, and on the other hand, death will be their torment. Blood will flow on all sides. Who can overcome if God does not shorten the time*

of trial? By the blood, tears and prayers of the righteous, God will permit Himself to be moved. Enoch and Elijah will be put to death. Pagan Rome will disappear. The fire of heaven will fall and consume three cities. The whole universe will be struck with terror, and many will be led astray because they had not adored the true Christ, living among them. It is the time when the sun will darken. Faith alone will live.

[33] *Behold the time. The abyss opens up. Behold the king of the kings of darkness, behold the Beast with its subjects, calling itself the savior of the world. He will rise with pride into the air in order to attain heaven. He will be suffocated by the breath of Saint Michael the Archangel. He will fall, and the earth, which for three days had been in continuous convulsions, will open its bosom full of fire. He will be plunged forever, with his subjects, into the eternal chasms of hell. Then water and fire will purify the earth and consume all the works of men's pride, and all will be renewed: God will be served and glorified!"*

IV
The Rule and the Last Warnings

After She had given me, also in French, the Rule of this new religious Order, the Holy Virgin continued her speech in the same manner:

"If they convert, the stones and rocks will change into wheat, and potatoes will be found sown in the earth.

Do you say your prayers well, my children?"

We both replied, "Not very well, Madame."

"Oh! My children, you must say them well, evening and morning. When you can't do better, say an Our Father and a Hail Mary and when you have the time to do better, say more.

Only a few old women go to Mass. The others work on Sunday in the summer. In the winter, when they are at a loose end, they only go to Mass to make fun of religion. During Lent, they go to the butcher's like dogs.

Have you ever seen spoiled wheat, my children?"

We both answered: "Oh no, Madame." The Holy Virgin turned to Maximin, saying:

"But you, my child, you must have seen some once near Coin, with your father. The farmer said to your father: "Come and see how my wheat has gone bad!" You went to see. Your father took two or three ears in his hand, rubbed them, and they fell to dust. Then, on your way back, when you were no more than half an hour away from Corps, your father gave you a piece of bread, and said: "Here, my child, eat this year, for I don't know who will be eating next year if the wheat spoils like that!"

Maximin replied, "It's quite true, Madame, I didn't remember." The Most Holy Virgin finished her speech in French.

"Well, my children, you will pass this on to all my people."

The beautiful Lady crossed the stream, and, two steps away from the stream, without turning herself to us who were following her (because we were attracted so much by her brilliance and even more so by her kindness which melted my heart), She repeated to us:

"Well, my children, you will pass this on to all my people."

Then She walked on up to the place where I had climbed before to look for our cows. Her feet touched only the tips of the grass and without bending it. Having reached the top of the little hill, the beautiful Lady stopped, and I rushed to stand in front of her to look at her closely, to try and determine which path She intended to take, because for me it was over. I had forgotten both my cows and the masters I worked for. I was forever and unconditionally attached to my Lady. Yes, I never wanted to leave her! I followed her without any thought but to serve her for the rest of my life.

In the presence of my Lady, I felt I had forgotten paradise. I thought of nothing more but to serve her in every way possible. I felt I could have done everything She could have asked me to do, for it seemed to me that She had a great deal of power. She looked at me with a tender kindness which drew me to her. I would have thrown myself into her arms with my eyes closed but She did not give me the time to do so. She rose imperceptibly from the ground to a height of around a meter or more, and, floating thus in the air momentarily, my beautiful Lady looked up to heaven, then down on the earth to her right and then her left. Then She looked at me with her eyes so sweet, so kind and so good that I felt She was drawing me inside her, and my heart seemed to open up to hers.

And while my heart was melting in sweet delight, the beautiful face of my good Lady began to disappear little by little. It was as if the scintillating light was intensifying around the Most Holy Virgin, as to prevent me from seeing her any longer. In this manner, the light took over her body so that it vanished before my eyes. Or rather it seemed to me that the body of my Lady changed into light while melting away. Then, the light in the shape of a globe rose gently straight upwards.

I cannot say if the intensity of the light diminished while She was rising, or whether the growing distance made me see less and less light as She rose. What I do know, is that I remained a long time with my head raised up, staring at the light, which was always moving away and diminishing in volume, until it finally disappeared. I unfastened my gaze from the heavens and looked around. I saw Maximin looking at me, and I said to him, "Memin, that must have been my father's Good Lord, or the Holy Virgin, or some other great saint."

And Maximin threw his arms into the air and said: "Oh! If only I'd known!"

V
The Return to their Employers who Conduct the First Inquiry

On that evening of September 19th, we went down a little earlier than usual. When I arrived at my master's farm, I was busy tying up my cows and tidying the stable, and had not yet finished when my mistress came up to me in tears and said, "Why, my child, why didn't you come and tell me what happened on the mountain?"

Maximin, not having found his masters at home as they were still working, had come over to mine and reported everything he had seen and heard. I answered: "I did want to tell you, but I wanted to get my work finished first."

A moment later, I went inside the house and my mistress said to me: "Tell me what you saw. The "Noisy Shepherd" (the nickname given Maximin by his employer Pierre Selme) has told me everything."

So, I start telling her what happened, and about halfway in my story, my masters came back from their fields. My mistress, who was weeping at hearing the complaints and warnings of our sweet Mother, said: "Ah! You were planning to harvest the wheat tomorrow (Sunday). Beware! Come and hear what happened today to this child and Pierre Selme's shepherd-boy."

And turning to me, she said: "Repeat everything you have said."

I started again and when I had finished, my master said: "It was the Holy Virgin or else a great saint, who has come on behalf of the Good God, but it's as if the Good God had come Himself. We must do what this saint said. How are you going to manage to tell that to all her people?"

I answered him: "You tell me what to do, and I will do so."

Then, looking at his mother, his wife, and his brother, he added, "I'll have to think about that." Then everyone went back to their business.

After supper, Maximin and his masters came over to see my masters and to recount what Maximin had told them, and to figure out what to do. They said: "It seems to us that it was the Holy Virgin sent by the Good God. The words She spoke make this apparent. And She told them to pass it on to all her people. Perhaps these children will have to travel the world to make it known that everyone must respect the commandments of the Good God, lest great miseries come upon us."

After a moment's silence, my master said to Maximin and me: "Do you know what you must do, my children? Tomorrow, you must get up early and both of you go to the parish priest and tell him everything you saw and heard. Tell him exactly what happened and he will tell you what you must do."

(The Visit to the Pastor)

On September 20th, the day after the Apparition, I left early in the morning with Maximin. When we reached the presbytery, I knocked on the door. The priest's housekeeper opened the door and asked us what we wanted. I said to her in French (I, who had never spoken French): "We would like to speak to Father."

"And what do you want to tell him?" she asked.

"We want to tell him, Miss, that yesterday we went up to watch over our cows on the mountains of Baisses, and after lunch, etc." We recounted a good piece of the Holy Virgin's words. Then the church-bell rang. It was the final call for Mass.

Father Jacques Perrin, the parish priest of LaSalette, who had been listening, flung open his door with a crash. He was in tears and beating his chest. He said to us: "My children, we are lost. God is going to punish us. Oh, Good God! It was the Holy Virgin who appeared to you!" And he left to offer Holy Mass.

We looked at each other, and at the housekeeper. Then Maximin said to me: "Me, I'm going off to my father in Corps." And we parted company.

As my masters had not told me to return to work immediately after speaking with Father, I saw no harm in going to Mass. And so, I went into the church. Mass began and after the first Gospel, Father Jacques Perrin turned to the congregation and tried to recount to his parishioners the story of the Apparition which had just taken place, the day before, on one of their mountains, and he urged them to stop working on Sundays. His voice was broken with sobs, and everyone was very, very moved. After Holy Mass, I went back to my masters' house.

Mr. Peytard, who is still today the mayor of LaSalette, came to question me about the Apparition, and having felt satisfied that I was speaking the truth, he went away convinced.

I stayed on in the service of my masters until All Saints' Day. Then I was placed as a boarder with the Sisters of Providence, in my home town of Corps.

VI
Description of the Virgin

The Most Holy Virgin was tall and well-proportioned. She seemed so light that a mere breath could have stirred her, yet She was motionless and perfectly balanced. Her bearing was majestic, imposing, but not like the nobility of the world. She compelled a respectful fear, but radiating so much love, that She drew us to herself. Her gaze was soft and penetrating. Her eyes seemed to speak to mine, but the conversation came from a profound and vivid feeling of love for the ravishing beauty which was liquefying me. The softness of her gaze, her air of incomprehensible kindness made me understand and feel that She was drawing me to her because She wanted to give herself. It was an expression of love which cannot be expressed with the language of the flesh, nor with the letters of the alphabet.

The clothing of the Holy Virgin was silvery white and shone with brilliance. It was quite intangible, composed of light and glory, shimmering and scintillating. There is no expression nor comparison to be found on earth.

The Holy Virgin was all beauty and all love; the sight of her made me long to be dissolved into her. In her finery, as in her person, everything breathed the majesty, the splendor, the magnificence of an incomparable queen. She seemed as white, immaculate, crystalline, dazzling, celestial, fresh and new like a virgin; it seemed that the word, Love, escaped from her silvery and pure lips. She appeared to me like a good Mother, full of kindness, amiability, love for us, full of compassion and mercy.

The crown of roses that She wore on her head was so beautiful, so brilliant, that it defies all imagination. The roses, of many colors, were not from the earth. It was a floral bouquet that surrounded the head of the most Holy Virgin in the form of a crown. But the roses kept changing and replacing each other, and then, from the heart of each rose, there emanated a beautiful captivating light, which gave the roses a shimmering beauty. From the crown of roses, there issued something like branches of gold and a host of other small flowers mixed with diamonds. The whole thing formed a most beautiful tiara, which alone shone brighter than our earth's sun.

The Holy Virgin had a very pretty Cross hanging from her neck. This Cross seemed golden, I say golden rather than gold-plated, for I have sometimes seen objects which were golden with varying shades of gold, which had a much more beautiful effect on my eyes than simple gold-plate. On this shining, beautiful Cross there was a Christ. It was our Lord on the Cross. Towards each end of the crossbeam there was a hammer, and at the other side a pair of pliers. The Christ was flesh-colored, but He shone luminously. The light that shone forth from his whole body seemed like brightly shining darts which pierced my heart with the desire to melt into Him. At times, the Christ appeared to be dead. His head bent forward and his body seemed to give way, as if about to fall, had He not been held back by the nails which held him to the Cross.

I had a deep compassion for Him, and I would have liked to tell the whole world about his unknown love, and to infuse into the souls of mortal men the most heartfelt love and most lively gratitude towards a God who had no need whatsoever of us to be everything He is, was and ever shall be. And yet, O Love incomprehensible to man, He made Himself man, and wanted to die, yes, die, so as to better imprint in our souls and in our memory, the passionate love He has for us! Oh, how wretched am I to find myself so poor in my expression of the love of our good Savior for us! But, in another way, how happy we are to be able to feel more deeply that which we cannot express!

At other times, the Christ appeared to be alive. His head was upright, his eyes open, and He seemed to be on the Cross of his own will. At times, too, He appeared to speak. He seemed to show that He was on the Cross for our sake, out of love for us, to draw us to his love, and that He always has more love to give us, that his love at the beginning, and in the year 33, is the same today and will be forevermore.

The Holy Virgin was crying almost the whole time She was speaking to me. Her tears flowed gently, one by one, down to her knees; then like sparks of light, they disappeared. They were glittering and full of love. I wanted to comfort her and stop her tears. But it seemed to me that She needed the tears to better show her love, forgotten by men. I would have liked to have thrown myself into her arms and say to her: "My kind Mother, do not cry! I want to love you for all the people in the world!" But She seemed to be saying to me: "There are so many who do not know me!"

I was in between death and life, on the one hand seeing so much love, so much desire to be loved, and on the other, so much coldness and indifference [... Melanie's ellipses] Oh! my Mother, most beautiful and lovable Mother, my love, heart of my heart!

The tears of our tender Mother, far from diminishing her air of majesty, of a queen and a mistress, seemed, on the contrary, to embellish her, to make her more beautiful, more powerful, more loving, more maternal, more ravishing. I would have gladly lapped up her tears, which made my heart burst with compassion and love. Is it possible to see a mother cry, and such a Mother, without doing everything imaginable to console her and change her grief into joy? O Mother more than good, you have been formed of all the prerogatives of which God is capable. You have seemingly exhausted the power of God. You are good and then good from the goodness of God Himself. God has magnified Himself by making you his terrestrial and celestial masterpiece.

The most Holy Virgin had a yellow pinafore. What am I saying, yellow? She had a pinafore more brilliant than several suns put together. It was not of tangible material, but composed of glory, and this glory was scintillating, and ravishingly beautiful. Everything about the Blessed Virgin moved me deeply, and inspired me to adore and love my Jesus in all phases of his earthly life.

The most Holy Virgin had two chains, one a little wider than the other. From the narrower one hung the Cross which I mentioned earlier. These chains (since they must be given the name of chains) were like rays of brightly shining glory, sparkling and dazzling.

Her shoes, (since they must be called shoes) were white, but a silvery, brilliant white. There were roses around them. These roses were dazzlingly beautiful, and from the heart of each rose there shone forth a flame of very beautiful and pleasing light. On her shoes there was a buckle of gold, not the gold of this earth, but rather the gold of paradise.

The sight of the Holy Virgin was itself a perfect paradise. She had within her all that could satisfy, for the earth was forgotten. The Holy Virgin was surrounded by two lights. The first light, closer to the most Holy Virgin, reached as far as us. It shone with a radiance both beautiful and sparkling.

The second light extended a little farther around the beautiful Lady and we were situated within that light. It was motionless (that is, it did not shimmer), yet much more brilliant than our poor earthly sun. All this light did not hurt nor tire the eyes in any way.

In addition to all these lights, all that splendor, there were also beams of light or rays of light emanating from the body of the Holy Virgin, from her clothes and from everywhere.

The voice of the beautiful Lady was sweet; it was enchanting, ravishing, warming to the heart. It satisfied, smoothing every obstacle. It calmed and softened. It seemed to me that I would never want to cease drinking in her beautiful voice, and my heart seemed to dance and leap towards her, so as to dissolve into her.

The eyes of the most Holy Virgin, our tender Mother, cannot be described in human language. To speak of them, one would need a seraph. You would need more than that. You would need the language of God Himself, of the God who formed the Immaculate Virgin, the masterpiece of his omnipotence. The eyes of the majestic

Mary appeared thousands upon thousands of times more beautiful than the rarest diamonds or the most sought-after precious stones. They shone like two suns; but they were soft, softness itself, as clear as a mirror. In her eyes, you could see paradise. They drew one towards her as if She wanted to give herself and bring you to her. The more I looked, the more I wanted to see her. The more I saw, the more I loved her, and I loved her with all my might.

The eyes of the beautiful Immaculate were like the door of God, through which one could see all that can intoxicate the soul. When my eyes met those of the Mother of God, I felt within myself a joyous upheaval of love and a solemn declaration that I loved her and was melting with love. As we looked at each other, our eyes spoke to each other in their fashion, and I loved her so much that I could have kissed her between those eyes which touched my soul and seemed to draw it towards them and cause it to dissolve into hers. Her eyes caused a gentle tremor in my whole being. I feared to make the least movement that might cause her the slightest displeasure.

Just the sight of the eyes of the purest of virgins would have been enough to make the heaven of a blessed soul, enough to satisfy the soul with the will of the Most High amid the events which occur in the course of mortal life, enough to cause the soul to offer uninterrupted acts of praise, thanksgiving, reparation and of expiation. Just this sight alone concentrates the soul on God, and makes the soul dead to earthly things, even the things which had seemed most important, but are now as mere child's play. Such a soul only desires conversation about God and of all that concerns his glory.

Sin is the only evil She sees on earth. She will die of grief unless God sustains her. Amen.

Castellammare, 21st of November 1878.
Mary of the Cross, Victim of Jesus, born Melanie Calvat, Shepherdess of LaSalette.

Nihil obstat and Imprimatur.
Datum Lycii ex Curia Ep. die 15 Nov. 1879.

[Given at Lecce from the Bishop's tribunal, Nov. 15, 1879 (Feast of the Poor Souls in the Carmelite Calendar)]

[Salvatore Luigi Zola, Bishop of Lecce, Italy]

Vicarius Generalis: Carmelius Archus Cosma.

[Vicar General: Archpriest Carmelo Cosmas (†1886)]

DISCLOSURES ABOUT THE LAST TIMES: "THE OTHER SECRET" OF MELANIE?

"Here the Blessed Virgin gave me the Rule, and then She told another Secret about the Last Times."

This affirmation of Melanie, in the Secret written on August 14, 1853, has never been taken into consideration by historians of LaSalette. Still Melanie refers to it, by answering the following question: "Why not reveal the whole Secret?"

"Because it reveals such amazing Secrets of the Divine Mercy, that if they were made known to mankind, instead of praying to ward off events, people would be rushing to see them happen, so as to rejoice all the sooner in the unheard triumph of the Church"[25]

Father Felicien Bliard gets specific:

No one in the world therefore knows the entire Secret of the shepherdess. From what we have until now, I am inclined to think that the complete Secret will form an admirable unity, including the anticipated history of the main events which will occur until the end of time. Will the other part be revealed later on? I have serious reasons to think so.[26]

Father Émile Combes, the priest of Diou, who knew Melanie during the final years of her life, revealed the following statements [speculative interpretations][27]:

The *Antichrist*, Melanie declared, will announce all over the world the day he will rise up to heaven, and from everywhere crowds will go to Jerusalem. He will ascend in the midst of a pompous cortège of false angels of light. He will already be high up, and enjoying applause from those millions of spectators and worshippers, when Saint Michael the Archangel will appear with an army of Angels with an incomparable splendor, and at the sound of:

"Who is like God? *Quis ut Deus?*" Immediately the demons will lose their borrowed brightness and their power, and will distance themselves from the Antichrist whom they had supported with their power. A tremendous fire will burst out of the ground, opening up all the way to the feet of the spectators in the front row, due to their dignity and wealth. Together with the Antichrist and demons, they will be swallowed up in a vast crater which will close upon them. Then straight away, the Jews will convert and will become the most faithful and ardent Christians. The whole earth will be Catholic.

Until the end of the world the laws will remain Christian, and there will no longer be any legal persecution. During quite a number of generations all men will be good Christians. However, little by little they will begin again to become lukewarm, forgetting God and finally committing great crimes. The Christian laws, which at first the secular authorities will observe with great severity, will little by little end up not having any sanctions anymore, as a result of a false mercy for those violating them. Therefore, the good won't be protected anymore. They will become the object of all sorts of humiliations and mockery. They will suffer much from society and from oppression by evil persons, and they will become a minority.

God will pursue mankind with his anger. The heavenly plagues will be horrible. The waters will be poisoned. Earthquakes and fires will be more destructive than anything the world had seen thus far. The sun will no longer give its light. Finally, the world will end up in the wrath of God. The poor, the humble, destitute of all help, will lift up their eyes and hands to call for the help of God. The coming of Christ will be sudden... all men will die.

Will some of them be "set apart" for the "renewal"? The renewal will take place, but not in the way that some good priests might imagine. All men will die without exception.

The elect will resurrect first, and with them those in limbo. God is more gracious than some might think. In his mercy, He will let these souls know their origin, the rebellion of our first father. They will humble and prostrate themselves before God, and God will have them restored to their innocence, by means of the Blood of Our Lord which they will have applied to themselves. The resurrected from limbo, nevertheless, won't have the same glory as the elect. They will stay in obscurity compared to the elect. The elect, having suffered with Our Lord, will have a glory far higher than the human race would have had in their state of innocence.

When the "rehabilitated" ones see the rejected pass by, they will humble themselves all the more. They will not be a part of the judgement.

The judgement of the elect will take place in a flash; they will be taken in front of Christ to be rejected. Our Lord will preside over the judgement with his Cross, the one on which He died; but it will be the Archangel Michael who will pronounce the judgement.

Immediately after the rejected ones are engulfed in the center of the earth and the assumption of the elect, this part of the Secret will be realized: *"Water and fire will purify the earth and consume all works of pride by man."* The surface of the earth will be reduced to burning (boiling) mud, as far down that man had been so that all the works of man will be pulverized, scattered in this mud of fire. There will be no traces left. It will be a cataclysm looking like chaos; and the surface of the earth, newly ordered differently, will become an earthly paradise.

The resurrected from limbo will be designated to live on the renewed earth. They will be immortal, impeccable, perfectly happy.[28] They won't know any suffering. They will see God. They will talk to God. They will be completely content, depending on the different degrees of the scope of their faculties. The enchantment of their stay will be nothing compared to their joy in serving and honoring God. In this way "God will be served and glorified."

The stars, are they inhabited? Only the earth is inhabited.[29]

A) 1847, age 12: at LaSalette one year after the Apparition
B) 1861, age 26: medical student, after several years in the seminary
C) 1865, age 30: serving as medic in the Pontifical Guard of Pius IX
D) Last photo before his death on March 1st, 1875, age 40

CHAPTER 5

WHAT TO THINK ABOUT THE SEERS?

The shepherds of LaSalette suffered from ongoing calumnies. For a long time, in order to discredit the fact of LaSalette, people tried to morally assasinate the two children.[1]

Their lack of education has been emphasized, their "instability":

Maximin: the impulsive one, constantly moving from one place to the other, his plans always failing (seminary, medicine, the marketing of an elixir under his name which brought him nothing but debts and criticism)

Melanie: a false mystic, whose egocentrism would have damaged the testimony and spirituality of the message.

Thanks to numerous new discoveries, today we are better equipped to answer the above question.

Are the Seers Uneducated and Witless?

The young shepherds of LaSalette, just like Bernadette of Lourdes, had rarely attended school. They could neither read nor write. They spoke in patois and hardly knew any French. These mountain shepherds had a disarming naivety. Father Émile Combes, who had welcomed Melanie in Diou and its surroundings from 1900 to 1903, was amazed by her inability to do simple arithmetic:

> She had come to me to prepare a large bowl of quince jelly. The juice with the bowl weighed around 8 kilos. "Now," she said, "we have to add an equal weight of sugar."

It was absolutely impossible to make her understand that from those 8 kilos she had to subtract the weight of the bowl, in this case 3 kilos and 250 grams:

> She kept repeating slowly: "My Father, we need the same amount of sugar as of juice."

I became impatient and she guessed my thought:

> "I am stupid," she said smiling.
>
> "Yes… How can you not see that the weight of the bowl is not the weight of the juice and that therefore you have to substract it? There isn't 8 kilo of juice here, there is barely 5 kilo. You don't understand that?"

Her answer: "No." The next morning she walked up to me all happy: "My Father, I understand what you told me yesterday," she said.

> "That took awhile, dear Sister! You must have discussed this with 'your little Brother,' and you always understand Him."
>
> She smiled.

He brings up this story to show the simplicity of her thinking in daily life, whereas when she spoke about the Apparition, she exhibited a supernatural wisdom.

> [This] strange fact of unintellgence in such an intelligent person seems to confirm that it is really from her "little Brother" that she has learned everything she knows.[2]

This "little Brother," who continued to appear to her after her childhood, she was ultimately able to identify at the age of 22 as the Child Jesus, because He showed Himself in his glory.

Maximin, whose unpolished common sense was much in touch with, and well-grounded, in reality had nevertheless an overflowing imagination. He liked to invent stories, tell funny jokes and tales. Sister Valerie, his teacher in Corps, recalls:

> Maximin had a lot of imagination; we always said that. Even as a small child, he told me what he would do when he would be pope. Or he saw himself as a king on the throne, and he wanted "Mama" Thècle at his right, while "Aunt" Valerie would be his minister. It made us laugh, Father. How many times he told us such stories, sitting on the ground, between our Mother [Thècle, the superior] and myself during recreation.[3]

Maximin acquired an education at the minor seminary, and then privately with Father Champon, his tutor, who prepared him for entry to the major seminary of Aire, where he studied for two years, (24th of February 1856 to July 1858). A letter written in that year shows the maturity of his reflection:

> Now it is so easy for me to draw my reason close to my faith, to compare humanistic writings with theology, and civil society with the Church. I see more and more deeply how these large matters blend and interweave. I see how obvious it is that I should always acquire more knowledge and virtue so as to save souls from their failures in faith, and the bitterness of doubt, of which perhaps I will be a connecting point which they will encounter in order to strengthen and console them.
>
> If only you knew how much I love more and more, with a sweet and pervasive joy, a religion that moves all the fibers of my soul, increasing my intelligence and fortifying my will, elevating and

strengthening my character, giving more meaning to my life! How much I appreciate my religion which inspires me with respect for myself and shows me at the same time, what goodness and loveliness there is in others; a religion that achieves that, in the likeness of this Providence in which power marries sweetness. Those two rare qualities, namely a kind heart with a strong reason, one day will be more in balance with one another. To walk, and have others walk, on the difficult road of duty and obligation! Having blessed me with a fiery soul and filled me with generous aspirations, God has carefully preserved me, early in life and under your protection, from worldly seductions and distractions, being eager to show me its vanity and peril. As if I should be a priest before coming of age, He inspired me with sublime thoughts, a taste for more serious things, keeping my spirit and heart always on a higher level. I have no idea if I will do his works well, since, of myself, I can do absolutely nothing! What I do know is that good priests are asked for everywhere, priests who have the spirit from above: a great spirit of faith infused with the light of God, to bring about Christian happiness within the conditions of our times, the peace, concord, and the charity of the Gospels at the heart of families, as well as society. There is a need for apostles who work, and want to place their spirit and body at the service of the Lord, throwing themselves into all kind of hazards, to sustain his so much unrecognized and persecuted religion. Isn't that a soldier's role coinciding with my somewhat belligerent temperament? So, should I be a soldier? Yes, a soldier of a better Fatherland; a soldier fighting in the world for the Church of Jesus Christ, for the triumph of his Cross and my dear LaSalette; a soldier who, the more he encounters trouble, the more he will be like his divine Master, and the more he will acquire knowledge and virtue to combat them.

That has always been the foundation of my desire, if ever the good God calls me to the priesthood and does not send me far from the Pyrenees, as you have separated me from our Alps.

I have to warn you, if his Excellency, Bishop Ginoulhiac, nevertheless has the intention to prevent me from advancing, as to not to allow me to act, speak and write of my mission as the apostle of LaSalette obliges me to do, please ponder this, so as to give me advice. Such an intention of my superior would be a positive sign of a non-vocation.

God can never make me have a priestly vocation, diametrically opposed to the vocation coming from Mary: to make known, everywhere and always, depending on the circumstances, her warnings to the people. In that case I can only take part in the new religious militia that fights voluntarily and unhindered, be it also with risk and peril, without undertaking the responsibility of a pastor.

Please forgive me for ending this letter with such a serious question! But it involves the destiny of your pupil who, while recognizing his capabilities and tastes for sciences and ecclesiastical matters, only wishes to do the will of God.

It is best that you be clear about this to your most affectionate and obedient Maximin.[4]

When Maximin left the seminary, he sought employment in Paris, like so many young people of his time, but he couldn't find any and ended up in misery. Aided by the intervention of Divine Providence, he completed his secondary studies at Tonnerre College, from March 1860 to August 1861. He went to LeHavre, returned to Paris ill, where he was cared for at the hospital of Saint-Louis. There he acquired an enthusiasm for medicine and studied for two years (end of September 1861, and 1862) to become a healthcare worker. Simultaneously, he took courses in a Catholic boarding school in Paris, on the Rue d'Enfer, and presented himself for the final exam. He failed. He more or less succeeded in editing his memoires (in 1863 and 1865), compiled and published after his death. [*Maximin Peint par Lui-même par Père Adrien Peladan* - Maximin Self-Portrait by Father Adrien Peladan] In 1866 he responded wittily to a satirical article in La Vie Parisienne, and took the opportunity to publish his version of the Apparition.

Melanie received less schooling, like the women of her time. In spite of her deficiencies in mathematics, she mastered penmanship perfectly. In Corenc she studied a teaching course, and she taught children in several countries (France, Greece and Italy). She is not a learned person, but if one defines intelligence, like many psychologists do, as a means of adapting oneself, she was quite intelligent. She adapted herself to the changes she encountered in different environments: convents, countries and languages (French, English, Greek and Italian, the latter of which she spoke and wrote quite well). She was able to dialogue at different levels: with the children of the orphanage whom she directed in Greece and Sicily, with bishops, cardinals and Pope Leo XIII himself. During a private audience with the Pope, alone with him, she expressed herself in a wise, responsible way. She made him understand that his advice for her to go to LaSalette to make Mary's message better understood and to found the Order of the Mother of God, would not be accepted, which was absolutely true.

She was able to maneuver with flexibility between projects and proposals, in a stream of constant contradictions, which she encountered in almost continuous succession. From the papal audience until her death (the account will be presented later in this volume) one cannot discover a single error in judgment that she made deliberately from her heart. She left Italy at a time where everything was going well (as never before) so as to take care of her mother, who had caused her much suffering in her childhood.

Melanie returned to Italy in 1892, at the request of Bishop Zola, one of her supporters.

On the 18th of September 1897, [Saint] Annibale DiFrancia asked her to take the leadership of his community of the Sisters of the Divine Zeal and their orphanage in Messina, Italy. He would regard her thereafter as the co-foundress of this new religious family. It was at his request that she wrote her biography, in which she expressed, with elegance and accuracy of doctrine, her spiritual experiences, even though she did not have any particular education in the matter.⁵

To put it concisely regarding Maximin and Melanie, the culture of their natural environment and the peasant wisdom of the time were not empty words. It was, with the assistance of grace, the root of their ability to adapt to a life of continual setbacks, as we will proceed to show.

The stylistic and poetic quality of their writings, the accuracy of their words, especially when they speak of the Apparition and their mission, give evidence of a deep enlightenment and infused Faith, and of the charism that guided them, to various degrees. Melanie's words were consistently more profound and coherent than Maximin.

WERE THEY UNSTABLE?

The shepherds have been criticized for adopting a lifestyle of the gyrovagues of former times [wandering monks, who, rather than being attached to a particular monastery, roamed about from place to place] Maximin wandered all across France: the South of France (le Midi), the West, LeHavre, Tonnerre, Paris, his trip to Italy and his six months as a Zouave (a French light-infantry company) in Rome, where his friend Louis-Marie-Urbain Similien had already taken him in 1854.

But it was not of his own will that he did not remain long in one place. His impulsive character is not the sole reason for his "instability":

> "I dismissed Maximin from the minor seminary," wrote Bishop Ginoulhiac to the priest Melin on the 5th of February 1854.⁶

It is through the advice of his professors that Maximin gave up the seminary for a secular life. His lofty appreciation of the priesthood and his status as a "seer" could not be joined together in his experience of ecclesiastical life.

And it was one of his teachers, Dr. Chassaignac, surgeon and director of l'Hôtel-Dieu, who dissuaded him from pursuing a medical career, by saying in essence:

> People won't consult you as a doctor but as a seer, healer and miracle worker. You will never be in balance (i.e. they will always consult you for the wrong reasons).

There again, Maximin followed reasonable advice and considerations. He did not act on mere impulse.

The same applies to his military engagement in Rome, where he wanted to offer his life for the Pope, to defend him from Garibaldi. On the 24th of May 1865, he enlisted in the pontifical Zouaves while concealing his identity as a seer, up to the moment when another Zouave, LeChauff DeKerguennec, discovered his name in the registration list. However, in 1865, there were no battles. The life of the Zouaves was less than edifying and did not correspond to Maximin's high ideals. When it was time to renew his engagement, he chose not to do so.

It was his status as a seer, and the efforts to separate him from LaSalette, that made him oscillate, for better or worse, between several intellectual or generous choices, while supported by the hospitability of priests or laymen. Father Champon received him at the presbytery of Seyssins (1854-1856) after he was dismissed from the minor seminary. The Jourdains adopted him for twelve years (1863-1875).

Maximin wisely understood that he was not called to the priesthood nor to marriage, for that matter. He lived out his celibacy honorably, in chastity. His coherence, his lucidity, his intelligence concerning the Apparition and Our Lady to whom he had devoted his life, are beyond criticism.

After the war of 1870, Maximin was without income, to which a physical handicap was added (as an aftermath of the cold nights wandering around in Paris). In 1860 he tried to generate an income by working with a company that exploited him by attaching his name to an elixir. For this he was sharply criticized by the self-righteous press, whereas the elixirs of monks, like "Benedictine," or "Chartreuse," were beyond blame, although they were also invented as a means of income.

His last year in Corps was a *via dolorosa*, ending with a holy death on March 1st, 1875.

In the appendix the reader will find autobiographical excerpts published in 1881 by Father Émile LeBaillif, as well as letters to Maximin's adoptive parents, Mr. and Mrs. Jourdain, who fell into financial ruin (because their house was sacked during the occupation of Paris). The letters testify to Maximin's difficult life: a fruitless search for a place in society, of a job, of support from the LaSalette sanctuary. Above all, they bear witness to his attitudes and feelings, not to mention his ability to express himself in writing.

The "instability" attributed to Melanie, who did not have the lively character of Maximin, can be explained with similar reasons. (See the Chronology.) "I would like to send her away from the community of the Providence," declared Bishop Ginoulhiac, on the 5th of February 1854.[7] Indeed, that is what he did, although the Sisters had voted unanimously (October 1853) to accept Melanie for profession of vows in their congregation.

Later [in 1863], the Bishop [of Marseille] tries to pressure her to join the Sisters of Charity in Vienne and take their habit. Since she refused, Melanie was confined to inactivity, until she sought help by throwing a note out of the window. [See below] Surely, the root of the problem is that the mountain shepherdess saw confinement as a hindrance to spreading the message: *"You will make this known to all my people."* We see Melanie vigorously defending her vocation, her mission and her freedom in the service of our Blessed Mother, to whom she felt deeply connected. The fact that she had gone away to England for six years was not her idea, but that of others who had a strong and persevering desire to hide her far away.

At the beginning of her exile to England, Melanie had established good contacts for the foundation of the Order for which she had received a mission on the 19th of September 1846. She acquired helpers, vocations and support, but because of the intervention of

Bishop Ginoulhiac, she was put rather quickly behind cloistered bars, notwithstanding the fact that in 1850, during a long thought-out decision, she had *excluded a cloistered life* as a vocation for herself because of her mission, and chosen instead an apostolic life.[8]

Here is how she announced to her dear Sisters in Corenc her entry into the novitiate of the English Carmel:

> Today... should be a feast-day, since it is today that the nuns voted to admit me. This is the day on which I think the most of you, and that is natural. This day makes me think I will have to leave you forever, that I won't see you here on earth anymore! But we will see one another in heaven, hopefully!... Being separated from you is a big sacrifice. You know how much I love you. My love has not changed. Oh! Let us talk about other things; my heart is breaking!!!... *Fiat!...*
>
> I think it is a great advantage for me, who am inclined to be rather lazy, to become a Carmelite. First of all, I don't have to turn the mattress of my bed, nor fluff up the straw; for fifteen days now I have slept in a comfortable [!] Carmelite bed, and I sleep well; I don't move too much while lying down, since my skin would get wounded from the sheets; secondly, you certainly remember how I hated changing sheets at Corenc; here I don't have to go through that trouble: one only changes tunics every two weeks, and, even without a rash, the tunic itches non-stop. And then, in the morning we do not bother to take breakfast. Oh! However, here is a thing I don't like. I think you know how Carmelites take the discipline. It is really hard for me when I have to use it like they do[9] during the *"Miserere"* [Psalm 50/51] with chants that are so slow, followed by many prayers. However, if the good Lord wants it, he will give me courage.
>
> In the rule, it is prohibited to run or to jump, even on days of recreation, which total five days a year. I think that is pretty severe. On the day the chaplain, sent by the Bishop, examined me for becoming a Carmelite, he also asked me a question, namely, if I

would be able to observe the rule in all its details or if I wanted to ask some dispensation? To that I answered, to make him laugh and also to lower the high esteem he had for me, I told him I needed to run sometimes. I was accustomed to running and galloping behind the cows, and that during the days of recreation, he should allow me to go to the yard to run and jump a little.[10]

Here she is forced to live the very opposite of her life in the open air, of her outgoing and intrepid temperament, and of her vocation and mission. In 1856, she professed her vows, as she was urged [virtually compelled] to do so, but it was with hesitation and with a mental reservation regarding the enclosure. Four years later [1860] she will reject the state of permanent enclosure because it hinders her mission, of which a new phase had begun in 1858. She throws a number of notes over the cloister walls asking for help to escape. This request is granted to her rather quickly and silently, out of English "fair play" and the fear of noisy rumors from the Anglicans. Here is the second of these notes, addressed to the Chief of Police in Darlington:

Having desired for several years to leave the Carmelite monastery, I have not yet succeeded in doing so, in spite of the efforts I've made. I am kept here by force. Whatever it takes, I want to leave. Therefore I urge the Darlington police to come here and to oblige the religious of this convent to let me out. For several days now, I sent you notes on the matter. Those notes have been collected by a servant who, instead of sending my letters to the indicated address, placed them in the hands of strangers, who have opened and read them. I require that this offense be punished according to English law. I know the people who are responsible for this, and I have far more to tell you, but I prefer to do so face to face. I sent several other letters to the same address by means of some birds. Those letters must have fallen close to Darlington.[11]

Next, she is welcomed by the religious of the Congregation of the Compassion in Marseille, where she takes the habit. The pious founder does not hesitate to send Melanie with an assistant, Mother Presentation, to restore order to an orphanage on the islands of Cephalonia in Greece (November 21, 1861 - July 28, 1863).

But when she returns to Marseille, Melanie is obliged to enter Carmel once more. She will stay there for ten months. Her determination is well known:

> She wanted to leave. The nuns seemed to object.[12] She started making noise, to the point of climbing into a cellar and screaming that she was locked up by force and without consent.[13]

[†Editor: Melanie was undoubtedly invited as a guest, and then trapped in the convent of the Carmel's *Extern* Sisters. Externs have separate living quarters, and their own constitutions and horarium. Their mission is to serve the cloistered nuns with the care of the sacristy and chapel, the shopping, and the greeting of visitors. Melanie was not canonically at liberty to join any cloistered community, having received a papal dispensation to exit the Darlington Carmel.]

After this ordeal Melanie returned to the Congregation of the Compassion, where she was employed as a teacher in the suburbs of Marseille, under well-guarded anonymity, until the year 1867, when Bishop Place, loyal to Napoleon III, dismissed her from his diocese. One has to concede that Melanie was not well-understood by her superiors. Father Beaup recalls their [biased] opinions:

> It was impossible for superiors to correct her. She still has the same character defects as in her childhood... But still her religious reputation remains intact, in relation to faith, piety and manners. Here is one proof of this lack of submission, namely, it is impossible to make her get up with the others in the morning. She does not sleep. This staying in bed is seen by her roommate as necessary because she was very much convinced that Melanie was sometimes tormented by a diabolic influence.

In Marseille, as in Corenc, a satanic influence is identified, although her superiors do not take it seriously:

> At times she is in a kind of daze and sometimes becomes

desperate if one contradicts her. Does this explain the rumor that she went several years without making her Easter [annual] Communion because her superior, whether to humiliate her, or out of respect for the Blessed Sacrament, had prohibited her from approaching Holy Communion unless she got up with the other Sisters to take part in the morning meditation? Since Holy Mass was usually scheduled after the morning meditation, Melanie was remaining a "long time" without receiving Holy Communion. However, this span rarely exceeded eight days, fourteen at the most. This same witness (Mother Presentation) has assured me that Melanie very often complained about being exhausted because of bad nights. The cause of that tiredness, she does not know, since it is not a physical ailment.[14]

Without official examinations, there isn't enough information to discern the exact nature of the demonic temptations [†Editor: or perhaps flare-ups of the painful stigmata?] Sent from Marseille to Grenoble by Mother Presentation, but dismissed by Bishop Ginoulhiac, Melanie was accompanied by this religious to Castellammare-di-Stabia in Italy. Bishop Petagna was head of that diocese and had been Melanie's confessor during his exile in Marseille. The bishop, with his friends, Bishop Zola and a Cardinal (either Sisto Sforza or Filippo Guidi, OP) grants her all the space she needs to accomplish her "mission": the release of her complete Secret, and the foundation of the Order asked for by the Apparition. In this way, direct connections are established with Pope Leo XIII and the Roman [Sacred] Congregations.

From that moment onward, all the alarming symptoms disappear. Bishop Petagna attributes this to the liberty which he offered Melanie in his own diocese, something "most unusual" for her.[15][16]

The story of Melanie, therefore, is a story of achieving balance, acquired through intense struggle, from Corenc (1851) to Castellammare-di-Stabia (1868), through exterior and interior difficulties, and complicated by the fact that she was subjected to a culture that was so contrary to her own intense nature.

Were They Coherent?

This third question finds its response in the proceeding ones. In their lives strewn with contradictions, without power or great personal resources, they were often tossed about, both because of their limitations and because of these oppositions. Maximin's well-ordered testament shows his concern to properly manage his life and his death. When Father Crevoulin visited him from Rome, one year before his death, Maximin told him:

> Pray for me, that I do only the will of the most Blessed Virgin, because all other things are of no importance to me.[17]

Their consistency is remarkable, in their self-sacrifice, their availability, their generosity, the magnitude of a soul that rejects all revenge. They both kept their own vocation, the concern to bear witness without fail, and to serve the crucial message of LaSalette without ulterior motive.

Maximin suffered for not finding a job, or the opportunity to consecrate his life to his mission as a seer.

Melanie persevered unrelentingly to convey the entirety of Our Lady's message, and ultimately succeeded, without fully realizing her own thwarted mission.

Each of them maintained the integrity of the message, despite the difficulties in their lives which thwarted each seer's individual desires for their vocations.

What About their Mental Equilibrium?

As for Maximin, this question has never been an issue. He was good natured, sociable, joyful, communicative and generous. The small side-issues he has been blamed for as a seer, don't affect his basic balance, on the contrary.

Sister Valerie, who taught the children at the boarding school of Providence in Corps, confided to Father Émile LeBaillif:

We fear that Mrs. Jourdain has treated him like mothers do who love their children too much and don't see any faults in them. I tell you this confidentially. She does not know about them, because she would blame me if she learned that I had said something bad about her dear child... This child has a lighthearted, unpredictable and very jovial character. This unpredictability, this levity in his behavior, causes others to belittle him. From any other young man, this behavior would be acceptable, would have passed without remark. However, the lightheartedness of such a privileged child has been regarded as inappropriate. Now you might ask: What kind of caprices for example?

Well, he didn't hesitate to go to the café. He accepted wine in cabarets, in the company of young people who liked being with him because he was always friendly and cheerful. Later on, they would say: "He is just like us." I don't believe he has ever done anything wrong, never."[18]

Melanie was subject to the most elaborate rumors: "(given to) hysteria, egocentric," and said to distort and interpret the message of the Apparition in a subjective way. Being more introverted, and often reacting to incidents, she became a prey to [the theories of] psychologists, and later on to psychoanalysts, at the time when these upcoming disciplines could afford the luxury of projecting their dogmas and schemas onto anyone, by denouncing their "repressions," their failures, and explaining everything through the subjective efflorescence of the subconscious. Following the hypothesis of the English Jesuit, H. Thurston, Father Jean Jaouen, M.S. tried to establish that Melanie's autobiography reveals a kind of rebellious egocentrism, that she would have [unconsciously] substituted the Virgin's message for the emanations of her totalitarian ego. According to him, when the Apparition was barely known, everything took place during the years 1852-1853. That is where he thinks he can grasp "the progressive symptoms" of her "morbid complex."[19] But the root of the problem would go back to July 1847: the superior of Corps feared for the humility (!) of Melanie.[20] Finally, officially, per [the corrupt]

Bishop Ginoulhiac, Melanie, "attached to her own ideas" would have sunk into hysteria.

Maritain reacted! Since the journal *La Vie Spirituelle* shortened Maritain's response, Massignon decided to publish Maritain's text unabridged in his *revue Dieu Vivant*.[21]

Father Jaouen maintained his thesis in the recasting of his book *La Grace de la Salette au regard de l'Eglise*[22] and makes it even worse by denouncing the "half-spontaneous, half-provoked delirium in which the poor woman had ended her agitated life."[23]

In 1991, Father Jean Stern [M.S. of the LaSalette Congregation] defends the thesis of Father Jaouen, "my master," as he calls him gratefully. Stern declares unequivocally and with clarity:

> By dreaming ceaselessly, Melanie cannot make the distinction anymore between the real and the imaginary... She refashions reality to fit her egocentrism.[24]

He specifies:

> The egocentrism is at the root of this reversal, and explains the emergence of the famous Secret.[25]

Notwithstanding, Leon Bloy, Maritain, Massignon and many others see in the autobiography of Melanie "a magnificent testimony of the invisible light that is not understood by darkness."[26]

For Father Stern, *the reality is quite different*,[27] as he qualifies an extreme statement of Father Jaouen:

> We think it does not make sense to refer to the concept of hysteria, a very extendable concept by the way, to understand the psychology of the seer.[28]

Father Stern's thesis, launched in 1946 for the 100th anniversary (of the visions) was still making its impact at the approach of the hundred-fiftieth anniversary [1996]:

> Melanie was "transformed into a kind of cult object by the Sisters who had welcomed her at school [...] indoctrinated by the attention that the Mistress of Novices gave to her, and by

the spiritual apocalyptic readings offered to the novices as texts for their formation."29

Such is the accusation. Facts contradict this! Father Antoine Bossan, investigator and witness, mentions that the religious of Corps and their superior, Sister Sainte-Thècle,

> made a point to humiliate Melanie and Maximin, in private and in public, to prevent them from becoming conceited over the special favor they had had, to see and hear the Blessed Virgin. They [Maximin and Melanie] hardly ever talked about the Apparition. And when they [the nuns] spoke to them in passing, it was almost always to rebuke them on their character, their rudeness and their faults.30

The seers accepted these rebukes, and countless similar ones. As to the apocalyptic literature in Corenc, Canon [Jean Baptist] Emile Millon, an historian comparable to Father Antoine Bossan, did an investigation:

> In November 1935, I wrote to the convent of Corenc on the subject of possible literature that Melanie read during her time in the novitiate. To my letter I joined a list of some works about private revelations, of prophetic visionaries that might have inspired Melanie, for such and such paragraph of her Secret, for such and such subsequent prophecies. The answer was: "The mentioned works are not in the library of the community of Corenc. Moreover, postulants and novices can only read a work with permission of the Mistress of Novices. Sister Mary of the Cross (Melanie) certainly never had permission to read books dealing with prophecies or revelations."31

Numerous saints, martyrs and confessors have been, like Christ, suspected of artifice, illuminism and falsehood. It was too easy to attribute the shepherdess' "deviation" to the excess of honor that she received. People around her made certain that this was not the case and, moreover, that honor was compensated by many humiliations, sequestrations and persecutions.

Cahier de mortifications To gain clarity in all this, with the aid of excavated documents, one must turn to the facts and the causes without any prejudice. First of all, let us remember these facts:

1. Her writings of 1850, *Cahier de réflexions avant que de se faire religieuse* [Notebook of Reflections before becoming a nun] and even her *Cahier de mortifications* testify to an uncommon spiritual maturity.
2. After a variety of trials (human and satanic, well-discerned by the Sisters) that disturbed her life, sometimes in strange ways, once she arrived in Italy she achieved a balance facilitated by an endurance and control which she progressively acquired. So it is, in fact, just the opposite of the imbalance that supposedly settled in.
3. The things she later supposedly invented, and which were attributed to her "schizophrenia," and which inspired her to long renderings of the Secret, are neither invented, nor late. We can find these essentially in the very first section of 1851, intended for the Pope. From 1848 onwards, Melanie mentions the troubles of the Pope (see below) and of Paris. She warns Benjamin Dausse about it (see below).

Now let us narrow down the questions.

Among the unfortunate actions that she was blamed for, some are of a natural, others of a supernatural, character.

NATURAL REACTIONS

At first sight, as we have seen, Melanie had difficult moments in her religious life. This had first of all to do with the fact that she was accused of having difficulty enduring confinement and immobility because she spent much of her childhood living alone in the open air from early morning to late in the evening as a shepherdess in the Alps. She was naturally rather uncomfortable with a regimen of life that was overly constrained,[32] such as the cloistered life of the English Carmel, for which she seemed destined, in spite of her own wishes.

The confinement was repugnant to Melanie, but made more suffocating by the suspicions and severe sanctions (e.g., exclusion from Holy Communion, threats, isolation, etc.). However, when for reasons of politico-religious convenience, this became a kind of sequestration incompatible with the mission that she felt she had been given by the Virgin, she reacted in a very understandable way. It is not easy to untangle a legitimate claim of human and Christian freedom. In the face of a moral harassment that puts any person on edge, it was aggravated by overwhelming mystical ordeals. This brings us to the supernatural level, in which Melanie extricated herself from a difficult situation.

THEIR SPIRITUAL TRIALS

A. The Mystical Dimension

The supernatural resizes man, from within, to the measure of God. This trial can involve secondary phenomena, positive as well as negative: charisms, asceticism and harsh temptations in chosen souls. Melanie, concerned about her spiritual formation, took on all this as best she could. On the 18th of April 1867, she confided to Father Sylvain Marie Giraud, M.S., the superior of LaSalette and a great spiritual expert on the contemporary current of victim souls:

> Allow me to let you know some of my miseries, and you will judge whether or not I can enter another community. When I was in Corenc, the desire to suffer led me to ask God for suffering, and indeed this came shortly after (although I don't know how my condition was at the time.) What I do know is that the more I suffered, the more I wanted to suffer. Therefore, I asked to suffer more, and to suffer, if it were possible, the suffering of the damned in hell, etc.
>
> After a few days my condition was such that it is impossible for me to describe, and sometimes I remained two or three days without realizing if I was still on earth or in hell. Six years later, I suffer less. However sometimes thoughts of despair invade me, and sometimes I would not know what I should do if I had to

be alone. Well, that's enough about that.³³

She does not dwell on it or allow it to develop into depression. Her brevity, and the serious question she asks herself, are proof of her lucidity. The phenomena she goes through are classical and well-known by spiritual persons.

But her desire to suffer gives way to suspicion: is she a masochist? No, she only wants to identify herself with Christ and continue her work through the victorious Cross. In the Apparition, Mary presented this to her, and Melanie accepted it deeply. It is the instrument of salvation for sinful and threatened humanity, over which Melanie weeps. "Let us think of Love. Let's not think of sorrow," said Melanie.³⁴

Like Saint Paul, the children of Fatima, and so many more Christian followers of the voluntary suffering of Christ for our salvation, Melanie wanted to share in his Passion. On this road she met Father Sylvain Marie Giraud, M.S., an enlightened theorist on the current of victim souls which flourished from the 17th century and blossomed in the 19th century. I, [namely René Laurentin, primary author of this book] studied this movement in my thesis.³⁵ Paul Claudel wrote to me after I was awarded a prize by the Academy for my thesis. He related that these mystics of reparation had inspired him to write his masterpiece *L'annonce à Marie* [The Annunciation to Mary], and also L'échange [The Exchange], and *Le soulier de satin* [The Satin Shoe]. Bishop Petagna, confessor and later protector of Melanie, preached the "martyrdom of love." In this spirit he had founded the religious community of the Victims of the Sacred Hearts. He had understood the soul of Melanie in Marseille. He invited her to his diocese where she could finally breathe, humanly and spiritually speaking. (As for her penances, we will talk about them extensively below).

B. Abuse by Satan

To the interior growth which signaled a new mystical direction, Melanie suffered traumatizing afflictions by the devil, well-certified by the Novice Mistress, Sister Therese. She, as well as the chaplain,

Father Gerente, understood these battles. Strange assaults from the devil disrupted her life during the novitiate of Corenc.

> After the first month that Sister Mary of the Cross (Melanie) had taken the habit of the religious Sisters of Providence, she asked Our Lady for the grace to suffer what the damned are suffering.
>
> Within three weeks Jesus and Mary granted these sufferings, and the young Sister began to feel a total disgust for prayer and the sacraments. This disgust grew every day, and at last she suffered terribly when she was forced to partake of the sacraments and to pray. At the same time strong thoughts of despair assaulted her, thoughts against the Faith, and many other things, as to make the young novice think she was in the abyss of hell. She suffered so much that it is impossible to explain this to someone who has not gone through it. Often one would find her having climbed onto a wall or a window, ready to jump if she had not been prevented from doing so. Later on, her pain intensified even more, in such a way that she had no freedom at all anymore. If one wanted to talk to her about God, she did not hear anything. If one wanted to have her explain how the demon tormented her, she could not talk about that either. Sometimes she went five or six days without being able to utter a single word, and for months she did not hear anything. Often, she did not recognize the people around her.

This testimony seems strange, and many exorcists who deal mainly with sinners possessed or mistreated by demons, are ignorant about these assaults on privileged souls, holy persons who are a threat to their infernal kingdom. They are not possessed, because the core of their soul is beyond the demons' reach, but the demons besiege them, like an enemy vehemently attacking the fortress of a city which has already foiled all his tricks. In such a case, this is an "obsession," in the sense of the Latin word obsessio, which has nothing to do with the psychological sense of the word, and which describes a profound, violent situation, which does not affect the deep union with God. The demonic actions look similar on the possessed as well as on the assaulted (Latin: obsessi), such as the Curé d'Ars, Mother Yvonne Aimee and many others. Like them, Melanie reacts by making fun of the adversary.

> When she went to church (noted the Sisters of Corenc), the demons would appear visibly to her and make her fall on the ground. If she held a breviary, demons would take it out of her hands and throw it noisily in the middle of the church. For more than a year they would beat her up without mercy, wherever she was, but mostly at night. When they did not know what to do anymore, they would throw her bed from one side to the other. And when the young Sister did not move anymore, they took another bed and emptied it out on her. And when they beat her heavily, she just said:
>
> "Ah! Dear companions, I had assumed that you were somewhat remarkable, but you are really not worth much, since you only do what blacksmiths do. Beat, beat hard! I will remain at the mercy of the One who puts me in your hands, and when He will find me well-polished, He will take me out, and I will be very grateful to you. So be good workers, work for me."
>
> This would put them in such a rage, that if they could have killed her, they would have. Sometimes they appeared disguised as frightful animals.
>
> These harassments lasted approximately two years and a few months. It is impossible to tell everything that happened to her. But we affirm that in 1854 she was at LaSalette and from that time the demons did not manifest themselves to her anymore.[36]

The ordeal continued, according to the letter of Father Burnoud to Bishop Ullathorne of Birmingham after his pilgrimage:

> The superior of LaSalette himself... was convinced that Melanie was subject to obsession (by Satan, who assaulted her psychologically) and that this was the only explanation for certain behaviors she exhibited. For example, she would scream:
>
> "There is no God!"

and it would only be with great efforts that in those situations, the priest could induce her to make short acts of faith.[37][38]

It is not only sinners who are attacked by demons, but also saints, like [Saint] Gemma Galgani or [Saint] Padre Pio, who are purified by spiritual nights that are not always cleared away by exorcism. I know many of these cases, be they historical or actual.

Christ was subject to such trials, as the Gospel tells us (many exegetes try to mitigate this). At the start of his mission, He was strongly tempted in the desert (Mt 4:1-11; Lk 4:1-12) and the demon went away, but only "until an opportune (kairos) time" (Lk 4:13), namely, the agony in the garden, the night of suffering and desolation, which made Him cry out on the Cross: *"Eloi, Eloi, Lama Sabachtani!"* [My God, my God, why have you forsaken me?] (Lk 15:34).

Melanie endured this, as did Saint Bernadette and Saint Therese of Lisieux. Those situations are difficult to untangle, because the mystical trial deriving from God can be intertwined with abuses from the demons and humans.

God draws good for the soul, through this persecution, saturating it with grace and purifying it as described in the book of Job. But in the moment that suffering occurs, even if the soul asked for suffering in an impulse of generosity, the soul can feel lost, because pain is an overwhelming and destructive evil. Therefore, it is impossible to love suffering as such; one can only bear it by way of an even stronger love. Even Christ uttered this very human prayer during his agony: "Father, take this cup away from me," before consenting out of love: "Nevertheless, not as I will, but as You will" (Mt 26:39).

First, Jesus repels the chalice as unacceptable, but then He embraces it, out of love for the Father. Significantly, in the Spanish language there is only one word for "desiring" and "loving." Melanie ended her intimate disclosure to Father Sylvain Marie Giraud, M.S. rather abruptly with the words: "Enough about this! Period."[39]

Like all suffering souls, Melanie does not linger too much on herself, nor on her suffering. She immediately takes shelter in surrender, detachment and love. As Father Jean Stern points out, we should never forget what Our Lady showed to the seers after her tears: the Cross. This is hardly an isolated case. Christ has shown others the Cross, among them, Sister Yvonne Aimee on the 5th of July 1922, to indicate to her, after her mystical marriage (June 1922), *her crucial mission*. The Cross is scarcely an empty concept: it is the necessary foundation of the salvation of men in Jesus Christ. That is the reason why He pushed his love up Calvary, and why the Cross remains the instrument of salvation today. Saint Paul preaches that this is the secret of all sanctity and of all effective apostolates. The power of God manifests itself in the moment of weakness, life in death (2Cor 11:12, 1:11). That is what Pope John Paul II lived heroically in his last years.

What is remarkable about Melanie is her non-rejection of suffering. She was more accustomed to it than ecstasies, and she ran "to the occasions to suffer as a glutton runs after delicacies."[40]

The thing that authenticates the suffering of Melanie, is the fact that this intolerable yoke made her spiritually robust in following her mission through so many impositions, and the forced exiles that plagued her until she found an open and understanding haven in Italy. It is because she knew how to align her suffering with the continuity of her life, with projects, with a rich creativity in initiatives, combined with a phenomenal perseverance. Moreover, she was never tedious, domineering or obsessive about the projects that were dear to her. During her life, so constantly thwarted by her adversaries, she was able to recognize the providential encounters of two Italian priest-founders of religious Orders, now beatified, who esteemed her and benefitted from her help (see below).

C. The Stigmata of the Passion

To the exterior suffering caused by temptations, afflictions and aggressive attacks from the devil, was added a completely different kind of suffering: the stigmata. This form of suffering is very different from the hideous and tormenting belligerence of hell. The stigmata is a communication with Christ. It qualifies suffering as a "suffering of love," in a straightforward and clear manner.

The stigmata of Melanie were considered, by her superficial critics, as pure inventions or as self-inflicted. "Bishop Ginoulhiac has always stated that Melanie did not have any stigmata."[41] This opinion is widely repeated: Father U. Paiola regards the stigmata of Melanie as "mere melodramatic fantasies."[42]

My study on the stigmata of Sister Yvonne Aimee[43], and personally meeting with several stigmatized persons, have taught me the prejudices that arise towards them from all sides, be they scientific or ecclesiastical.

Physicians, even those who are Christian, who take part in commissions of investigation, react negatively when they merely hear about stigmata, labeling it "self-harm." However, personal observation is another matter. Brazilian doctors in San Nicolas, and in certain parts of the world allowed physicians to see the pooling of blood with their own eyes, in a carefully controlled clinical examination. For this they offer no explanation. Observation of such phenomena is the only thing that can convince a physician, and I have known several doctors who have acknowledged this, starting with the pioneer in this subject prior to 1900, namely Doctor Imbert-Gourbeyre. He mentions Melanie, by the way, in his study *Les Stigmatisees*.[44]

The bright luminosity and cheerful sanctity of Francis of Assisi was necessary for the Church to accept such a paradoxical and repulsive phenomena (which can only be understood by love).

How to regard the stigmata in relation to Melanie? I shared in the general doubts about it but Michel Corteville, in his extensive research, has gathered for the first time twenty independent witnesses of the stigmata of Melanie, from all the phases of her life: childhood and youth in Isère, successive stays in Darlington England, Marseille France, in Castellammare Italy (1868-1882), and Cannes France (1885). The stigmata became invisible from 1889 to 1897, but at the same time she went through all the pains of the Passion without external outpourings of blood.

The stigmata were noticed again in Messina, Italy (1898), by [Saint] Annibale DiFrancia, and later in France by an acquaintance of Melanie, Father Émile Combes in Diou (1901), and Canon Hector Rigaux and his aunt, in Argoeuves in 1903.

In spite of the ambiguous character of the first testimonies which left a certain doubt as to her childhood stigmata, these other observations cannot be ignored. The similarity in numerous testimonies is undeniable and leaves no room for ambiguity. Father Gerente assumes that they were neither witnessed nor known, but the *argumentum a silentio* only demonstrates an extensive ignorance of this phenomena because Melanie tried to keep it as secret as possible.

It is possible to misinterpret the following words of Melanie spoken to Father Combe: "My executioner, (that) is my love," which she immediately corrected to apply to Christ: "His executioner, (that) is his love."[45] In this little phrase there is a lot of modesty, and a little bit of humor: "my love" can personify Christ, and it is with a mixture of sweetness and humanity, and a mystical sense of our identification with Christ, that she unifies the love of Christ who sends her the grace of the stigmata, and her own love, which receives them wholeheartedly.

One can read in the document, published in Appendix I [Section D: Marseille, 1860-1867] a summary by Mother Marie of the Presentation, assistant of the community of the Compassion, who lived for a long time in direct contact with Melanie.

SHOULD WE ACCEPT THE MYSTICAL EXPERIENCES OF MELANIE'S CHILDHOOD AS FACTUAL?

Alerted by some indications of the existence of charisms in the past, François Sibillat, Melanie's spiritual director, ordered her to write her childhood memories soon after her novitiate began in Corenc. In September 1852, Melanie recorded in a hasty manner, and with rather deficient spelling, an initial autobiography, the "abridged version" of her difficult childhood[46]: the first visits of her "Brother" and the stigmata. The document aroused perplexity in her critics.

Bishop Ullathorne, who was in communication with the Grande Chartreuse, notes two objections, sufficient enough to him for the whole document to be disregarded:

1. At the Apparition Melanie had not immediately recognized the Blessed Virgin.
2. And foremost, she was not a good pupil at catechism.[47]

Bishop Ullathorne:

> She had been at the parish nine months and nevertheless, the priest did not recognize her. She was hardly ever at church because of her work. Her superior said that a year later, she was still incapable of reciting from memory the Acts of Faith, Hope and Love, although they were taught her twice a day.[48] She only showed an improvement of character after the Apparition. Yet, in this (autobiographical) document, she described having learned songs and engaged in intimate conversations with Our Lord in several apparitions during her childhood. If she was familiar with such holy apparitions of Our Lord, how could she not know that it was the Blessed Virgin [on Sept. 19th]?[49]

As to the apparitions of Our Lord, the answer can be found in the document itself. The child who first appeared to Melanie in moments of distress had not presented himself as "Our Lord," but as a little "brother." The Child Jesus appeared to her incognito, and little by little completed the spiritual instruction begun by Melanie's father, Pierre Calvat, when he was home, by showing her the crucifix. (In the same way in Fatima, a long time after the Apparitions, Sister Lucia dos Santos had two apparitions of the Child Jesus, whom she did not recognize as such, in spite of her "experience."[50]

On the other hand, Our Lady had not yet been presented to her as weeping, or wearing a crucifix. Surely Melanie is not mistaken by indicating to Maximin (who only sees a "beautiful Lady") that it must be "a great saint, the good God... or the Blessed Virgin."

So what should we think about the catechism and the prayers that Melanie could not learn by heart? Next to the difficulty of the French language, the silent shepherdess was used to another form of prayer.

After having questioned her, [Saint] Annibale concludes:

> When the Most Blessed Virgin appeared to Melanie at LaSalette, the 14-year-old, was a totally different person than some "rugged, simple girl incapable of learning the Our Father," as some historians on the Apparition would have us believe. However, it is true that she did not even try to learn the vocal prayers, because her own prayer was mental and supernatural. She told me that when she was working for her masters, at the time the [family] would recite the Rosary of the Most Holy Virgin, she would go to the stable as to not hear this recitation, since it seemed to her that Our Lord would be bored to hear it. Then, with the passing of time, she came to know the excellence of vocal prayer, and she adopted it, and she always had it adopted by others. I remember that I sometimes found her, before Holy Mass, with the rosary in her hands.[51]

WAS MELANIE A MASOCHIST?

Of the inspired mystical sufferings on which we commented, Melanie added voluntary sufferings to which she felt called from above.

These sufferings are appalling and can make a negative impression. Our principles of pleasure and of desire (according to Freud), or of cleanliness and tidiness to better serve the Lord, have superseded the love of the Cross (central to the messages of LaSalette and Pontmain) and to the spirit of mortification, which was much esteemed in earlier times.

To judge Melanie well, let us consider three testimonies that mark out her penitential life.

[1] Firstly, is what she famously confided to Father Sylvain Marie

Giraud, M.S. about the follies of her youth, at the time when she was a shepherdess on the mountainside without any education. He asked her what she did for God. She answered that she first humiliated herself excessively: "My life was woven with infidelity, with sin and ungratefulness. I should have done much more for Jesus Christ, because the same Jesus Christ, mad with love for us, has done so much for the most miserable of all creatures."[52]

The way she describes her efforts as a child to compensate the mediocrity of her love, is the complete opposite of bragging:

What did I do? Follies and nothing more, and if, to humiliate myself, I have to confess and tell you the little that I did do, and did with so much imperfection, I will tell you that when I received the benefit of knowing God, I did all kinds of things that came to my mind. I fasted, maybe even on Sundays out of ignorance. I discovered that the Fool of Love was dying of a desire to be loved, and that He thirsted for souls. I also, out of ignorance, wanted to die of thirst... and I never wanted to drink. Being rebuked by my little Brother (Jesus, not yet identified) I changed my way of penance out of obedience. Reaching the age of seven or eight, I began to pray a little vocally, and to do some penance according to my lack of knowledge. That is to say, I tried to put myself almost completely in a stream and then I stayed there with wet clothes. I placed thorny rose branches on myself and I did all kinds of stupid things that I could imagine. However, as I could not do much to expiate my sins and those of the whole world, the Lord in his mercy provided for the need I felt within as an absolute necessity to suffer. He gave me patrons [saints] agreeable to my sentiments, and my little brother (Jesus) was happy with this little bit. He taught me to always pray and to offer myself to the Eternal Father, day and night. If, out of weakness, I failed, He gave me remedies to utilize in the best possible way.

But I did not do anything for God. That is the truth. I don't know what you want to say dear Father. If I look at what I have done, everything vanishes. Help me yourself...[53]

Whereas she notes the ardent motif of her penance, out of "pure love" and "for the expiation of sin," she also indicates that the "brother" Jesus, her advisor, had admonished her for her excesses. This is an important notion. Besides some of her penances at the time of the Apparition, her indifference to sleep in the midst of bad weather, to remain in wet clothes, are also confirmed by the testimony of her employer, Baptiste Pra.[54]

> [2] Secondly, a subsequent letter deals with the time she was still a Sister of Providence. She was in LaSalette, before returning to Corps, from whence she would be taken to England. This letter to her spiritual Father reveals her frightening and worrisome penances, but also her prudence, since she had already said that her mortifications were inspired by her love for the suffering Christ. As she did not get any answer, inspired by his silence, she writes him the following:

"Your silence authorizes me to continue my penances and even to add some other regimens; twice a day sackcloth; manacles every day, etc. Often, I sleep on the floor, other times I put a board with sharp points in my bed, and all of that is nothing to me. I would like to do more, but I think this will come. In fact, every day I am constructing penances. I run after occasions to suffer like gourmands run after candy. What bothers me is that sometimes when there is a lot of suffering, I don't feel anything. It is like I am dead. ry day I have intense headaches, pains in my heart, etc., and on Fridays when all this increases, I hardly feel anything. That makes me angry with our brother [Jesus], and I am furious at myself, because I am nothing but a shadow of a religious person. I don't dare being called that because I am distorting religious life. Tell me what I should do to become perfect. I cannot become humble because I have no idea what that is. Last Sunday I wanted to know how much virtue I had gained since I entered religious life. I did my personal examination of conscience on this subject, and, after a long examen, I found myself without even half a virtue. Then, instead of humiliating myself towards God, I was glad about it, thinking, well, if I don't have any, God has them all [...] the way I am writing should not make you think that I am sad. I have never been so happy since I came here. I believe God wants me to be here."55

One should take notice that she does not want to do anything without informing her spiritual Father about it, and notice her sincere effort of discernment, and finally the positive and profound conclusion inspired by God: she understood that she has nothing of herself, but all is from God, which encompasses Christian spirituality, starting with Saint Paul (Php 4:13; 2Cor ch 11)

[3] Thirdly, the penance is excessive. The motivations are profound and justified: Jesus "mad with love," his Passion, and expiation in a radical humility. The last proof of the fact that she continued her penances until the end of her life, in Italy (Messina, 1897-1898), comes from the servant of God, Nazarena Majone, first Daughter of the Divine Zeal of the Heart of Jesus.

"During all the time she stayed with us, every Friday she would lock herself up and not come out all day. And that is not all. Since that day was for her a day of penance, she would not eat or drink, not even a little sip, even if she suffered terribly from thirst. If she ever drank, she would always mortify herself and drink very slowly. Meanwhile, she was for us a continuous model of edification. Her virtue was always the same. We have never seen her angry, but always calm and serene. Her virtues were always hidden."56

Melanie seems to have forgotten the reminiscences of her little brother, Jesus, who rebuked her for not drinking in her youth (refer to Ch 5 Sec I, and above in this section). She seemed to forget the elementary rules that health requires, since the human body needs water and dies after six days if it does not have any. She never went to that extreme as her common sense prevented her. Besides, next to an unbearable fasting, stigmatists draw a mysterious energy from the Eucharist.

Sister Nazarena continues:

> We have seen the instruments of penance that she used. It amazed us how she could stand it all. She had a cross made of nails. She put in on her back and then let herself fall (on the ground) face upward. This we heard about later; we saw the instrument full of blood (same text).

So was she a masochist? In one sense, yes, but we have seen how her excessive actions were inspired by the "mad love of Jesus," who suffered for us and invited his disciples to follow Him, which is an invitation to reflection.

Without much advice, she improvises these penances to meet Jesus suffering, at the highest mystical level. She is beyond her body, as she sometimes has noted.

To this, we must add an historical explanation. After the era of persecutions, when the Church at peace became an important power in the Empire, the fathers of the desert replaced martyrdom with asceticism. To the mortal violence of persecutors, they substituted a series of corporal penances, which the Church did not cease to cultivate. Reading the fathers of the desert became common among the religious Orders, and among the laity of the Church, up until the middle of the 20th century.

Instruments of penance are reported to have been worn in the 17th century by zealous Christians as immortalized in the theatrical comedy of Molière who makes Tartuffe exclaim:

> "Laurent, do tighten my hair shirt, and do it with it my discipline!"

The use of instruments of penance were still common in the 18th century like Saint Louis-Marie DeMontfort[57]; in the 19th century, the Cure d'Ars; in the 20th century between the two World Wars, Mother Yvonne Aimee DeMalestroit; all of them radiant and dynamic personalities in their life and actions. (We could mention the flagellants of the 16th and 17th century whom the Church would moderate up until their disappearance, with the exception of a few places in Spain.)

In all the monastic Orders, and in other Orders as well, until the Vatican Council, flagellation with the "discipline" (a whip of rope to which some substituted a whip with iron spikes, as was the flagellation of Christ), was very common on Fridays, during the recitation of the Passion Psalm 51, the *Miserere*.

Regardless - that these generous devices, except in some religious Orders, having nowadays almost disappeared - during my childhood, at school and within my family, we were trained to make small daily sacrifices. That is what we did, without masochism, out of the desire to do well. This Biblical tradition of thousands of years, in our time almost forgotten, was largely and officially promoted within the Church, up until the middle of the 20th century. Driven out of western society, asceticism is nowadays the asset of oriental wisdom.

Having said that, the Church never withdrew the austere invitation of Christ to "renounce" oneself and to "take up one's cross" (Mt16:24; Mk 8:34; Lk 9:23), nor the exhortation of the Apostle Paul to die to oneself and to live in Christ (Col 3:9-11; Gal 2:19-20) In what way? In all kind of ways, depending on the vocation, on the individual and on the circumstances of life, since holiness brings about charismatic excesses in various ways.

In the end, all this can only be judged from the point of view of love, genuine and humble love. The testimonies on Melanie and others clearly reveal that her penances were inspired by the love that Christ crucified has for us, along with the concern of "filling up in our flesh what is still lacking in regard to Christ's afflictions, for the sake of his body, which is the Church," as the Apostle Paul formulates it (Col 1:24). That is the basis of the stigmatists, like Saint Francis of Assisi. I came to understand their exceptional but authentic meaning, by studying the history of stigmatized people, of whom many have been canonized, or are living hidden today, and they are far more numerous than some might imagine. I have personally met more than ten of them.

To ever-reappearing objection of "self-harm/masochism" the only scientific answer that I can offer, is to bring about the (multiple) cases in which doctors and theologians have seen, with their own eyes, blood welling up from under the skin, without any intermediary instrument or possible natural cause, and, by the way, in a variety of circumstances. All this must be taken into account before accusing Melanie of masochism. Within the Church there is a vocation to suffering, in union with Christ, of which Father Sylvain Marie Giraud, M.S., one of her spiritual confreres, was among the great theorists in the 19th century.

WAS MELANIE SELF-CENTERED?

As for the egocentrism and subjective projections to which some would reduce Melanie's spiritual development, the texts as a whole defy this hypothesis that has been projected onto her, attributing as a late product of her imagination what the recently discovered documents attest to earlier.

The seers differ much from each other, and are even opposite in characteristics: Maximin, extrovert, Melanie introvert. He was sociable, whereas she liked to be alone with God. She was interior, contemplative, *however not at all self-absorbed*. She was able to make room for social relationships, but without thrusting herself into the lead. She made friends everywhere, and at all levels; she engaged in very frequent verbal exchanges, written or spoken. In those communities in which she was not dragged in by force, she lived an exemplary life, and even in the ones she was forced to live in, she sometimes adapted herself for years on end. From the Sisters of Corenc, where she was happy, to the exile of six years in England (acquiesced until the Blessed Virgin called her to something new), then in Greece and in Italy - she was a consenting soul, getting along with "everything

God wanted," and "as long as He wanted."

WAS MELANIE AN ANTI-SEMITE?

She has been accused of anti-Semitism. Some have said that Maritain, whose wife was Jewish, would not have defended her if he had known about her letters to Canon Alexander DeBrandt at the beginning of the Dreyfuss case. And it is true that when Melanie was given articles from *La Libre Parole* to read, wherein the editor Edouard Drumont, an anti-Dreyfusard and a notorious anti-semite, displayed his ideology for a traditional France, and against an anti-clerical government of "Freemasons, Carbonaros, Jews, Protestants, Socialists, Anarchists," as Melanie relates.[58] And she even added some more resounding anathemas.

Nevertheless, Maritain was not ignorant of her Letters to Father DeBrandt, edited by Father Combe in 1913. They were copied by Vera, his sister-in-law, and he even cites them. If he did not protest, it was because Melanie, who was not anti-Semitic at all, had reacted on her own to the article submitted to her. She wrote to Mr. Schmidt: "I am far from approving the data of Drumont."[59]

At the time Pius IX preached: "Outside the Church, there is no salvation," without bringing in the important nuances elaborated by the Second Vatican Council, and at a time when he denounced without hesitation the opponents of God and the Church, Melanie, by the same logic, is severe on these same enemies: non-Christians and bad Christians (including Napoleon III) displaying the fiery anti-clericalism of Drumont with even more severity on bad priests. Her colorful words are sharp, in the Romanesque and traditionalistic style of the time. Ecclesiastical authorities have criticized her for her comments on unworthy clergy. In the message of LaSalette itself (the message that is contrasted to the "excessive" Secrets), the Virgin compares bad Christians with "dogs," just like Melanie in her younger years compared Napoleon III to a "pig," and in her later years President Combes, who expelled the religious from his country and confiscated their goods, to "Nero or Attila." Let it be said, once and for all, that Melanie's prophetic and hyperbolic language should be situated in her time, and cannot be taken literally. Her words are directed to sins, not persons.

As to the Jews, in spite of the anti-Semitic sentiment that pervaded France in that era, including Bishop Fava and the Catholic press, Melanie prays for them and speaks about them with a hopefulness similar to that of Saint Paul, in his magnificent chapters of the Letter to the Romans (ch 9-11), where he is ready to become "anathema" to save his people, and expresses his confidence in their future.

Melanie spoke of the Jews with esteem and respect: Jesus wanted to be circumcised "so as to give merit to the circumcision done by the Jews," she writes.[60] She prophesies: "After the Antichrist, the Jews will convert and will live out a penitent and exemplary life."[61]

What is even more, when the French will lose faith, (refer to Ch 4 Sec II: 4 and Sec III:8 [11]), returning to their origins the Jews will replace the apostate Christians who fall from grace: "It is possible and even certain, that the Jews will take over the title of 'People of God,' while Christians will be rejected."[62] "The last pope will be Hebrew, like Saint Peter," she concludes.[63]

She discerns three personifications of the Apocalypse and she generously makes way for the Hebrew people:

1. The first represents Jesus Christ;
2. The second represents the Church, the mystical Body of Jesus Christ, who has to resemble Him in every way;
3. The third represents the Hebrew, or rather, the generations until the end of the world, represented by the Hebrew.[64]

In brief, as one can find severe judgments made by Melanie on all those outside the Church or unfaithful to the Church, one cannot find any anti-Semitism in her words. She offers warmhearted congratulations to Canon Alexander DeBrandt on the beatification of his friend, Father [Saint] Liberman, a Jew who became a priest through his intervention, in spite of their diverging ideas at the

Eudist novitiate.[65]

WERE THE SEERS CORRUPTED BY POLITICAL INFLUENCES?

As for the influence of royalist or esoteric groups on Melanie or Maximin, to whom a considerable role is attributed, we will see the limitations of their arguments below [Ch 7: III. Royalist and Apocalyptic Influences?]

ARE THEY SAINTS?

MELANIE

In analyzing the mental balance and psychology of Melanie, we have already probed into her life, laden with exterior and interior trials, and her mystical impetus towards sanctity. It was identified by her superiors during her novitiate, in which she asked for the name of Mary of the Cross (9th of October 1851): a very significant choice and decisive decision.

Let it suffice to support the preceding observations with a sketch of some of the principal virtues and with testimonies of her holiness.

We know the fundamental importance of humility.[66] After examining all the testimonies, it is a false statement that the Sisters of Corps or Corenc, or even her most devoted acquaintances had indulged in some kind of cult towards her. Two answers of Melanie to Father Lagier, around February 1847, prove once again her indifference, be it for criticism or for praise, a sign of spiritual health. He attacks her to test her:

- *Well, my poor Melanie! It must have been the devil that you saw.... and since she did not react) What I just told you, did that hurt you?*
- *No.*
- *Are you sure?*
- *No. What would you want me to do? (She said this with so much calmness and such an angelic look that tears started to well up in my eyes...])*[67]

> - *It must be an honor for you, my child, to be chosen to tell us about this great marvel?*
>
> - *I don't know what you want me to say.*[68]

Melanie does not like engravings in which she is represented with the Virgin (and with Maximin). On the 11th of September 1849, Marie DesBrulais presented to her one of the images for a dedication; Melanie took a pencil... and pierced the image of her own head! At the time when they are saying goodbye, Marie DesBrulais insists on "having a little souvenir from her":

> I asked her for it. "I don't want anyone to remember me," she answered. "I don't want to be thought of as a saint."[69]

On the 31th of May 1849, Louis-Marie-Urbain Similien, having finished praying at the site of the Apparition, finds himself suddenly face to face with Melanie, accompanied by a teaching Sister from the Providence [Convent]:

> Taking into consideration my previous dealings with her community, the teacher accepted my greetings cheerfully, and entrusted to me her pupil, who was willing to answer all my questions.
>
> This young girl, of normal proportions, did not seem at all the 16 years that she was supposed to be. At this age she had an oval face. Her skin was pale. She had rosy cheeks and dark hair, and she appeared quite graceful. Her appearance, of a most beautiful candor, breathed a ravishing modesty. Her personality manifested a great reticence.
>
> She did not want to be shown off in public, rather she sought isolation. That was the reason why she only spoke about the Apparition out of necessity. When she did so, it was in a low voice, a serious tone, her eyes usually looking down, and her hands falling down and somewhat being crossed beneath her breast. In this way her attitude corresponded truly to the dignity of her words. In short, everything about her expressed the sublimity of her mission, and the influence of the Holy Spirit.
>
> However, as to downplay the reflection of her virtues, since in

every mortal creature there has to be some imperfections as the consequence of original sin, Melanie's superiors accused her of not having a more open character, and feared in her a tendency towards pride, because of the high favors that she had been granted. Other than these two recriminations, everything in her actions was praiseworthy.[70]

Marie DesBrulais, another well-known witness, questioned the guide who led her on the mountain, and received almost the same explanation:

- So, the young lady, is it true that she has become proud?
- No, that is not true. She is not as cheerful or friendly as Maximin, but she is alright. He is more distracted.[71]

DesBrulais typifies the seers accurately: Melanie, discreet, reserved and ponderous; Maximin, spontaneous and provocative, but with healthy human warmth.

At the end of Melanie's life, the suspicious priest of Diou, thinking of welcoming her in his parish, submitted her to a common test:

> Vigil of Pentecost 20 [May 1899] My first impression this morning at the [train] station: naïve appearance of [...] or 7 year old girl [she was 67], being somewhat lost.[...]

> As soon as we came to my house, I wanted to know if she was humble, and I started out scrutinizing her with the malice of a magistrate! Lifting up my eyes every time, to see if there would appear any traits of pride on her face, I read to her the *"Memoirs of Good Father Sibillat"* from one end to the other. It was a waste of effort.

> Then, suddenly, I started to tell her the bad things about her that people had told me, without omitting the most horrible stories, which I don't dare to write down here. This also was a waste of effort. Not only did she not reply to these calumnies, all along she even kept a childish candor on her face, and with simplicity she answered all my questions.[...]

> When I told her the bad things that were said about her, she seemed lost in God, or otherwise as if she might not have grasped the meaning of what was said. I have never seen such a level of humility or purity![72]

Melanie's humility, the consciousness of her littleness before God, her transparency, all explain her inexhaustible patience in trials and contradictions.

Unfeigned love towards her neighbor was the motif of her life, all the more obvious in certain situations, especially after 1860: serving the Sisters of the Compassion, in Greece, then at the school in the suburbs of Marseille, where she appears to have worked in a satisfactory way. Service also characterizes her life in Italy, even during her stay at the Visitation Convent in Rome, to do the work that Pope Leo XIII had asked her. The superior of this convent, who gave hospitality to the "very good Melanie," wrote: "For us, she is a model of edification, because of her virtuous and holy behavior, and she charitably serves a younger Sister who is very ill; she takes care of her day and night, according to the need. Her mortification is also remarkable, and, like I said, we are very much edified by her."[73]

Melanie left Italy in 1884 to take care of her mother until the latter's death, five years later.

In his unpublished manuscript of 1917, Maritain investigates the "Virtues of Melanie" and researches them systematically. The testimony of this great philosopher, confidant of popes, ambassador of France at the Holy See, humble investigator and spokesman of the "ignorant shepherdess," is the most impressive of all:

> I asked those who have known Melanie what impression her physiognomy made on them at first sight [...] that astounded them most, was the extraordinary candor appearing on her face, and her incomparable sweetness and simplicity. But above all, it was her meditative recollection. A picture taken of her in LaSalette while she was praying without her realizing she had been photographed, allows us, with this spontaneous document,

to form an idea of this 'recollection' of which people marveled who saw her in church. She was constantly in the living presence of God, and her prayer was really in complete oblivion of her surroundings, a pure gaze of love and light.

Melanie was always very silent and sweet. To the most sharp or hurtful observations, she used to answer quietly and calmly, which Father Combe, who had a more explosive character, sometimes found "exasperating." If in the first years after the Apparition she was thought to be gloomy, it is because she was a shy person, and up till then, she had only been a "wild child" accustomed to divine contemplation, and not to human courtesy. Moreover, she was rather afraid of people, of their stares, their noisiness, and she preferred to turn herself ardently to the God of her heart. If on the other hand, an amazing vehemence seemed to emerge from some of her words and from many of the letters she wrote, it has to do with the fact that they were seeing her in her mission. In any other circumstance, her sweetness would prevail.

By the way, don't we know that sweetness and power, far from being incompatible, are in fact inseparable? Wasn't Moses, called by the Holy Spirit, the meekest of all the children of men? And Jesus, meek and humble of heart, did He not chase the merchants in the Temple away with a whip, and didn't He overturn their tables?

The *zeal of your house consumes me*. As soon as the rights of God or of Mary are at stake, Melanie becomes uncompromising. On those occasions she drops a stunning verdict on men and things: she will use terribly harsh and straightforward language, and a vengeful outrage, which impels the imagination to form a bridge over twenty centuries, to connect the shepherdess of the Alps to the majestic inspired men of the mountains of Judaea.

That which gives Melanie this special power, is the fact that she is fixed in the truth, with an unshakable love. It's a kind of impossibility for her to express anything other than the truth, or to act differently than along the pure lines of her conscience; a complete incapacity to compromise. She hated lies with an angelic hatred, as the most direct offense to the subsisting Truth, like an absolutely unbearable disorder. It is so much rooted in her soul, that it manifests itself from her earliest childhood onwards. To the "theatrical performances" or "comedies" to which her mother wanted to take her, the "wild child" is incapable of attending without making a scene of shouting or stomping. When she was only five or six months, her mother wanted to take her to the evening parties where there was amusement; but she would shout, cry and tear up her cloth. In this way, she made it impossible for people to hear what was said, and her mother had to take her outside. Melanie felt badly about that. She considered it a disobedience and a sin.

> "One day," she added, (she was about five or six years old) "my mother, thinking I was more docile, wanted to take me to a comedy, and I really did not resist in any way. I had decided I would obey, although inside I felt a strong aversion. However, I had given my senses to God. I begged Him to preserve me from seeing or hearing anything that would offend Him. In this play someone announced to the public that we would see amazing things, that one would cut off a man's head and that it would be put on again, without it leaving a trace of injury. My mother, seeing me quiet, was happy; but when the moment arrived, my mother said to me:
>
> - Look, look, look there!
>
> - I screamed: It's not true! It's not true! My eyes cannot stand fakery! And I cried so loud that my poor mother had to take me away, much to her displeasure. Once home, I was sent away as being incorrigible, and I really was terrible. I constantly caused grief to my dear mother.

The three theological virtues are the sap of all holiness. Melanie, as we have seen, lived from faith, and lived only from faith.

In "these times of dead faith," as she used to refer to it, Melanie appears like a sign of God to remind people, in all walks of life, of the integrity of faith. And when she grieves, if she groans, if she exhorts to adjure Christians - her lengthy correspondence bears admirable witness to this - it is to regulate their thoughts and actions of faith alone, and on the practice of the faith. Here as everywhere, she is the faithful interpreter of Our Lady of LaSalette. She does not offer some social or political remedy. Neither does she require of everyone to ascend to the heights of Christian life and spirituality. What she does require, unceasingly, is that everyone remains faithful to the duties of his state of life. The religious should strive towards perfect charity, the priest to sanctify the people, the priest and the laity to keep the promises of their baptism and to practice the commandments of God. Melanie had a holy and strong devotion to the commandments of God, and one can say that she practiced the fourth commandment in a heroic way, not only during her childhood, but also when she traveled from Italy to France to care with the utmost tenderness, and to prepare for a pious death, "this dear mother" who in the past had been to her an unnatural mother, and who had never ceased to make Melanie suffer terribly.

The virtue of *hope* within Melanie, was necessarily commensurate with the interior and exterior trials which the poor shepherdess had to undergo, trials which sometimes reached as far as dereliction seemingly without remedy.

As to the virtue of *charity*, let us remember that Melanie's entire life was one long testimony of faithful love of God and his Mother. Let us remember also, in regard to loving our neighbor, that Melanie imposed upon herself the bloodiest penances on behalf of her most virulent persecutors. How many among those who had wanted to annihilate her, had cause to bless her at the hour of their death, because they obtained their salvation through her prayers! Jesus had taught her: "God does not forbid us to love our neighbor. On the contrary, He asks us to do so, no matter who he is, friend or foe, for pure love of God, in whose image he is made." And Melanie applied strictly what she had been taught, loving with a perfectly pure heart, people of all kinds, for God alone, and first of all those whom she had a special duty to love: her "dear mother" and her "dear masters" (for example, The Monk [nickname of a terrible employer] and his family).

Melanie had a small pension, assured by some people devoted to Our Lady of LaSalette, but the money disappeared in her hands, since she would give everything to the poor.

Melanie loved the most Blessed Virgin with an unparalleled love. She cherished "her mama," with the confident and simple tenderness of a little child. And Melanie knew, like the great doctors Saint Bernard and Saint Grignion DeMontfort, the magnificent depth of Mary's mystery:

> "Only God can speak worthily of the magnificence of the Virgin Mother and of her power, because, to begin to understand the mystery of the elevation of this most sublime Virgin, one would have to know God. Now the Angels themselves do not perceive the mysteries of God; but they know God in proportion adapted to their angelic state, and this knowledge ravishes them and keeps them in a continuous ecstasy of love, joy, admiration and happiness, incomprehensible to the inhabitants of the earth. When we claim that Mary is the masterpiece of the Most Holy Trinity, nothing more can be said. Mary was, is, and will always be, beneath God, but the most perfect, sublime and exalted of all creatures. Mary is by grace, what Our Lord Jesus Christ is by nature. Neither Saint John, nor Saint Peter, nor any other saint can be compared to Mary, neither in love, nor in suffering, nor in faithfulness, nor in grace, nor in knowledge. If Saint John represents the Church, because from the Cross Jesus gave him to Mary as her son, Mary is no less a Mother, a mother with authority over her son. Thus, Mary is the sanctuary of the Church. She

is the life, support and eye of the Church."[74]

Particularly significant was Melanie's perpetual faithfulness at the service of her mission in spite of opposition, persevering until her death in Altamura, despite the contradictions.

- Bishop Ginoulhiac made her leave the diocese of Grenoble after having forbidden her to make her vows.

- In England, where he sent Melanie, people were willing to help her in the project to found the Order of the Virgin, but it was frustrated by the advice of Bishop Ginoulhiac.

- Therefore, Melanie was obliged to join the Carmel of Darlington, in spite of her preference for "the great outdoors," but the cloistered vocation inhibited her mission. She pronounced her vows with mental reservation, so as to remain available to the Virgin. She was finally able to leave the cloister on the 19th of September 1860, so as to be able to reveal the Secret.

- In Marseille, a new episcopal interdiction prevented her from living as a religious teacher, as she had begun to do with the Sisters in Corenc.

- In 1879, another bishop, Fava of Grenoble, paralyzed her ability to start the Order at LaSalette, which had been approved by Bishop Petagna and submitted to the Pope.

- Giagomo [Jacques, James] Cusmano, a friend of Melanie, recently beatified, wanted to put his congregation under the patronage of Our Lady of LaSalette, but was prevented from doing so by a "supposed" papal interdiction.[75]

- From August 1892 to March 1895, Melanie rightly defends a legacy, received in proper and due form, for the foundation of her Order. Anxious to obtain this gift [for his own purposes], the Archbishop of Autun excommunicated her.

- Despite the Order of the Mother of God being encouraged by Leo XIII, trials and obstacles interfered with the realization of the foundation, in particular the rising anger over the contents of the Secret once it was published, leading to the slander of Melanie herself, who endured all these trials - to use her own adjective - "cheerfully."

Father Francois Michel Sibillat, among the very first Missionaries of LaSalette, and spiritual director of Melanie in Corenc, one day exclaimed:

> If Saint Teresa [of Avila] would have had to go through the trials over which Melanie triumphed, Saint Teresa would have succumbed![76]

[Saint] Annibale DiFrancia wanted to introduce the cause of her beatification:

> "I am on the verge of promoting the process by gathering information on the virtues and gifts of our beloved Melanie, through the Diocese of Messina [...] I don't know if you are aware that Melanie has performed a miracle by suddenly healing a person who was seriously ill, appearing in one of my Institutes."[77] [78]

MAXIMIN

The two shepherds kept up no particular ties. Their destinies were totally independent from one another. Melanie explains why:

> Although I beheld many good qualities in Maximin, I fled from him as much as I could because he was the opposite of my solitary nature. During the four years we stayed in the same boarding school, I tried not to encounter him; we rarely stayed more than 15 minutes together without becoming upset.[79]

However, she appreciated Maximin, his candor, his unbounded generosity, and his simplicity in a world which, at the time, was very conventional:

> Maximin was good by nature; he would not have been able to hurt anyone. He loved the poor. He would often give them everything, even the clothes he was wearing. Several times he was scolded because he had given away his clothes, his shirt, his

hat, etc. (He was so good, a Sister told me, that he once came back to school with only his shirt on, and he did not dare to go inside. When he saw me at the window, he begged me to get him one of my dresses, which I did. Decked out in this manner the Sister let him go in with the girls... but when he handed in his boy's underclothing, the story turned humorous once more! He started to cry because she did not allow him to remain dressed like us... once again the Sister corrected him. As soon as she had finished punishing him, I saw Maximin jump up to embrace her. When I was alone with him, wanting to know what he was thinking, I said to him:

If the Sister would have punished me that way, I would not have embraced her afterwards!

Oh, Maximin answered, *it was to console her. She already had so much trouble.*

Now, a word about his simplicity. One Sunday in the church filled with people, he ran after the priest, making his confession out loud so he could communicate at Mass: "Father, give me absolution before Mass! I embraced the niece of a Sister, and the Sister said I committed a sin!"

He was of great simplicity, and without mistrust. When the pensionaries sometimes wanted to get rid of him because he distracted them from their lessons, they acted as if they had lost something in the garden or elsewhere. And Maximin, always inclined to help, would run here and there to find the lost object, and when he would come back, they started laughing, and he never figured it out. Really, he would not have been able to believe that a person could say one thing, yet mean something else.[80]

Maximin has been slandered frequently, just as Melanie. Even Bishop Ginoulhiac, in a letter to his friend, the Minister of Culture, was not afraid to present him as a "liar" whom he had to chase away from the minor seminary.[81]

Melanie called for people's repentance in the style of Saint John the

Baptist, by her words and by her penances. Maximin, on the contrary, to fulfill the directive of the Holy Virgin "to pass" the message to "all her people," played, ate and drank with all sorts of persons. That is what scandalized the devotees, so much as to openly criticize him. Nevertheless, in his life there was no drunkenness, no frivolous habits, as Father Claude DeLeon pretends, as do some others:

> Maximin, after the Apparition, was confided to the care of the religious Sisters of Corps as a pensionary. He would escape their attention ten times a day, run off to the village to play and drink strong liquor,[...] he excels among his comrades by his cursing and by the unbelievable liberty of his actions and his language [...] Everywhere he is noticed because of his debauchery [...] Grenoble... . .] has the privilege of seeing him often in its cafés.[82]

Sister Valerie, his dear adoptive "aunt" brings the facts back to their true proportions. She writes to a biographer, on the 4th of September 1879:

> - This child had a lighthearted character; he was flighty and very jolly. This flightiness, this light-heartedness, made him commit some caprices that depreciated him in the eyes of the public. People would have accepted this from any other young man and such conduct would not even have been noticed. However, levity in such a privileged child gave rise to calumny. Now you might ask:
>
> - What kind of caprices for example?
>
> - Well, he didn't hesitate to go to the café. He accepted wine in cabarets, in the company of young people who liked being with him because he was always friendly and cheerful. Later on they would say: "He is just like us." I, personally, don't believe he has ever done anything wrong, never.[83]

A Program for the Rehabilitation of their Reputations

After his death, the most absurd calumnies against Maximin came to the ears of Bishop Fava, of Grenoble. Influenced by the rumors circulating at that point in time, he tried to prevent Father Émile LeBaillif from publishing a biography based on the documents provided by Mrs. Jourdain.

One of the most negative reports was sent by a Parisian priest, who collected the following malicious rumors:

> In the opinion of Rev. Father Caillard, Maximin "has for ten years scandalized the people of Versailles, by his laziness, his drunkenness, and even his immorality, since everyone knows that this man has supported a woman for some time."

Father Billard, Vicar of Saint-Germain-l'Auxerrois and a nephew of Mrs. Jourdain, accused him of an "intimate relationship" with his adoptive mother![84] Henri Dion who reports this accusation, indicates where it comes from: the inheritance of the Jourdains, which was turned away from Father Billard because of their adoption of Maximin. Master Isnard, notary at Corps, revealed the calumniator.

> Only the sacred character [of ordination] which covered him could have spared him [this priest] from indictment.[85]

Melanie was scarcely treated any better. Bishop Zola affirmed that:

> she is neither possessed, nor deluded, nor proud, nor disobedient [...] nor a miserable woman left to carnal passions[86], as has been rumored to Pius IX.[87]

Both seers suffered character assassinations from certain clergymen, to whom the Secret undoubtedly was directed. Those kinds of attacks [directed against saints] are not uncommon. Closer to our time, [Saint] Padre Pio's bishop sent to the Vatican the darkest accusations about him. Since this bishop was known to be very respectable, the discovery of those calumnies in the archives immediately halted, for awhile, the cause for Padre Pio's beatification. Perhaps he had been deceived by good apostles, or tempted, as it sometimes happens... ? A good number of saints have been calumniated. Don Bosco was slandered to Pope Pius IX, and he suffered from it.

Propagated everywhere, the calumnies against the shepherds of LaSalette - visionaries who were living in the world without being able to realize their desire for a religious vocation, and being very often on their own - (unlike the seers of Lourdes or Rue de Bac, who were members of religious communities) these calumnies have been perpetuated even until the present. Their calls for conversion, the urgent call of Mary to unworthy priests, were not much different from Christ's preaching, which was condemned by religious authorities.

The Secrets of Mary did indeed disturb Robert Masson:

> Ah! Those Secrets... in a strong manner, they confuse my pen beforehand. Real or false (and in fact I don't want to know), they make a noise around me like a noise that covers the words. An uproar of intrigues and conjectures: of calumnies... [on the clergy]; of gossiping birds that unfortunately feast more on the commentaries than on the message itself. I'm reluctant to dip into this greasy fortune-teller water - that tumbles down from Our Lady to Madame Fraya - without hope of being able to keep my feet dry, since I know not whether the splash of the puddle will dirty the entire landscape.[88]

Maria Winowska on the other hand, gets out of this muddy water:

> The Secret of Melanie is so thoroughly drenched by the tears of the Virgin, that all hell will work together to drown it in waves of ink and gall. Propaganda of the lowest kind will force the Church to prohibit its diffusion. It conjures in the imagination a text in the style of Jeremiah, violent and bitter, as are some verses of the Magnificat. The rose-water devotion of the 19th century could be offended by it: in those days no one read the prophets very much.[89]

Facing the disinformation, and at the same time, defending the truth of the Biblical language of LaSalette, Matagrin the Bishop of Grenoble from 1969-1989, dared to speak about the need for the "rehabilitation" of the [reputation of the] seers:

> It is the task of historians: let the historians help truth make its way. [90]

The holiness of the poor, the coherence in their testimony, their classic spiritual ordeals: our new study blazes trails for this rehabilitation.

We conclude this chapter on Maximin and Melanie with three testimonies, that will help to show things in a clearer light. First, Melanie's opinion about her companion, when reading his biography, written by Father Emile LeBaillif:

> Every night I read several pages of the life of good Maximin. I am moved by, and envious of, his various and continuous suffering. I am so far from having his naive generosity and, most of all, his virtues. In short, he has been a martyr for the accomplishment of his mission. But glory be to God, one can truly say: he now dwells in glory and gathers what he has sown in tears.[91]

His weeping continued the tears of Our Lady, in a filial communion.

About Melanie, Sister Josephine, Servant Superior of the Daughters of Charity at Galatina, wrote to Father Émile Combes on October 15, 1907:

> Melanie often came to Mass in our church, which was open to the public. She would stay near the door. I had a lot of trouble to make her accept a place on the children's bench. Her humble and modest attitude was very edifying to them. At the moment of receiving Holy Communion, she would prostrate on the floor. During the acts of thanksgiving, she seemed to be delighted and in ecstasy. I have never seen her otherwise [in church] than kneeling. The same applies to feast days. She spent her days working, reading and praying and a large part of the night writing. The little time of sleep that she took, was always on the bare floor, the bed was only there for the sake of appearances, to mislead. She

never slept there. Her paternal home was very poor and humble, as can be deduced by the fact that in winter the rain fell indoors, as if on the street. To pass from one part to the other she needed an umbrella. During the short visits that we [Sisters] made to accompany some people wanting to meet Melanie, it happened that, out of curiosity, I entered her small kitchen, where I saw that the fire had never been lit. On a very small stove some potatoes were cooking, and that was her meal for the entire week. Never, Father, have we been able to make her accept a few food supplies, and if we secretly put some in her drawer, a month later they would still be there.

Dear Melanie has been twice with us during the break. We asked her a thousand and one questions on the Apparition, to which she would answer vaguely and humbly; but if we asked her if the Blessed Virgin was very beautiful, Melanie's countenance became radiant and she would answer: "Who can describe this beauty? It cannot be explained!" Her conversation always revolved on the offense to God by the profanation of the sacred day of Sunday and of blasphemy. When she went to the cemetery, her preferred place to walk, she instructed the children on the way and taught them the Sign of the Cross. One day two women asked her for a medal. She gave a medal to one woman but refused a medal to the other. When the woman asked why, she answered:

- Because you curse.
- The woman blushed, saying: "How does she know? She has never met me."

It is certain, Father, that she was inspired by God. I had the occasion to talk with her about some difficulties I encountered in my duties, and with a few words she always helped me out. I cannot say more about this holy soul, Father, except that I felt a great consolation when she prayed near me in our church, and when she fixed her eyes on our beautiful Immaculate Virgin whom she loved so much. People who approached her were edified by her modesty and her meditative prayer. Her humility shone through her writings. I so much regret having burned her letters. I only kept two of them. The last she wrote to me from Altamura, before her death [...] Therefore I count on you, Father, on [...] your ardent prayers, to take advantage of the examples that she, as the beloved and privileged one of Mary, has left us.[92]

The Servant of God Nazarena Majone, first superior of the Sisters of the Divine Zeal of the Heart of Jesus, who hosted Melanie for a year in Messina, writes:

> Her life was a model of virtue, and of continuous mortification, without her ever getting tired. Her behavior was one of a saint, sweet, modest. We admired her holy virtues. Her mortification was unrivaled; she ate very little. She drank almost nothing, although she always suffered from thirst [...] At night she hardly slept. We could see her in the corridor, in the dormitory, checking on one after the other while carrying a lighted taper in her hand. Sometimes she would go to the bakery when the girls were sweeping the grain, at night of course, and she would join them for a while to clean the grain with them. She was always meditating, and during Holy Mass, she was so deep in prayer, that she seemed almost ecstatic, especially after Holy Communion. Sometimes, even during recreation, we saw her so absorbed in prayer that she was a continuous edification to us.

> Once we forced her to tell us about the Apparition of the Virgin of LaSalette, by doing so in the third person as if she was not the shepherdess. She started out, foremost to satisfy us, because she was very docile and she had a very kind heart, and also because she was very fond of us. She started out the story in the third person, as if it were not herself. Sometimes she forgot about this, and instead of talking in the third person, she would start talking in the first, and when she noticed this, she got lost, because of her great humility which did not want anyone to know who she was. She did not want to continue, but moved by the fact that we acted as if nothing was the matter, she went on. When she repeated the mistake, she began to laugh, and we replied: "It is

nothing, Mother, just go on." Encouraging her in this manner, we reached the end of the story.

I can't describe with how much love and zeal she guided us in the ways of holy virtue, be it by her example, her warnings or her maternal advice. Her words were always sweet, she was docile like a little lamb.[...]

She was for us a continuous edification. Her virtue was always even. We never saw her become angry; she was always calm and serene. Her virtues were always hidden. She took no pleasure in us seeing or knowing about her [acts] of virtue, because she always wanted to live hidden from everyone. I remember when she came to Galatina, the entire community welcomed her. According to our custom we gathered in the visiting room to greet her.

She wanted to flee and said: "I am going away, right now."

We esteemed her very much, since she really was a saint of steadfast virtue and a hidden life.

Melanie also edified Father Veillard, Missionary in the LaSalette community, historian and respectable theologian, friend of Father Jean Stern:

"It doesn't seem possible to deny - and it has not been denied [?] - that Melanie was, especially towards the end of her life, a very beautiful soul in the eyes of God."[93]

ADDITIONAL TESTIMONIES

1. THE STIGMATA OF MELANIE: AN OVERVIEW OF THE TESTIMONIES

Because of the statement of Bishop Ginoulhiac (refer to Ch 5: Sec IV:C), Melanie's stigmata were considered imaginary. Here is a list of sources which give testimony to the stigmata, regardless of some apparent contradictions.

A) 1847, age 15: at LaSalette one year after the Apparition
B) Date uncertain, location possibly at Castellammare-di-Stabia
C) 1903, age 71: her last visit to LaSalette, unnoticed by most pilgrims
D) 1898, age 68: Messina. Death at Altamura: Dec. 15, 1904, age 72

A. Childhood in Corps and its Vicinity, 1835-1846

Melanie herself relates how she received the stigmata in her early childhood. It is not a late invention. As early as 1852 she mentioned it to her confessor at Corenc.[94] She repeated the story in a less explicit way, in her autobiography (see below). The first autobiographical text explains that she also had incognito visits of the Child Jesus, "the little Brother," who will reveal his identity much later. One day, she spoke about this in the third person:

> The little Child [Jesus] who visited sometimes [...] took her by the hand and led her along the road of the Department of the *Hautes Alpes* [High Alps], speaking always about the Passion or the hidden life of Our Lord Jesus Christ. They were in a forest when Melanie started complaining that she would not leave if her good Jesus did not allow her to suffer everything that He had suffered, and in every place that He had suffered. She was almost breathless but the Divine Guide told her to keep on walking. He tried to dissuade her by saying that the sufferings of Jesus Christ were ineffable and that they were too difficult for her, but she was too stubborn to believe it.
>
> - So you think you can bear them my Sister! Well, make the Sign of the Cross!
>
> Then the Child touched her head first with his two little hands and immediately pain came over her head. The "wild one" [Melanie herself] placed her hands on her head thinking she would be able to feel something there [thorns], but there was nothing. Then the Child continued to touch her. After touching her head, He touched her hands, her feet and her side. This caused a tremendous pain every day, and more specially on Fridays, and the more she advanced in age, the more the pain increased as well.[95]

These various traits are common to stigmatists. Her autobiography describes how her teacher at the school for the poor, could not comb her hair because it was stuck together by the blood of the stigmata from the crown of thorns:

The teacher tried to comb me with affectionate patience; but my hair was all matted with clumps because of the blood that would often run and then dry, if I had no water at hand to clean my head. The good teacher did not succeed in combing me that day. So, she just lifted up my hair in front and tied it together at the back.[96]

Her family had noticed her stigmatization:

Her younger sister, Marie, informed the Sisters of Corps, where Melanie went to school from 1847 to 1849, interpreting what she saw in her own way: "My sister Melanie is well-behaved and very mortified. Sometimes she inserts a knife in her hands and makes herself bleed..."[97] Here she confuses the mortifications of her older sister (fasting and physical penance) with the stigmata that affected her hands and feet: "under her stockings."

Her mother confirmed this in the same period as Marie Calvat, to Father Seignoux, priest at Courdemanche during her pilgrimage of September 1854:

- Melanie [...] has almost no strength in her arms, to such a point that if she were here, she would have to pick up the glass one would offer her to drink from, with both hands.
- And where does that infirmity come from? How would you explain this?
- Well, she practices mortifications. She hurts herself. She has here (pointing out the top of her hand) wounds like Our Lord, wanting to suffer like Him.
- But who opened these wounds to her?
- Herself.
- How do you know? Has she told you this explicitly?...

I then saw that she did not have the information straight from Melanie. Soon, thereafter, the sister of Melanie, [Marie], a young girl of around 14 at the time, with a prettier physical appearance than Melanie, was telling me with a tone of shyness and modesty that I admired:

- Father, I have seen it. She has shown me (and putting her hand at the top of her foot) here, there was blood leaking from her stockings.
- Well, my child, who hurt her there like that?
- It was herself.
- How do you know? Has she told you so positively?
- Yes Father, she told me that it was herself who had done that...[98]

Marie had seen the wound but not their formation, nor the action of a knife. When Marie had insisted on an explanation, Melanie had left her to this idea, either to cut short any discussion, or out of discretion and humility. And Marie (eight years younger than Melanie) accepted it without pondering any further.

At the end of his improvised inquiry (see below), Father Seignoux accepts this interpretation of self-mutilation, as the fruit of her "extreme desire to bear in her body, like the Apostle [Paul], the mortification of the Savior," and he tells this to one of the priests of the [LaSalette] sanctuary, who was quite surprised by Seignoux's explanation.

What is certain, is that Melanie practiced a fearsome asceticism, which was recommended in the spiritual books in that era. She wanted to suffer the Passion of Christ. She desired his sufferings like Francis of Assisi. The first autobiography bears witness to this.

This explains her answer to Father Combe who questioned her on the 12th of January 1901: "My executioner, it is my love."[99] It is out of love, and at her insistent request to suffer like Jesus (first autobiography), that she received the stigmata. Nevertheless, she immediately modified her statement: *"Her executioner, it is his love."* Christ never self-mutilated himself. He underwent his Passion because of the cruelty of man, as Melanie had undergone the attacks of the devil, well-documented elsewhere. However, the sufferings of the

Passion, as horrible as they were, are something completely different. She desired them, and received them out of love, and they were given to her out of love (that is how the stigmatized, whom I know, regard their stigmata). She is so identified to Christ and his Passion, that she mingles the suffering love of the Crucified with her own suffering, in one and the same shared suffering.

Her own father, who gradually became her confidant, will mention in 1855 a stigmatization on her shoulder granted by Jesus (see below, n° 8). What preceded are the observations made at home when Melanie was living there. The stigmata could have been seen by the family in the short respites when she lived at home, in between the times when she was hired out as a shepherdess. But it was primarily after the Apparition, when she became a specific object of interest. Her penances and stigmata, which she tried to hide, could not escape the attention of her young sister Marie, who conflates these separate phenomena.

B. Her Youth at Corps, Corenc and LaSalette: 1847-1854

After the Apparition, there are many indications and testimonies. It is with hand trembling that Melanie writes, at Corenc in 1853, the Rule of the Holy Virgin which she hands over to Father Sibillat. She excuses herself by saying: "On Fridays, I cannot write any better."[100]

In 1863 Father Antoine Bossan, having learned of her stay at Corenc from 1850 to 1853, interrogates Father Gerente:

- Did Melanie have the stigmata?
- No, never. I have never seen anything like it, nor anyone else around here. If there had been anything of this nature, the Sisters certainly would have noticed.[101]

Therefore, there was ignorance of the stigmata because Melanie had learned to hide them when they started to become visible, just as Padre Pio did with his gloves.

Sister Dosithee, companion of Melanie during their novitiate in Corenc, when questioned by Father Antoine Bossan in 1871, informs him without hesitation:

- She [Sister Dosithee] had seen wounds on the hands of Melanie very often, foremost on the inside of the palms. They were carmine red, purplish. This happened mainly on Fridays. Then she would be pale, sick, and walk with difficulty. One day Melanie sat down and fell asleep. With her thumb and index finger, Sister Dosithee probed the inside and outside of Melanie's hand, where it was reddish. Instantly Melanie woke up as if she felt pain. She asked who touched her. Sister Dosithee admitted it was herself. Melanie said nothing, because she realized that Sister Dosithee knew.[102]

On the 21st of September 1853, Canon Rousselot allowed the Vicar General Lusagnet to remain with the assumption that Melanie was indeed stigmatized.[103]

In February-March of 1854 Melanie stayed at the sanctuary of LaSalette, as she went there sometimes as well as in summer. Father Antoine Bossan reports:

She usually kept her sleeves over her hands [as did Our Lady of LaSalette] However sometimes by gesticulating, or when she served herself during meals, her sleeves would fall back and one could see her hands... Father Denaz told me that on those occasions he had seen a red stain on the hands of Melanie without knowing what it was.[104]

Halfway into September 1854 Father Seignoux improvised an inquiry. After the aforementioned testimony of the mother and sister of Melanie, he interrogated the pastor of Corps [where the seers were baptized]. The subject is delicate. Bishop Ginoulhiac has expressed himself against the stigmata of Melanie... Father Melin "seemed to want to avoid the question, and answered that he had not been preoccupied by it."

After that the same priest of Courdemanche met Father Sibillat, M.S., a confident of the seer, and asked him about her "stigmata":

- Well yes, I have seen them, last Christmas; they disappear and then come back.
- Where do these phenomena come from? Is it the demon, or is it from God?

Finally, he questions Canon Gerin, the holy priest at the Cathedral of Grenoble:

> O dear, I could not say anything [i.e., make an official statement] It is an event which is completely separate from the great wonder of the Apparition. I won't pronounce judgment on the subject. The future will tell us what to think about it. (PS II p.148-149)

C. Melanie as an Adult in Darlington, England (1854-1860)

In September 1855, Pierre Mathieu, Melanie's father, affirms to Louis-Marie-Urbain Similien

> that she had received from heaven the stigmata on her shoulder, at the place where the Cross was carried.[105]

Bishop Newsham, present at Melanie's Clothing Day at the Carmel in Darlington, stated that the stains of the stigmata:

> which had healed, as you might know, but reappeared several days after her taking the veil. On the day of the celebration, they were red like blood. And indeed, they were bleeding on that day, as Lady Dodworth confirmed who assisted her then. The prioress of the convent, myself and some others have seen these stigmata, red as blood.[106]

> [†Editor: Significant feasts are normally chosen for these events. In 1855, February 23rd fell on the Friday after Ash Wednesday, and the Roman liturgy designated the Mass and Office: *Spinæ Coronæ, DNJC, Duplex Maius* [The Crowning with Thorns of Our Lord Jesus Christ] having the rank of a Double Major which was just below the level of a feast. In Carmel, it was customary on Clothing Day to appear in the public chapel dressed as a bride, then to enter the enclosure and reappear at the grille

wearing the habit. Lady Dodworth was undoubtedly a benefactor for Melanie's apparrel and was allowed to assist in dressing the bride.]

Bishop Ullathorne of Birmingham wrote to Bishop Ginoulhiac on the 25th of April 1855:[107]

> She professes having visions, performing miracles, having stigmata.

Father Leopold Sebaux of the Diocese of Le Mans [the future holy Bishop of Angouleme], writes to Father Auvergne, on the 5th of July 1855:

> The superior of the Carmelites of Darlington has written several days ago to a priest in Le Mans, that Melanie certainly has the stigmata.[108]

D. Marseille, 1860-1867

In April 1867, Mother Marie of the Presentation, assistant of the community of the Compassion, gives a crucial testimony to the Fathers of the sanctuary of LaSalette. She had close ties to the seer for seven years (1869-1876). This unpublished text is transmitted integrally by Father Louis Beaup:

> Here is an important question that I can resolve today - the one about Melanie's stigmata. Many will assume what I had assumed in the past, namely that the thing was a pious invention or a trickery. However here is the truth, because I heard this from a religious [of the Compassion, Mother Presentation]. She is utterly convinced about the reality of the stigmata, which she has been able to observe regularly for seven years, either on the hands, or on the feet, or on the head, but on the head only within particular circumstances. That is, it only showed on one side of the forehead.
>
> These stigmata appeared every year all thru the season of Advent, all of Lent [this is classic] and usually the week before the 19th of September. Normally it is only a red mark [so no self-mutilation],

but at some periods there are fresh stains, producing a certain amount of blood, at such point that I had to make her wear gloves or mittens, so the children we taught would not notice it. The intensity of the wounds seemed to depend on the tranquility and calmness of her mind. When in trouble or contradicted, nothing is evident, or almost nothing. However, I am convinced that she does not do anything to make them appear or disappear. Now that today is Wednesday in Holy Week, she must certainly have them. I have not inquired about it because she usually keeps them hidden, [holy discretion] but it would not surprise me that now there is nothing; she is quite upset about all the changes, about everything that is happening.[...]

This nun from Marseille is therefore very much convinced of the stigmata, albeit, she says that Melanie does not deserve this grace, since she has a very unhappy character, and her piety, although sincere, does not show extraordinary signs of fervor (!) Father Calage, who directed Melanie during all those six or seven years, is very convinced about the stigmata. The chaplain of the Carmelite convent, where Melanie stayed in England, has also admitted to being convinced. Another priest, who had gone to England to meet Melanie, said he was convinced.[109]

[†Editor: Mother Presentation, "fond of alcohol," had left her religious community. She was basically forced upon Melanie as her assigned companion for thirty-three years. "I needed her to exercise my patience!...I did novena after novena so that the Good Lord might deliver me from that creature." Letter to Mr. Schmid, 30th March 1895]

On the 18th of January 1872, Father Felicien Bliard reports the testimony of Father Calage, SJ, who directed Melanie during her stay in Marseille:

The discovery of the stigmata in her hands caused the decision to allow her to change houses [...] he had visible stigmata, above all, during Lent and towards the anniversary of the Apparition.[110]

E. Castellammare-di-Stabia, Italy: (1868-1882)

Virginia Bonifacio, pupil of Melanie in Castellammare, reports:

> One would think she suffered from the crowning with thorns, but I could not see any marks because she had her forehead covered. Meanwhile, on her hand, I saw what looked like a scar...[111]

F. Cannes, 1885

Mother Eymard (Marie-Louise Girard, superior of the Camaldalese of the Seyne), wrote on the 16th of August 1943:

> I saw her sitting in a chair, her eyes closed, her head raised, supported by her left hand, and her right hand rested on her knee, having on the backside a purplish print in the form of a diamond, a little bit larger in the middle... She withdrew to her room, as she did every Friday [...] she also had these signs on Saturday after Mass.[112]

Melanie mailed letters stained with blood: on the 20th of February 1881 to Father Émile LeBaillif, and on the 30th of January 1891 to Canon Alexander DeBrandt.[113]

On the 11th of May 1897, Melanie wrote to Father Émile Combe:

> One calls 'stigmata' those wounds that arise in certain places: on the feet, on the hands, on the side of the head [...] I hasten to tell you, my dear Reverend Father, that for twelve years now I have been restored as to the exterior condition, that is to say, there is no blood anymore, no visible wounds, there is only a sweet, though vehement, pain remaining. So, let's not talk about it anymore.[114]

G. Messina, Italy (1897-1898)

On the 18th of August 1897, Melanie arrived at Messina, at the request of [Saint] Annibale DiFrancia, to direct his religious Sisters and their orphanage. He testified to:

> her prodigious and singular stigmatization [...] have been an eyewitness, and so were [...] he Sisters of my Institute; moreover,

> I have a letter from Melanie, in which she tells me about her stigmata in terms of utmost humility.[115]

Therefore, the stigmata, invisible since 1885 as Melanie had related, have reappeared.

On the 15th of October 1897, she writes to [Saint] Annibale DiFrancia:

> For my great and manifold sins and to humiliate my pride, the Lord allows that on Friday a small stain appears on my hands, etc., and a small amount of blood comes out. But thanks be to God, this has only happened three times since I have come to Messina.[116]

Here is a fragment from the second autobiography of Melanie, written at the request of Canon Annibale (1898), afterwards translated [from Italian] into French and completed in Diou. Melanie relives her first stigmatization in the light of her experience.

> When I asked how I could stay faithful to the Eternal Love, I saw in myself...a real nothingness - only suffering as a means, and even then it would be necessary that the Divine Mercy grant me this grace, only for his glory and the salvation of souls. I was kneeling. I had given myself totally to Love, but deep in my soul, I would have been afraid for myself, if the effects of the great [divine] Light would have departed from me and had not engulfed my entire being, all the powers of my soul, in his divine and devouring Love.
>
> Then I made the Sign of the Cross and immediately my Brother appeared, but now He was higher than me (I mean, he was tall). He was very handsome as always, and very high also in love. He was vested like priests when they offer the Sacrifice of the Mass (many years later I saw vestments when I entered a church for the first time). Everything was beautiful and resplendent and attractive. I cannot express this loving beauty. On his chest there was like an open heart: from the inside, rays of light suddenly poured out like burning flames, peacefully, lovingly.

My Brother put his hand on this living wound and with two fingers he took out a small round thing, very white, on which there was a likeness, the living portrait of my loving Brother. I say a portrait, but it was of living flesh, with eyes that moved and a mouth that spoke; He made a move to call me, wanting to give Himself. My heart could not resist this loving impulse that attracted me to Him. He said to me: "Sister of my heart, receive the Eternal Love of the God of the strong."

Hardly had I received this, hardly had he touched my heart, that I felt new life, and an even greater and purer desire to suffer, to endure contempt, abandonment, immolation and a thousand deaths for the unique glory of the Most High. My nothingness was destroyed, my self vanished from sight. The one who is All, had placed me in safety, penetrated, fulfilled me. It was like I did not exist anymore. It was like my heart leaped in desire to dissolve in my breast. I felt some of the effects of this invigorating love.

I won't give an explanation of what cannot be explained. I don't have words to tell what cannot be named. The two extremes embraced: the extreme eternal and infinite magnificence, with extreme, infinite nothingness. Whereas my heart quivered for joy, I felt as oppressed, crushed by the immense mercy of God for me, who am not more than an earthworm. I said to my Brother: "If I belong to my Lord, to my Almighty Savior, then with my God, using his eternal will, I want to profess my intense gratitude for the gift of suffering of every single day of my life, by walking on the road and the truth of the Most High, with my God. I adore the Cross more than the glory of all the saints!" (Saying: 'with my God', I meant: with his grace; at the time the word 'grace' was unknown to me).

- My Brother, lifting his eyes to the sky, said while drawing near: "What favor does this small miserable creature desire?"
- I answered mentally: "With the will of the eternal light, I ask the utmost glory on this road of crucifixion with God."

At that very moment my Brother blew on my lips, put his hands on my head, his right hand in my right hand and then in my left hand, on my two feet and on my heart... That is enough! I cannot say more about it. O, true painful and delightful drunkenness of the one that lives and dies. O Jesus! Cause yourself to be known and loved by all people. May I know You and love You the way You are worthy to be loved. O fire, may I love You as You love yourself, and then I will be happy.

Since I was touched by my Brother, as I have related above, I felt great pains in those mentioned parts of the body, especially on Friday. On those days blood would ooze from the wounds which appeared on those very parts of the body, and then they would close again without leaving any trace. I have to admit that I suffered more at the time these wounds appeared for one or two hours - and at other times, on Fridays. And the wounds would appear from two o'clock in the afternoon till half past four. Other times they would last all of Lent. On some Fridays the wounds would open on Thursday evening until Friday evening. I felt great pains through my entire body, bitter and sorrowful pains, this being a great joy for me. I was very happy and I would have liked to suffer even more, if possible. It was a sorrow of ecstasy and love. While I suffered, and also loved, my dear Jesus, it was like I was not myself anymore. My "all" had become the owner of my soul and my faculties. He said He wanted me totally for Himself: word and action were one sole living act.

O, the goodness of the works of the Sovereign Good! He corrects. He embellishes. He deprives, enriches, wounds and heals. If one knows his will, one must align oneself with that grace. Though it is even better to abandon oneself, to be passive, to be without will apart from the Divine Will.[117]

H. Melanie in her Seventies: Diou, Argoeuves (1899-1904)

Father Émile Combes, priest of Diou where Melanie stayed, noted an increase of the phenomena of the stigmata during the first days of 1901.[118] He preserved the cloth that had soaked the wound of her side on the 10th of January 1901.[119]

Father Hector Rigaux, who had hosted Melanie at Argoeuves in September 1902 and August 1903, wrote:

> Witnessing this miracle, renewed before my very eyes, I saw the blood flow from this privileged woman; my good aunt has seen the [wounds of Melanie's] crown of thorns bleeding right before her.[120]

The diversity, the convergence, the precision of so many witnesses independent of each other, surely prove the mystery of Melanie's supernatural stigmata: hands, feet, side, head, following the variable models, multiplied since Saint Francis of Assisi, with or without bleeding. It is a major new aspect in the story of the seer of LaSalette.

2. WHY WERE THE SEERS REJECTED?

In spite of positive support at all levels from the common people to the Pope, the two shepherds have been an ongoing target of critics. This is a fact, even though Bishop DeBruillard officially recognized the Apparition (on the 19th of September 1851) accompanied by the Agreement of Rome. Why the criticism?

The reasons can be found on different levels, with a cumulative effect.

A. Tension between Institutions and Personal Charisms

A primary, and very common, factor has been identified by Karl Rahner: the tension between institutes and charisms, because the prestige of charisms, notably that of a visionary to which people attribute a direct connection with God - without restraint and sometimes quite excessively - can be embarrassing for existing authorities. Many people believe much more easily in a seer than in a bishop, regardless that he officially represents the magisterium. It is needless to insist on this general, unambiguous fact. It explains why seers are often marginalized or exiled. For Bernadette, the solution was to tear her away from her family and to put her in a community, albeit a very good one, which had the mission to more or less lock her up, to screen and choose which visitors she would be allowed to receive, to funnel her testimony to a focus on "humility." Until 1866, the superior at Lourdes presented her as a mediocre girl, unworthy of what she had seen. Bernadette spiritually profited from the daily constraints and humiliations.

B. The Pastoral Factor

To organize pilgrimages in an orderly manner, an instrument was needed in the hands of the bishop. The foundation of an Order connected to the Pope, was one of the requests of Our Lady to Melanie. In Rome, Bishop Fava obstructed this, so as "not to harm good and peace."

C. The Political Factor

Bishop Ginoulhiac was well appreciated by the imperial regime, inaugurated on the 3rd of December 1851. This will help him rise to the Archbishopric of Lyon, as Primate of Gaul. However, the seers did not like Napoleon. Their Secret announces the downfall of the emperor, "The Eaglet" as the clear description of Maximin states, or "The Eagle" as Melanie calls him. Bishop Ginoulhiac was obligated to Bishop DeBruillard and to Pius IX to support the LaSalette pilgrimage, but he could not oppose the empire (in view of the passage of Saint Paul to be loyal to the authorities). The only political solution was to dissociate as much as possible the pilgrimage from the seers, which Bishop Ginoulhiac expressed in a very strong formula: "The mission of the shepherds ends where the mission of the Church begins."

This motto will determine his incessant actions to remove and marginalize the seers, to prevent Melanie's vows and the admission of Maximin to the priesthood. This is what Bishop Ginoulhiac prescribed for the religious of the Providence at Corps on the 5th of February 1854:

> I vehemently prohibit you, [...] by virtue of holy obedience:
>
> 1. to allow Melanie to go up to LaSalette, either alone or

accompanied;

2. to have her meet anyone on her own in the parlor, except her father at Corps, without having obtained my written permission beforehand;

3. if Melanie refuses to obey these orders [...] you will tell her that you are forced to send her away and to have her go back to her father;

4. and this will also be the case if, in your convent, she indulges in whims, cries, threats, and battles to which she has so often abandoned herself in Corenc or elsewhere.

D. Pseudo-Mystical Incidents

On the 1st of June 1854, the Countess Pauline DeNicolay, a person who appeared to be gifted with mystical tendencies, wrote to Father Burnoud, first superior of the LaSalette sanctuary:

> The religious don't meet the expectations. We need people with a certain character. The Sisters are not suitable for the work. We need people of such and such a character, with certain skills, "like yourself," the Lord tells me interiorly, spontaneously.
>
> At the same time, I experienced such a deep sentiment that it penetrated my soul and filled it completely, even now, with as much sweetness as sorrow. [...]
>
> I also have to confirm what I told you earlier regarding poor Melanie. Yes, there is illusion in her, and sometimes, sadly enough, something worse than illusion. She wrote her Secret entirely for the Holy Father. Therefore, her mission is over and yours begins. The Rule of which she told you, does not come from God [...] my spirit, enlightened me about this poor child two years ago, and is even more certain about it now. [...]
>
> In my opinion, her presence, far from being useful to your work, can only do harm. For this reason, and for her own benefit, it would be preferable that she would be sent to a convent much further away. [...]

Then after that, your ties with the Bishop of Grenoble will become simpler and easier. And I don't think a new examination of Melanie will be necessary.

At the time when the project of Bishop DeBruillard, namely the foundation of a missionary congregation serving the message of LaSalette, was still the norm, Father Burnoud, dazzled by the new personality of the countess, wrote to his successor Bishop Ginoulhiac: "*[The countess] is exactly the right person as a superior.*"[121]

So, Pauline DeNicolay showed up at the right moment to discredit Melanie in the mind of Father Burnoud, and to remove her from LaSalette. Sadly enough, this pseudo-mystic, and several other women who encircled the sanctuary (Adèle, Marianne, Victorine, etc., like the several dozens of visionaries competing with Bernadette in Lourdes in the spring of 1858), required much caution (see below). The project of LaSalette, recommended by Pauline for the sake of the Church and the world, as well as her "Marian revelations" to Pius IX, led to nothing. She left for the Holy Land and founded a "sanctuary" for her so-called Emmaus: *Goubeibeh* [†Editor: there is no English translation for this French word which was probably based on a Hebraism]

E. The Cultural and Philosophical Factor

Criticism had been prompted by the direction of a culture, which pushed heavily against the Faith, the Gospels and theology, from modernism up until the present. It is necessary to, at least briefly, bring up this factor, modern idealism, which derives from Descartes and especially from Kant and Hegel. This philosophy starts from a critique that subordinates the object to the subject: "to be" to "me." "I think, therefore I am," said Descartes. The first and fundamental evidence is not being ["to be"] according to the realism of Aristotle, but for Descartes it's the "ego."

Hence the current trend of idealism has made the subject prevail over the object. This revolution has not been without fruit: its positive aspect consists of having promoted the exploration of the subject by way of existentialism, and subsequently psychology and psychoanalysis, the youngest among human sciences. However, this legitimate exploration has suffered from the totalitarian tendency of the subjective method: the Gospel is explained, not through the historical Jesus, but through communitarian enthusiasm, creating Christ from faith: his words, his miracles, his divinity. The reign of "everything is psychology" has weighed heavily against mystics and seers, as well as on exorcism.

Following these assumptions, Father Dhanis dissociated "Fatima I" (the Apparitions) from "Fatima II" (the Secrets and visions of Lucia) as subsequent inventions of Lucia. Father Alonso has refuted this thesis. But in the same way [as Father Dhanis], Father Thurston and Father Jaouen have tried to make a distinction between LaSalette I and LaSalette II[122], proposing that the revealed Secrets and the religious Order to be founded, are subsequent inventions of Melanie's imagination and egocentrism.

The philosophical reductionist method was promulgated through the quiet revolution of idealism, which became more and more radical from Kant to Brunschvicg (died 1944). For Brunschvicg, reality was displaced by [subective] knowledge. The subject is therefore everything, while the thing in itself - which according to Kant *cannot* be known - is nothing: it does not even exist. It is needless to assume its existence, since it is of no use. In this philosophy, we can only know our own knowledge, in a closed circuit.

Regarding the Apparition of LaSalette, Father Jaouen or Father Jean Stern are far from this philosophical radicalism, since they brilliantly preserve the central vision of the Virgin in tears, as well as her primitively attested words. Their position dissociates the Apparition (acknowledged by the Bishop), from the Secret. They regard the Secret as a subsequent invention of the seers. However, the logic of their analysis reaches further. Following their line of logic, it would be coherent to also attribute the Apparition to the "psychology" of the seers, just as many are doing today, here and elsewhere. One cannot dissociate the Apparition from the Secrets, nor the Virgin from the seers, who subordinated their entire lives to her message.

The idealistic criticism of knowledge has also deformed the notion of criticism itself, not without severe consequences for theology and spirituality.

For ancient Greece - the founders of philosophy, mathematics, history and our western society - criticism means reflection, verification and discernment, so as to obtain an objective penetration of reality.

For Descartes, "criticism" means suspicion, systematic questioning. He personally extricated himself quite easily from this dilemma, and in a constructive manner, by re-establishing God and everything else from "me" outwards, making the ego the primordial certitude. His successors however, did not proceed the same way. Negative, reductionist and disintegrating criticism has prevailed, and has caused the crisis of modern times, and still continues to do so. Although Pius X reprimanded modernism authoritatively, the pope did not unmask its causes, values and limitations. Many theologians have stopped talking about God, and are studying instead the "language about God." According to this same suspicious criticism, any revelation from heaven is subjective. At LaSalette (and elsewhere), the Apparition and the message are just inventions, projections, dreams of the seers.

The growing awareness of these presuppositions invites us to reconsider the seers, not in the reductionist and dissociative manner, but in an integral and penetrating manner, starting out from their healthy human nature, the fundamental evidence that surpasses them, and their irreversible commitment despite so much opposition.

Father Jaouen goes too far when he wrote: "The Apparition did not have as a goal to make saints out of the two children, but rather to convert people."[123] Usually, a grace given to everyone also involves, in the first instance, the two witnesses. The tendency is to affirm that charism is meant to build up the Church and not the charismatic. This is incorrect according to the Apostle Paul: "The one who speaks in tongues builds up himself" (1Cor 14:4). Even more so, the personal encounter with the Mother of the Son was not intended to use the two seers as mere instruments. That encounter affirmed and fortified them as persons.

And this gave them strength and peace to endure the trials. The Apparition was not in vain for them personally. They had been instructed by the Cross from their early childhood, since they both had to suffer misery and the absence of maternal affection. Several years after the Apparition through which they experienced esteem from many, they underwent the process of rejection, including rejection from the hierarchy.

Marginalization, exile, confinements, uprooting, made it impossible for Melanie to accomplish the mission to which she devoted herself incessantly, towards and against everything that opposed it. Maximin, who persevered for many years towards his vocation, was left empty-handed, but without bitterness or resentment. In these situations, the seers sometimes reacted too quickly, more or less regrettable, particularly Melanie, when she perceived that human constraint (combined with diabolic trials) was incompatible with her mission. Being esteemed under the episcopacy of Bishop DeBruillard, then rejected by his successor, she once expressed her distress to Sister Butruille, superior in Vienne, who wanted to be good to Melanie and had gained her confidence:

The Bishop has sent me here to get rid of me![124]

If the seers were sometimes overcome by such hard ordeals, they consecrated themselves first and foremost to the Virgin, each one in his own way, and this kind of holiness is proper to the poor, the little ones, the marginalized, whom the Gospel ranks in the first place (Lk 1:52-53; Mt 5:1) Some overlapping analyses will conclude this book.

19th c. Lay Defenders of the Secret

A) Louis Veuillot: convert and journalist
B) Paul Verlaine: celebrated his reversion to the faith with poetry
C) Joris-Karl Huysmans: satirist, found solace among Catholic colleagues
D) Leon Bloy: best known writer in the French Catholic Literary Revival

CHAPTER 6

IMPORTANT UNEXPECTED TESTIMONIES

WRITERS

Excluded and belittled by the main stream, for reasons that have not been deeply analyzed until now, Maximin and Melanie have been acknowledged by a number of famous witnesses: writers, philosophers, religious, pastors and successive popes. Here is a brief overview.

20th c. Lay Defenders of the Secret

A) Raissa Maritain: convert, hosted philosophy circles with her husband
B) Jacques Maritain: convert, philosopher, ambassador to the Holy See
C) Louis Massignon: pioneer of Catholic-Muslim mutual understanding
D) Paul Claudel: French poet, dramatist, diplomat

LOUIS VEUILLOT (1813-1883)

editor of *L'Univers* [The Universe] and defender of the Apparition, embraced it with a popular devotion. On February 6, 1849, while thanking Father Louis Perrin for the water from LaSalette, for the baptism of his child, he revealed to the priest his militant conviction with the following words:

> What could be better and more reassuring, in the times we live in, than to count on the pledges of protection from the Blessed Mother, and to see the people not completely blind and ungrateful? Our hope is only there and nowhere else. Society, so terribly threatened and more and more in danger than it realizes, won't be saved by its own wisdom or power. Proof of this can be found every day. As soon as it wins a victory, this victory turns against itself. It can only defend itself with help from on High. It can only find refuge in the arms of God, and God will not open his arms except through the prayer of Mary.[1]

PAUL VERLAINE (1844-1896)

a leader of the Symbolist movement, evokes his tormented faith in Our Lady of LaSalette, in the collection called *Bonheur*:

> You who are multiplying miracles and promises
> From Sainte-Chapelle to LaSalette and Lourdes,
> Deign to make promises bloom for us
> Even in these times of horrors of unethical and deaf nation-states,
> Mother save France. Intercede for us.
> Give us a living faith and above all a humble faith,
> May the soul of all our ancestors burn in us all
> In life and in death....

His distress invokes her in other poems:

> She is goodness.
> Like the Mother
> In the Trinity

The Daughter and the Mother
She is goodness,
Compassion
Endless and unceasing
The intercession
Which sustains and upholds
Compassion[2]

JORIS KARL HUYSMANS (1815-1907)

does not like the statue of LaSalette, the head dressed with a "Mohican bonnet," a kind of pastry mold. He does not appreciate "Maximin curly like a poodle" nor "Melanie wrapped in a beehive bonnet." He ignores their human value and their peasant culture. However, he affirms:

> How can one explain, except by divine intervention, that two creatures, incapable of remembering one single word, could keep so tenaciously and lively the memory of a long speech, which they heard only once? If the Virgin had addressed herself to intelligent children, one would have blamed them for having invented these speeches! The imbecility of these confidants is a guarantee of the truth. God nearly always makes use of what is most feeble and low, to confuse the powerful and wise.[3]

His conversion began in LaSalette: "It was there," he told Father Bessede, "that, overwhelmed by sinister forebodings, I saw the perfect liberation."

In 1905, being ill, he prayed to the Virgin to bring him "up-there." He sees in the Apparition a reward for the faith preserved in the Dauphine province:

> There the Virgin is more honored than in the other provinces. The chapels dedicated to her abound in this area.

FOR LÉON BLOY (1846-1917) LASALETTE IS CENTRAL

LaSalette has been the starting point of my intellectual life and, as far as I can see, of my religious life. I was born in 1846 at the time God wanted, seventy days before the Apparition. So, I belong to LaSalette in a mysterious way.⁴

Similarly, Pius XII was consecrated bishop on the 13th of May 1917, the date of the first Marian Apparition at Fatima, and thus he felt a bond with Fatima.

Bloy was a pilgrim to LaSalette in September 1879 with Father Tardif DeMoidrey, and again from the 14th of September to the 16th of October 1880, and finally in 1906. In his books on LaSalette

- *La Femme Pauvre [The Poor Woman] in which he describes his first pilgrimage*
- *Celle qui pleure [She who Weeps],*
- *La vie de Melanie par elle même, Le symbolisme de l'Apparition [Melanie's autobiography, The Symbolism of the Apparition],*

he is not afraid to denounce what he regards as:

> the horrible crime of having gagged the Mother of God for so many years, of scorning her warnings, her clear orders, her prophecies, of having warned her children against her, of having persecuted and dishonored her witnesses. Melanie, a madwoman! Maximin, a drunk! There are no words to express the horror of the ambiguity of choosing what pleases among the facts of LaSalette, and of rejecting as despicable reverie or lies whatever displeases.⁵

The day after his death, his wife wrote to Vallette, director of *Mercure de France*:

> If one wanted to raise a monument to him, it would have to be, apart from a granite cross, a statue of Our Lady of LaSalette.

His last words appeared in a posthumous edition:

> The Apparition took place on the 19th of September 1846. It was the last of the Ember Days of September, a Saturday, the Eve of the feast of Our Lady of the Seven Sorrows that year, at the time of First Vespers, at the moment in which the Church sings, during the Divine Office [the Stabat Mater in mode II], a

hymn with a Christian sentiment so heartbreaking and so deeply sorrowful!

Oh! In what flow of tears! In what sorrow is the pitiful Virgin Mary engulfed when her bloodied Son is taken down from the tree. She gazes at Him laying in her arms!

The Sorrowful One bathes with tears his sweet face, his breast so tender, his side so soft, his pierced and injured right and left hands, and those feet red with blood. A hundred times and a thousand times, She tightly embraces this chest and these arms. She clings to his wounds and melts entirely in sorrowful kisses.

O Mother, we beg you by these your tears, by this sad funeral of your Child, by the purple of his wounds, this sorrow of your Heart, to enclose your heart in ours!

I have tried to translate into the least colorful of all languages [French], this sublime [Latin] hymn that made our fathers cry. There is none more penetrating in all the sacred Office. It pleased the Blessed Virgin to appear [on LaSalette] at the moment this cry of sorrow burst forth in the Church. This miraculous occurrence has the natural power to strongly affect the heart and spirit, especially if we consider that the devotion to the Sorrows of Mary is seen by theologians as one of the most certain signs of predestination. Those who know the dogma of the Communion of Saints and the universal impact, in millions of destinies, of the least human event, these can ask themselves what were the mysterious effects of this unheard-of manifestation, at such a time, in the three concomitant empires: of Church Militant, the Church Suffering and the Church Triumphant. Those effects, totally hidden from our physical senses, developed silently, under the eye of God, like immense waves in the infinite space of suffering and prayer. At this privileged hour in the history of the world, when the Queen of Heaven sounded forth in LaSalette the sorrowful Magnificat of her prophetic Lamentations, the eighty thousand agonizing and the eighty thousand newborn who fluctuate each day towards time or towards eternity, must have felt in their souls something of the divine thrill of Saint John the Baptist in the womb of his mother. Some were brought to the foot of the throne of their judge in an irresistible flow of tears from their [motherly] Advocate. The others began their earthly pilgrimage in a reflux movement of these same healthy waves which one day would tear down the walls of the city of pride. One day, when all hidden things will be manifested to man, the real importance of this great event, which they have dared to silently disdain if they did not dare to persecute the witnesses, will be known. We will finally know, how many desperate souls were saved on this occasion, how many supernatural vocations were decided upon because of this day, and from how many latent and inevitable catastrophes the multitude of ungrateful people were delivered by this tearful Queen descending from paradise.[6]

JACQUES MARITAIN (1882-1973)

a young philosopher unfamiliar with Christianity, met Leon Bloy whose ardent faith converted him, and he became Maritain's baptismal godfather. Jacques' wife Raïssa is baptized with him. Falling gravely ill the following year, Raïssa recovers after praying to Our Lady of LaSalette, on the advice of Bloy. The Maritains, regarding this as a miracle, decided to make a pilgrimage to LaSalette the same year. This brought about other conversions: Raïssa's father, and then the writer Psichari, at the Maritains' home in front of the statue of Our Lady of LaSalette.

In *Grandes amitiés [Great Friendships]*, Raïssa recalled their first pilgrimage to the high mountain site, starting with a Homeric ascent in a kind of

> carriage so old that all parts were held together by ropes. This gave it more flexibility than sturdiness. It was drawn by two horses and two mules. We climbed the steep road, which is known to be very dangerous. At that time it was still a difficult path [...] narrow as the gate to heaven, an immense wall at our left and an

abyss at our right. The weather was warm and lovely, the air of admirable purity. It seemed to me as if we were pilgrims to the earthly paradise, hidden up there close to heaven.

Raïssa concluded:

> We learned of LaSalette through Leon Bloy. The Apparition is one of the most important spiritual events that has happened for centuries. Lourdes is more famous but less extraordinary, in spite of all its miraculous healings.

In 1915, Jacques started a significant *Mémoire sur LaSalette* [Memoir about LaSalette], which he did not publish. However, he kept his writings in his archive and took some articles from them.

> To really serve the Blessed Virgin, I think it is important to return to the question of LaSalette in its entirety [...] without any passion but only truth.[7]

In 1918, on the advice of Pope Benedict XV, he placed "the enormous memoir," which in those difficult times did not seem appropriate to publish, into the hands of Cardinal Billot.

Thirty years later [1948], having become ambassador of France to the Holy See, he pleaded one more time in favor of LaSalette and the seers, this time with Pope Pius XII.

> The Apparition of LaSalette has a place in the hearts of French Catholics. Maybe it is more hidden but not less important than Lourdes. It was the first [public] Marian Apparition of the nineteenth century [8] and in the passionate discussions that ensued during the first ten years, LaSalette inscribed itself deeply in the Catholic devotion of our country. In this Apparition the Blessed Virgin wept and it was because of those tears of the Mother of God, along with the prophecy of great trials, suffered in our times by the world, that many faithful regard the event of LaSalette with an especially fervent respect. They find in it the lesson of penance that would be reiterated in Lourdes and in Fatima, a source of inner conversion and spiritual life which makes LaSalette very cherished among them. [...]

At the Apparition in 1846 Melanie was 14 years and 10 months old. She lived for many more years after that. Everyone who knew her affirmed that her long life, lived in solitude and poverty, was a life of high virtue, dignity, unshakable faith, humility, Christian ardor and perseverance in doing good. In their eyes, this woman who is presently being labeled a hysteric, was gifted with the highest supernatural gifts. Her spirit of mortification and penance was exemplary, as was her devotion to the Blessed Virgin and to the Eucharist, which was almost her only food. I have interviewed two priests, now deceased, who were her confessors during her stay in France, who have confirmed all this to me. Having lived a long time in Italy, Melanie was the protégé of Bishop Petagna of Castellammare-di-Stabia, who served for eighteen years as her director, and of Bishop Zola of Lecce, and of Bishop Cecchini of Altamura, who esteemed her greatly. The Canon Annibale DiFrancia, who called her to Messina to become the novice mistress of his Institute, considered her a saint and bore witness to her, highly praising her virtues in the oration he preached at her funeral. Her memory is venerated in Altamura, where she lived the last seven months of her life and where she died on the night of December 14-15, 1904 at the age of 73. She has a tomb in the cathedral. Father Garrigou-Lagrange could testify that she predicted, to a lay brother who knew her, the date and the circumstances of her death.

1. Doesn't all this cause a serious problem? If one wants to throw light on the Apparition of LaSalette, isn't it best to first collect and examine all the documents and witnesses regarding the long life of the seer and about the virtues attributed to her? Only then, once a judgement on this fundamental matter has been made, can the other questions of the Apparition of LaSalette be addressed in a sufficiently reliable and objective way.

2. I had collected, in a voluminous memoir, the results of my research on the question of LaSalette. I brought this memoir

to Rome at the beginning of April 1918. In such a compilation it is impossible to avoid the question of the Secrets of the two shepherds, therefore I wanted to know - in light of the Decree of the Holy Office of December 21, 1915 - if I might be granted the authorization to publish the memoir. I talked about this in a private audience with His Holiness Benedict XV. During this meeting, the Pope told my wife and I, on the subject of the Secret of Melanie: "*Quoad substantiam, credo; quoad singula verba, nego*" [As to the basic meaning I agree. As to the particular words I do not agree.] He asked me to bring my manuscript to Cardinal Billot, and to ask him, on behalf of the Pope, to read and examine it. After several months, Cardinal Billot told me that he did not find anything reprehensible in my work. However, it was not appropriate to publish it. Since then, the memoir has remained unpublished. I have here a copy. Although now after thirty years, this text seems to me badly written and clumsily presented, I am willing to make it known just for information, if it is of any use.

3. Several months after my journey to Rome in 1918, Cardinal Billot wished to inform me about a confidential memoir he had received through the mediation of Bishop Giray, on the account that Melanie had made about her childhood at the request of her confessors. In it, the testimony of her younger brother was evoked. (Eugene, born in 1836, must have been four or five at the time of Melanie's childhood memories, or maybe he was not even born then). So, I wrote a detailed answer and sent it to Cardinal Billot, in which I showed the inanity of the arguments employed in the memoir in question. This answer I also hold at the disposal of the competent authorities.[9]

LOUIS MASSIGNON (1883-1962)

Islamist and high-level mystic, very active in ecumenism, was secretly ordained a priest in the married clergy of the Melkite rite. One day when he was celebrating Mass in the grotto in Bethlehem, some pilgrims were astonished: "He looks like Massignon!" He made his first pilgrimage to LaSalette at 28 years of age, on the night of December 24, 1911. The following year (1912) he went to Altamura where Melanie had died.

"A misunderstood saint," he said to her detractors.

He made other pilgrimages, in 1915, 1930 and 1934.

> In 1946, in his magazine *Dieu vivant* [The Living God] he publishes *Une défense du secret de La Salette* [A Defense of the Secret of LaSalette] by J.B. Wilfrid, a letter of Maritain's: *Autour du grand drame de la Salette* [On the Great Drama of LaSalette], and another text by his own pen *Le voile de ses larmes sur l'Eglise* [The Veil of her Tears over the Church.] He refutes those who separate the Apparition from its seers, according to their popular slogan: "Their mission is over, LaSalette begins!"

In January, 1912 he writes to Paul Claudel:

> To accept the message of Melanie on the Apparition and to repudiate it because of the charisms and the autobiography, is a clumsy imitation of Renan expunging the Gospels of their miracles. To accept the testimony of Melanie in 1846 [...] and to argue that her narration after 1852 is a lie [...] is, coming from the devil's advocate, more than a deficient method, it's an admission. In short, the existence of the Secret is certain, and the authenticity of the present text is highly probable.[10]

Massignon considered his fifth pilgrimage (1953) as the highlight of his spiritual destiny. It was on the anniversary of the Apparition, the 19th and 20th of September when he observed from his profoundly ecumenical view:

> The Feast of Our Lady of LaSalette coincides with the *Day of Atonement*, not only for the Jews (*Yom Kippur*), but also for the Muslims (Ashura). [†Editor: In 1953 Yom Kippur fell on Sept. 18/19. In 1846, it fell on Sept 29/30.]

His zealous archival work, and his authority, contributed in keeping the discussion open.[11]

Massignon left an unforgettable memoir of his first pilgrimage of Christmas day, 1911:

> I arrived yesterday evening. I walked through Corps and the winding path of Saint-Julien. I thought I would die in the snow as it was so thick and soft. Rarely have I been more clearly in peril of death. In the middle of the night, after an amazing pale pink sunset above the furthest valleys, I still had to walk for more than an hour, half stumbling and falling, and taking a breath every five or six steps. The thought of sitting down and letting myself go, did cross my mind... At that moment, a clear and delicate crescent moon rose between two clouds. A little further, near a hill, beneath the evening star, I glimpsed the dark structure of the church and the lodging. In a deliberate rhythm, to prevent breaking anything or using up my last strength too quickly, I said my Rosary, one syllable at every step (I said it all and even a third more). Finally, I collapsed against the wall of the lodging and noticed a small light. I shouted in vain. The wind started to blow and I thought the frost would bring me to the [pearly] gates. But I managed to drag myself through the - more than one meter thick - snow piled along the lodging, and then, thank God, I discovered a bell chain which I rang. I was saved![12]

PAUL CLAUDEL (1868-1955)

who had read Melanie's complete story, wrote to Massignon:

The story of the Apparition is so beautiful, and the words of the Virgin are admirable!"[13] Massignon sent him a picture taken by the Blessed Annibale DiFrancia at the exhumation of Melanie eighteen years after her death. Claudel got the publication rights to use the picture for the cover of *Le symbolisme de LaSalette*. He answered Massignon: "How, by seeing this holy mask, can one not remember the exclamation in the Canticles: "I am black, and I am beautiful" [Song 1:5]

Claudel made a pilgrimage to LaSalette in August, 1930 and wrote *Les revelations de LaSalette* for one of his daughters. He published

Maximin's testament. The message of LaSalette resonates in Claudel symbolically:

> Was not the Blessed Virgin right in announcing that a great famine would return? All we have to do is look around us. It is there because, if we possessed a spiritual vision, we would see around us *souls* reduced to skeletal destitution, like the pictures coming from India [...] The potatoes are rotting away. All the humble family treasure, the visible reserves of patience and unselfishness... is exhausted and spoiled.[14]

The book appeared in 1946, and later in 1952 was re-edited with a meditation added, in which he writes:

> Above LaSalette, there is a three-peaked mountain which, apparently, resembles Mount Sinai. The central peak is named the Obiou. [...] Here at the foot of Obiou, the Mother of God specially descended from heaven, where also infallible authority affirmed her assumption [back to heaven]. She rushed away, as if she could not take any more horror and sadness, after delivering her solemn warning to her ungrateful and rebellious people.

The message of LaSalette had taken Paul Claudel aback at first, but progressively he discovered "its seriousness and richness." What struck him so much (just like Huysmans), was the eloquent contrast between "its symbolic regalia and the simplicity and intimacy of her conversation with the two poor children, as pure as baptismal water [...]

> Look: those are real tears, like the tears that once rolled from Christ's cheek at the death of Lazarus. You philosophers, do what you want, but you cannot make me believe that it is not for a serious matter that the Blessed Virgin is mourning and weeping over us [...]

Claudel recalls his pilgrimage to the exceptional mountain as follows:

> Mourning countryside, deep cleaves of black shale, rough and raw rocks folding and unfolding, ice-cold and piercing air, houses of sinister poverty with their very small windows. La Mure,

Corps [...] here is the great solitude of the Alps. Here the mountains throng in dramatic attitudes all around us, like the group of holy women gathered around the Cross.[15]

Spiritual Persons

Sylvain Marie Giraud, M.S. (1830–1885)

According to Father Henri Bremond, the LaSalette Father, Sylvain Marie Giraud is one of the greatest spiritual leaders of modern times. Poet, musician, sacred orator, disciple of Father Olier and Father DeCondren, this Provençal charmed his fellow countrymen in many ways. He preached to the pilgrims of the mountain. He guided priests, religious and communities, and he died in the odor of sanctity. His writings are mainly directed toward priests, to instruct them on the excellence of the state of victimhood, as he himself lived it, just as Melanie did.[16]

In a very inspired description of the *Apostles of the Last Times* as prayed for by Saint Louis Grignion DeMontfort and by Melanie, Father Giraud foresees the triumph of Mary through the Apparition whose shrine he served:

> LaSalette! The world, in its last ordeal, in its last throws of agony, will turn towards her, as from a vast ocean. When the storm worsens, the whole crew will turn towards the lighthouse shining afar and pointing out the harbor of salvation.
>
> Oh! Mountain of Our Mother! Blessed are the souls of those, who fleeing the persecution of the wicked, will direct their steps to you! Blessed are the souls, in this hard and hazardous march, who carry in their hearts a full and unlimited devotion for the Church and for Jesus Christ which no sacrifice can stop......nd a thousand times blessed the souls who will finally rest on your heights! Down in the world, rejected by God, charity will cool

19th c. Defenders of LaSalette

A) Fr. Sylvain Marie Giraud, MS: LaSalette Superior, friend of Maximin
B) Gustave Thibon: convert, philosopher, nobel prize nominee
C) Desire Cardinal Mercier, Archbishop and Primate of Belgium
D) Canons Auguste & Joseph Lemann: Jewish converts, theologians

and the Faith will die out. Scandal will have its time of triumph, and *the sinful man* will install his one-day reign.

But God will prepare the triumph of his Church. And in the meantime, before the hour of his glorious victory, you, LaSalette, will be his consolation and joy.

And after all this, I see the Church climbing from your sanctified heights up to heaven, to reign forever with her eternal spouse Jesus Christ, the Son of God.[17]

GUSTAVE THIBON (1903-2000)

has written several pages on LaSalette, notably in the anthology *LaSalette, témoignages* [LaSalette, Testimonies] As a farmer he is sensitive to its message:

> It is to the whole universe that the Immaculate Virgin addressed herself a hundred years ago through the intermediaries Maximin and Melanie. However, the fact that She chose two poor local children to pass on her message, proves how deeply concerned She was with the peasants' world. We were the first witnesses of the message, so it is to us that it is directed in the first place.
>
> Some superficial minds were shocked by the terrible threats contained in the words of Our Lady of LaSalette. I heard people saying: "we cannot believe in such a cruel God." This is to forget that divine threats are assurances repulsed. God is only cruel in as much as men, by closing their hearts to his grace, prevent Him from being good. 'I cannot hold back the arm of my Son anymore.' The initial refusal comes from us. This hand of God that strikes us, is a very merciful hand, full of gifts prepared for us for all eternity, and that we force, by our indifference, to close against his presents. God doesn't have to positively punish us. It is sufficient that He turns away from us, for us to roll inevitably to the bottom of the abyss, abandoned by the heaviness of our sins, the spectacle of the modern world whose pride has repulsed God, testifying to the truth with vehemence.

For us farmers, the call from Mary for penance and prayer, together with her material threats, is vested with a very specific meaning. The message of the Virgin could be summarized in these simple words: if one does not look towards heaven, one will lose the earth. And this warning applies to us, more so than to anyone else. Bent towards the earth by his work, the farmer always risks being entangled in it. His realism and his sense of effort have as a counterpart materialism and avarice. These fruits of the earth, these carnal goods obtained through such hard work, tempt him constantly to make idols of them and to forget that God, as Mistral points out, "shares the work with him." Mary descended from heaven to remind him in his own language, and using images which best suit his spirit, that the realism of the earth, if not expanded and crowned by prayer, sooner or later will lead to the ruin of man. The "potatoes that will rot away" are also the souls of the farmers who love only the earth. And this earth, these excessively loved goods from down here, will be lost, as everything comes from God and matter, cut away from the spirit, withers in our hands, like a branch separated from the tree. To he who searches for God, everything is added unto him. However, to he who has nothing (i.e. who has only earthly goods) even what he has will be taken away from him [Mt 25:29] Mary has come to teach farmers that roots can only thrive if their grip on the earth is united with the branch reaching towards the sky.[18]

19th c. Saints who Promoted LaSalette

A) Saint John Mary Vianney: the holy Curé of Ars
B) Saint John Bosco: founder of the Salesians
C) Saint Peter Julien Eymard: founder of the Blessed Sacrament Fathers
D) Blessed Cusmano: founder of the Missionary Servants of the Poor

THE SAINTS

SAINT JEAN-MARIE VIANNEY (1786-1859)

the priest of Ars, made a complex journey towards LaSalette. As a priest ordained in the cathedral of Grenoble (1815) he willingly believed in the Apparition. However, his puzzling encounter with Maximin on September 25, 1850 created a long-lasting misunderstanding. Finally on October 12, 1858 he affirmed to Canon Gerin of Grenoble:

> Now, it is no longer possible for me to not believe in LaSalette anymore.

He said to Father Archier,

> Ah! LaSalette has already done a lot of good, but it will do still more; and later it will do good everywhere, and always more and more.

According to Bishop DeLangalerie of Belley, the priest of Ars died declaring his faith in the Apparition.[19]

SAINT JOHN BOSCO (1815-1888)

educator of young people, devoted a book on LaSalette in his series *Lectures catholiques*, which has been re-edited several times:[20]

> The Apparition of the Blessed Virgin on September 19, 1846 is an established and marvelous fact, confirmed by thousands of people who can certify this up until today. This loving Mother has appeared as a beautiful Lady to two children [...] She showed herself on a mountain of the Alps, [...] for the benefit of France [...] and the whole world. She did this to warn that the anger of her Divine Son was aroused against humanity, especially because of three sins: blasphemy, profanation of Sundays and feast days, and disregard of the laws of abstinence.

Prodigious facts have confirmed this Apparition, written down in public documents or attested by people whose sincerity and conviction exclude all possibility of doubt on the matter. Those facts are precious to strengthen good people in their attachment to religion, and to refute those who, perhaps just out of ignorance, want to put a limit on the power and mercy of God, claiming that the time for miracles is over.

Jesus promised that, in his Church, there would be miracles even greater than the ones He performed. He did not limit the amount nor the time in which those miracles would be performed. So as long as the Church exists, we will always see the hand of the Lord manifest his power by way of prodigious acts [...] However, these signs, proof of divine omnipotence, are always an omen of serious events which manifest God's mercy and goodness, as well as his justice and indignation; and this always to his greater glory and to the greatest benefit of souls.

So, let us act in a way that these prodigies will be for us a source of grace and blessing. May they contribute to arouse a lively faith in us, a faith of action, a faith that brings us to do good and to avoid evil, so as to make us worthy of the infinite mercy, through time and for eternity.

SAINT PIERRE JULIEN EYMARD (1811-1868)

born thirty kilometers from LaSalette, was ordained a priest on July 20, 1834 by Bishop DeBruillard. He is the one who relates and confirms the healing of Marguerite Guillot (on September 8, 1848). He exchanges letters with Canon Rousselot to defend the Apparition before the Bishop Jean-Iréne Depéry of Gap. At first a Marist (1839-1856), Father Eymard founds the priests of the Most Holy Sacrament after a pilgrimage to LaSalette. He knew Maximin, kept a copy of the Secret given to Engineer Dausse, and was the spiritual guide to Maximin's adoptive mother, Mrs. Jourdain.

He celebrated his last Mass in the chapel of the Missionaries of LaSalette in Grenoble. On August 1, 1868 in La Mure, his final act was to press an image of the Apparition to his heart. In the album of the Shrine, he wrote the following words:

> I had the honor of being the first one to proclaim, in Lyon, the miraculous event of the Apparition. And today I am happy to kiss, with love and gratitude, this blessed earth, this mountain of salvation... If I had not been a Marist, I would have requested my bishop, as a great favor, to consecrate me to the service of Our Lady of LaSalette.[21]

BLESSED GIAGOMO [JACQUES, JAMES] CUSMANO (1834–1888)

a doctor in Palermo having become a priest, founded the Servants of the Poor. He visited Melanie, welcomed her for several days in Palermo and begged her to help him found his religious family based on the Rule received from Our Lady. However, 'Rome' did not consent. Dying at the age of 43, he was beatified by John Paul II as a real 'Apostle of the Last Times.' At his second visit to Castellammare, Melanie encouraged him in his foundation:

> I was surprised at my arrival to see Melanie open the door herself, with a respectful and charitable welcome, and furthermore, to have found on the table a copy of the Rule and a little statue of the Apparition of the Great Mother of God on the mountain of LaSalette.
>
> Reading quickly through the Rule, it seemed to me to fit remarkably harmoniously with my desires, since I found in it the outline of an institute of Brothers and Sisters, living in real poverty and in a spirit of evangelical self-denial, so as to relieve others of their misery and suffering. Also, there was an institute of Missionaries, devoted to the direction of the two institutes and to the apostolic evangelization of the poor. And finally, I found

1897-8, co-foundress Melanie instructed the novices of a congregation that St. Annibale DiFrancia was attempting to found. In 1910, Luisa Piccaretta came under the direction of the same priest. Both women were revered by the "Daughters of Divine Zeal," but neither felt called to join.

in it the concept of two confraternities, one of women and the other of men, who are therein called disciples, whose aim is attracting people towards the Missionaries, and in this way to win them for Jesus-Christ. These ideas have been, and still are, the object of my desire.

To my great surprise, Melanie told me in confidence her story and the reasons why she lived confined in this village. It seemed right to me to beg her to help me, as it was not possible for her to dedicate herself to the Order she thought she was called to. In all humility she showed me her incapacity and also her powerlessness because of a severe law that kept her there. However, she promised me to do whatever she was allowed to, a visit of only eight days, and after that, everything the Holy Father wished. In the meantime, she encouraged me to have the Sisters wear a habit, and to try to unite and begin the Community in the way the Lord would inspire me to, and to trust more in the help of God and the Most Holy Mother, so that things would thrive for his glory and for the salvation of souls.[22]

BLESSED [SAINT] ANNIBALE DIFRANCIA (1851-1927)

apostle of prayer for vocations[23] welcomed Melanie for one year (1898) in Messina. He considered her a "wise co-founder" of his religious institute. He preached her funeral eulogy in Altamura, opened a house of the Daughters of Divine Zeal to care for her tomb in their chapel, and he expected her beatification. On the 20th of December 1902 he wrote:

> I was very fortunate to be able to welcome Melanie for a year and eighteen days in one of my religious institutes of Sisters, *The Daughters of Divine Zeal of the Heart of Jesus*. Melanie arrived on September 14, 1897, the day of the exaltation of the Holy Cross, the fifth day of the novena to Our Lady of LaSalette. The coming of Melanie to my institute was preceded by remarkable signs. She undertook the direction of my religious institute which was just starting to take shape, and of the orphanage attached to it.

Before her arrival she had promised me to stay one year. Within this time, she gave my community such a stimulus, that one could rightly call her its foundress.

During her stay in my institute, I took the opportunity to examine diligently this amazing creature. I discovered in her the most astonishing virtues, which could rank her among the greatest saints. I might be wrong, but this is my impression. [...]

She is very pure, very innocent, very lovely, strong, prudent, very humble, full of zeal for God and for souls, natural as a dove, an excellent counselor. She possesses discernment of hearts to a very high degree. She is patient, perfectly peaceful, quiet, sweet, but prompt and quick to put into action what she knows to be the will of God.

Her life was a continuous interior martyrdom, mainly for two reasons: because of the offenses made to God, and [the anticipation] to see the two religious Orders realized of which the Most Blessed Virgin had given her the admirable Rule on the mountain of LaSalette. [...]

Though hidden, even seeing her humble exterior, peaceful, inalterably calm and sweet, a great holiness shows through her.[24]

Innumerable are the pilgrims and friends of LaSalette: Saint Leonardo Murialdo, Antoine Chevrier, Daniele Comboni, Sophie Barat, Emilie de Rodat, Euphrasie Pelletier, Francesco Spinelli, Edouard Rosaz, Don Orione, founder of the Sons of Divine Providence.

Defenders in the Hierarchy: Italy

A) Card. Lambruschini: served 3 popes, encouraged Bishop DeBruillard
B) Dominican Cardinal Filippo Guidi: offered his services to Melanie
C) Dominican Fr. Lepidi: Master of the Sacred Palace, papal theologian
D) Dominican Archbishop Cecchini: Melanie's confessor, final protector

Bishops

Bishop DeBruillard, and later his successors in the Diocese of Grenoble, have promoted the devotion to Our Lady of LaSalette through many different documents. Apart from Grenoble, three bishops, Villecourt, Dupuch and Ullathorne, have written on the history of the Apparition.

CARDINAL CLÉMENT VILLECOURT (1787-1867)

was the first Bishop to make a pilgrimage to LaSalette. On July 21, 1847 he arrived at LaSalette and spent the day with the two children. His *Nouveau Récit de l'Apparition* [New Account of the Apparition] presents them to us. He describes Melanie as follows:

> Add together in your imagination all the characteristics that you think would depict the most perfect and striking modesty, and you will barely get an idea of the modesty of Melanie. She has regular features but her eyes are full of gentleness, and her voice is of an angelic amiability which immediately fills you with esteem and a certain respect. Nothing points to the rusticity of mountain shepherds. Change her clothes, and you would never guess that she was born in the most miserable shack, and that her parents, brothers and sisters live on alms to help them in their profound poverty. Melanie is almost sixteen; one would think she were barely twelve. She does not say much; she only speaks if questioned. Then she speaks with a grace that gives a delightful sound to her voice and an inexpressible charm to her restraint. What she says is so right that it delights. However, she is not aware of it. A child of six would not express himself with more simplicity and less pretentiousness. She seems to attach much importance to the explanation of Christian doctrine. She simply says what she thinks regarding matters that might have different interpretations. However, if they express another point of view, she makes known with a modest smile, that she approves of it. She is not without liveliness. One can see that she knows how to contain it with a natural disposition to propriety. She

is candid and straightforward. She does not always agree with Maximin, who doesn't get angry. But, if she has a different opinion, she does not emphasize its value or importance. That is all I have been able to assess about Melanie. Maximin, because of his good-naturedness, has given me much more means to form his portrait. I begged the Mother Superior of the Providence to carefully ensure that the multitude of curious people, attracted by the Apparition, to Corps would not mar the simplicity of these intriguing shepherds. She promised me to do so, adding that she was not worried in the slightest on that point for Maximin, and that she would do everything so that Melanie would be saved from the danger of pride.[25]

Healed by Our Lady of LaSalette and appointed cardinal by Pius IX in 1855, Bishop Villecourt was one of the first and most constant defenders of the Apparition, according to his own words to Bishop DeBruillard:

> Yes, my venerable Lord and Father: like you I believe that the Immaculate Virgin, having shown herself so tender towards France, has to be considered as the one, after God, who had the greatest part in an event, of which no one can have been more amazed than myself. In the end I gave in to the will of the sovereign Pontiff who told me officially that he had followed divine inspiration in choosing to vest in purple he who sees himself rightly as the least of all bishops. May I now respond to the will of Providence in the new situation I am in! Perhaps She desired that in the holy City, where some have tried to send many arguments against the Apparition of the Blessed Virgin on the mountain of LaSalette, this Apparition would find in me a zealous defender. So far, I have already succeeded in dispelling the clouds that deceit had sown. With God's help, I will continue; and I hope it will not be without success...[26]

Maximin will visit him in Rome in 1865 and will accept a few of Maximin's personal belongings to look after when, thanks to a word from Villecourt, he joins the pontifical Zouaves.

CARLO MARIA MARTINI (1927-2012)

Bishop of Milan from 1979 until his death in 2012, at first exegete and then rector of the Gregorian University in Rome, was a pilgrim of LaSalette. His meditations on the Apparition were published under the title: *Maria soffre ancora* [Mary Still Suffers].

> For the new evangelization and for the renewal of society, the first and foremost resource will be new women and new men, plunged in the mystery of God, and integrated in society, saintly and sanctifying people. It is not enough to update pastoral programs, languages and instruments of communication. Charity is not enough either. A flourishing of sanctity is necessary. [...]
>
> All this - namely holiness - is possible with the grace of the Holy Spirit. However, it requires a progressive and persevering way of personal conversion, dictated by the Sacrament of Reconciliation. [...] This message of penance and Reconciliation is the message emanating from LaSalette, which we want to bring to our communities, so they will become communities of penance and able to reconcile themselves."[27]

French Bishops favorable to LaSalette

A) Card. Clement Villecourt: first Italian prelate-pilgrim to LaSalette
B) Bishop Wm. Ullathorne: wrote book to promote devotion in England
C) Bishop Jacques Bailles: promoted devotion in western France
D) Bishop Pierre Parisis: approved a Confraternity of Reparation for Blasphemy and the Profanation of Sunday, but later opposed devotion to LaSalette

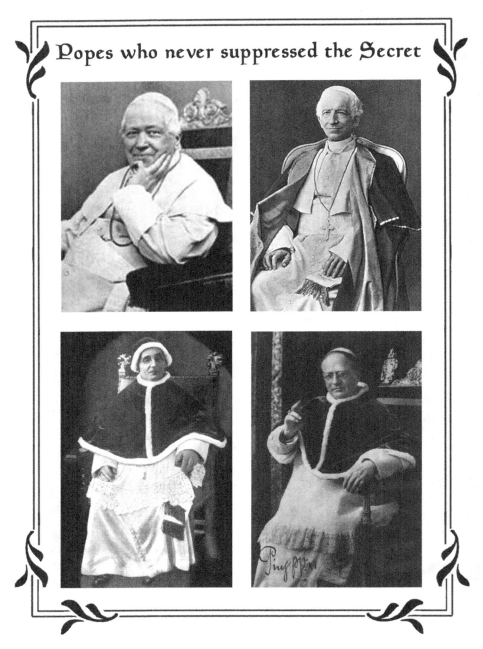

A) Blessed Pius IX: received the handwritten Secrets in 1851
B) Leo XIII: a dozen Rosary encyclicals, urged Melanie to initiate OMD
C) Benedict XV: strong devotion to the Sorrowful Heart of Mary
D) St. Pius X: (not shown) "Slave of Mary," a DeMontfort devotee
E) Pius XI: instituted feast of the Theotokos, October 11

POPES

PIUS IX (1792-1878)

raised to the pontificate in the year of the Apparition, was a personal adherent, albeit in a discrete way. He wrote several letters in Latin on the subject.

In this first letter (September 20, 1848) Pope Pius IX thanks Canon Rousselot:

> We were particularly happy to hear your story about the multitude of pilgrims who rush from all sides to this mountain site to honor the Blessed Virgin Mary there, and, especially, to know that those people, having arrived at this place, implore for Our humble person the all-powerful protection and help of the Mother of God. Likewise, we have the greatest desire to let these people know that We cover them with Our Apostolic Benediction.

This last letter, dated August 30, 1854, enlists Bishop Ginoulhiac to defend the 'reality' recognized by his predecessor against the calumnies of some priests:

> It is obvious, that by some discourses and writings of anonymous persons, today a suspicion of doubt is posited on the *reality* of LaSalette, and that even the legitimacy of the veneration of the Most Holy Mother of God on this mountain is questioned.
>
> As to the *reality* which has been published in many ways, and which has been recognized by the Bishop [DeBruillard], your predecessor, based on evidence and documents which you undoubtedly have at hand, there is nothing to prevent you, as soon as you find it appropriate, from studying it anew and *demonstrating it publicly*. You should use all your zeal, venerable brother, so that the piety and the filial devotion to the Queen of Heaven and the Sovereign of the world, so happily flourishing in your diocese, may continue there and increase day by day. And, if necessary, it will be a duty of your pastoral solicitude to inform your flock of the dangers that surround this same devotion and

to guard against them. Finally, raising our eyes to heaven and invoking the powerful protection of the Most Holy Virgin Mary, let us pray to God, venerable brother, and beseech Him through our Lord Jesus Christ, to maintain everything that is good in this diocese, and by his benevolence to guard what He has protected. As a pledge of our special affection for you, and as a portent of every heavenly blessing, receive the Apostolic Benediction which We grant you from the bottom of our heart, to you, venerable brother, and to your flock.

Did Pius IX pronounce himself on the Secrets of the shepherds? Yes, as soon as he read their letters, according to Canon Rousselot and Canon Gerin who were mandated to deliver them to the Pontiff personally:

Each child had written and sealed his letter containing his Secret, in the presence of witnesses who stated on the envelope that the content was by his own hand.

His Holiness opened the three letters [one presumably from Bishop DeBruillard] in our presence, read them, and commenting on the one from Maximin, he said: "In this there is the candor and simplicity of a child."

We answered that these were young children from the mountains, who had been receiving education only in the last few months.

To see better to read the two letters, His Holiness rose and walked to the window to open a shutter. We followed him. After having read the letter from Melanie, His Holiness said: "I must read this letter again with a clear head."

While he read this last letter, a certain emotion appeared on the face of the Holy Father. His lips stiffened and his cheeks puffed. Having finished, the Holy Father said: "These are scourges with which France is threatened. She is not the only one guilty. Germany, Italy, the whole of Europe are too and they deserve chastisement. Proudhon is less to be feared than religious indifference and human respect. Your soldiers kneel down when they see me but only, after having looked to the right and to the left, to be sure that no one sees them. It is not without reason that the Church is called militant, and you see here its Captain (bringing his right hand to his chest). I had your book examined by Bishop Frattini, Promotor of the Faith. He told me it was good, that he was happy with it, that it breathes the truth.[28]

The good reception of the Secrets by Pius IX, and the faith of his main collaborators in LaSalette, encouraged Bishop DeBruillard to formally recognize the Apparition. By the end of his stay, Pius IX accorded another audience to Canon Rousselot, and gave "to the children [i.e., the seers] of LaSalette his benediction in a very gracious manner."

LEO XIII, POPE (1878-1903)

is even more engaged in the Apparition. On the positive testimony of the Curiae of Naples and Castellammare, on December 3, 1878 in the first year of his pontificate, he received Melanie in private audience. (Her account of the audience, in which the Pope invites her to promote, in France, the Rule of religious life given through the Apparition, is reproduced further down in this book). The Pope encouraged the community of LaSalette presented by Bishop Fava. He bestows the title of Minor Basilica to the LaSalette Shrine, and allows the solemn coronation of the statue of the Virgin of Reconciliation.

It is during the time of the next Pope, Pius X, that Melanie dies. A strong eulogy about the seer appears in *Osservatore Romano*, neglected by the French religious press. Thanks to Father Cornuau, a friend of Leon Bloy, the holy Pope knew the autobiography of Melanie. "What about our Saint?" he asked Bishop Cecchini,[29] the bishop who had presided over the funeral of the seer, who died in the odor of sanctity.

Popes who never suppressed the Secret

A) Ven. Pius XII: Overcame theologians for the Assumption dogma
B) St. John XXIII: "The Pope of Saint Joseph" husband of Mary
C) St. Paul VI: "From paradise he will be close to you." MMP159f-g
D) St. John Paul II: "Totus tuus ego sum--I belong entirely to you, O Mary"

BENEDICT XV (POPE (1914-1922)

received the Maritains in audience. They left a written testimony about the meeting:

He received us with great benevolence and goodness. [...]

"LaSalette!" he said, with a lively and interested glance. And he explained at length his own feelings on the question: "The Apparition is beyond doubt. However, the words of the Blessed Virgin to Melanie, in particular when in the Secret message they express such severity with regard to the clergy - are they certain? This is what is debatable! It is very well possible that, while speaking in general she complained about the clergy, but the terms used might have been exaggerated by Melanie's fantasy (imagination), no matter how sincere and good her disposition. In short, considering the Secret Message, *quod substantiam concedo; quoad singula verba nego* (Latin: As to the basic meaning I agree. As to the particular words, I do not agree). The Holy Office wants to avoid scandal, to pacify souls, to prevent the Christian people from turning away from priests, whom so many enemies are ever ready to overwhelm." [...]

Then, with great gentleness he asked:

- But you, do you believe the Blessed Virgin has spoken this way, literally? [...]

- [Jacques] Yes, Most Holy Father, I think that Melanie was a saint and that what she reported was literally true. I have many details about her life. She was stigmatized. She has suffered much because of her faithfulness to her mission...

- "Yes I know." The Pope said. He did not seem to be offended by my answer. "One cannot say of her all the things of which the other seer has been blamed."

- [Jacques] He was also very much calumniated. He did not receive the extraordinary graces that Melanie was favored with. Nevertheless, he was a good Christian.
- [Raïssa] A simple heart.
- You believe in it too, Madam? You also have devotion to Our Lady of LaSalette?
- [Raïssa] "Yes Most Holy Father." She said this with emphasis, in spite of her fear of having intruded too much by intervening.
- Yes, I know. There are many people in France who have a real devotion to Our Lady of LaSalette. Some of them even more than for Our Lady of Lourdes, is that not so?
- [Jacques] It is because the Blessed Virgin wept at LaSalette. It is because of her tears.
- [Raïssa] Tears are the right answer to the current state of the world.

The Pope remained silent. He seemed to be touched. His face was very serious. Then after awhile he said to me: "Well this is what you must do. Go and see Our brother, Cardinal Billot (a slight smile appears on his lips...Jacques) knew that the two prelates did not like one another very much). He is in charge of studies. It will be a natural introduction for you. When you have talked philosophy with him, do as you have just done with Us. Open up your heart. He will listen to you. Tell him you don't want to ask him anything concerning the Secret of the Holy Office, but say that you have written a work, and that you want to submit it humbly to the Church, ready to acknowledge its judgement if you have been mistaken. There is not, is there, any pride on your part? If the Good God wants your service on this occasion, He will inspire in Cardinal Billot a suitable response.[30]

PIUS XII, POPE (1939-1958)

encouraged the celebration of the centennial through a signed letter to the Superior General of the LaSalette Fathers:

> Our devotion to the Blessed Virgin Mary, to her Immaculate Heart to which we have consecrated the Church and the world, can only expand with the sweet prospect [...] of the centennial of the Apparition of Our Lady of LaSalette, of which the canonical process, guided at the time by the diocesan authorities, revealed itself favorable.

THE FUTURE JOHN XXIII

Angelo Roncalli, residing in France to serve as nuncio, diplomatically saved the centenary [1946], which would have been celebrated under the shadow of criticism of the seers and the burial of their Secret. Rome had refused a legate, and Pius XII had warned Ambassador Maritain about the doubts heaped against the Apparition. It was in the context of the Marian Congress of Grenoble that Nuncio Roncalli participated in the centenary celebrations, and presided at the Feast of August 15, 1946 at the Shrine of LaSalette. He exhorted the crowds: "Pray, pilgrims of the Centenary! Pray for those who are currently in Paris in the process of building peace [...] Pray for Reconciliation among men [...] ! The message of LaSalette - what is it, if not a moving call for Reconciliation?"

In his Apostolic Letter: *Haud paucae* of June 16, 1961, John XXIII, designated "the Blessed Virgin of LaSalette as [...] Reconciler of Sinners."

POPE [SAINT] JOHN PAUL II

"I pray to her every single day!" John Paul II said in June 1990, after having blessed a painting of Our Lady of LaSalette in Castel Gandolfo.

For the hundred and fiftieth anniversary of the Apparition, he wrote this Apostolic Letter to Bishop Louis Dufaux of Grenoble:

> Such a commemoration can be full of graces. It is important for me to be associated with it, in union with the pilgrims who come to venerate the Mother of the Lord under the title of Our Lady Reconciler of Sinners [...]
>
> The Apparition of Mary to Maximin and Melanie represents a significate step. At LaSalette, Mary, most loving Mother, showed her sadness regarding the moral evil of humanity. Through her tears, she helps us to better grasp the painful seriousness of sin, of the rejection of God, but also of the passionate fidelity which her Son bears towards her children, He, the Redeemer, whose love has been wounded by negligence and rejection.
>
> The message of LaSalette was given to two young shepherds in a time of great suffering for people who were afflicted by hunger and facing many injustices. [...] The indifference, or even hostility, towards the evangelical message increased. Our Lady [...] wearing on her breast the image of her crucified Son, shows that She is associated with the work of salvation. She is affected by the trials of her children and She suffers to see them drift away from the Church of Christ, to such a degree as to forget or reject the presence of God in their lives and of the holiness of his Name [...]
>
> The message of Mary is not excluded to the suffering expressed in her tears. The Virgin calls us to composure. She invites us to penance, to perseverance in prayer, and particularly to faithfulness to the Sunday obligation. She asks that her message be "passed on to all of her people" through the testimony of two children. [...]
>
> The words of Mary at LaSalette, in their simplicity and severity, are still relevant in a world which still undergoes the scourges of war and of famine, and dries up with misfortunes which are the sign, and often the consequences, of the sins of man. [...]

Even today, the one whom "all generations will call blessed" (Lk 1:48) desires to lead "all of her people" who endure the trials of this time, to the joy born from the peaceful fulfillment of the mission given to man by God. [...]

Mary is present to the Church as at the day of the Cross, the day of the Resurrection and the day of Pentecost. At LaSalette She has clearly manifested the constancy of her prayer for the world [...] May She lead all the nations of the earth towards her Son!

The World

A) Guissepe Garabaldi: Italian Guerilla Commander, Freemason
B) Napoleon III: French Commander-in-Chief, Freemason
C) Count DeChambord: aspired to become King Henry V of France
D) Victor Emmanuel II: first King over the Papal States, Freemason

CHAPTER 7

THE SECRETS

THE SHORT AND THE COMPLETE VERSIONS

For the first time ever (in Chapter 4) we were able to edit the eight versions of the Secrets, of which three were unknown until now. They are of two different types:

A. THE SHORT VERSIONS

The first two were transmitted to Pius IX: one by Maximin on July 3, 1851 (version 1) and one by Melanie on July 6, (version 2). These are authorized documents, recorded by the Bishop after having consulted two of the Canons of his diocese, and then officially transmitted to the Pope.

Next are the confidences of Maximin to Mr. Dausse, culminating in the handwritten version of August 11, 1851 (version 3).

The two new versions requested by Bishop Ginoulhiac of the two seers: one from Maximin, of August 5th, 1853 (version 4), and one from Melanie, of August 12th, 1853 (version 5), re-written more carefully on the 14th of August (version 6), are completely revised, according to their memory and their understanding at that time. These versions are revealing, be it less faithful and less authoritative.

Those first six versions (three from Maximin and three from Melanie) each consist of ten to twenty lines. On average, the versions of Melanie are twice as long as those of Maximin.

B. THE COMPLETE VERSION

Melanie could only reveal the Complete Version from 1858 onwards. It was subsequently edited three times.

1. The first version, intended for the Pope (1858), which was located in the archives of the English Pontifical College thanks to Father Jean Stern, definitely reached Pius IX, however this version has not been recovered. (We have numbered it [7] with brackets, to signify its loss as well as its proximity to version 7, taken up literally, with additions, in the definitive version 8).

2. Having returned to Marseille, by the end of 1860 or in the course of 1861, Melanie rewrites her Secret on a five-page leaflet (version 7), omitting the passages (designated with: "etc.") which she did not yet want to make public. By the end of January 1870, she handed over an accurate copy to Father Felicien Bliard, published and commented by others, and then by himself, in 1873, with the Imprimatur of the Archdiocese of Naples.

3. The very last version (8) dated November 21, 1878 at Castellammare-di-Stabia onwards, is literally identical yet more complete, and published the following year in 1879 with the Imprimatur of Bishop Zola of the Diocese of Lecce.

The redactions of the longer versions (1860-1861 and 1878) are all made solely by Melanie. She has received the Secret in a more extensive, more difficult and more compromising way than the younger Maximin. With the Secret of Melanie, it is the heavy task of a prophet which mobilizes her, because she and her companion are assigned a role of primordial importance: "*If, after you have told the people what I told you* [...] *they don't convert* [...] *my Son will make his power burst forth*" (on the 6th of July 1851).

NORMS FOR INTERPRETATION

What is the value of the prophecies and predictions contained in the Secret of LaSalette? Before we begin, let us note the difficulties of evaluation and interpretation.

In general, predictions are not history before history. They are generally partial, vague and symbolic, as Cardinal Ratzinger emphasized when commenting on the Third Secret of Fatima.

The Secrets mainly concern the future of the Church. Nevertheless, they also touch upon political and conjectural phenomena that are important for the salvation of mankind: the overthrow of the king, for Saint Catherine Labouré, the Russian materialistic power, for Lucia of Fatima.

The seers had some difficulty to express, five to thirty years later, what they had received in one single Apparition, with its density of words and images that were difficult to situate in time. This explains the variations in the order, precision and content of their successive versions, conditioned by several factors: changing circumstances, different missions, the variety of addressees, special assistance of grace according to the importance of the revelation and its legitimacy, and the maturation of memories.

The two seers did not have exactly the same perception of the Apparition: Maximin began to see it later than Melanie. His receptivity was different. His attention and his understanding was less profound. The beautiful Lady, who ended up charming him, remained unknown to him, although not as a stranger.[1]

In general, seers do not discern well the temporal planes, often juxtaposed in a typological way, because, in the designs and the thought of God, the historical events are stages of the mystery of salvation, with analogous structures which correspond to each other in different periods.

In fact, the seers are overwhelmed by what they relate. Their interpretation is intuitive. They refer to current events using the language of their time, not according to reasoned exegetical methods. Melanie, more thoughtful than Maximin, acknowledges her part in interpretation, notably the delay before the realization in her different versions of 1851, 1853 and 1860.

"The time is not far off: there won't be more than twice 50 years" (before it becomes reality; July 6, 1851).

"The end of the world will come before twice forty years," she specifies without caution on August 12, 1853.

"His birth" (of the Antichrist), "won't exceed twice fifty years" she writes in 1860. She has trouble perceiving the time frame.

Finally, the version of Lecce does not give any qualifying period of time.

Melanie explained herself on this, writing to Father Roubaud on January 3, 1891, that it was not "words that came out of the mouth of our sweet Mother Mary."[2] These were perspectives seen as *images*.

ROYALIST AND APOCALYPTIC INFLUENCES?

Prior to the recent discovery of the very first documents addressed to the Pope, royalist and apocalyptic influences were attributed to a considerable part of the Secret of LaSalette. The excitement of pilgrims, fond of popular prophecies, and the supposed animosity of Melanie towards Bishop Ginoulhiac would have been enough to produce the fictitious additions of "LaSalette II," in the long version of Melanie in 1879: "the ruin of Paris; the Antichrist; revolutions; the sanctification of priests and consecrated souls, etc."[3] were relevant to these extrapolations. To recover the authentic message of "LaSalette I," it was sufficient to reject "with resolution all esoteric and political speculations as foreign to the Apparition."[4]

The recovered documents at least mitigate this objection. In fact, all the themes listed as "LaSalette II" are present in the first redactions (1851) of the Secret, gathered officially in Grenoble and Rome several months before the official recognition of the Apparition. Moreover, the Secrets of 1851 confirm what the seers had already confided, as early as 1848 or 1849, to B. Dausse, to Miss Dastarac or at the school of Corps (e.g., Paris, Antichrist, revolutions, even

"Prussians 1870")... The incriminating themes thus have their roots very deep in the history of LaSalette. The political and esoteric influence is not, as far as Melanie is concerned, between 1851 and 1879.

Does this supposed influence exist before 1851? Had it contaminated the official Secret of the visionaries, sent by Bishop DeBruillard to Pius IX on July 6, 1851?

We know that in September, 1850, two pilgrims, Mr. Houzelot and Mr. Verrier who were "legitimist" supporters of the so-called Baron DeRichemont, (†1853) pseudo-Louis XVII, arranged for Maximin to meet the pretender on his return from Ars in September, 1850. In Maximin's memoirs, published by Father Émile LeBaillif, Maximin testifies to the vivid, but ultimately disappointing, impression that this character had aroused in his childlike imagination. In his Secret, written in 1853 at the request of Bishop Ginoulhiac (presented earlier), he does indeed speak of a "son of Louis XVI." To his friend Perroud, Maximin will even imagine himself as his Prime Minister! But in the official Secret of 1851, there is total silence - not the slightest mention of a king! His adventurous imagination does not interfere with the legitimate exercise of his mission. Many witnesses noted it: as soon as it was a matter of publicly giving an account of Mary's message, the seer displays a seriousness that is not natural to him.

Melanie, on the other hand, in her first version of July 6, 1851, does announce to Pius IX "a great king" (with or without a crown, as emphasized by Maritain[5]) who "will reign for a few years." Could it be that the royalist influence had been decisive for her? No, precisely because it was she who did not want to follow Houzelot and Verrier in their expedition. She stopped in Grenoble, at her Bishop's rectory. According to the countless pilgrims who approached her, Melanie was not a woman who could be told what to say. She would not like to walk beside a king. She does not like them, she told her compa-nion, Sister Dosithée.

In short, we cannot reduce the Secrets to foreign influences. The prophecy of a "king," or a chief guarantor of peace, is found in several saints, including Don Bosco, and the Church does not canonize charlatans. At the troubled hour when Bishop DeBruillard himself spoke of "popular agitations," "thrones overturned," "Europe in upheaval" and "society on the brink of destruction" (in his instruction for the construction of the sanctuary on May 1, 1852) the Secrets of LaSalette were centered on the Faith but embodied in the flesh, like the prophecies of the Bible, bringing their Christian, social and even political aspirations, however diverse and surprising it may be. After the public message was given to the two shepherds, the expenses incurred in preserving the Secret and for the recognition of the Apparition were assumed, secondarily, but not incidentally, by the Bishop DeBruillard of Grenoble and by Rome (summer 1851).

What Do the Secrets Say?

It remains to discern the object and the value of the Secrets, through their successive, halting and diversified expressions, even while they are always referring to the same unforgettable, intensely lived memory.

In what order shall we begin? We first tried to group the predictions in the order that the seers related them in 1851. However, that order was not constant. It differs in three of the ten points that can be distinguished. In the next versions, there are also differences in the order. This all seems to show that the seers each received the same Secret, but with a different perception and a different perspective. So, the clearest way to proceed will be to regroup everything around four key points:

1. France
2. The World
3. The Church, the Pope and Rome
4. The Antichrist and the End of Time

1. FRANCE

Christian France is naturally a priority in the attention of the two shepherds of the Dauphin province. The most consistent prediction is that *apostasy* will occur. This can be retraced in all versions. Therefore, it is of major importance. The time frame is recurrently predicted "in another century," or "in the year 2000 at the latest," says Maximin (on July 3, 1851).

The verification of this prediction is only too accurate. France suffered anticlerical persecutions from the end of the 19th century and the beginning of the 20th century. However Catholicism, united and motivated, resisted in its faith, while allowing itself to be stripped of material and juridical resources. Subsequent persecution, more discreet, obtained a large collapse of faith and religious practice from 1968 onwards, by a massive secularization of the culture largely consented to, without resistance on all levels: exegetical, moral and educational, etc.

The Secrets also promise a *return to faith* at the beginning of the third millennium, because it appears through the examination of the writings of Maximin, that the "year 2000" indicates the first part of the 21st century. Without doubt the admirable elect which we see emerging or developing themselves in France (and elsewhere) under different forms, are a sign of this. However, one cannot yet measure either its extent or its impact.

The disappearance of faith was already a temptation in Melanie's time. She saw "chastisements" in the immediate future, in the countryside of the Isère, and of Europe in general. Indeed, the rotting away of potato harvests, and of wheat affected by diseases, provoked a general famine the following year (1847), but this particular point - also prophetic - belongs to the public message, not to the Secret part.

The first version of Melanie's Secret predicts a long-term *famine*. Her 1860 version would enlarge the famine to other parts of the world. This disaster, which first afflicted Ireland, is occurring today in the Third World. There are more hungry and underfed people than ever, because of the increase in population (from 1 to 6 billion within a century), notably in the poor countries. The phenomena are sharpened by the capitalistic accumulation of wealth.

In five versions (all from Melanie) Our Lady speaks about destruction, at least a partial destruction, of *Paris*: "infallibly" Melanie specifies. Up until now [the time of this writing] the Capital has not been destroyed, but it has been seriously threatened:

- In 1871, the Prussian invasion was followed by the Communist uprising and a civil war.
- In 1914, the advance of the Prussian armies to Paris was the next threat. According to several witnesses, an Apparition of the Virgin had distressed the Prussian invaders during a battle at the Marne. An imposed silence suffocated news of that Apparition. However, some wounded German soldiers in French hospitals have testified about this Marian Apparition. The question remains unresolved so far.
- In 1917-1918 there was the heavy bombarding of "Big Bertha" [German canon] on the Capital. Many were the alerts, as recalled vividly by Yvonne Aimée.[6]
- In 1945 the destruction of Paris was prepared by Hitler, but it was stopped by various intersections of fortunate situations during the Liberation.

All of this cannot be underestimated. If Paris and France today continue in the moral and spiritual degradation, those successive threats could one day become reality.

Another city, *Marseille*, is associated with Paris in the Secret of Melanie.

"Marseille will be engulfed shortly" (i.e. shortly after the destruction of the Capital) she writes in 1851. She explains this catastrophe as the sinking of the earth. Marseille seems to have experienced this partially already, because the city was flooded on September 19, 2000, the anniversary of the Apparition.

Melanie makes her prophecies depend on Paris and Marseille:

> When these things will happen, [moral] disorder will be complete on the earth. The world will abandon itself to the most impious passions.

The seer also speaks (to Father Combe) about the destruction of two cities she knows: Piera (in Greece) by an earthquake, and Gallipoli (in Italy), even "more engulfed" than Marseille. She also mentions tremors in Lyon, a city she also knows.[7] Her complete Secret addresses the end time, as Christ in his eschatological discourse (Luke 21:11) spoke about fearful earthquakes and other signs in the Gospels.

Three versions criticize *Napoleon III*. Bishop Ginoulhiac was not pleased by this. He was a friend of the regime, and in 1870 it recognized him as supreme Primate of the Church of Gaul. This explains his tense relationship with the seers and his reluctance regarding the Apparition. Before the recent discovery of the older texts, the earlier version of Melanie's allusion to the fall of the "Eagle [...] who always wanted to fly higher," might have seemed apocryphal. But Maximin said it very clearly from the 5th of August 1853 onwards:

> An eaglet will rise. When he will have grown a bit, he will turn upon himself. Then he will rise even higher. Then his feathers will start to fall. Then, finally, without feathers, he will fall on some daggers. After his death there will be chaos.

This last remark is not precise. Napoleon III was not killed by daggers. However, his empire ended under the Prussian armies, then prison, and finally exile which led him to his grave in 1873.

Lucia of Fatima made a similar "error" in the Third Part of her Secret. The Pope is "killed" by several projectiles, whereas Pope John Paul II survived an assassination attempt. Prayers can change the course of events. Cardinal Ratzinger explained that, according to Scripture and Christian Tradition, nothing [about prophecy] is final. The Secret of LaSalette is in the good company of the Third Secret of Fatima.

The pictorial expression of "daggers," conveys the resounding fall of a reign which was not without economic advantages for the nation.

After Napoleon III, Maximin predicted the coming of a "viper, today in the heart of France." Should it be identified with the anarchy of Communists, or with other anticlerical and pernicious regimes, which occurred, or will occur?

Maximin predicted afterwards, a *king*, as did Melanie. This almost happened when a parliamentarian majority offered the throne to "Henri V" in 1871. His resistance to the tri-colored flag [of the Revolution instead of the pre-revolution white flag] caused the negotiation to fail by a narrow margin. Nevertheless, the word "king" can be considered broadly, just as in the Bible.

Is the prediction of good kings after bad ones (in the versions 2, 4, 7 and 8), born from the influence of minor political groups on the seers?

This is not evident. Of course, they are children of their own time. The pilgrimage to Ars, made by Maximin in the company of pious but highly-placed royalists, may have fanned the flames of his childish imagination. However, around 1865, he told the so-called "Henri V": "You cannot reign, and you know why." (*cf.* this chapter)

As for Melanie, she criticized the opulent and dissolute monarchs. This is what the companion of her novitiate, Sister Dosithée, said about it:

- She did not like kings.
- Why not?
- Because their lives were not beautiful enough. When Melanie studied the history of France, she would exclaim: "Ah! Those kings, those kings... I don't like them; I don't like their lives.[8]

In fact, Maximin had no bias. He charitably warned Napoleon III: "Sire, just know that the day you will abandon the Pope, you will fall."[9]

Moreover, Maximin met the Count DeChambord in Austria, in Troisdorf, near Gorlitz, for the purpose of dissuading him to aspire to the throne. The meeting, confirmed by people of the Count's entourage, is known to us through a letter of Father Brissaud, Missionary of LaSalette. He reports in an amusing manner, the interrogation conducted by his superior:[10]

- "Where do you come from Maximin?" asked Father Joseph Perrin, M.S., our current superior.
- I will have you guess.
- Well, I won't search, just tell me.
- I cannot say. But I don't have to be silent about it. I can tell you, but keep it to yourself as long as I live. I come from Troisdorf.
- From Henri V?
- From Henri V.
- And why?
- Because I had something to tell him.
- From who?
- Well that I won't tell anybody.
- And what did you say to him?
- That he could not become King of France.
- Well, well! Why not?
- Why? Why? What do I know about it? I was not told why not.
- And did you reach Henri V?
- Yes, but not without a lot of effort. Important gentlemen were there, who wanted me to write down my message in a closed envelope. I did not want to, and I told them that I only wanted to talk to him, and that I would wait at his door until my death, if necessary. They treated me as a fool. They

thought I was an assassin. They searched and searched me. At the end they gave in. Two of those gentlemen and four soldiers led me to a beautiful room, and they pushed open the door. I walked in. I did not see anyone. Then near a window I perceived a movement, then someone started talking to me.

- Come here.
- Is it you Sir Henri V?
- Yes. What do you want to tell me? Who are you? Who sent you here?
- I am Maximin, the shepherd of LaSalette. I came here to tell you that you should not try to become King of France. It will be impossible anyhow. And you know very well why... (Here Henri made a weird face! a weird face!) Who sent me here? I don't know myself. But I do know that I did not want to come here. Also, I know that I was not able to not come here. Well now, my duty is done, so just let me go.
- Make this boy go away!
- And here I am.

After Cardinal Lavigerie delivered the "Toast of Algiers" on December 3, 1890, Melanie accepted African unification to the Republic, in accordance with the doctrine of the Apostle Paul: respect and obedience towards the established authorities, even the persecutors. She did so with judicious distinction, as shown in her letter to Canon Alexander DeBrandt on December 3, 1890:

> Here the ignorant poor don't know what to think of the words pronounced by Cardinal Lavigerie, in which he adheres to the Republic. Certainly, we all have accepted the Republic as a form of government. Whether we have a Republic or a king, we need to be indifferent, as long as this Republic or this king walk in justice, truth and the holy fear of God. However, at the moment the representatives of the Republic chase away God, by

persecuting his ministers and men and women religious, denying the existence of God by blaspheming Him, etc. tt hardly seems appropriate to declare oneself a full adherent of the Republic without adding: Yes, to the *form* of government but not to its acts of barbarity...[11]

2. THE WORLD

The Secrets announce persecutions, revolutions or wars (version 5) affecting France, Russia, England and Spain (version 7-8); civil wars in France and Italy; then a "general war which will be horrible" (version 7-8). The two World Wars 1914-1918, 1939-1945 could not be better characterized, since there never had been any "general war" before. The announcement of real peace after this is not random. After the First World War a peace treaty was never signed. The Second World War resulted in the Cold War, several countries divided in half, and a multitude of local wars, until the armament race between the USA and the USSR ended up with the collapse of Communism. Mentioning only the Middle East, it has known four wars since the 1960s, to which the war in Afghanistan must be added.

The LaSalette seers also announce, as did Lucia at Fatima, a famine beyond the locality, beyond France and Europe. This prediction is accurate, since, in our time of technical progress, the number of underfed or badly nourished persons has increased because the profits of capitalism tend to be concentrated in certain areas, and other regimes starve their inhabitants deliberately (Nazism, Communism, Cambodians and Koreans).

Instead, the "new Christian kings" of whom Melanie speaks - opposed to the *"ten kings of the Antichrist"* - have not yet appeared. The return of kings in Spain, and in Bulgaria, where the monarchy was thought to be out of fashion (and the canonization of the murdered Tsar by the Orthodox Church) represents only a small part of this prophecy.

Finally, after all these troubles which reflect the themes of Biblical prophecies (revolutions, wars, persecutions, apostasy), the Secrets of the Virgin predict a period of prosperity and peace (versions 1-8). Will this be for the 21st century?

3. THE CHURCH, THE POPE, AND ROME

A. Conversion of the Nation(s)

The Secret recorded by Maximin for the Pope on July 3, 1851, foretells the conversion of a Protestant nation in the North of Europe. Maximin names England, in his version of August 5, 1853. Three years later, through Don Bosco, Saint Dominic Savio announced the same thing to Pius IX.

Cardinal Mercier clung to this hope until his death bed. He had tried to accomplish it with Lord Halifax. However, the project did not succeed. The Roman Curia slowed, and then halted, the process by unilaterally denouncing the validity of Anglican ordinations.

However, are these glimpses of fresh conversions? Melanie (versions 2, 5, 6, 8) and Maximin (versions 1, 3, 4) foresaw the conversion of other nations, and Maximin beheld the rise of one single nation (version 4). Melanie, in rather radical language, concluded her complete Secret (8): "God will be served and glorified," an echo of Biblical prophecy.

B. The Pope and Persecution

Several predictions, especially concerning Rome, the eternal City, as the seat of the Antichrist, do not correspond to any event so far (version 8).

On the other hand, there will be "a pope whom no one expects" (3, 4). "He won't be Roman" (3). "French"! exclaims Maximin, proud of his country.

This Pope will be persecuted (versions 1, 2). "He will be shot at" (version 2). In 1849, before editing the Secrets, one connects this to the palace of Pius IX, the Quirinal, the actual residence of the

President of the Republic, where Msgr. Palma, one of the Pope's secretaries, had been killed. However, the attempted assassination of Pope John Paul II is more apropos to this prophecy.

"Nevertheless, the Vicar of God will triumph once again." This could indicate the respite accorded to the Papal States in 1850. But it could be applied to the successes of John Paul II, notably during his last travels, in spite of his suffering and poor health.

"The head of the Church will win the palm of martyrdom" (versions 5, 6) illustrates well what Saint John Paul II said in the spring of 1998: "The Pope must suffer." With the Apostle Paul, the Pope continues within himself the suffering of Christ for the Church (Col 1:24). Melanie inferred the same concept when she wrote her Secret for Pius IX: "A Pope must love suffering."[12]

According to the official interpretation, the Secret of Fatima symbolically expresses such a truth. The two long versions of Melanie (versions 7 and 8) insist on this persecution, and this suffering, and on the divine assistance.

Melanie foresaw the two subsequent Popes, particularly John Paul II, and Pius IX, who lost the crown of the papal kingdom. "Let him not leave Rome after 1859," she recommends. Just like Don Bosco said ten years later.

Certain years, 1850-1860 (version 4) and then 1863 (versions 5, 6), 1864 and 1865 (versions 7, 8) return, in several versions, to characterize the critical period for Pius IX and the Church. He will lose his crown at the same time as Napoleon III, a supporter of Garibaldi. No open revolution yet (versions 4-5-6) as the shepherds said would occur, but the 1st International was launched by Karl Marx.

As in many prophecies, plans are intermingled. The two seers have difficulty discerning them in the right order, and since all of it seems to them very serious, they resort to pictorial formulas, not without symbolic coherence.

Nevertheless, the essence of the message is that the rejection of

God by men, by hierarchs and even priests, is linked to these disasters, persecutions and temptations of Satan.

C. Unworthy Priests or "Cesspools of Impurity"

The thing which caused the most damage for the seers, apart from their criticism of Emperor Napoleon III, was what Melanie, in five of the eight versions (2, 5, 6, 7 and 8), said about the sins of priests.

From the very first version (July 1851) brought to the Bishop and then to the Pope, Maximin announced "great trouble in the Church" (version 1). Melanie was the first to mention persecution of "priests, religious and true servants of Christ." This has been verified up until today: expulsion of religious from France in 1901, hundreds of millions of incarcerations and deaths in the Soviet gulags, persecutions in Spain and Mexico, and in Latin-American or Islamist dictatorships.

However, among "the ministers of God and the brides of Christ, there will be some who will give in to disorders, and" Melanie adds "that is what will be the most terrifying," (version 2). In 1853 she specifies: "Consecrated persons will fall into a great loosening of morals, almost completely forgetting God" (Melanie, on the 12th and 14th of August, versions 5 and 6). Secularization, the relaxation of asceticism etc., prove all of this.

Melanie's long versions of 1860 and 1878 become more and more dramatic. The word 'priest' is still mentioned. Both versions start as follows:

> *The priests, ministers of my Son, by their wicked manner of life, by their irreverence and impiety in celebrating the Holy Mysteries, by their love of money, honor and pleasures, priests have become cesspools of impurity. Yes, the sins of priests cry out for vengeance, and vengeance looms over their heads. Woe to those priests and persons consecrated to God, who by their infidelity and wicked lives, are crucifying my Son again! (par. 2)*

To this the version of 1878 adds: "Priests have become cesspools of impurity." And finally:

The heads, the leaders of God's people, have neglected prayer and penance, and the demon has obscured their minds. They have become those roving stars that the old devil will drag with his tail in order to cause them to perish. (par. 5)

Two questions can be posed:

1. Why did Maximin not develop this theme in his three versions? If he had not received this part of the message as clearly, was it because he might have been too young? Would a woman, in the footsteps of famous saints, be more inclined to prophesy reform of the Church?

2. Could the progressive dramatization of the Secret by Melanie, not without poetic intensity by the way, have been provoked by the rough treatment that she had received from certain priests? And did she perhaps downplay this shocking and painful revelation (proof!) for the Pope?

From 1871 onwards, and preeminently from 1879, an outcry arose. The Secret was disqualified as an outrageous and sacrilegious attack. The expression "cesspools of impurity" has been particularly deplored, while forgetting that the prophetic language of the Bible is by no means moderate either. In spite of herself, the seer uses the hyperboles of the great saints of the Middle Ages (Catherine of Sienna, Bridget of Sweden, etc.).

Msgr. Roncalli, the future Pope John XXIII, writing about chastity in his *Journal of a Soul*, recalled the Biblical image of "fallen stars" as mentioned in the Secret (version 8): "My Lord Jesus, I also tremble for myself because "stars have fallen from heaven" (*cf.* Apoc 6:13). And I, who am but dust, how can I flatter myself?"[13]

The Latin *sacerdoce* [priests] consecrated to celibacy in a world in which nothing is celibate anymore, is a real challenge, a risky climb up a steep wall, that becomes more and more slippery as time progresses. "Disorders and the love of carnal pleasures will spread all over the earth" Melanie accurately foresees (versions 7 and 8). It is the reign of the principal of pleasure and lust, according to Freud. In view of human weakness, instability and the disappearance of every rule of prudence, including the ecclesiastical cassock from 1968, there are failures, and sins, sometimes very serious sins, because the demon puts forth great effort to engage saints and consecrated persons in arduous ordeals. The prophetic tone of Melanie does not deny, but rather supports this evidence.

Wondering about the relevancy of this shocking point [i.e., cesspools], it must be admitted in all objectivity, that there is nothing to blame other than the tone and the inconvenience. Every priest, having the mission to exclusively serve the infinite love of God, feels himself small and unworthy, as does every Christian called to a mystical ascent towards Him. He becomes aware of the horror of his sins, no matter how venial. This is what Melanie's prophetic tone denounces. The sins of priests, venial in the vast majority of cases, (Melanie does not deny this) are often hidden, and most priests repent before God as they should. If, however, exceptionally, scandals do occur, the Church, like any self-respecting profession, will do everything to bring these to light. The violent tone in Melanie's final version, does not surpass the words of Christ: "So, because you are lukewarm, and neither hot nor cold, I will vomit you out of my mouth!" (Apoc 3:16)

Beyond the common errors of this sinful world, the "great troubles in the Church" have become reality "in the 20th century," (Maximin version 1) when the renewal of the clergy was compromised in the western world. Right after the Second Vatican Council, and more precisely from May 1968, more than 40,000 priests (10% of the workforce) left the priesthood. [†Editor: These oft-cited statistics were inflated by including deceased priests who "left the priesthood."] Many left to get married, contrary to the promises they had pronounced when they received the subdiaconate. This degree of ordination was eliminated by the post-conciliar commission. This spiritual decimation is without precedent. It might be excused, due to the insistent request of several Bishops - not to the Council where this question was forbidden, but directly to Pope Paul VI - to have mercy on priests who had left their service to get married. Paul VI, who had prohibited debates on the matter during the Council as to avoid noise and scandal, began allowing priests to marry, through a canonical innovation, the "reduction to the secular state." In spite of himself, he unintentionally contributed to the public storm of criticism directed at the rule of celibacy. Soon media campaigns demanded a sabbatical year in which every priest could be allowed to re-evaluate his commitment to celibacy which may have been made under "undue pressure." This wave of publicity badly weakened the priesthood in those post-conciliar years.

Thus the prophetic message expressed by Melanie - *"The Church will undergo a harrowing crisis"* (versions 7-8 par. 13) - has been historically fulfilled in multiple and contrasting ways: in the first place in the Church of France, where the collapse of Christianity and the universalization of agnosticism have been pushed to the limit, in spite of the admirable rise of the elect.

4. THE ANTICHRIST AND THE END TIMES

Like many prophets since the eschatological predictions of Christ, of the Apostle Paul (1 and 2 Thes) and of the Apocalypse (the last book of the Bible), the prophetic message of LaSalette employs images and formulas of Biblical eschatology of which the young seers were ignorant. Yet they have recourse to end-time genre to apply it to the world they knew, a world which attracts disaster by forgetting or despising its Creator.

A. Antichrist?

The Secrets of 1851, and all the other versions, mention the *Antichrist*. Maximin designates this mysterious Biblical figure by the apocalyptic image of monster, whereas Melanie asks for the spelling of a word unknown to her. He will be *"born of a nun"* she writes. *"His father will be a bishop"* she specifies in 1860 (7). After the example of Christ, Melanie adds, the Antichrist will also have a prophetic forerunner in keeping with 1Jn 2:18-22; 4:3. The version of 1879 goes on: *"A forerunner of the Antichrist, with his troops of several nations...*

will shed much blood and will want to annihilate the worship of God" (par 22) He will stand up against Christ and every idea of religion, *"in order to have himself considered as god."* (7-8).

This prophecy, on several levels, both individual and collective, tangible and ideological, deserves more attention than at first sight. Let us remember the prophetic words of Charles Baudelaire [French poet similar to his contemporary, Edgar Allen Poe]: "The greatest contrivance of the demon is to cause us to imagine that he does not exist." In *Le Demon* (by Laurentin, published by Fayard 1995) I have studied this closely to show that the persecuting and homicidal actions culminating in the Nazi and Communist exterminations, were subsequently followed by a successful underground effort to uproot spirituality and asphyxiate the Faith. From the open and severe anticlericalism in the 19th and 20th centuries, to the discrete impetration in all layers of society, an agnostic secularization, the strategy and tactics of diminishing Christian Faith have been led by a master's hand. The anti-religious offensive developed itself behind the scenes, through a majority of rulers who claimed to be Christian and politically correct. Their politics however have nothing to do with the heroic faithfulness of a Saint Louis XVI, but more with the dubious religiosity of a Napoleon III. In this so-called reassuring leader, Melanie foresaw the rising specter of the "Antichrist."

The Secrets describe, in various yet converging terms and images, the disasters linked to the rise of this personality. Just as in the first letter of Saint John, the Antichrist is individual as well as collective, since he is evoked under different forms. There will be talk about the *"resuscitates"* (version 7 and 8), but they will be bad spirits, young agents of Satan, who will *"carry out brilliant victories"* by their armaments and prodigies. Melanie glimpses this "cult of spirits:" Satanic cults have abounded surreptitiously since the middle of the 19th century. (*Le Démon*, p.174-213, gives details about what is known about this cult and explicitly satanic music, and formal but occult ceremonies: Sabbaths, black masses and ritual murders, which have been multiplying since 1950).

B. Last Times?

The Secret of LaSalette does not situate the persecution of the Antichrist immediately before the end of the world. The "monster" will disturb the peace, as Maximin writes to Pius IX (version 1): "He will be asphyxiated by the breath of Saint Michael," Melanie writes (version 8).

Towards 1900 Melanie entrusted to Father Émile Combes some elements of her "second Secret on the end times" (refer to Ch 4 Sec III:7 and Sec IV). She outlines the main points to Miss Vernet:

> Real peace in the world will only reign after the death of the Antichrist: two or three brief periods of peace before the Antichrist, one peace after a war. I wish that this war will not occur. It will be horrible, terrible! Then a short-lived peace. All this time I have not seen a king on the throne of France. That does not matter. If France turns herself back to God, God will lift her up and give her a very Christian king. Nineveh was condemned to perish, but when the city did penance, it was forgiven.
>
> The earth will open itself in the presence of thousands of spectators from all parts of the world. Gathering to witness the ascent of the Antichrist to Heaven (as he will have predicted) but the Antichrist will fall, body and soul, into hell. They will all convert; they will all glorify the one and only God of heaven and earth. The Gospel of Jesus-Christ will be preached in all purity all over the earth. Churches will open again; kings will be the right arm of the Holy See. There will only be one shepherd and one flock, and charity will reign in all hearts. The world will last for many more centuries, then charity will cool again and once again the earth will stop bearing fruit [...][14]

THE IMPORTANCE OF THE SECRETS

It is always difficult to form a conclusion about the value and authenticity of prophecies. Even those from the Scriptures are puzzling for exegetes.

The great eschatological prophecy of Christ himself in the synoptic Gospels concerns the *end of Jerusalem and the end of the world*, by the fact that those two events correspond to one another in a typological way as the end of the old and of the new covenant, not without far-reaching implications. Because God's plan for the salvation of the world continues in the perpetual conflict between the light of grace on the one hand, and the frenzies of the world stimulated by the temptations from the demon, on the other hand. We should not be surprised to find this same ambiguity in Maximin and, above all, in Melanie, which explains her hesitation regarding a time-table which she nevertheless attempts to discern and substantiate to provide clarity, albeit without success.

A first series of data spread over the years between 1859 and 1865, mainly concern the threats of Italian unity versus the reign of Pius IX. Other data deal with the 20th or 21st century at the latest. (version 1). In the Scriptures, the term Antichrist designates a person (in the Letters of Saint Paul) and also a collective movement (Letters of Saint John). In some confidences, Maximin first talks about a "general Antichrist"[15]

It can mean a large atheistic movement (for example. the anticlericalism of the 19th century or Communism), but also a long period of famine (versions 5 and 6), of revolutions, wars (7 and 8), attacks against the Pope in a background of antireligious struggle (versions 2, and 5-8) combined with apostasy in France (versions 1, 3, 4) and elsewhere (version 5-8), and the failures of priests (versions 2 and 5-8). After this the reign of "the Antichrist" will come (all versions mention this).

What is the truth, the accuracy, the relevance or the irrelevance of these predictions? This is always difficult to establish, as the following two examples show:

With surprise, I discovered that Yvonne Beauvais (Mother Yvonne Aimée), obedient to her spiritual director, had a considerable number of prophecies put in writing in the 1920s, that came to pass in the 1940s. The most improbable one (her reception of six decorations because of her heroism during WWII) was filmed in 1947: 16 photographs of the decorations are reproduced on the cover of the book *Predictions de soeur Yvonne Aimée* (1995). She felt ashamed to write these things down in 1929. However, they did literally come true in 1947. This case is not only exceptional, it is unique. When I asked Bollandist historians if they had ever encountered a similar case (the undeniable and anteriority of the prediction and accuracy of its realization), their Dean Halkin, after having consulted the work of Bollandists who had ceaselessly studied the Lives of Saints for more than three centuries, answered me: "No, we have not" (*Predications*, p.9).

Now let us consider the third part of the Secret of Fatima (less exact and less specific than the second). To justify this Third Secret, Cardinal Ratzinger insisted on the symbolic character, the metaphoric transpositions and the fact that prayer can always change the course of events and therefore contradict the prophecies, something that upset the prophet Jonah (Jon 4:2). This explains why John Paul II did not get killed as the Third Fatima Secret predicted, but was seriously wounded. Our Lady still needed him on earth. When the Pope acknowledged his attempted murder by having the text of the Third Secret brought to his hospital bed, it could be a confirmation in spite of the differences. The attempt had not taken place on the top of a mountain but on Saint Peter's square. The Pope was not tired or afflicted then, nor was he surrounded by hostile soldiers, but by a fervent throng. And there were no other martyrs in Rome at that time. Cardinal Sodano explains that the prediction symbolically unites around him all the victims of atheism. The shot did not come from an army but from an assassin who had been paid for the job. The Cardinal [tries to] justify the accuracy of the prophecy by saying that one has to see it on a different level: it deals with organized religious persecutions on a third of the planet, culminating in the action against the Pope who accelerated the fall of Marxism. This interpretation justifies the prophecy beyond the literal meaning.

The prediction of LaSalette is more detailed than the one from Fatima concerning the Pope: *"He will be shot at,"* Melanie writes (2), and *"he will triumph once more."* The prayers of the faithful, the composure of the driver and the guards, and the skill of the doctors in the Gemelli Hospital all contributed to prevent his death.

As to the authenticity of the Secret of LaSalette, one has to emphasize its prophetic character. Just like all authentic predictions, it is not a matter of arousing curiosity about the future, which is God's concern, but to generally prepare Christians: priests, religious and the lay faithful for the drama that awaits them, by stimulating the courage and faithfulness that God expects from them in sufferings endured for Him. Likewise, the predictions of Mother Yvonne Aimée were not comprehensible before their realization.

Prophecy in Biblical semantics, is speaking *in the name of God* to designate his plans and intentions for the future. All the versions of the Secret of LaSalette speak in the name of God, formulated in different ways as to stimulate Christians for the spiritual battle, to complete abandonment to God in the various trials awaiting them: wars, famine, persecutions.

Melanie, by her very life, has particularly given testimony to this. She was constantly contradicted and persecuted, and several times locked up. In her chaotic, fragmented life journey, she never let herself be discouraged, but continued her mission with perseverance. She held to the firm conviction that she was to reveal the Secret given to her in the course of time: "You won't say anything until I will tell you to do so" (version of July 6, 1851).

In all the various versions one theme is constant: through threats and woes that will come, but also through happy events (conversions, peace, testimony and faithfulness of the righteous), it is necessary to refer to the plan of God and the teachings of his Church. This has nothing to do with curiosity. And this has not changed in the hearts of the seers, nor in the written versions of the Secrets.

According to Saint Louis-Marie DeMontfort (as we will see in the next chapter of this book) Our Lady wants to call the *"Apostles of the Last Times:"* disciples faithful to Christ, from this day on, living

> *in poverty and humility, in contempt and in silence, in prayer and in mortification, in chastity and in union with God, in suffering and unknown to the world. It is time that they come forth and enlighten the earth! (par 30-31)*

Aspiring Founders of Mary's New Order

A) Ven. Francesco Saverio Petagna: Bishop of Castellammare-di-Stabia
B) Fr. Alexander C. M. DeBrandt: Canon of the Cathedral of Amiens
C) Father Alfonso Fusco: Italian Redemptorist priest
D) Father Paul Gouin: scholar, pastor, biographer of Melanie

CHAPTER 8

THE RULE OF THE ORDER OF THE MOTHER OF GOD, A PRACTICAL COMPLEMENT TO THE SECRETS

A Final Secret is Reserved for Melanie

Melanie affirmed that after she was given the Secret, Our Lady went on to give her a Rule of life for a new religious family. Melanie revealed the essence of it in 1853. But she would have to wait until 1876 to fully explain herself. The Rule was accepted by Bishop Petagna of Castellammare. On this part of the message, unlike the Secret, Melanie is the sole witness.

Let us consider the Rule in this sequence:

- How the message of LaSalette laid the foundation for the Rule
- How Melanie received the Rule and tried to have it recognized
- Finally, how Melanie overcame many obstacles and opposition

1. HOW THE "MISSIONARIES OF LASALETTE" WERE ESTABLISHED

The mandate of Bishop DeBruillard of May 1, 1852, provided for the foundation of a missionary community in addition to the construction of the shrine. The Apparition itself called for consolers of the weeping Mary, for the mystery of the Cross to be lived, and to announce her message "to all her people." This was immediately understood by the Church.

The first Missionaries at LaSalette shared this general ideal. At the end of 1851, Father Sibillat, Melanie's director, put himself at the disposal of Bishop DeBruillard, specifying:

> Canon Rousselot drew up a draft of the Constitutions for this body of diocesan *Missionaries who would be called Missionaries of Our Lady of LaSalette* and who would perpetuate the name of the immortal shrine forever.[1]

Father Bernardin Burnoud, first superior, and Father François Sibillat soon pronounced, in the hands of Bishop DeBruillard, their "provisional promise, which would later become a vow, to begin to live and work according to the spirit and the Constitutions"[2] of the Missionaries of Our Lady of LaSalette. But the commitment of Father Burnoud did not last, and others would resign after him. When he left LaSalette, on the eve of September 19, 1855, he asked Bishop Ginoulhiac, successor to DeBruillard, to be released from the vow he had pronounced a year earlier, using this formula:

> My Savior Jesus Christ, prostrate at the foot of your Cross, all covered in your Blood and the tears of your Holy Mother, whom I take as witness of my commitments, I vow to devote myself, from this moment and forever, to the work of Expiation and Reconciliation which Mary came to inaugurate herself on the Holy Mountain of LaSalette.[3]

Father Berlioz had submitted to Bishop Ginoulhiac similar ideals;

> All your desire, your Excellency, is to see your work grow, to see the seeds sown by a divine hand on the Holy Mountain finally

rise up, watered by tears as fertile as they are maternal [...]

It follows, your Excellency, that to enter into the thought of Mary, to perpetuate her Apparition in a living institution, and produce in the world the blessings that She promised, there must be in LaSalette a very serious religious Institute, perhaps one of the most serious which has ever been founded up to now, and essentially an expiatory institution, for men and for women [...]

Father Denaz, one of the most enlightened in the ways of God, wrote to me several days ago: "I remain convinced that Jesus and Mary are asking for a foundation in the expiatory sense, and they desire and expect some voluntary *victims* on this new Calvary."[4]

The final thought of Father Berlioz, the superior who did not remain at LaSalette, will be cited at the end of this chapter. Father Sylvain Marie Giraud, M.S., one of the "great witnesseses" of LaSalette, would himself become a Missionary. However, he did not succeed in gaining unanimous support for his life project. Having sacrificed his personal aspirations, he would transmit his spiritual ideals to a female community for which he did much to help found: the "Sisters of LaSalette of Lyon."

Father Antoine Bossan, who joined the Missionaries' team very early and became the first historian of the pilgrimage, shared the same sentiments. His *Association de prières et de pénitence pour consoler et aider N.D. de la Salette* [Association of Prayer and Penance to Console and Serve Our Lady of LaSalette] did not receive approval from the Grenoble Diocese. He left the Missionaries in 1868.

Bishop Ginoulhiac, in his Provisional Rules for the Diocesan Missionaries of Our Lady of LaSalette (February 2, 1858), captured well the spirit of the apostolate and sacrifice of the disciples of the Weeping Virgin, but at the same time he curbed their preaching. Is this the reason of the accelerated attrition of its early members? Generous women, after a few intriguers, also came forward. This letter of March 8, 1860 of Sidonie Petitjean to Canon Rousselot bears witness:

Father [...] cannot watch this impiety which reigns in so many hearts, and this Christian indifference in many others, without recalling the Apparition of our good Mother Mary of LaSalette, and without my heart burning with desire ever more ardently to go to this Holy Mountain to consecrate my life in expiation for so much iniquity and to pray there for the conversion of all miserable sinners [...] Is not the Church in need of our sacrifices, devotions and good example? Are not the prayers offered in a religious house offered with more recollection and ardor in a Shrine? While the wicked are uniting to attack religion, should we not unite ourselves to obtain from God that He watch over and sustain us? In the past, during the greatest calamities of the Church, did she not draw consolation from the foundation of religious congregations and convents?

Father, I think [...] often of the impression you perceived in the countenance of the Holy Father while he was reading the Secrets of the children of LaSalette, and I say to myself, perhaps it was a reflection of the martyrdom, and persecutions they were predicting [...] think that the Order of the religious of LaSalette would be able to bring him some satisfaction. This idea thrills me! Oh, how I wish to be able to bring him some comfort and consolation! How happy that would make me! [5]

The zeal and enthusiasm coming from LaSalette, and the Apparitions of Rue du Bac, merged with the apostolic and missionary current launched in France after the violence of the Revolution, by the popes as well as the founders of new religious communities.[6] The zeal was augmented by the publication of *True Devotion to Mary* by Father DeMontfort (d. 1716), which had lain hidden, *"concealed in a chest,"* and discovered in 1842, four years before the Apparition of LaSalette. Saint Louis DeMontfort inspires hope for the *"Apostles of the Last Times"* which one also finds in the message of Melanie.[7]

2. HOW MELANIE RECEIVED AND REVEALED THE RULE

In his funeral eulogy, delivered in the cathedrals of Messina and

Altamura, Blessed Annibale Maria DiFrancia summarized when and how Melanie received this Rule of life:

> The Most Holy Virgin, after She had confided to Melanie a Secret, went on to reveal to her that there would emerge from the Holy Church a distinguished religious Order, that of new apostles, the Missionaries of the Mother of God. These would spread throughout the entire world, inspiring a great return to Catholicism. This religious congregation would be comprised of a second Order and a third Order. Its members will be burning with zeal for the glory of God and the salvation of souls, with a fervor comparable to that of the first Apostles. [...] The Most Holy Virgin, after having announced this future event, gives to Melanie the Rule to be observed by this new religious Order. This Rule, Melanie keeps in her memory, deep in her spirit. [...] Later, when the moment chosen by the Most Holy Virgin for revealing the Secret arrived, Melanie wrote down this Rule, because it was no longer possible for her to keep it only in her memory.
>
> This Rule was submitted to the judgment of a commission of cardinals of the Holy Church. It was deemed irreproachable, like a chapter of the Gospel, containing the quintessential Christian perfection to be practiced with the greatest gentleness and charity.
>
> Melanie suffered a spiritual agony during her whole life, waiting to see the fulfillment of the words of the Most Holy Virgin, and the organization of the new Apostles of the Holy Church. Far from seeing these goals attained, she witnessed the persecutions that those devoted to Our Lady of LaSalette would have to undergo by the will of God, to such a degree that each new persecution would seem to annihilate the devotion. Her eyes were always turned toward Rome, waiting for the supreme authority of the Church to crown LaSalette with glory and honor, and the foundation to emerge for which she sighed. But the prudence of the Holy See in this matter, and the Divine Providence which

rules over and disposes all things was bringing this holy woman to a continual and perfect resignation to the Divine Will.

She might have said, as Isaiah 38:17: "*Ecce in pace amaritudo mea amarissima!*" ("It was for my welfare that I endured great bitterness!") Often, Melanie considered herself to be an obstacle to the accomplishment of the divine plan, and so she abased herself before God, mortifying herself in various ways and wishing for death, sighing after it and begging for it in her prayers.

If She who appeared on the mountain of LaSalette was truly the Most Holy Virgin Mary, the Immaculate Mother of God, if it was indeed this incomparable Mother who confided her Secret to Melanie and to Maximin and gave a most holy Rule for a new religious Order of numerous *Apostles (of the Last Times)*, who could doubt that the promise of the Queen of Heaven would necessarily be completely fulfilled? Rejoice, then, O innocent Shepherdess of LaSalette, rejoice in the Lord, O soul chosen from among many! Your long martyrdom has been but a preparation for an ineffable grace! The sacrifice of your simple life, offered in holocaust through sufferings and mortification of every kind, will be blessed by Jesus and Mary, and its fruit will be a generation of chosen souls. Who will be able to count them?"[8]

A. The Initial Confiding of the Rule

It is in 1853 that Melanie reveals for the first time the Rule she received, she says, at the time of the Apparition;

> I had just heard from Father Sibillat, in 1852[9], that several priests from the Diocese of Grenoble were gathering to form an Order of Missionaries of Our Lady of LaSalette, and that they were going to work on developing a Rule. I immediately told Father Sibillat that the Holy Virgin had provided all that was needed for the religious, and that if he would give me a bit of time, I would quickly write a little something about the Rule.
>
> After I had submitted to him a few articles, he left. A few days later, he returned and told me that Bishop Ginoulhiac took me

to be an egotist, delusional and insane.[10]

On August 14, 1853, Melanie mentions the Rule, as an acknowledged writing, at the end of the Secret requested by Bishop Ginoulhiac. In January 1854, Melanie speaks of this foundation, desired by the Apparition, to the superior from Vienne. But by this time, the Bishop had passed from doubt[11] to rejection.

B. Resistance to the Growth of an English Foundation

From the heart of England, Melanie was valiantly learning the English language, accepting the turn of events with good humor, and giving the latest news to her dear Sisters at Corenc;

> As soon as I arrived here, I was urged to found a convent of LaSalette (I had shown the Rule of the Holy Virgin and was told that the Bishop Grenoble did not believe in it.) A Lady, newly converted, who is quite wealthy, is having a convent built. I am in distress because I am being asked how it should be built, in what place, how many cells, etc. etc. [...] "

> The persons who desire to enter as religious are very rich, and I am in difficulty to receive them, because the house of the Holy Virgin must be founded on humility, poverty, and all the solid virtues. However, many believe they have a vocation but they do not have one. When I perceive a vocation, I receive[12] all, the poor and the rich. Next week I enter the Carmelite convent to learn English more quickly, so as not to make errors when speaking to the postulants. But I would like to be dispensed from being in charge of this foundation. I see often that I am nothing, that I am a heap of dung.[13] I think I have said it all, dear Sister Assistant. I am an unworthy Sister of the Providence of Corenc and I will die a Sister of the Providence unless Our Reverend Mother Superior tells me to stop being one. I will obey her always, however great a sacrifice this may be, but I hope to die a Sister of Providence. I have already been told, that I must become a religious of LaSalette, since I am going to found a convent, and I say to myself: No, no..."[14]

Bishops of Grenoble: Detractors

A) Jacques-Marie-Achille Ginoulhiac: sent Melanie to an English convent
B) Pierre-Antoine-Justin Paulinier: refused alms to the dying Maximin
C) Amand-Joseph Fava: refused the Rule of Mary for the LaSalette Fathers
D) Paul-Emile Henry: took over the LaSalette shrine and the revenue

Detractors of the Secret: Cardinals

A) Cardinal Caterini: in 1880, forbade Melanie to write about the Secret
B) Cardinal Guilbert: 'The Secret is nothing more than a tissue of lies."
C) Cardinal Bianchi: employed by Bishop Fava to spy on Melanie
D) Cardinal Perraud: virtually stole property willed for Mary's Order

Melanie's humor overcame, in peace, the heartbreak she felt by the exclusion from the Providence community. She had the key in her hand, convent, vocations ready to fill the convent and observe the Rule of Our Lady, yet she recused herself. Everything indicates that it was Bishop Ginoulhiac who flatly obstructed the project which had begun so well. His secretary diverted this letter of Melanie[15], which never reached the Sisters at Corenc.

C. The "Sight": a Prophetic Vision of the Apostles of the Last Times

[†Editor: As mentioned in Chapter 4, under Bishop Petagna at Castellammare-di-Stabia, Melanie gave Version 7 of the Secret to be copied by Father Felicien Bliard sometime before the end of January 1870. Father Bliard passed this on to the canon lawyer Father Regis Girard, who published it in France with the blessing of Pius IX. Henceforth, it became generally known that, after the Secret, Our Lady had given Melanie a Rule. "While the Most Holy Virgin was giving me the Rule and speaking about the *Apostles of the Last Times*, I saw an immense plain..." In 1876, at the behest of the same Bishop Petagna, Melanie was asked to respond to the questions of the same Father Bliard, to describe what she had seen and understood about this new religious Order, apart from the text of the Rule which Our Lady had dictated. This vision-within-a-vision came to be known as the "*Vue*" or "*Sight*" to distinguish it from the Apparition itself. There are a handful of extant variations of the 1876 version of the Sight, all very close to the definitive version of 1879. Melanie may have made copies herself, or she was writing from memory. We can only speculate why Father Corteville and Father Laurentin chose to offer the readers a condensed text of the earlier version in their 2002 *Découverte*. Father Corteville was still working on the second half of his doctoral dissertation which would focus on the Rule and would not go to press until 2009. The primary subject of *Découverte* was the Secret, and not the Order of the Mother of God. In 2002 he probably wasn't prepared to present the Sight in a scholarly manner. Our English translation of this massive dissertation is well underway, so we are pleased to offer the reader the definitive 1879 version of the Sight, with the addition of paragraph lettering.]

It was in Italy, after the first publications of the Secret, that Melanie was questioned about the Rule.[16] Father Felicien Bliard received a mandate from Bishop Petagna to question her. On October 3, 1876, Melanie answered him and this was eventually published by Father Émile Combes[17]:

Introduction:

It is quite true that in the Apparition of September 19, 1846 on the Mountain of LaSalette, the Most Holy Virgin manifested to me that She wanted the creation of a new religious Order, which She herself designated under the name *"Apostles of the Last Times."* The proof is in the Rule that She herself gave me, in a strong voice, after giving me the Secret, and which you have had for a long time, and also in the "Sight" of this Order, which I will describe shortly. This Order will include:

1. Priests, who will be the Missionaries of the Holy Virgin and the *Apostles of the Last Times:*
2. Religious, who will depend upon the Missionaries:
3. Laity, engaged in the world but desiring to unite and commit themselves to this Order.

The goal of this new Order is to work for the sanctification of the clergy, for the conversion of sinners and to extend the reign of God over all the earth. The religious are called, like the Missionaries, to work zealously for the good of souls, through prayer and the spiritual and corporal works of mercy. As for the spirit of the Order, this must be the spirit of the first Apostles. The Holy Virgin sufficiently characterized this spirit, both in the Rule that She gave to me, and in her call for *Apostles of the Last Times,* the climax of the Secret.

The apostolates to which this Order will be employed are indicated in the Rule given by the Most Holy Virgin. and in the Sight which I will now make known:

a. While the Most Holy Virgin was giving me the Rule and speaking about the *Apostles of the Last Times*, I saw an immense plain, dotted with small hills. My eyes could see everything. I do not know if I saw with my bodily eyes. It would be closer to the truth if I said that I saw the world beneath me, so that I saw the whole universe and its inhabitants, going about their business, each according to his state in life (not always out of justice, but mainly out of ambition. And by a just chastisement from God, they were at war among themselves).

b. And so, I saw this immense plain with its inhabitants. In some places, men were white, in others, they were the color of wood, or various lighter and darker shades. In other places, I saw men who were almost yellow, the color of light straw with red eyes. In other countries they were as black as coal. I saw countries where the inhabitants were of small build, and others where they were of very large build. And then, I saw that Missionaries and Sisters were in these countries and in every part of the globe.

c. I saw the *Apostles of the Last Times* in their habit. They had a black cassock, not very fine, and snaps instead of buttons, on the cape as well as the cassock. Their hats were rather rough, with well-formed corners. [†Editor: It resembled the attire of the priests of her era. She mentioned a tri-cornered biretta to Fr. Combe.]

d. Their belts were white, of a coarse cloth. The waistband was about as wide as this line [11 cm. or 4"] and the streamers almost reached the bottom of the cassock. On the end of one streamer were these three letters, in red: M. P. J. *(Mourir pour Jésus—To die for Jesus)*. On the other end were these three letters in [sky] blue: E. D. M. *(Enfant de Marie—Child of Mary)*.

e. They all wore quite a large crucifix, which hung from the neck on a thick, black cord. The foot of the Cross tucked into the belt, on the left-hand side. But when they preached or performed some religious function, it hung on the breast.

On the right-hand side of the belt hung a Rosary, and on the Rosary was a Cross without a Christ. I saw that the *Apostles of the Last Times* had white shoes (black when traveling long distances) with a buckle on top. [†Editor: In his biography, Maximin notes that Our Lady wore white shoes with gold buckles.]

f. The religious, who were the first to enter the Order of the Mother of God, were the Sisters of the Providence of Grenoble. I saw two of them with just one lay Sister. They were among the first to wear the habit, having taken first the spirit of the Order, and then the habit, on the day of the Incarnation of the Divine Redeemer. [March 25]

g. I saw that their dress was coarse and black, roughly shaped like a sack, with wide sleeves. Their shoes were white (except on missions) with buckles on top. The belt, the Rosary and the Cross were like those of the Fathers.

h. They did not have a bonnet, but some white material which surrounded their faces. Over this was a black veil which hung quite low at the back. They wore a kind of white cape [i.e., an outdoor hooded mantle, not a choir mantle.]

i. I saw the Missionaries preaching, hearing confessions, assisting the dying, giving retreats to priests, to kings and their courts, to "grands" [e.g., leaders, employers, heads of families], to soldiers, workers, the poor, to children, to all religious, to women and virgins. I saw, in some places, Missionaries at the side of the sick, of the poor, of prisoners, and baptizing children and adults.

j. In other places, I saw *Disciples of the Apostles of the Last Times*. I understood quite clearly that these gentlemen, that I have called the Disciples, were part of the Order. These were unattached men, young people who did not feel themselves called to the priesthood, yet wanted to embrace a Christian life, achieve their salvation by accompanying the Fathers on some of their missions and working with all their might for their own sanctification and for the salvation of souls. They were very holy and very zealous for the glory of God.

k. These Disciples were at the side of the sick who did not wish to confess their sins; and at the side of the poor, the wounded, in attendance at meetings, in prisons, with sects, etc., etc. I even saw some of them eating and drinking with the impious and those who did not wish to hear about God or priests. And these terrestrial angels endeavored, by all imaginable means, to speak to them and lead them to God, and save these poor souls, each one of whom has been redeemed by the Blood of Jesus Christ, who is madly in love with us. (Oh! If I could die not once, but a thousand times a day, to win souls for our good Lord! Oh, love, love!)

l. This "sight" was very clear and precise, and left no doubt in my mind as to what was taking place. I was filled with admiration for the greatness of God, his love for souls, and his holy ingenuity in trying to save them all. And I could see that his love cannot be understood on earth, because it surpasses everything that even the holiest can conceive. Thus, I saw that the Gospel of Jesus Christ was preached in all its purity to the ends of the earth and to all peoples.

m. I saw that the Sisters were fully occupied in all sorts of spiritual and corporal works, and, like the Missionaries, spread across the earth.

n. With them there were women and girls filled with zeal, who helped the religious carry out their works. These widows and girls were persons who did not wish to bind themselves by religious vows, but desired to serve the Good God, to work out their salvation, and to lead a life apart from the world. They were dressed in black, very simply. They wore a pectoral Crucifix, as did the Disciples, but a little smaller than the one the Missionaries wore, and it was not worn on the outside.

o. I saw and understood that the *Apostles of the Last Times* and the Sisters took the three religious vows. In addition, they made a promise to give themselves, and to give to the Most Holy Virgin—for souls in purgatory and for the conversion of sinners—all their prayers, all their penances, in a word, all their meritorious works. The Disciples and the women also made this promise or oblation to the Most Holy Virgin.

p. I saw that the Missionaries lived in community, and that they chanted the Divine Office together in choir. Some of their houses had few members. I saw that the Disciples, who could read, recited the Little Office of the Blessed Virgin in their chapel.

q. I also saw that the Sisters, like the women, recited the Little Office of the Blessed Virgin.

r. I understood, in God, that the *Apostles of the Last Times* should follow in the footsteps of the Apostles of the early Church of Jesus Christ, except that the Superior General should take care to call together, when possible, every year, the members of the Order to the Central House for a ten-day retreat. And I saw that when members of the Order were very far away, the retreat took place in each separate house, or they gathered in the central house of their Province.

s. These retreats had the aim of reinvigorating their fervor and the observance of the Rule.

t. I saw that the Superiors changed. And [the Superiors] sent some members to one of the houses of the Order, established expressly for the care of the infirm and for religious who had lost their early fervor through the influence and contagion of the great ones of the world, and had become slack [*mous*] and lost their charity and zeal. The sick were well-cared for in this house.

u. I saw that our gentle Savior looked down on the workers of this Order with great kindliness, for they were serving the Good God with complete and utter devotion, without a thought for themselves. Being completely detached from the things of this earth, they were entirely in the hands of God's providence, filled with faith and trust in Him.

v. I saw the souls in purgatory as if celebrating the benefits they were receiving from the *Apostles of the Last Times* and the Sisters. And I saw that souls who had been delivered from purgatory, or were still there because they have something to atone for, whichever of them had the power to do so, were interceding very much, thus many conversions were brought about through their prayers. For I saw that God wanted the Missionaries and the Sisters of this Order to place all their prayers, penances and good works in the hands of Mary, their first Superior and Novice Mistress, for the souls in purgatory, and for the conversion of sinners *throughout the world.*

w. I saw and understood that the Good God wanted this Order to fight against all the abuses that lead to the decadence of the clergy and the religious life, and to the ruin of Christian society.[18]

x. *Many religious Orders and Congregations returned to their first fervor, thanks to the care and example of the Fathers, or based themselves on the Order of the Mother of God.* I saw that this Order never, ever received candidates, as Missionaries or as Sisters, whose parents needed other people's charity, or required their son and daughter to assist them. And if the parents of one of the members fell into misery, the Community, out of love for the Fourth Commandment, out of prudence, out of charity, and for the tranquility of its members whose parents were afflicted, would give generously, according to its abilities, to that family. And this was done with great charity, with great joy, and gratitude to God, for having given the Community an opportunity of easing the burden of the followers of Jesus, who gave Himself to us all.

y. I saw that the members of the Order of the Mother of God were making every effort to divest themselves completely of the spirit of the corrupt generation [cf Act 2:40], to advance in the love of God and to acquire the virtues of Our Lord Jesus Christ. They had a very low regard for themselves. They were very united among themselves, for they had neither ambition, nor envy, nor jealousy, desiring in all things only to please their Divine Master, desiring nothing outside of the Heart of Jesus, where they dwelt in varying degrees of closeness, depending on the purity and generosity of their love. This love of Jesus produced in them the fruits of great obedience, profound humility and simplicity, of great mortification, ardent zeal, and perfect abandonment into the hands of the Divine Master.

z. I saw that this Order was like the hearth of all apostolates,* as a perpetual altar of unceasing prayer for the manifold needs of holy Church, for lukewarm souls and for the conversion of sinners everywhere.[19] [*Editor: *"foyer de toutes les oeuvres"* can be equally translated "home of all religious Orders." Melanie often interchanged *ordre* and *oeuvre* because she saw the "Order" of the Mother of God as Mary's own "work."]

Melanie concludes:

Yes, despite my unworthiness, I believe I have received a mission for the Order in question. I have the desire of all my heart for the glory of God and the good of souls. I have the desire for the cause of the urgent needs of the whole society. I have the desire because it is necessary to reanimate a priestly spirit in the clergy. I am not able to assure others that that which drives me to establish this foundation is of the Spirit of God. That is for my superiors to judge. What I know for certain, is that I, in the depths of myself, feel strongly compelled, and persuaded that it is the good God who wants this Order, so useful for the Church and for the good of souls. But if an authority, a superior, a confessor tells

> me to remain at peace and not to think of it, ah! that would be an act of charity toward me, because I feel as if crushed (though gladly) by the grandeur and sublimity of the weight of this *ark of salvation* for the whole world. However, I would believe myself to be sinning, that is, failing gravely in fidelity and obedience to God, if I set aside the foundation, and did not make every effort to have it established.
>
> I recently sought from His Excellency, the Bishop of Castellammare, the authorization to work without further delay toward the foundation of this Order, because everything in the world seems to tell me that the moment has arrived, so I feel myself powerfully compelled to work on it without delay. I feel as though driven in an irresistible manner to desire this Order, and it seems to me that I always hear an interior voice that is asking me for combatants of Jesus Christ and of his doctrine.

The complete Rule was submitted to the Ordinary of Castellammare. He authorized its observance:

> Bishop Petagna of Castellammare, believes with all the ardor of his soul, that the Rule which I presented to him on November 15, 1876 came from the Most Holy Virgin. It's for that reason that His Excellency permits me, with all his heart, to begin the foundation of this new Order in his diocese. I can show the permission signed by his hand, which I still have, in case of doubt.[20] [†Editor: November 15th is the Feast of All Carmelite Souls.]

D. Encouragement in Rome, Opposition in France

Bishop Fava, the third bishop after the Apparition, took his seat at Grenoble manifesting favorable sentiments toward it. In his Pastoral *Letter for the Thirtieth Anniversary of the Apparition*, he presented a good impression of the seers and compared them to the Christmas shepherds, the first heralds of the good news:

> These two little ones, unconcerned with their dignity as apostles, were descending with their herd to the next village. [...] When the Angels announced the Gospel, that is to say, the Good

News, did they not speak to shepherds in the fields of Judea? This is the ordinary way of the Almighty. "He chooses the weak of the world to confound the strong." *Infirma mundi eligit Deus ut confundat fortes* (1Cor 1:27). This great God deigns once again by this means to be served so that we may be able to glorify Jesus and his Mother.

Our goal, our very dear brothers, is to awaken more and more your faith, hope and charity in recalling to your attention the instructions given at LaSalette by the Holy Virgin in that discourse which one could call: her sermon on the mount. It seems to us, in effect, that She presented herself there as Apostle and Queen of Apostles.[21]

[Quick Background: In the summer or autumn of 1876 Melanie felt that the Order should begin. She presented the Rule and the *Sight* to Bishop Petagna on November 15th, who had it examined by two Bishops: himself and Zola, and by two theologians: one of whom was Don Caraso, secretary of Cardinal Sforza of Naples. As the ordinary of his territory, Petagna authorized Melanie and Mother Presentation, as well as a few priests (Father Fusco, and others whose names we don't know) to begin to follow the Rule of the Mother of God at Castellammare. Meanwhile, one of Bishop Petagna's first steps was to write to Bishop Fava, the new Bishop of Grenoble [installed one year previously Nov. 18, 1875] and suggest that the Order of the Mother of God be formally started at LaSalette. Instead, Fava held the first general chapter of the small community of Diocesan Missionaries which Bishop DeBruillard had founded at LaSalette. His successor, Bishop Ginoulhiac, had not been able to decide whether to endow them with a rule. Father Sibillat conveyed to him several articles of Melanie's Rule but this was rejected. He and Father Bossan resigned in 1858. The Missionaries on the mountain were divided on this essential question. The Father Superior, Father Giraud resigned also, reducing the number to about a dozen men. Bishop Fava took the matter into his own hands. He drew up himself the plans for its Constitutions, and for an Apostolic College to be associated with the Institute of Missionaries. In October 1878, Father Fusco read in a newspaper the intention of Bishop Fava to come to Rome to have his rule approved for the Fathers and Sisters of LaSalette, as well as to seek the title of Basilica for the shrine and to commission a new statue. Melanie decided that she should hasten to send a copy of the Rule of the Mother of God to the Holy Father himself. Father Fusco took it to Rome. (cf MC vol. 2, and Gouin *Shepherdess*)]

Pope Leo XIII, having received the Rule proposed, summoned Melanie to Rome to take part in the deliberations. A "congress" was organized, between Melanie and Bishop Fava, at the Sacred Congregation of Bishops and Regulars. Cardinal Ferrieri offered the Bishop the Rule that Melanie received, but Fava refused it, straightaway, before even reading it (!) He explained himself in his letter to Monsignor Bianchi, secretary at this "Congress" [which had convened for this purpose], dated November 26, 1878:

> I, Bishop Fava of Grenoble, have the honor of revealing to the Sacred Congregation of Bishops and Regulars, that I received, about two years ago [1876], a letter from the current Bishop of Castellammare, which spoke to me of a religious Order to be founded, called the Order of the *Apostles of the Last Times.*
>
> I responded to His Excellency [Bishop Petagna] that this appellation, of which I am unfamiliar, is based upon an Apparition, and which must be referred to the Holy Father. His Excellency wanted me to consider proceeding to found the Order [at LaSalette], then consult Rome later [†Editor: the normal canonical procedure is for a bishop to test a community in its first stages]. I responded to the priest, who had transmitted this opinion of Bishop Petagna, that I did not share his opinion and that I could not undertake something in that manner, until the Sacred Congregation itself had decided this question.
>
> Arriving in Rome, I learned that the Bishop of Castellammare had written to the Sacred Congregation of Bishops and Regulars,

and that it was a question of founding at Rome, or at least in Italy, the said religious Order, according to a Rule that Melanie is said to have received from the Holy Virgin and had submitted to the Bishop [Petagna] of Castellammare. He examined it and then had it examined by Abbot Zola, now Bishop of Ugento, and two theologians, one of whom was Don Caraso, Canon and Secretary of the Archbishop of Naples. No one raised any doubt about the testimony of Melanie, and so the Rule was recognized as worthy of the origins attributed to it.

I object to the judgment of this venerable Congress, with all due respect, and I continue to defer the cause of this particular case to the decision of the Sacred Congregation. What I promise to do is to study the said Rule if it is transmitted to me, to take advantage of what is contained therein to draft the Constitutions of the Fathers and Religious of LaSalette, whose Constitutions are being reviewed so as to be presented for the approval of the Sacred Congregation.

This conclusion is surprising. The Bishop of Grenoble:

- ignores the Rule of Melanie
- but then he asks that it be transmitted to him
- yet instead of engaging in a proper examination of the Rule, he objects to its authenticity.
- nevertheless, he promises to be inspired by it(!)[22]

But this concession will never be followed through. Bishop Fava aligned with the policy of Bishop Ginoulhiac, who had blocked the English foundation in mid-course. He insinuates that the existence of the community of Castellammare, founded around Melanie, is a source of discord:

> Furthermore, I ask that, if the religious Order in question, for both men and women, were to be founded in Italy, it would be good to reach an agreement with me so that this foundation, which has already been authorized, they say, by the Bishop of Castellammare in his diocese, would not harm either the good

or the peace.[23]

[From the notebook of Mother Saint-John: The whole Congress was favorable to the Apparition and the Rule, and decided that it should be given to all the Religious of LaSalette to put to the test. Bishop Fava, irritated by this decision, rose up, and said: "When the Church proves to me that it came from heaven, I will accept it, but not before."... All this was reported to the Pope.... The Holy Father replied, "The Church has never done so, and cannot make a dogmatic decree on an Apparition. If I were to be asked to do this even for Loretto, in which I have so much faith and trust, I could not grant it. Apparitions and miracles are not the domain of the Faith and cannot be imposed." (cf MC vol. 2, and Gouin *Shepherdess*)]

Five days later on December 3, 1878, Leo XIII received Melanie in a private audience. She left this written account:

It was, I believe, Tuesday the 3rd of December 1878, that I had the grace of an audience with Pope Leo XIII. The Holy Father greeted me with kindness and spoke to me in very good French.

- [Pope Leo XIII] "Very well! You will leave right away for the mountain of LaSalette, with the Rule of the Most Holy Virgin, and you will have it observed by the priests and the Sisters.

  These words of the Holy Father confirmed my suspicion that he had not yet learned of what took place at the "Congress." I had gathered this when speaking to his Eminence, Cardinal Guidi, on my way to the audience.

— [Melanie] Who am I, most Holy Father, to dare to command that your orders be obeyed?

- [Pope Leo XIII] But yes, I tell you, you will leave with the Bishop of Grenoble and you will have the Rule of the Holy Virgin observed.

— [Melanie] Most Holy Father, permit me to tell you that for a long time these priests and Sisters have led a more than secular life, and it will be very difficult for them to comply with a Rule of humility and self-sacrifice. It seems to me that it would be easier to found an institution with lay persons of good will, rather than these religious on the mountain who are far from being good Christians.

- [Pope Leo XIII] Listen. You are going to go up there with the Rule of the Holy Virgin, which you will make known to them. And those who do not wish to observe it will be sent by the Bishop to another parish.

— [Melanie] Very well, Holy Father.

- [Pope Leo XIII] So you will leave right away. However, because it is usually the case when the Good Lord deigns to give a Rule for religious life, He gives, He communicates to the same person the spirit in which the Rule must be observed. This is why you must write it down [i.e., Constitutions] when you arrive in Grenoble. So when you arrive at the mountain of LaSalette you must send [your text] to me."

— [Melanie] Oh! Most Holy Father, do not send me to Grenoble under Bishop Fava, for I will not have freedom of action."

- [Pope Leo XIII] How, how so?

— [Melanie] Bishop Fava would command me to write what he desires, not what the Holy Spirit desires. [p.18]

- [Pope Leo XIII] No, no. You will go alone into a room and write. When you have written a few pages, you will send them to me.

— [Melanie] Most Holy Father, please forgive me if I show you my difficulties. When I have written two pages, the Bishop of Grenoble will demand that I hand them to him, and, under the pretext of improving them he will change everything, and order me to copy down his explanations on the way to practice the Rule of the Holy Virgin.

- [Pope Leo XIII] Oh, surely not! This is what you will do.

When you have filled a page, you will put it in an envelope yourself and seal it firmly, and you will put my address on it like this: "His Holiness Pope Leo XIII, who is myself (sic). (As he said this, he put his hand on his chest.)

— [Melanie] Most Holy Father, please forgive me if I dare to express the revulsion I feel within myself at the thought of writing under the authority of the Bishop of Grenoble. His Excellency will break the seal on my letter, change what I have written, and have his version copied out by another person. It will not be what I have written which will come into the hands of your Holiness.

- [Pope Leo XIII] Oh, surely not! The Bishop of Grenoble would not do such a thing!

— [Melanie] Most Holy Father, I know his ways through experience. The old serpent never sleeps.

- [Pope Leo XIII] So what is to be done?

— [Melanie] Send me, Most Holy Father, to any other country, anywhere that I am not under the Bishop of Grenoble.

- [Pope Leo XIII] But what to do? I have given orders that you are to go to the Mountain of LaSalette, to have the priests and nuns observe the Rule which the Blessed Virgin has given you, and that before going up, you would write the Constitutions that you will send me! And you know that, when the Pope has given an order, he cannot go back on it.

— [Melanie] Most Holy Father, Our Lord has entrusted you with all power on earth to govern his Church. The earth is spacious to come and go. [p 19]

[Variant in the 1900 "Combe" edition: "Most Holy Father, forgive me if I add that you are the head of God's Church, you have the keys to lock and to unlock. Our Lord Jesus Christ stated categorically to his disciples that He would not go to Jerusalem for the Passover Feast. He did go, most Holy Father.]

- [Pope Leo XIII] Listen. Pray well tonight, and tomorrow I will give you my decision.
- [Melanie] Yes Holy Father. In the waiting room there is a priest and a companion whom the holy Bishop of Castellammare assigned to me for this journey. They would like the favor of your blessing.

Immediately, the Papal Chamberlain, looked annoyed and said a couple of words to the Holy Father which seemed to be a refusal. Having understood, Melanie repeated her request. Finally, the Holy Father said to let them enter.[24]

[†Editor: If this conversation displays some naivete on the part of Pope Leo, he had only been elected the previous February. He had been a supporter of papal infallibility in the First Vatican Council, and had not yet learned firsthand the practical limitations of this power.]

In the end, the decision of the Holy Father was that Melanie should stay in Rome with the Salesians [i.e., the Visitation Nuns founded by St. Francis DeSales] on the Palatine Hill, while she drew up the Constitutions to specify how the Rule would be implemented. Melanie edified the community that received her, while enduring the opposition of Bishop Fava. So that she would not disturb him any longer, it was Fava who obtained that she would be confined in the cloister, explained Father Carra, one of his secretaries.[25]

Melanie finished writing the Constitutions on January 5, 1879. The Dominican Cardinal, Filippo Maria Guidi, reviewed them, then submitted them to a consultant [Father Daum] from the Sacred Congregation of Bishops and Regulars, at the same time that the Constitutions [for the LaSalette Fathers] were presented by Bishop Fava, having been drafted, not by Fava, but by a Vicar General.

The Roman consultor, Father Daum of the French Seminary, was not very favorable to the seer of LaSalette. The formula of the *Apostles of the Last Times*, dear to St. Louis-Mary DeMontfort, was seen by him as schismatic; the *pure love of God* was too ambitious an ideal... The Constitutions, written by Melanie at the request of the Pope, were attributed to the Virgin by Father Daum, contained too many "novelties" he thought. But Melanie, who was not listened to, only attributed the brief Rule to the Virgin; the rest was penned by herself. The consultor explained, however, that there would be no difficulty in adopting certain points from the Rule of Melanie, and concluded that it could be tested by other Bishops [i.e., than Grenoble]. The Sacred Congregation concurred with his conclusions.

As for the Missionaries of LaSalette, on May 27, 1879, their Constitutions received the customary "Decree of Praise." The religious [on the Mountain of LaSalette] were encouraged to follow the Constitutions, presented by the Bishop of Grenoble, on condition that they remove all reference to the Apparition of LaSalette (!!!) The Sacred Congregation transmitted Melanie's Rule to Bishop Fava, hoping to *inspire* him. [Father Gouin remarked that there was a certain Roman dilatoriness of deliberately delaying the process. Only in 1909 in the pontificate of Pius X were their Constitutions approved for a ten-year period, and definitively approved in 1929. - The directive also resulted in the Congregation's title being changed from Missionaries of *Our Lady of LaSalette* to simply Missionaries of LaSalette, but the earlier title was eventually regained in 1934.]

As for the suffering seer, on May 7, 1879, she had been authorized by Leo XIII to return to Castellammare. Bishop Petagna was dead and buried. After Petagna's death, the foundation begun in the rented Ruffo Villa didn't benefit from any further support of his successor and had to disband. Despite the support of Leo XIII, it was an evident setback.

The Irresistible Radiance of the Rule

Melanie's project, buried like the grain of wheat that dies (Jn 12:24), sprouted after the initial setback.

Father Bernard, Missionary of LaSalette, Apostolic Prefect Emeritus of Norway, who visited Melanie in 1886 and 1888, rallied for her

Rule:

> The Rule given by the Mother of God is a framework of incorruptible wood and vivified by a divine breath, for the constitutional body of the of the apostolic Missionaries, who are desired and called by the heavenly Messenger, and against which gnawing human worms will not be able to puncture or perforate until the end of time.[26]

In 1895, Father Berlioz, former Superior of LaSalette, invites priests and laity to fulfill the desire of Father DeMontfort:

> In this supreme hour in which we are living, namely the approach of the *Last Times*, the Mother of the Apostles appeals to the priestly tribe. She wants to multiply the number of true apostles, *supra modum apostolic* [apostles beyond measure]. She calls them close to her, to the foot of the Cross; since one must return to the source to be steeped in primordial perfection. Saint Grignion DeMontfort had foreseen this marvelous intervention of the Mother of God in the *Last Times*, breathing life into the apostles who, as apostolic giants would in some manner prepare the mission of Enoch and Elijah, and share it in their time.

[†Editor: Leo XIII beatified DeMontfort in 1888. The Pope chose the date of the 50th anniversary of his own priestly ordination to celebrate his Golden Jubilee with the beatification of this Marian priest whom he admired.]

> We think that the heavenly messenger is thus fashioning an apostolic Order of great perfection, of which She must direct and guide its formation, protect its existence, assure its propagation and longevity. It's the Queen of the Apostles who has appeared to reveal her desire and to establish her Order. In this apostolic role, the Queen of Heaven is actively involved in the Christian life. [...]

> Here is, in our view, the signaling of a vast three-tiered Order of penance and reparation, united in a life of immolation, of the desert and of apostleship, to help and to serve, gathering the

entire Christian people, without distinction of class or nationality, into the mystical tradition of these holy observances: *You will pass this on to all my people.*

Here is what we believe needs to be understood from the heavenly vision. It is that which, by the grace of God and the virtues of Mary, will give to the Christian world a new strength to oppose evil with a powerful barrier.... we ask through Mary the realization of all the designs of her mercy for us. We hope for chosen souls to be docile to her and to grace. God loves prompt and eager obedience. [...] It's been half a century that the Holy Virgin has been waiting for this, and She calls to us with tears: *"For how long a time I have suffered for the rest of you."*[27]

The Blessed Giagomo [Jacques, James] Cusmano, from Palermo, founder of congregations today comprising 489 Sisters and 125 male religious, adopted secretly, about the year 1880, the "Rule of the Mother of God." But his early death impeded him from uniting the congregations under the patronage of LaSalette.[28]

In 1897, while Melanie assisted him at Messina, Father Annibale DiFrancia [canonized 1989], founded the "Rogationists." Their zeal for the cause of vocations must prepare the coming of the *Apostles of the Last Times* (of which he shared the expectation with Father Jordan, founder of the Salvatorians). Father Annibale's congregations now include 315 male religious and 650 Sisters, who name Melanie as the co-foundress.

Melanie had much love for the fledgling community of religious called Daughters of the *Divine Zeal of the Heart of Jesus*, [...] in particular for the mission to which they were consecrated by a fourth vow, to pray every day for good laborers in the Holy Church, in response to the commandment of Our Lord Jesus Christ: *Rogate ergo Dominum messis* [Pray to the Lord of the harvest that He send workers. Lk 10:2]. The symbol that they wore on their breast is the Sacred Heart with precisely those words *"Rogate...* Melanie saw in this prayer the means to stimulate the *Apostles of the Last Times*. One day she said to me: "I belong to your congregation" and she was wearing on her heart, under her habit, this holy emblem.[29]

On July 5, 1890, Henriette Deluy-Fabry (Mother Saint-Joseph), foundress of the Sisters of Reparation of Our Lady of LaSalette, began a new foundation with the Rule of Melanie. Harassed by critics, the new congregation spread itself nevertheless to the Somme, in Belgium, then to Anjou [western France] The whole Maritain family, and Louis Massignon, were members of its Third Order. But at the time of the Second World War, a decision of the bishop closed the house of Saint Lambert-du-Lattay [in the Anjou] and dispersed the community of about 20 Sisters. Writing to a friend of this work, Father Laurent, the rector of the LaSalette shrine at the dawn of the centenary, wrote:

> For our dear LaSalette, the apparent contradictions that would oppose Missionaries, such as ourselves [on the mountain], with the Missionaries of the Mother of God, hardly matter. There is only what Providence has willed, and that is to console this good Mother who is weeping, by devoting ourselves to her. There will never be enough of us for this task.[30]

SPIRIT AND CHARACTER OF THE RULE

A. THE INSPIRATION

Melanie refers constantly to the Order and its spirit, to a design of Mary that she was commissioned to make known:

> This Order must have the spirit of the first Apostles. The Holy Virgin sufficiently characterized this spirit, both in the Rule that She gave me, and in the call to the *Apostles of the Last Times* which concludes the Secret.[31]

Father Annibale DiFrancia highlighted that inspired character in these lines:

> The words contained in the Secret of Melanie, and by which the Most Holy Virgin announced the foundation of this great

religious Order, in truth, have nothing from our humanity. They breathe a divine breath. They are simplicity situated in harmony with the sublime!³²

He saw in the Order an antidote to the rise of the Antichrist and his disciples, in this "call" of the Virgin (Secret, versions 7 and 8):

> [30] *I address an urgent call to the earth;*
>
> *I call the true disciples of the living God who reigns in heaven;*
>
> *I call the true imitators of Christ made Man, the only and true Savior of men;*
>
> *I call my children, my true devotees, those who have offered themselves to me so that I may lead them to my divine Son, those whom I carry in my arms, so to speak, those who have lived by my spirit;*
>
> *Finally, I call the Apostles of the Last Times, the faithful disciples of Jesus Christ, who have lived in contempt for the world and of themselves, in poverty and humility, in contempt and in silence, in prayer and in mortification, in chastity and in union with God, in suffering and unknown to the world.*

The call addresses itself to all those who are engaged by a three-fold relationship of being members: first with "God, living and reigning in heaven," secondly with "Christ made man³³, the only Savior," and finally with Mary, the path leading to Christ in spirit and in life. But they will not be *"Apostles of the Last Times"* unless they have matured in this relationship of daily consecrated life. The triple relationship that is proposed is the entrance into the Trinitarian life.

Father Annibale especially highlighted their "humility," according to the self-emptying of Christ (Col. 2:7) and the virtues of the hidden life, its preaching and its cross. That which is reflected in the three successive proposals of the Apparition:

> The three poses of the Holy Virgin in her Apparition correspond symbolically to the three degrees or ascents of the soul toward perfect charity, indicated by the doctors who have taught mystical theology. These three degrees, or ages, are called the purgative way, the illuminative way and the unitive way, corresponding

to the three theological virtues (faith, hope, love).³⁴

In the first stage, the soul weeps with Mary over sin, choosing to serve the only true God "living in the heavens," and no longer in the errors of this world (Jn 17:14). He burns his idols, meditating on the mystery of God.

The second stage is that of listening to and imitating Christ, the stage of doctrine and of the virtues.

Finally, *the third stage* is the New Pentecost of the Spirit, inseparable from Mary to whom one gives oneself to be carried to her Son. From thence springs forth the apostolic life of the *Apostles of the Last Times* and the new Evangelization.

The response to the three calls of Mary will be a triple confession of love, following the example of the triple questioning of Jesus to Peter at the moment of entrusting him with his flock (Jn 21:15-17).

The Rule recorded by Melanie makes explicit the pedagogy of this design. Many of its articles have a tri-part structure. The Trinity is contained clearly enough in the above three articles. The term *Apostle of the Last Times* appears further on, embedded in an "ordinary" life. The Rule illustrates the virtues indicated in the Secret and previously enumerated by Saint Vincent Ferrer:

> They will be poor, simple, gentle, humble, vile to their own eyes; they will love one another with an ardent charity.³⁵

B. REVIVAL OF THE GOSPEL, AND OF THE PRIMITIVE CHURCH

Here then is the Rule that Melanie received on September 19, 1846, confident that Our Lady was assisting her memory as with the rest. She felt herself compelled by this last point, by the final words of Our Lady: *You will pass this on to all my people.*

Like many of the Rules inspired through the ages, this one is a return to the simple and profound source of the Gospel. It's spirituality proceeds from love, beginning there with the rest developing the form of religious life. It all returns to the primitive community of Jerusalem so well described in the Acts of the Apostles:

> The company of believers were of one heart and soul, and... they had everything in common. (Acts 4:32)

All proceeds from the interior: the true life in God which comes from God alone. This total gift is expressed in particular through adoration of the Eucharist, continuous during three months of the year, accompanied with fasting, in a complete, fraternal and communal gift, which inspires the *"Apostles of the Last Times* with a sense of urgent evangelization."

C. SIMPLICITY

The Rule is consistently simple, evangelical, and attentive to the human dimension. If it insists on penance, it's with a magnanimity of spirit and great care of the body as of the soul, without forgetting sufficient nutrition for one and the other. This conciseness explains why Leo XIII invited Melanie to write some Constitutions, to specify without misrepresentation the mode of life, with the assistance of the Sacred Congregation of Bishops and Regulars.

The lucid text of the Rule has not ceased to inspire the foundation of previous and new communities. It reflects the life of the Virgin Mary, who conserved, meditated upon and grasped in her heart the words and actions of Christ (cf Lk 2:19,51).

> Is it a Rule of so sublime a simplicity? One who knows how to read it is penetrated by religious amazement. It represents precision and depth united with discretion. There is in it a logic, a marvelous plan that links the thirty-three articles.[36]

Melanie, like Maximin, considered the words of the Virgin, although limited by human vocabulary, as "music for the soul," at the same time a bittersweet food, and a healing balm for sinners.

D. THE ORDER OF THE MOTHER OF GOD AND ITS DEVELOPMENT

The Rule develops harmoniously in three steps:

The first part begins with the new commandment of love revealed by Christ, which is to be lived in the community framework, according to the three universal precepts [i.e., love of God, neighbor, and self] (Art. 1-3) and the three evangelical counsels (4-7). They are connected by a perfect fraternal unity, which constitutes not so much a fourth vow as it is the result and the witnessing of the three counsels well-lived.

The second part (9-18) invites superiors and members to the same attentive love, to be inspired by the necessary virtues of a communal and apostolic life, and always living in union with God, centered on the Eucharist.

The third part (20-25) concerns the formation of the members, and the apostolic objectives, in the same context of communal unity.

The final articles (16-33) specify the essentials of daily life: community life (26), unity of hearts in prayer, as in the food taken in common, care of the sick (28). The second-to-last article suggests the local example where Melanie was formed in religious life: "Daily Office like the Sisters of Corenc" (32). The Rule ends on the Cross, which Melanie had carried [in her life] and brought with her to the Apparition of September 19, 1846, and that all the members of the Community are to carry with the crucified Christ, and Mary crucified in spirit by her very suffering, by and for our sins.

Here we present the text that was in Melanie's handwriting, photographed at the Archives of the Sacred Congregation of Religious (ENS, funds de l'abbé Gouin) studied by Dom Dennis Huerre, Abbot of Sainte-Marie-de-la Pierre-qui-Vire 1952-1978, and published his approval.

Nihil obstat: Abbey of Sainte-Marie de la Pierre-qui-Vire, August 22, 1952. Dom Denis Huerre, Abbot.

Imprimatur. Diocese of Sens, on the Feast of Christ the King, October 26, 1952. Frédéric Lamy, Archbishop.

The titles of the works are cited in a simplified manner with references to the Gospel. To illustrate the text or explain certain expressions, the relevant citations are given in the notes. The inspired Rule of Life, delivered to Melanie, recapitulates in effect the spiritual doctrine of the Church.

The Authentic Text of the Rule

Melanie, what I am going to tell you will not be a secret. This is the Rule that you will make my daughters, who will be here when the Rule will be approved by the superiors, follow exactly. My Missionaries will follow the same Rule.

1. The members of this Order of the Mother of God will love God above all things and their neighbor as themselves for the pure love of God.[37]

2. The spirit of this Order is none other than the spirit of Jesus Christ in Himself, and the spirit of Jesus in souls.[38] [†Editor: in contrast to the "spirit of the corrupt generation" in Act 2:40, see the Sight par. y]

3. The members of this Order will apply themselves to study Jesus Christ and to imitate Him, and the more they know Jesus, the more they will humble themselves in the sight of their nothingness, of their weakness, and their incapacity without divine grace, for doing real good in souls.[39]

4. They will be perfectly obedient in everything and everywhere.[40]

5. Each of them will preserve themselves in great chastity of body and spirit, that Jesus Christ may make his abode in them.[41]

6. The members of this Order will have only one heart and one soul in the love of Jesus Christ.[42]

7. They will not have anything of their own as their own, but everything must be held in common, without having any ambition for the least transient thing. I want my children to be naked, deprived of all things.[43]

8. They will have a great, unbounded charity. They will bear the suffering of everyone, following the example of their Divine Master, and they will not make anyone suffer.[44]

9. The members of the Order will obey their superiors and they will render them the honor and respect which are due to them, with great simplicity of heart.[45]

10. The superioress will be vigilant with sweetness to see that the Rule is obeyed. From time to time, she will discuss matters with the Missionary Father who will have the care of your souls, that she may be assisted in governing the house well. She will be the humblest, and more severe with herself than with others. She will correct the faults of her Daughters with great sweetness and prudence. She will always raise her soul to God before making a correction.[46]

11. There will be exposition of the Blessed Sacrament, day and night in the chapel during the months of September, February and May, where the members of the Order will delight themselves in happy hours, when charity or the salvation of souls doesn't detain them elsewhere.[47]

12. They will lead a very interior life, although laborious, uniting the contemplative life to the active. They will sacrifice themselves, and all will make themselves victims of Jesus and Jesus crucified.[48]

13. Every day they will receive the Bread of Life with true piety. You will, however, be able to withhold Communion from some members when you see that they are not following in the steps of Jesus crucified.[49]

14. In addition to the fasting commanded by the Church, they will also keep the months of September, February and May in fasting. They will make use of some instruments of penance. Those who are too feeble and unable to do works of expiation will offer, with humility and sweetness, their infirmity to Jesus Christ.[50]

15. They will fast every Friday and will do some penance. All these works will be offered for the souls in purgatory, on behalf of the conversion of sinners, and for their own advancement in the love of God.[51]

16. The members of the Order will act with great humility and great sweetness towards the laity. They will receive them with great kindness. Those who will be the most humble will have

the first place in the Heart of Jesus, as well as in mine.[52]

17. The members will have only one heart and one soul: no one will hold fast to his own will.[53]

18. They will be of an angelic purity; they will observe a great modesty everywhere and in everything.[54]

19. All will guard a great silence, carefully avoiding useless conversations with strangers.[55]

20. Subjects who will want to be received will be of a very sincere disposition to give themselves entirely to God, and to sacrifice themselves for his love. They will attach themselves well to obedience, which will conduct them to heaven.[56]

21. They will only be admitted among the postulants after having completed a retreat of twelve days, during which they will make a general confession to the Missionary Father, the confessor of the community. If they are disposed to labor with all their strength to sanctify themselves and to acquire the virtues which are proper to victims who desire to immolate themselves, every day for the God of heaven and earth, they will be received into the novitiate. After three months they will be given the habit of the Order, and they will remember well that they have only been admitted to the house of the Mother of God to labor towards their sanctification through prayer, penance and all the works concerning the glory of God and the salvation of souls.[57]

22. My Missionaries will be the Apostles of the Last Times, preaching the Gospel of Jesus Christ in all its purity throughout the earth.[58]

23. They will have an indefatigable zeal: they will preach the reform of hearts, penance and the observance of the law of God. They will preach on the necessity of prayer, on contempt of the things of the earth, on death, judgment, heaven and hell, on the life, death and resurrection of Jesus Christ. They will fortify souls in the Faith so that when the devil will come, a great number of people may not be deceived.[59]

24. New subjects will be well-formed in Christian virtues and in the practice of humility, charity, obedience, renunciation and sweetness.[60]

25. The novitiate will last six years. Those who will have given proof of solid virtues and who will want to be counted among the number of the combatants of Jesus Christ in this Order, will beseech this grace from the superioress on their knees. After you will have made them acknowledge their obligations to the Rule which I am giving you, and if they promise you to observe it faithfully, you will receive them.[61]

26. Prayer will be made in common in the chapel, at a suitable and set time.[62]

27. They will eat in common, in the refectory, that which will be necessary to sustain life and labor for the glory of God. At the same time the body is given what it needs, the soul will be fortified by holy reading which will take place during the meal.[63]

28. You will have the greatest care for infirm and sick members.[64]

29. If one member offends another by word or some other act, this one is to repair the fault as soon as possible.[65]

30. All members of this Order are to genuflect each time they pass before the tabernacle where Jesus Christ is present.[66]

31. Each time the subjects encounter one another, one will say: "May Jesus be loved by all hearts!" The other will answer: "Amen!"[67]

   [†Editor: "May Jesus *and Mary* be known and loved by all hearts! This is always my first cry when I wake up." Letter of Melanie written in 1853 for an article for the pilgrims. Refer to Documents: Melanie II Sec 4]

32. The Sisters are to pray the Office as the religious of Correnc near Grenoble. The Chapters and other practices will be made in a similar manner.[68]

33. All the members will wear a Cross like mine.[69] Observe well my Rule!

O quam bonum, et quam jucundum habitare in hoc corde!
O how good and how delightful to dwell in this heart!
Holy card painted by Melanie of LaSalette
Reconstruction of poorly preserved photograph

CONCLUSION

Following the discoveries of Michel Corteville of essential documents in the archives of the Vatican and elsewhere, the present work has tried to shed light on the principal questions and previously unresolved polemics. Let us briefly review the results.

Insight on the Secrets

It was over the Secret of LaSalette where the shadows fell more heavily. In the absence of the first two official documents, certified by the Bishop of Grenoble and transmitted to Pope Pius IX, they have been discussed only by hypothesis and conjecture. It was these very documents and the encouragements of the investigators from Grenoble, from the Pope and from his collaborators, that caused Bishop DeBruillard to recognize the Apparition on its fifth anniversary, September 19, 1851. And it was Pope Pius IX himself who encouraged Bishop Ginoulhiac, DeBruillard's successor, to confirm the authenticity, by refuting the criticisms of one of his protesting priests. But then this very bishop, more a friend of the government than the seers, launched an enduring campaign of criticism to undermine the credibility of the seers, in spite of the mission they received from the Virgin: *You will pass this on to all my people!*

A sizeable current of theological reflection (priests, bishops, cardinals), academic (Maritain) or popular, had reacted against criticism of the Apparition from which developed a serious polemic, that was eventually neutralized by a decree of the Holy See on December 21, 1915 which forbade, until Conciliar reforms, to *publicly discuss* the Secret [†Editor: that is, to publish commentaries, but it was never forbidden to publish the Secret.] The opening of the archives of the Sacred Congregation of the Doctrine of the Faith *de facto* marked the end of this constrained silence.

NEW INSIGHTS ON THE SEERS

Bishop Ginoulhiac's reluctance hardened because of the revelation of the Secrets that he had requested of the seers, which announced the fall of Napoleon III, the man who had advocated his promotion to the episcopate against the opinion of the pontifical Secretary of State, who was fearful of his Gallicanism. Bishop Ginoulhiac was torn between the opposing influences of the Emperor and the Pope. There was only one politically correct solution, namely, to dissociate the seers and their Secrets from the Apparition and the Pilgrimage, of which the fruits had to be cultivated according to the formal approval of Bishop DeBruillard of the Apparition with the encouragement of Rome.

A. MELANIE

The Countess Pauline DeNicolay, pseudo-mystic, warmly recommended to the Bishop by the Superior of the Sanctuary, came to his aid:

> Poor Melanie [...] there is in her some delusion and sometimes alas, worse than delusion. [...] *Her mission finished when yours began.*

Supported by several other persons, Bishop Ginoulhiac appropriated this idea in his anniversary sermon on September 19, 1855:

> The mission of the shepherds is *finished*, that of the Church is beginning.

It was said that Melanie was influenced by some mystico-political groups. This was not true for Melanie, but rather these words applied to the influence of the Countess on the Bishop. "Inspired" to denounce Melanie for the purpose of taking her place at LaSalette, the Countess chimed in with Melanie's detractors, providing a formula (literally) to resolve the antagonism between the religious and the political spheres, thus saving the pilgrimages by abandoning the seers. The spiritual authority in the name of whom she wished to impose herself, namely, the Patriarch of Jerusalem, Bishop Gori, disqualified her in a letter:

> She was a capricious lady, well known to me, who knew not how to endure any inconvenience. She was a cross to her servants, whom she continually tormented in diverse ways. After having served her for some time, they felt compelled to leave, bitter and afflicted from maltreatment. She had a tongue that did not spare persons in the highest positions of the ecclesiastical hierarchy, and I am a witness to that. Her stigmata (which, according to her canonizers, lasted until the death of the late Bonaventure of Solero, formerly the Father Guardian of the Franciscan Order), were made of gum arabic, as it was recounted to me by her servant, Angelina.

Melanie was progressively and definitively discarded: from LaSalette she was sent to England, tolerated at Marseille, then exiled to Italy where, thanks to the confidence of Bishop Petagna of Castellammare, she finally found some stability in her peregrinations and received the esteem of several Italian bishops, of Pope Leo XIII and some founders destined for beatification: Annibale Maria DiFrancia, Giagomo [Jacques, James] Cusmano, as well as other "Servants of God."

Melanie, advanced in the spiritual life (in a manner analogous to the seer Bernadette of Lourdes). She received the stigmata in childhood, and was consecrated to Mary under the sign of her tears and of the Cross of Christ, to carry her own cross with Him "for his Body which is the Church" (Col 1:24). Melanie offered her trials, of every kind, particularly for priests. Father Sylvain Marie Giraud, M.S., and subsequently Bishop Petagna, assisted her in her vocation of victim soul. This vocation is more common than one might think, austere and privileged, and apt to provoke misunderstandings and disbelief.

Melanie exhorted her French correspondents to reject all compromise with liberalism. She had recourse to a passionate and even sometimes violent manner of speaking, recognized by Maritain as accents showing "zeal for the House of God." (See the Letters from Maritain, Documents 10-11 below.) But Melanie did not mind conversing with some youthful unbelievers, people in the streets of Castellammare. She also gave spiritual counsel to priests, religious and laity, with the patience and moderation of an authentic spiritual director, praised by Father Georges Nalin. (See the Letter from this priest, Document 14 below.)

Beyond any false hypotheses, which are now invalidated, and the prejudices commonly held against many servants of God, this recently discovered, and more complete documentation, compels us to recognize in Melanie a mystical life of a very high degree. Her heroism in penance, patience and perseverance is attested by her original expression of rare experiences, which she manages to convey in very ordinary language. (See Documents 11-16 and the Chronology of her life, below.)

B. MAXIMIN

Without reaching Melanie's level of spirituality, Maximin loyally lived out a destiny equally exceptional, challenging and sown with deceptions, yet he remained faithful to Our Lady, to her message and to the law of God. Dismissed from a minor seminary by the intervention of Bishop Ginoulhiac, he rebounded to the major seminary of

Dax and Aire, which he left at the end of two years, because it was impressed upon him that his condition of seer was "incompatible" with the ecclesiastical state. After two years of study of medicine to become an officer of health, he halted, thanks to a professor who helped him take into consideration the ambiguity of one day becoming visionary-healer.

In those difficult conditions, Maximin did well in his studies, not brilliant but respectable, and he knew how to obey his professors without argument (even when faced with poor counsel). Prevented from high success by turmoil and poverty, he persevered in his Christian life with great abandonment to God, and unreserved fidelity to the "message" profoundly engraved on his heart. Afflicted with sickness after the financial ruin of his adoptive parents, he believed he could take advantage of a good opportunity to avoid destitution by marketing an elixir, an endeavor which earned him strong reproach... *only* because of his position as seer, whereas monks who converted food to alcoholic drinks were regarded as irreproachable (Benedictines, Trappists, Chartreux). Maximin was bitterly betrayed by those who sought to capitalize on his role of seer.

THE UNIVERSAL DIMENSION OF HOLINESS

We have already responded to the open question: Are Maximin and Melanie poor, famous wretches, fickle and unbalanced, or even deviant? No! There was no deviance on their part, nor in their unwavering allegiance to their Faith and their mission, received during that single Apparition, laden with such a heavy and complex message, especially for Melanie. Their mission was fettered by their rejection, but they accepted their marginal and occasional role, not without deep regret.

The Apostle Paul generally described as "saints" the members of the first Christian communities, by virtue of the holiness all receive at their baptism with the gift of the Spirit, and by striving to live the true life in God. From this point of view, it is clear, in spite of the calumny, that Maximin and Melanie are not to be grouped with the incestuous Christians of Corinth (1Cor 5), nor with others who deserved to be excommunicated without delay, for tarnishing the sanctity of the community. They did not dishonor that grace, but esteemed it, each in his own way and in his own capacity. The Saints (meaning those canonized) are not formed by the Holy Spirit in the same mold, like commercially packaged cheese and other manufactured products. The Holy Spirit guides saints interiorly in an extraordinary diversity, according to their irreplaceable personal vocation. There could not be *more* diversity than among the saints: the Paraclete awakens them, with their free and active cooperation, to better themselves through identification with Jesus Christ... not as clones or look-a-likes, but as diverse reflections of Divine Love, in the image of the Persons of the Trinity. The Trinity has one single life, a single act, one in being, but are true distinct Persons: three different personhoods, distinct and inconfusable, in a vis-à-vis relationship, since "God is love." (1Jn 4:7) As an image of God, each Christian keeps his own temperament and his regional, familial and personal identity. All are called to reconvert our often egotistical, individualist desire into pure altruism, in Their image, to realize the prayer of Christ: "That they may be one as We are one (in love), You in Me and I in You, as the Father is in Me and I in Him." (cf Jn 17:21-22; 10:30). It's according to these particulars that the Holy Spirit brings each disciple to perfection.

The two seers of LaSalette sincerely pursued, though differently and to varying degrees, the austere ideals of their Christian identity, casting an influence, and benefitting many Christians of low and high cultural or hierarchical class, as we have seen.

Yes, the seers are singular (unique), as was Christ. He was unique in becoming man, the only individual Divine Person in the Trinity to do so. He was unique in becoming a man of distant royal lineage, while living a humble village life, a carpenter in his trade. Some of his relatives argued, wanting to bring Him back to his carpentry work by trying to turn Him from his "crazy" idea of being a prophet. He was excluded and condemned by the religious leaders of the People of God, and ultimately put to death.

The diverse contradictions undergone by the seers did not cause them to separate from Christ. In fact, contradictions had an opposite effect, bringing them closer in resemblance to Christ. Jesus was scorned for his marginal condition, the seers for their humble station. They were in good company and in solidarity with Him. The seers manifested their personality, because the human universal only exists in the particular. Each faithfully kept his roots, his essential singularities, his own unique irreplaceable personality in the eyes of God the Creator. Moreover, in a transcendent manner, Jesus Christ, Second Person of the Holy Trinity, God made Man, became the most universal of all men, but remained rooted deeply in human solidarity, by his selfless, creative and saving Love. He was also the most controversial of men, the most excluded, and that quality made Him especially attractive to Melanie. It's one of the lessons of this book. May it teach historians, especially Christians, respect for persons and for the sacred, an interior discernment which distinguishes the universal from the singular; love and its fruits in the hearts of the humble; God in the human; immanent Love in the weakness of men.

The Holiness of the Poor

Ours is a time when people are rediscovering the meaning of the universal call to become "saints" according to the Apostle Paul. It's an ideal time to promote unnamed saints, people who were spurned by the elitist system and the domination of rationalist, technical and critical intelligence. It is a time where there is a great desire to see, more widely publicized, the holiness of the people of God - not only the doctors or founders, kings or hierarchs, not only those who have the necessary financial backing to be pushed forward in the process of canonization, but the holiness of children for whom the Prophet Daniel fought... Also, that of mothers and fathers of families, those of low estate or an excluded caste, like Saint Benedict Labre. That poor man of little means was canonized first of all by acclamation, at the very moment of his death, by the underworld of beggars who cried out in Rome:

The Saint is dead! *(Il Santo è morto!)*

The Church assumes the voice of the poor.

I, [René Laurentin], was unaware of Melanie and Maximin, except regarding their wretched politico-neurotic reputations, for which our modernity, critical and reductive, prides itself. Numerous exegetes, historians and theologians tried to reduce the "historical Jesus" to a mere village prophet who was unaware of his divinity, and Mary, to an ignorant and submissive peasant. Deeper study of Christ and the Virgin over the past half-century, brought me to understand and defend them with an unfathomable admiration that continues to increase beyond my capacity. It's on the same basis that I acquired a fresh perspective regarding Melanie and Maximin, thanks to the texts uncovered by Michel Corteville. They have emerged into the light so differently, and so endearingly: straightforward, likeable and provocative, yet humble. Melanie is discreet and contemplative, more refined and more interior, nonetheless remaining peasant and alpine. Thanks to exceptional documentation, the seers have come to life. I admire the work of God in their sacrifices, long recognized by many great minds, spiritual leaders, churchmen and Saints.

According to the same investigative method - open wide to all aspects of reality, all points of debate and all points of criticism... as progressively permeated with fraternal admiration for the two shepherds of LaSalette, each in their capacity, in their simple and unique humanity, and in the way they observed one another but did not interact much with each other. Melanie avoided Maximin when he was placed with her in the girls' elementary class to remediate their illiteracy.

What I like about Maximin, is his robust nature, his taste for the encounter, his frank and sometimes provocative reactions, his straight-talk, but also his receptivity, his obedience, his capacity to rebound from the successive hindrances in his life. It's especially his fidelity to his Christian education, to his meeting with the Virgin, to his mission, which he served with all his strength and all his heart. It's his heroism in celibacy which he kept all his life, after the failure to attain his priestly vocation. Sociable and generous, he showed himself ready to lay down his life for the Church as a papal Zouave. And, he knew how to accept without bitterness all who rejected him.

Correspondents

A) Dom Paul Delatte: became convinced of Melanie's innocence
B) Garrigou-Lagrange, OP: "Melanie remained faithful to her mission."
C) Father Ciro Quaranta: Postulator of Causes for Beatification
D) Bishop Mario Paciello of Altamura, where Melanie died.

DOCUMENTS

These texts, most of them as yet unpublished, will allow readers to get in touch with the seers as they are themselves: their peasant authenticity, their style (for they do have style), their modesty, and Melanie's mystical dimension.

MAXIMIN

1. MAXIMIN TO BISHOP DEBRUILLARD: UNPUBLISHED LETTER OF DECEMBER 31, 1851[1]

Monsignor:

I beg Your Grace's pardon if I take the liberty of writing to you. But as She did not disdain to make me happy, and as She chose me among so many others to whom She could have done the same favor, and who would have been more worthy of it, it is my duty to express to her my deep gratitude for the benefits She has bestowed on me.

You have deigned, My Lord, to recognize in your flock the least of your sheep which you have had so much trouble guarding until now. Your zeal and your charity have not tired of pursuing him. You have always brought him back to the fold, and even now you spoil him as shepherds spoil the sheep that they love above the rest. O good shepherd, O my father, this sheep promises you that he will no longer flee from you, and that he will always listen to your voice.

Allow me, My Lord, to address this prayer to God: My God, grant the good shepherd a blessed year. For the good of his flock, may he live a long time to come and may his diocese give him the consolations which his love, generosity and devotion deserve.

Deign, Your Excellency, to bless the child you have kindly adopted and to receive the sincere expression of his respect and gratitude.

Maximin Giraud
December 31, [18]51
Minor Seminary of Côte

2. MAXIMIN TO HENRY LECHAUF OF KERGUENEC, BEST FRIEND IN THE PAPAL ZOUAVES[2]

Carpineto, September 8, 1865

My dear Henry,

Since you've been gone, a lot has happened, at least for me, if not for the whole battalion. The fifth company has been sent as a detachment, and God knows to what country! I was the first to apply, then first by my number, but the last one to have served in the battalion of the first company.

Therefore, I was not able to carry out your commissions with the brave and worthy Zouaves, of whom you mentioned to me in your kind little letter. I only received it on the morning of the 7th, although it is dated August 23rd. I am going to tell you a little story which will undoubtedly interest you. Considering your love for everything connected with the battalion, the slightest bit of information is for you a source of pleasure or sorrow, depending on whether things are going well or badly!

We left on July 26th, around two o'clock in the morning. For the first time, while I was hauling my fresh-packed rucksack on my back, it seemed a bit heavy for the first three or four miles. But then I got used to it. We came as far as the station at Albano and from there we took the railway to Segni where, without having eaten anything, we had to climb a steep hill, eight or nine miles in the dreadful heat. Even though I arrived about an hour, or an hour and a half earlier, some of the detachment did not arrive until about two o'clock in the afternoon. We did not eat for the first time until about four o'clock. The detachment remained there for the night. Jouin, Vergnaud and I were sent on a two-hour march further on, through forests, brush and rocks, to Monte-Lanico, ahead of the luggage and in the vanguard! We stayed in this village until about three o'clock in the morning. Then, not seeing anything coming, we walked with a guide to the town of Carpineto. We entered there only around six o'clock in the morning, still with our backpacks and all our weapons. We did not stop climbing because we were in the midst of high mountains which look very much like those of my Dauphine. You are going to ask me, very naturally, what we came to do there and so far away from Rome and Frascati. It was to chase away the bandits who were making a terrible mess. Around September 5th they had entered a small town called Maenza, five hours from Carpineto. There, after having stuffed themselves, they engaged in all sorts of orgies, [even murder.] They killed three people - two men and a woman - and, later on, eleven other people, terrorizing the land; no man dared to oppose them. This punishment (meted out by the bandits) is said to have been retribution upon the people of that village for sending them poisoned food.

As for us, we still do patrols, but they are very tiring. There isn't a single flat path. We are always climbing on sharp rocks and stones, so every day we need to repair the soles of our shoes, which imposes a serious financial burden upon the government. Every day it is necessary to repair them!

To the eye, Carpineto is beautiful. The views are delightful, but the city inside is awful: pigs, dogs, cats, horses, even mules and donkeys, are housed together with the inhabitants. The streets are not streets: they are stairs, so there are no wheeled carriages.

As for the food, it is very bad. The wine is absolutely vinegar, but that does not prevent us from drinking it. The fatigue, food, heat and this chilly mountain air sickens many people. I was trained as a medic. I did it first of all out of charity but drew back when they wanted to pay me. However, I have now resumed my services and I am very happy about it because in the mountain it is only the wind that chases us - rather than robbers. However, we still see some of the bandits from time to time. I need to finish, though I still have much to tell you about this town and its inhabitants. But there is no stationery or envelopes. I have to write to you, using my bag for a desk, with poor quality paper and a pen that does not mark. My ink is wax and water. We are housed in a convent.

Farewell, my dear Henry. Please take good care of your health. I pray to the Blessed Virgin of LaSalette that She may heal you; for though you may want to go to heaven soon, others want to keep you on earth, including me.

Farewell then! I kiss you with all my heart.
Your devoted friend,
Maximin Giraud, from La S.

3. UNPUBLISHED LETTER FROM MAXIMIN TO FELICIE BEROT, OF AIRE-SUR-ADOUR[3]

Corps, January 7, 1872

My good little sister,

I received your very kind letter on New Year's Eve. Therefore, I wish you, and my good friend Leon, a very happy and excellent New Year. You tell me that he still loves me very much. His concern is reciprocated, for I think of him often here on the Holy Mountain of LaSalette. I pray for him and his happiness. It goes without saying that you, my little sister, are not forgotten when he addresses Our Lady of LaSalette; for you are the mainstay of his happiness.

You ask me a lot of questions, but you know perfectly well that I cannot always answer, even indirectly. You speak to me of Paris, but it had only a small warning. Although it seemed impressive to many honest people, it did not open the eyes of either our rulers, or the impious. It even seems that this chastisement was not delivered by Divine Providence. The warning merely served to exasperate the demolishers of principle and virtue, of which Paris is the home.

As for your cousin, I don't know what to advise her. Paris will continue to face a lot of misery but, by taking precautions, we will be able to get out of the city in time. By praying to God very much, we will be able to escape punishment, for God does not abandon those who trust in Him. Paris is detrimental for young people, especially the students. That is what is most terrible and what is most to be pitied. It is not rare to see young men of 16-17 years insult their mothers, abandoning them and not wanting to see them again. Paris will be destroyed one day or another. But that must not prevent you, myself, or your cousin, [...] from furthering the best interests of the inhabitants of Paris.

Europe is threatened by ominous, black clouds. I fear for our unfortunate France, but Prussia is about to pay its debts, and so is Italy.

Let's come back to you and set aside discussing such terrible events. Trusting in God and prayer, we will be protected. My good little sister, I still hold you in affection. And I still love my dear Leon very much. I think of your charming children, whom I don't have the honor to know. I think, I think. [...] Then I ponder yet more. Can you guess? Ah, I dare not tell you. Should I divulge the words? Once again, I dare not. Never mind.

Well, I am thinking now of the good goose drumsticks that I ate in your country, served with mincemeat. If it were not so far for you to send one or two, I would beg for some, and then be content to never eat again! It was presented more artistically than any meal I have eaten since I left Aire.[4] I'll leave aside now the gastronomical comments, to send you my greetings and wish you a wonderful evening. It's evening now, so good evening my dear Felicie and Leon. I salute you both with deep respect.

Your devoted brother,
Maximin Giraud

4. MEMOIRS OF MAXIMIN (1865)[5] LETTER TO MRS. JOURDAIN, HIS ADOPTIVE MOTHER

Dearest and most excellent Mother,

Only you, in my eyes, deserve this sweet name. I have too often lavished it upon a few miserable helpers who, afterwards and many times, became a reproach to me [for having so unwisely applied it to them]

Already for nearly three years, my dear Mother, I have been overjoyed with your blessings. You have never made me feel estranged. You make enormous sacrifices for me, so as not to leave me at the mercy of anyone who [impiously] curious, was eager to know extraordinary things. Such people imagine that, because one has received a favor from the Queen of Angels, one lives like the angels and works miracles, especially in their presence. Such people are not afraid to ask me to petition or inquire on their behalf - as Herod did when Our Lord Jesus Christ stood before him. If their expectation is disappointed, they do not hesitate, in [the manner of Herod], to call me crazy.

Thank you, a thousand thanks, my good mama, for all you do for me.

I've never been able to fully appreciate what a mother is, having lost mine in the cradle. But since I have had the honor of knowing you, of living close to you in the intimacy of Mr. Jourdain: a father, a mother, a family, affection, all these things have been new to me because of you.

Alas! How unfortunate it is to be alone or in foreign hands! Life loses its charm. Faith itself loses much of its appeal, for there is little faith left in the sacred bonds that God has placed in the heart of man to bind him to his religion, to his homeland, to his family. People feel themselves in a complete vacuum, desire nothing, feeling indifferent to everything, if not worse than indifferent.

That was pretty much my existence before I came to you. Such is the life of many young people who have long been separated from their parents.

I lacked happiness until I came to know a Christian family life from the inside - before I became the darling child of a mother who really wanted to love me, to look at me, to adopt me with her heart as her own son.

Now you ask me to tell you my whole life's story, without any reluctance, and to retrace my history from as far back as I can remember, even my most tender years.

There is nothing I would refuse you, being quite unable to do so because of your many kindnesses. I give in. However, it is a very difficult task to talk about oneself.

What is hard and painful for anyone else is even more so for me, especially because you are very pious. In addition, the event which has forever made me famous in the eyes of pious people forces me to speak about myself without ostentation nor demeaning myself, but quite simply, to say only the truth without a shadow of change, the pure truth. This command was twice repeated by Our Lady of LaSalette: "Make it known to all my people!" So today, good Mother, I'll pass it on to you in writing, as I passed it on orally as a child.

This is my mission. Yes, now that I have more education, I pay homage to Mary and I wish to continue to do so before all her people!

The Apparition

Never before had we [Melanie and I] seen multi-colored rays spring from a lady of fire whose crown on her brow appeared to us to be made of blossoms in the form of white, red and blue roses. The most splendid of tiaras surmounted her headdress, all gold and silver, transparent, high and rounded at the top, and slightly inclined forward. On all sides there were small golden flowers, of which flames emitted from their centers. Between each branch of flowers was a branch of twelve sparkling gems. These branches were formed of stalks, sequins or stars. Nothing could be more resplendent.

The Apparition's headpiece was low enough to completely hide the hair and ears. The white cloth, adorned with garlands of light, that covered her breast and shoulders, was tied at both ends, surrounding the body as if it were a kind of belt. This shawl was rather like the humeral veil of the priests at the altar. The robe with which she was clothed, rose very high and concealed the neck as much as possible, with a charm of modesty which belongs only to our poor, humble, and chaste religious.

A starry robe with the shimmering of a thousand pearls and precious stones, and of a brilliant whiteness, stood out under a plain scapular or apron - along which flowed the tears of the Apparition. The apron was almost the same color as the robe; a light and shiny fabric which only the hand of angels can make.

Her immaculate shoes were topped with a golden buckle, as on bishops' shoes, and they were also adorned with incomparable roses of various colors, but smaller than the roses in the crown.

From the "chalice" of every flower of her mysterious adornment, a kind of flame of light and gold shown out, which rose like incense and mingled with the radiant light around her.

A large, shining chain, the width of three fingers, like the gold braid which borders the priestly chasuble, trailed along the garland of roses. From a smaller, ring-shaped chain hung a golden "crucified" whose extraordinary brilliance was distinct from that of the Cross. One could see pincers on the right and a hammer on the left, which seemed to hover unattached.

Her splendid light, by which, say I Maximin - the Immaculate Mother of God attracted us and kept us bound so closely to her that a person could not have passed between her and us - it neither dazzled us, nor tired us, nor blinded us, but on the contrary was infinitely sweet and pleasant. Mary permitted that in this way we experience how sweet and pleasant it is to be so loved by her. We, in particular little shepherds - however ignorant and boorish we may be - have reason to love the Virgin Mary more than anything else, for She was so kind to us in so many ways!

She was very kind to have appeared to us - without being seen by the forty other shepherds who, being placed to the right and left of the small ravine towards the source of the Sezia, four or five hundred meters upstream on the Gargas, would have been within reach of seeing a character of such extreme singularity - on a plateau that has never produced a single tree, not even a small shrub. [†Editor: the latitude is above the timberline]

The First Disclosures

I spoke first to old Mother Pra, Melanie's employer. [Melanie] had not yet spoken to anyone and was busy taking her cows to the barn to milk them. The words of the burning Lady, the second sun, made [Mother Pra] think I had lost my head. She asked me to tell her what I had seen and heard, which surprised her very much. I am quite surprised that she did not see, as I did, this bright light at the summit of the Holy Mountain, which should have been visible at a very great distance.

I did not imagine that I had received a special grace, but I felt a more intimate and tender love for the Lady of the Apparition. The same was true of the old woman, in whose bright, black eyes I saw big tears shining, and who, although I had stopped talking, was still listening to me, crouched by her fire, hanging on my lips, forgetting about the evening meal she was preparing.

Mistaking her attitude, her expression and her tears for doubt, I hastened to say to her, calling her by her nickname of "Mother

Carron" [†Editor: Carron/Charron was an old French surname for chariot-makers. Maximin affectionately called her "Mother Carrou"]: "Most certainly, I have seen and heard everything that I have just reported to you! And if you do not believe *me*, Melanie, your shepherdess, who was with me, will tell you the same thing!"

Immediately, I set off for my own employer's house, where I noticed an extra place setting at the table, and all eyes directed toward me. Already some shepherds were wondering what it was that I had wanted to say to them on the way down, and Mother Carron had not kept silent. Pierre Selme very politely invited me to sit next to him. With all possible deference, he offered me the best he had at table. When the meal was over... I saw him uncover his snow-white head in front of his children, his servants and his eagerly curious neighbors who were already filling the house. He asked me to recount what I had witnessed up there with Melanie. They all listened with the deepest attention - if not with equal respect and emotion - to the story I related to them with admiration, gentleness and dignity (and by no means with excess of words). The father, mother and seven-year-old son, without knowing what the wonder was I was recounting, said almost as one:

"It must be the Most Holy Virgin or some great saint. How happy you are, dear child!"

And they [these three] seemed under... I don't know what impression of happiness and piety which makes the soul, thought and feeling belong more to heaven than to earth. They had wept as they heard of the misfortunes which were going to affect the harvests, while the rest of the audience, smiling maliciously from behind, supposed that I had been fooled by some witch or a ghost. Dad Selme sternly rebuked his sons:

- "You laughed while listening to such serious words. This is not good, for in laughing you have not reflected on what you were hearing, nor have you understood its importance. You mock what this poor innocent boy says, as if he were capable of deceiving us and inventing such beautiful words. You declare that She was a ghost who came asking for prayers. The Apparition supports us [i.e., who say it was the Virgin] proving the contrary [of what you assert] by the prayers She herself insistently requested as necessary to hold back the arm of her Son, and by the conversion She demands of us, if we want to obtain abundant crops. She recommends to her two little witnesses to pray well every day. And if She suffers much, She does not add that it is because She's in purgatory, but that we must pray for her intentions. She is therefore neither a ghost who asks for prayers, nor even less a witch who wants to deceive and trick us. Witches do not shine like the sun at noon and do not rise to highest heaven. They are people like us who, far from preaching to us, far from converting us, seek only to take us away from God and our religion, and never do anything but evil by casting spells on people and animals. The Apparition did not say or do any of this kind, if you believe the little Memin."

Pierre Selme believed in Memin, for which he used a nickname which reveals the tenderness that mothers sometimes display toward their children, a nickname that was familiar to my companions in their dialect. [†Editor, as mentioned in Ch 4 Sec III:8 "V," *le Berger de Bruite* "the Noisy Shepherd"] Selme simply believed. This righteous and sensible old man was one whom the villagers often asked to serve as an arbitrator. Like a Christian mother or a pure-hearted young girl, Selme hastened to pay homage to the Apparition which penetrated him with love and gratitude.

The next morning, the scene of the previous day took place again at the home of the parish priest of LaSalette. Having consulted each other during the night, Melanie's employer and mine sent us before six o'clock in the morning in order to make sure that we would neither be deceived, nor misled.

As we walked along, without even meeting the country watchman, we wondered what good it would do to go to the presbytery, from where the globe of fire must have been seen, as well as the rest of the universe, because it was so bright. There we found the maidservant sitting back on her heels, kneeling in the dirt in front of the hearth, blowing and stirring the embers.

- What do you want with the priest?
- "To speak to him!" "To speak to him!" I said it twice, without thinking whether or not she was being indiscreet. The good Perpetua then resumed with a slightly displeased look:
- "Calm down! First you tell me, and if it's not complete nonsense then I tell the parish priest."

Since this was evidently the law or custom, we did as required. She listened to us with all the interest of someone with more piety than discretion. She was filled with wonder, and moved to tears by the story. I told it myself, since my too-timid companion had let me do all the talking. The maidservant remained motionless and silent, stunned, and delighted.

Then, just as I was about to finish, the parish priest, who had cracked opened the door of his room and lent an attentive ear, ran towards us, raising his arms to the sky. With eyes wet with tears, he cried out:

- "Oh! How happy you must be, my children! You have seen the Most Blessed Virgin!" And he began to cry even more, wondering what action had earned his parish such a distinguished honor.

Immediately Melanie turned toward me and said with liveliness,

- "Was I not right to believe that it was the Good God or the Most Blessed Virgin?"

Without paying attention to our exchange of reflections, so absorbed was he by what he had just heard, this new Simeon, the good priest, sang his *Nunc dimittis*:

- "Oh, what woe to the nations if they do not return by a straight path to God! The Queen of Heaven came down to earth for the ruin of many, as well as for the salvation of many. I regret to leave my parish, but I hope that God will bless the little good I have been able to do here!"

Father Jacques Perrin, an octogenarian, who had recently been appointed to a post of retirement and honor near Lyon, blessed us by exhorting us never to forget the immense grace which the Most Blessed Virgin had deigned to grant us. We returned to the Ablandins, absorbed, meditating on the pious exhortations of this holy priest, no less than that of the Apparition. His recounting of the story would provoke in simple and believing souls a filial and grateful love for the Most Blessed Virgin. Sobs affected his voice when the parish priest of LaSalette announced such "great news."

The Conversion of the Wheelwright, Giraud

On arriving at my father's house, at the end of the High Mass at Corps, we found only my stepmother, called *Marâtre*, in the dialect of the country, but without at all having the meaning of "bad mother." The proof that she was a fairly good Christian-believer, is the astonishment and dismay she felt when she heard my employer tell her twice the happiness and glory I had been favored with from Mary.

- "Yes. I can assure you, your child had, with the daughter of Mathieu Calvat, in service with Baptiste Pra, whom you know perfectly well and with whom Angelique, Maximin's sister, your child, had the glory and the happiness of seeing the Most Blessed Virgin. Besides, here he is. Question him. He will tell you the story as he did to us last night while we ate supper! And he's going now to join his father at the cabaret where business is usually done with customers."

While I told what I saw and heard the day before, my dear stepmother reflected and looked at me attentively like a person who wants to believe, who even does believe, but to whom it seems so surprising that she would like to see some miracle in me in support of my words. When the story was completed, she embraced me, she cried and she led me to my maternal grandmother. But already, as fast as lightning, the news had spread through the town, which was in a tumult.

No sooner had I crossed the threshold of my father's home, when women and children were pointing their fingers at me and greeting me as the privileged of Mary. They regarded me with a kind of respect. From several windows I heard voices saying, "There's little Memin with his mother!" A group formed and followed me. It seemed to me that, in the eyes of the crowd, I was no longer the same child as I was eight days ago. My grandmother saw me and greeted me from the top of a black marble staircase, common in the country, and which serves as a porch. She cried out:

- "Well, they are saying beautiful things all over Corps, that you have seen the Most Blessed Virgin! As for me, I don't believe it. It is rather your poor mother who must have come to ask for prayers or to remind you to be wiser than you are. What do you think, Marie?"

- My stepmother replied: "Come now, it is indeed the Most Blessed Virgin or some saint from heaven. Certainly, it is not your daughter, nor some other deceased soul who came to instruct him in this manner!"

Then, turning to me, she ordered me to begin my story again. It was in the presence of a multitude of people, whose numbers kept growing every moment.

During this first open-air sermon, did I make converts, supporters of Our Lady of LaSalette? Yes, I am convinced of it. Yes, three times yes! For I saw eyes filling with tears, and breasts swelling with sighs. I have heard people make public confessions of the following kind:

- "It's true, we no longer practice our holy religion. Yes, it is we who have been godless!"

I do not know if from my mouth it came out like a celestial light that radiates in docile minds, like a divine breath that makes hearts tremble, imparting to them a mysterious movement and drawing them into a new current. But by repeating to them the French part of the speech, which most of them hardly understood and which I would not have understood eight days before, I could only renew in their eyes the prodigy of Balaam's donkey, speaking and prophesying, and the next instant pooping like its predecessors (!)

My preaching or mission completed, I, as always, eagerly accepted my good grandmother's sweets. I do not think I was any less sensitive to her caresses that accompanied them. I was ready to join my playmates, but they didn't treat me the same, as in the past. Far from quarrelling with me, as was their detestable habit, and far from having their eyes gouged out rather than giving up a marble or a spinning top, they even offered these to me as a gift. I was confused by their respectful and cordial camaraderie. But I was no longer the popular Memin who was respected in the past. Their thousand kindnesses were designed to make me treat kindly those of strong opinion, among them our village teachers, who regarded me with irony, mocking me as if I was the son of the Most Holy Virgin, a little Jesus. Shrugging my shoulders, I reply placidly:

- "Say and do whatever you please. The one I saw and heard, was it the Most Blessed Virgin? She didn't tell me her name. She didn't ask me to make you believe it!" And I turned on my heels, neither offending, nor blaming anyone.

In the evening and after supper, I asked my mother to teach me how to pray. The day before, when I was sent to bed, I, who would never have thought of praying alone, now wanted to say at least the Our Father and Hail Mary. The Apparition had very much advised us to do this but, not knowing where to begin, and being able only to stammer a few words without knowing the rest of the prayer, I began to cry. At the same time, just making the Sign of the Cross when going to bed, would not have been without merit, nor would it have displeased the heart of our heavenly Father and Mother. On Sunday morning I did the same, for want of anything better. But in the evening, as I felt my heart filled with an ever-greater love for the Beautiful Lady, in whom my heart never ceases to find the most perfect object of its desires, I asked my stepmother to pray with me. She did so. Who knows whether, without Our Lady's recommendation, I would have applied myself so wholeheartedly to praying to God? I probably would not have grown up any more religious than my father.

I hadn't seen him all day, not since the previous week. I had fallen asleep under the dominion of the sweetest, most radiant vision, in the arms of the one who showed herself, today as yesterday, so kind to me and my family, when my father, reeking of alcohol, finally came home at ten o'clock in the evening. He went directly toward my bed and shook me with the increasing fury which had been aroused in him by the declaration of Pierre Selme. Indeed, during their meeting at the cabaret, after a polite exchange, Selme told Giraud about the great happiness his son had experienced. To the thousand arguments of my father, who is far from one who hypothesizes, my employer always answered him: "And better than that!" Selme ended up relating to him the whole event of the Apparition.

My father looked at Selme, almost angry, and said,

- "You big animal, do you believe that nonsense? I don't. Don't you see that it is some priest's maid who, in agreement with her master, wanted to deceive my child, or some old pious witch who abuses the innocence and ignorance of my little one by juggling tricks? And you, to whom I have entrusted him, you let it happen like that? And you come, with an imperturbable seriousness, to tell this tale to me, the wheelwright of Corps! Here, have a drink and say no more!"

- "The wheelwright," said our excellent Pierre Selme in a dry tone [addressing those at the cabaret] "you know him, gentlemen. He is as crazy as ever. But I can tell you that the matter is very true. The child was tending my flock on the mountain, and he hardly moved away from the flock, except to take a drink from the nearby fountain. There he saw, with the little shepherdess Melanie, a Lady very beautiful and luminous. I and the other witnesses would have known her if she had really just been an ordinary woman of the locality. This is what I have come to tell you, old wheelwright."

- "Do as you please with *your* children but I, Giraud, do not permit them such things. My son has been honest up to this day, and honest he will remain!"

And, without further ado, returning to his epithets of "fool" and "idiot," and other similar amenities, he angrily told Selme, in the name of the friendship that bound them, not to breathe a word of it to him. He even forbade him to tell anyone else about it, so they proceeded to drink and discuss business.

However, my father, who had forgotten nothing of this scene, ruthlessly made me get out of bed, in spite of my stepmother's protestations. Holding me upright in the dark between his legs, half asleep, I was forced to repeat to him the speech on the mountain.

First of all, he made fun of me at the expense of the Virgin who, according to him, had nothing better to do than to come and show herself to a kid like me. Thirty-six ideas rolling around in his head, he did not reflect that this boy did not speak any French.

At the place where I related that the harvest would be spoilt, he was furious and interrupted me and kicked me away. Walking with great strides and calling the Lady of the Apparition epithets, which modesty and respect do not allow me to record here, he got up and said to me:

- "Who is this Lady who in eight days [the time he was hired to replace the sick shepherd] taught you such a long lesson, while in eight years I have not been able to teach you an Our Father or a Hail Mary? You have the memory of a rabbit. You come back ten times without remembering the chores or the tobacco or the nails I send you to get. This Lady did not waste her time! What a pity that I don't know her. I would have sent you to *her* school! Go to bed, and don't you dare repeat such nonsense to anyone else. Otherwise... do you hear me?"

And he made with his eyes a most significant expression that made me tremble, more with fright than cold, as I returned to [the warmth of] my bed. The next day, Monday, visitors or curious people from the locality came to our wheelwright workshop and while my father was working, they were asking me questions and making me tell them about the great wonder. He said little in their presence but, after their departure, he scolded me and ordered me in the most formal way to stop talking about it, and even to declare, to anyone who would question me, that I knew absolutely nothing.

Visits followed visits. When I looked at my father, I saw nothing on his face that prevented me from responding to their requests, so I made it my duty to pass everything on to the people, without reflecting too much of my mission. As a reward, after the people left the workshop, I received sharp blows from my father with his added qualifiers of "little scamp" and "disobedient," saying that he did not want his family, so respectable from father to son, to deceive the public today through his child playing such an unworthy role. And he got so carried away that he passed by the newcomers outside, calling them big fools, swearing and blaspheming, and finally consigning me to the house with orders not to go out again.

There in the house, my stepmother, who was less shy, who neither beat nor scolded me and rather let things go their own way, did not refuse those with questions to approach, although she was quite surprised by the crowd of visitors who came from the town and beyond.

On the evening of the 21st, after supper, troubled by the visits of the day and perhaps a little by the Lady of September 19, my father asked me to tell him the story once again, but obviously with the firm intention of discovering, either in the words or in the circumstances of the Apparition, some trace of a hoax.

The scene was no calmer than the day before, when I came to the point about the crops going bad. My stepmother wanted to stop his threats. He mistreated her by calling her "crazy" a priest-follower, and quick to believe the first stupidity that comes along. I escaped with this poor stepmother who still willing, at my request, to pray with me. My father, Giraud, does not notice that his son, once so sullen when it came to prayer, no longer dared to lie down or get up without reciting the *Our Father and Hail Mary,* but even prayed that he would become pious. Giraud did not notice that his son was speaking French, and answered difficulties addressed to him in French that were raised against the Lady's speech at LaSalette. Everybody cried out for the miracle of my suddenly speaking a language that was literally unknown to me. But [my father's] prejudices blinded him to excess, so much so that on Tuesday he kept me hidden and kept a watchful eye on his door, and that it was necessary for people to use a stratagem to arrange an interview with the witness of the Most Blessed Virgin.

> The bailiff, our neighbor, Ambroise Pelissier, an upright, just man of great kindness, always took pity even on strangers who came from all sides to see me. Pelissier would come to his friend's house [Giraud] to talk and drink, and, under some pretext, asked my father to send Memin to speak to Mrs. Pelissier.
>
> Once in the Pellissier home, I would respond to believers who wanted more details about the event. I would often pulverize with a word the objections of curious investigators, more or less incredulous, who would have liked to embarrass me and make me look ridiculous.
>
> It was a contest that became more and more important every day, against which subterfuge was no longer enough, and against which also my father could not fight indefinitely. His conversion, nevertheless, was not to be ascribed to the good and generous Pelissier, nor to the intervention of the parish priest of Corps, nor to any outside influence. It had to be the result of a special grace of the Most Blessed Virgin.

Asking me every day at supper about the speech of the beautiful Lady, as soon as I reached the point about the harvest, as if before an impassable barrier, he suddenly stopped me, and furiously made me hurry off to my room.

One evening, although he seemed better disposed, I told him that there was more. Although grumbling very rudely, he allowed me to continue. I did so in our dialect, spoken by the Virgin Mary. But when I reached the part of the story where She mentioned Coin [a small village], and that I had replied to the Apparition that I had never seen any spoiled wheat, and then continued with the observations made to me by the Apparition, and how I agreed that I did not remember, my father was completely astonished, as if struck by lightning. His face changed expression and also his language, which went from being coarse to charmingly polite.

- "This is something extraordinary! You were too little to have remembered the story of Coin, being no more than two years old. There was, at that time of the night in such a place, absolutely no one, no living soul. It's astonishing indeed! I myself will have to climb the mountain and examine all this closely and seriously. And if it is as people are saying, then the Most Holy Virgin will only have to cure me of the asthma which has made me suffer for years, and *then* I will promise not to prevent you from publishing her goodness to yourself and to us."

I had never gone to bed happier. Had I not finally discovered that the sire of my early life had kept, in spite of his predilection for [secular] France, of which I had often heard him speak, a secret attachment to the one who had appeared to me from heaven, so kind and beautiful and who is par excellence, after God, beauty, love and happiness? The conviction had been entirely in his mind from the evening of our first pilgrimage, on the 26th, when his wife answered all his objections with this:

- "There is nothing up there but an immense carpet of greenery, where neither a shrub, nor a rock, nor any prominence whatsoever can be seen for more than a thousand meters. It would be impossible to hide something from the eyes of the children and, in this manner, to have deceived them, while they were guarding their herds along these vast rambling pastures, which only the foot of an obscure goatherd could reach."

Only fifteen days had passed since the Apparition that the belief had already spread to all the surrounding cantons. From Grenoble, Gap and other towns, crowds were coming to join in the pilgrimage. I had been going up the mountain three times a day, for more than a month, explaining what happened, and where I beheld the most surprising cures, which gave way to the most extraordinary conversions. My father's own conversion had not yet happened.

But he no longer scolded or beat me. He no longer prevented me from seeing and accompanying strangers. His asthma - without being entirely cured - was getting better since his promise to stop hindering me. He even made me a small cross of white wood, one and a half meters high for my dear Mountain. He told me to ask the parish priest to bless it so that pilgrims would not kneel before a simple piece of wood.

- "Later, when I have lumber to purchase, or work to do in the village of LaSalette, I will climb up that mountain!"

It was October 22nd. It was cold and snowy. The two young friends I took with me didn't mind because they were mountaineers like us. We did not omit any shortcut, so impatient were we to arrive and to plant the sign of salvation, the first Cross erected on those bitterly cold peaks, where the beautiful Lady ascended from the earth! The taller Cross of two and a half meters height, which Melanie would erect near the Fountain, in holy emulation - built by her father Mathieu, a carpenter - was set up on the occasion of her leaving the employment of Pra to enter the Sisters' school of Corps. The country watchman was fined, and the mayor of LaSalette cited Mathieu Calvat before the justice of the peace. [†Editor: probably near the feast of All Saints when summer employment for shepherds was customarily halted by the expectation of the winter snows.]

Finally, a fortnight after our raising these Crosses, my father, having some business to settle at Dorcières, travelled up there with two or three friends, and from there, they went on to Planeau. Until they arrived, they laughed and teased us, each one outdoing the other. Suddenly, at the sight of the little Cross at the place of Our Lady's assumption, they fell, as if in spite of themselves, to their knees. And these men, who had even less faith than my father and who did not even remember the whole of the Our Father, tried to recite it aloud.

One of them began: *Our Father, who art in heaven* and stopped. Another of them thought he could complete the prayer: "*Full of grace, the Lord...* and he stopped. The third continued: *Give us our bread! Pray for us sinners. But deliver us from evil. Ainsi soit-il!* [†Editor: the colloquial expression, "So be it!" concluded prayers in much of France in that era instead of "Amen."]

After this hapless prayer, they wept and promised to convert. And from the Cross, they went to the fountain; they drank, and more tears flowed from their eyes, and they swore fidelity to God and to his most holy Mother, in the practice of our divine religion.

My father came home at ten o'clock in the evening. His asthma was totally cured and he announced to his wife that he was going to find Father Melin and confess. And under the astonished gaze of my mother-in-law, who thought he was drunk with wine, he repeated seriously: "Yes, tonight, and no later!" But at the insistence of his wife, who made him understand that it was really too late, he gave in, said his prayers and went to bed. The next morning, he kept his word. He, who had not come near the Holy Table for more than twenty years, did so publicly on Sundays. And from that time forward, I have never heard him pronounce in vain the name of God, which he revered with every word. He attends Mass every Sunday and also on weekdays to make up, he says, for the Sundays that he did not go, and for all the other times that he should have gone, or when he did not send his workers to church, or whom he prevented from going.

Not knowing how to read [a missal], he recites his Rosary [during Mass] and, if he happens to [complete it] before the conclusion of the Last Gospel, he starts another Rosary. Although I often point out to him that the Mass is over, he gives me a strong shove by showing me what dozens of Rosaries he still has to recite. If I leave the Church without signing myself well with the holy water, he gives me a little slap and takes my hand to make me make the Sign of the Cross with proper respect.

Now, in all his business transactions at the shop or on the square, we notice that he is gentle and much more affable than before. He even goes so far as to inspire respect for himself and his words, both in private and public life.

It seems that since his conversion, his heart as a Christian, and father of a family, has become similar to the heart of the Blessed Virgin. He saw to it, as much as it depended on him, that I prepared myself well for First Communion. His dearest wish was that it be well made, and that he be able to attend it.

More Disclosures

Alas, I was not without faults. From the age of seven or eight, when, stealing fruit that I did not even enjoy eating, I took part in these pranks due to human respect, which led me to do as my little friends did.

No one was giddier than me. One day my father gave me a goat and a sheep to guard. In order be more at ease while I played, I tied up the sheep, which was constantly trying to rejoin its companions that were grazing on the edge of a precipice. I did not foresee that anything bad might happen to it. On my return, I saw the sheep hanging over the abyss, but instead of pulling her up or cutting the rope, I ran off with the goat to the house. In my fright, I climbed up to huddle in the attic, where I was planning to scrounge for food at night, rather than simply confess to my father the fault I had committed, who finally discovered me after three days of searching and sending out alarms.

When I was driving my cows to pasture, was it a case of lacking foresight or was it gluttony? On my way, I would eat the full day's provisions, of which I gave my small dog a large portion. When I was told that I had nothing left for the rest of the day, I responded without thinking ahead:

- "But I'm not hungry now!" And thus, it was a prophecy that I was destined for hunger for the rest of my life!

Was I not rude during the Apparition itself, and in my behavior and in my very impolite thoughts regarding the Beautiful Lady? Thus, saddened to hear her say that the main food of my father and my family was going to run out, I could not help crying out with a more than naive, even unseemly liveliness, which should have made her call me to order:

"Oh, no, ma'am, that can't be true!"

My behavior in this was more insolent than my thoughts. I only wanted to say that, surely, there would still be a few potatoes left. And if later on I told a lie in front of the Most Holy Virgin, by affirming to her that I had never seen spoiled wheat, one can only blame my dull memory. A child better brought up than myself would have begun by saying, "I don't remember."

Not being trained in politeness, I kept putting my hat on my head, then took it off, to spin it on my stick. Then I put it back on my head mechanically, as one distracted. Then again, while the Beautiful Lady was speaking to Melanie, I used my stick to roll stones toward her feet, but without touching them. I am extremely ashamed of this since Melanie said I should be, but she could have excused me, all the same. Fortunately for me that the Blessed Virgin is incomparably more indulgent than the world, and that She did not even get angry when, in my impertinent and childish tenderness, I leapt up to steal a rose from her feet.

After a little chat about what we had just seen and heard, I suggested to Melanie, with the lightness so natural in childhood, to start again our game of the preceding day. It consisted in pushing a knife into the grass, cutting a piece of sod, then making the one who had not had the skill or the happiness to push the knife deepest into the ground, carry it, and force the defeated one to stoop down and crawl on all fours towards the designated goal.

My seemingly perpetual movement, was an exuberance that only increased instead of diminishing. It seemed impossible for me to remain still, either when I was being questioned or when I was being instructed.

If I was surrounded by interlocutors, it's my poor hair which usually suffered the most. I never ceased to twirl it in my hands, as I even did under the gaze of the Blessed Virgin.

If we are under the arbor at the convent of Corps, I swing on a rope, or I tip over on a chair, or I doze off in the chair, especially if it is cushioned with springs like those at the chancery, or for lack of a seat, when I'm sitting on the grass at the Mountain. I sit there. I crawl or slide on my knees. I even roll in the grass without acknowledging the presence of other persons, or the importance or dignity of the person questioning me. I examine, without asking permission, the belongings of the pilgrim who has admitted me into his room, or I touch in a rather casual manner whatever I please, or I ask indiscreet questions.

Alas, if only my turbulence stopped there. How many practical jokes did I play on the good pilgrims whom I had promised to accompany to LaSalette! I halt them halfway to indulge my own amusement, looking for nests in the woods, the coppices, the fields and the brooms.

One day, the muleteer told the Canon of Evreux, the first historian of LaSalette, Father Bez, that I would reach LePlaneau before them, but I kept them waiting for four hours. The canon said that if he could have suspected me to be capable of such a misdeed, he would have tied me to the mule's tail. When hunger finally made me come out of the woods to join them, he took me by the ears. But contrary to my expectations, he very amicably gave me some of his bread.

Father Bez spared me a dressing down from the Superior, when I came back with my pants split in two and stained with egg yolk. He beheld in the tear, nature in its most primitive state, notwithstanding my efforts to mend the pants with tree bark. The debonair Father Bez kindly purchased for me new pants on our return. Like a multitude of other pilgrims who were nearly as kind and indulgent as the Most Blessed Virgin, he said to me on the way down:

- "I don't know why the heavenly Mother chose you. I really don't know why. She probably needed a scatterbrain like Maximin, who discerned nothing in the event of September 19 and did not even appreciate it himself. She left you with all your faults to make it clear that it was She, and She alone, who acted in this sublime Apparition, and that you are neither a visionary, nor an enlightened person, nor some mystic in perpetual contemplation."

5. MAXIMIN IN 1869: EXCERPTS FROM LETTERS TO HIS ADOPTIVE PARENTS:[6]

August 1, 1869

The Bishop is in Paris. He should return around August 5th and the thing will be done immediately. The canons will all present themselves to support my request for a charity pension. They all assure me that this time I will get it. I am leaving tomorrow to fetch Father Sylvain Marie Giraud, M.S. from LaSalette to join the canons. [†Editor: Giraud was the Superior of the Missionaries of LaSalette at this time, and always a faithful friend, devoted to Maximin.]

After having exposed my destitution to them, I told them that without the Bishop, I would be forced to stay in Corps or

LaSalette and beg for bread from the pilgrims. But what moved them most were my continual tears. I can no longer hold them back any longer. The emptiness is in me and everywhere you are not. Oh, how I suffer! Every day is a stab to my heart.

August 10, 1869

I only intend to leave the Holy Mountain to go and see the Bishop to definitively resolve this matter. The Fathers are for me. But it is very difficult to get them to loosen their purse strings. They will only open them on one condition, namely making me a LaSalette Father along with them. Every day I myself tell the story at the Fountain in the presence of a large audience, which makes all the pilgrims very happy. At present, I am making a fervent novena to the Most Blessed Virgin to find out whether I should stay in the world or not. Does She want me to be a priest and a free, apostolic missionary like Father Combalot? I am inclined to believe it, if the person - who promised to liquidate my two or three thousand francs of debts and to pay for my seminary keeps his word - or, if the Bishop and the Carthusians who seem to be disposed in my favor assure me a pension of two thousand francs. So, in November, in order to be closer to you in Paris, so as not to leave you again, I will enter Saint-Sulpice. [†Editor: a major seminary] Would that I could do a very great good to souls. Oh, how ardently I pray to the Most Blessed Virgin of the Mountain!

August 20th, 1869

I'm still up here [on LaSalette] I weep here all the time. In the morning they make me get up at five o'clock. I repeat my story several times a day. Often around midnight I am still signing pictures. I am dead tired. As I don't have a penny, I don't know what to do. Father Auvergne writes me to wait for the Bishop and Father Sylvain Marie Giraud, M.S., who are due to arrive here on pilgrimage at the end of August. The Fathers are pleased with me. They tell me that they can support my request to His Excellency. They promise me money to return to Paris. They preferred to see me stay in Grenoble, in the country, or to go to boarding school of the convent, at their expense. Many pilgrims have offered me money. My refusal had the best effect. For my precarious position is well known. "You see," I said to the Fathers, "I expect everything from you and the others. I ask the pilgrims to give you what they want to give me, so that you yourselves may come to my assistance... "

September 18, 1869

I know perfectly well what you're suffering. I know it myself. If I have taken so long to answer you, it is because I have nothing new to say. The Bishop of Grenoble is here. I will ask to speak to him. For I cannot stay on the Holy Mountain forever.

To be sure that the Most Blessed Virgin wants me to be a priest and a missionary, to preach wherever I am called and to compose in your house or on the mountain of LaSalette, in my spare time, little works all to her glory. Although She did not speak to me of this sublime vocation on September 19, 1846, and although I never had a clear idea about this, I ask her for a miraculous sign, namely that a benefactor pays all my debts and ensures a modest comfort to my adoptive parents whom I must not abandon in old age. If She wants me at this price, I am quite ready to give myself to her, to consecrate myself completely to her service, not as a lay missionary, but as a priest or a religious. The LaSalette Fathers, and all our friends, gather around the Bishop to plead our cause. But I am afraid that none of us will succeed, because it is hard, very hard to part with money. Tomorrow I will write to you and you will know everything.

Oh, how I pray to the Most Blessed Virgin Mary so that She won't abandon you! Pilgrims are pouring in. They are from two to three thousand. They overwhelm me with questions. They make me sign a lot of images. They touch my clothes from behind. I have to shake hands right and left. I don't have a minute to myself.

October 26, 1869

I cannot as yet set the day of my departure from the Holy Mountain and Grenoble. Under this cover, I am giving you the final decision of my dear and dainty Bishop. The Missionaries of Our Lady of LaSalette, led by Father Giraud, have been admirable for me and for you. They went to throw themselves at the feet of His Grace and beg him to come to our aid. His Bishop's heart was as hard and cold as ice. He spurned me and those beloved and very excellent Fathers. I ask nothing further from His Grace. Let him, his administration and his gold remain where they are.[7] I believe I have shown him my most respectful deference for his episcopal character. Nevertheless, from now on, I can no longer have recourse to him. Between him and me, it is over. As for the good Fathers of Our Lady of LaSalette, I am grateful to them.

Father LeBaillif comments [below] that they had attempted the impossible with the Bishop of Grenoble who refused alms to this needy person, the salary of a servant, and in particular the portion due to a little Benjamin. It was in this sense that Sister Sainte-Valerie wrote to him on November 4, 1878: [†Ed. Maximin had died March 1, 1875]

... Perhaps the LaSalette Fathers were not all wayward. Several times they offered an abode to Maximin who, having no vocation for community life, always refused it. So, they left him to his own devices. I should also add that the Fathers could do very little. They were only custodians of the gifts of LaSalette and could not make use of them without the approval of the Bishop of the Diocese. This is one of the messages we thought we should communicate to you. Since you are only asking for clarity, I think you will be very satisfied with it. Since you are writing his story, and it is an important one, it is necessary that it be true.

MELANIE

1. LETTER TO "MOTHER CARRON," WIFE OF BAPTISTE PRA, MELANIE'S EMPLOYER AT ABLANDINS[8]

Correnc, February 23, 1851

My dear Mother Carron,

I cannot tell you the great joy I feel in writing to you to express my gratitude for all the kindness you have had for me. I pray to the Lord for you, who has everything and can do everything. He will reward you in my place. I also pray to Him that He may grant you and your whole family a long and happy old age. This is what my heart desires.

My dear mother, if I left Corps without going to see you, it is not without regret. In place of the long conversation I would have had with you, had I gone to say goodbye, I am writing you this long letter.

I am very anxious to see you. You know that, when I was in Corps, every Thursday I asked about you. If I were a bird, I would fly there for a moment's recreation, but I cannot. O God grant that I be quickly given the habit of a nun, so that I might soon go to LaSalette, to see and embrace with all my heart my good mother Carron. Oh! It is on that day that I will make up for what I did not do before leaving.

My dear mother, I recommend myself to the prayers of the whole household. Yes, pray for me that I may be a good, holy nun. I would rather die than not be a good nun. You know that I always had the idea of going abroad to convert and baptize the poor savages who do not know the good God. That is why I see myself as a good religious, so that with the help of my God, I may win souls for Him and send them to our homeland, heaven, which was destined for us from the beginning of the world. Oh, if we knew a little about heaven, we would not hesitate to do God's will.

My good mother Carron, you may be surprised that I want to go so far, and thus expose myself to death at any moment. But do you think that after seeing the Queen of queens who had come to this miserable land to mourn the sins of men, Melanie doesn't bother to console her good Mother? I want to do all I can to please her, and I hope you will do the same, and never allow your sons to sully their hands by working on Sundays. Yes, my dear mother, always remember that the Blessed Virgin said that it was Sunday work which weighed so much on her Son's arm, and that, if it was continued, She would let it fall. Well then, let us always be ready to die, so that when God will give us death, we will live forever in heaven. Breathe God's love into the little children of Baptiste Pra, so that they may grow wiser than they are in age and that, one day, I may see you all in heaven. Oh, how happy we will be when we are in heaven, especially when we think that this joy will last forever, everlasting joy. When you will have the happiness to go to the holy Mountain of Our Lady, I beg you to pray for me.

Farewell, my good mother Carrou, I embrace you all with all my heart, and I'm your ever obedient and affectionate little girl,

Melanie Mathieu,

Shepherdess of LaSalette, postulant at the Providence Convent

2. UNPUBLISHED LETTER TO MAXIMIN[9]

J.M.J.
Corenc, March 16, 1851

Dear Maximin:

Your letter made me very happy, especially when I saw the resolution you made. Oh, how happy I am I thanked the Blessed Virgin. I hurried quickly to begin the novena that you advised. Yes, dear Maximin, if you desire it, you will be very wise. You will pass your exam well. Have confidence. Pray to the good God who can do everything. If, however, you have no success, yet you have done all that you could have done, thank the good Lord, because it will mean that if you had succeeded, you would have had *dirty* love[10]; and then believe that God has a better reward in store for you in heaven. Oh! Let us rejoice in advance that one day we will go to the house of our heavenly Father! There we will love him well; we will bless him! Oh, good Maximin, it's good to think that we will go to see the Child Jesus! We will always, always love Him! Oh, how this thought does good to my soul! We are here below for only a short time. Work for heaven. Love to suffer good Maximin. May it be your consolation here below because I believe that there are no other consolations.

Make your meditation well every day, and do all your deeds to please the Blessed Virgin, our good Mama. Up there we will always see her, O happiness of happiness!

In the meantime, let us do all we can to please her, good Maximin. Let us try to see ourselves one day well raised up in heaven, but for this let us make all the sacrifices that come our way. I will pray for you and for Victor Long.

Goodbye my dear Maximin.

I am in the Sacred Hearts of Jesus and Mary, your sister in Our Lord.

Melanie Mathieu, Postulant

On the 19th do not take the trouble to come and see me at Corenc for I will not be there. You can see me at one o'clock in the afternoon with my Sister Saint-Louis, in Grenoble.

Corenc March 16, 1851

J.M.J.

3. UNPUBLISHED LETTER TO HER PARENTS[11]

J.M.J.
Corenc, April 13, 1851

Dear parents,

I received your letter with much pleasure, but I didn't receive all its contents with pleasure. I did not reproach you to make you angry, but so that you could use it to your advantage. Do you think I am pleased to hear that you did not celebrate the jubilee? Certainly not. It tears my soul apart. I really do not taste an hour of pleasure here on earth. Everything falls on me, if I want to leave France to go to China, it's not without reason, believe me. I believe that God will not delay long in letting his anger fall on certain countries, and if something happens to Corps, I will believe that it is the anger of God. How, dear parents, after all the graces you have received, do you fail to celebrate the jubilee? Oh, God, come and hide me! [†Editor: 1850 was a Jubilee, a "50th year" from the birth of Jesus Christ, replete with indulgences and celebrations.]

Dear parents, what did God do to cause you to harbor hatred against Him? Don't you know that God said, "Whatever you do to the least of my people, you do to me"? (Mt 25:40)

The Blessed Virgin appeared one day to a person and said to her, "What weighs down my Son's arm so much is blasphemy, work on Sundays and enmity," etc.[12]

You see, dear parents, how much hatred of your neighbor displeases God? Our Lord forgave his executioners and had no hatred against anyone like them. If you want to go and enjoy eternal rest, ah! If you knew what heaven is like you would not seek to gain esteem, but you would want to be despised, following the example of Our Lord Jesus Christ.

Dear parents, would you finally do me a great pleasure? Well, it will soon be the 19th of September, the feast of the Blessed Mother. Go to confession and receive Communion because I believe that God wants to punish the world, and if you were to die suddenly, where would you go? In heaven, no one will harbor hatred against you. It is just your imagination, that's all. Don't hate yourself, because God will not ask you what others do, but He will ask what you have done to deserve heaven. Be ready to die and think of judgment, of heaven, of hell,[13] and let your conduct as of today show to which of these two places you would want to go to spend eternity.

I beg you, if you so choose, to ask the Mayor for a tree to make a Cross to put on the mountain of LaSalette, where the Blessed Mother spoke.[14] Let us love the Blessed Virgin well. Oh, how happy we are to have in heaven such a good Mother who takes such good care of us! What would have become of us, and what would become of the world, if we did not have a Mary to implore from her Son his forgiveness of the whole world, without which it would surely no longer exist Oh, let us ask her daily to beg her Son to delay still longer the evils He has ready to fall upon ungrateful men. Oh, never hurt Mary.

I am doing everything I can to be permitted to take the religious habit in two months, so as to be completely devoted to God and to have no more communication with the world.

Mela[nie]

Corenc April 13, 1851

Let us truly love the Blessed Mother, so that She may lead us to Heaven. Oh, how kind She is! Glory be to our Mother Mary!

4. DESCRIPTION OF THE VIRGIN, WRITTEN DURING HER NOVITIATE[15]

Corenc, June 26, 1853

Sir,

It is on the instruction of our Mother Superior that I am honored to write you a few lines, to speak to you about Mary, our Mother and our protectress. But what shall I say? I, who loved her so little before She showed herself to me on the privileged Mountain, and who still loves her so little! Alas! I am the most wretched of creatures!

I would like to say something about Our Lady of LaSalette, but I can only repeat what you have already read in books. I can add just a few details that are perhaps not written down:

The Most Blessed Virgin was surrounded by two of the most intense illuminations. I don't know what name to give to the color of the first light that we beheld, and which extended one or two meters around our Mother. In this light, which was motionless, the two little shepherds were enveloped. Then another illumination emanated from our good Mother, very beautiful and brilliant. It reached us, and shot forth rays. I could not look at her for a long time without my eyes filling with tears. However, at that moment I felt stronger, so as to support her, because, if all had not been supernatural, even at the approach of that first light, I would have been reduced to ashes. We were so close to the Most Blessed Virgin that a person could not have passed between us.

The Most Blessed Virgin had roses around the shawl on her shoulders. Around her shoes there were white, blue, and red roses.[16] From the center of these roses there came out a kind of flame that wafted, like incense and mixed with the light that surrounded our Protectress. In short, it is more than possible that God, without letting us know, changed our eyes, so that we could remain as long as possible, as it were, gazing on the sun. At the moment Our Lady spoke, the sun that we have on the earth seemed like a mere shadow. That is why I am not surprised that when looking at the sun now, to my eyes it seems less bright than before the Apparition.

While the Blessed Virgin was speaking to us, She wept, shedding many tears. Oh, sir, who wouldn't cry when seeing his mother crying? And our Mother continues to weep over the ingratitude of her children. The tears of our good Mother were shining. They did not fall on the earth. They disappeared like sparks of fire. Mary's features were white and elongated. Her eyes were very soft. Her gaze was so kind, so affable, that one felt drawn to her spontaneously. You have to be dead not to love Mary.

You would have to be more than that! You would have to never have existed not to love Mary! And not to make her loved! Ah... if I could make myself heard by the whole universe, then I could satisfy my desire to make her loved.

May Jesus and Mary be known and loved by all hearts![17]: This is always my first cry when I wake up.

Have the great goodness, sir, not to forget me in your prayers and, although I am unworthy, I will pray for you.

Accept the tribute of the deep respect with which I, your most humble servant, bear you, sir,

Sister Mary of the Cross
The least of the Sisters

5. AUTOGRAPHED PRAYER BY MELANIE (UNPUBLISHED)[18]
Chaplet of Our Lady of LaSalette

She makes a note to herself to use an ordinary rosary

Offering of the Chaplet
My sweet Jesus, mercy! And You, good Virgin of LaSalette, receive this chaplet that we offer to you to help you bear the heavy arm of your divine Son.

On the large beads:
Acts of Faith, Hope and Charity

On the small beads:
Our Lady Reconciler of LaSalette,
Pray for us who have recourse to you!

Conclusion:
O Holy Virgin of LaSalette, see our faith in your Apparition, our confidence in you, and our regret for having offended your divine Son. Obtain mercy for us from Him, and cover us forever with your mighty protection.

You can pray it, good Father[19], in fewer words, to make it even shorter.

6. LETTER TO HER MOTHER AND THE INHABITANTS OF CORPS[20]

On July 19th, Napoleon III declared war. On September 2, he surrendered in Sedan. Melanie drew lessons from this, according to the message of LaSalette:

September 11, 1870

My dear and beloved mother, may Jesus be in all hearts!

This letter is not only for you, but also for all the people of Corps and the surrounding area.

Seeing that his children were forgetting their duties, that they were deviating from the law that God had given them, and that they were becoming ungrateful, the Lord resolved to punish them severely. The wife of the father asked for mercy, and at the same time she went to the father's two youngest children, that is, the two weakest, and the most ignorant of the whole family. The Bride, who cannot weep in the house of her heavenly Bridegroom, shed abundant tears in the fields of her wretched children. She uttered her complaints and her threats, because we do not return, we do not embrace the path of piety and we do not observe the law of the Divine Master. The little ones, the very little ones, embrace the reformation of the heart and are attached to the observance of the holy law of the Father of the family. But, alas! The greater number remains in crime and sinks even lower. Then the Father of the family sends his punishments to punish them, and remove them from this hardening [...]

You have understood this, dear mother and dear people of Corps. The Father of the family is God. We are his children. Neither you, nor I, have loved Him as we should have. We have not kept his commandments as we should have. Now the good Lord is punishing us. We have many soldiers dying, many families and cities in misery, and it will not be over until we turn to God. Paris is guilty, and very guilty, because it has rewarded a wicked man who wrote against the divinity of Jesus Christ (the ungodly Renan). There is a limited time for men to commit sin; then God, who is eternal, punishes the wicked. [...]

It is necessary: 1) that France recognizes that this war is purely the effect of the hand of God; 2) that she humbles herself and 3) that she wholeheartedly calls for observance of his commandments without human respect. There are people praying and asking God for the success of our French soldiers. This is not what the good God wants. He wants the conversion of the French. The Blessed Virgin came to France......nd France is not converted. She is more guilty than the other nations. She does not humble herself before the good Lord. She will be greatly humiliated: Paris, home of vanity and pride, who can prevent her from perishing if fervent prayers do not rise to the Heart of the Divine Master?

Yes, let us pray, let us pray! Form processions, as you did in the year 1846-1847. Believe that God will listen to you. He always listens. Let us pray very much. I never loved Napoleon because I have in my memory his whole history. May the Divine Savior forgive him for all the evil he did, and will do again. Let us remember that we are created to love and serve God, and outside of that there is no true happiness. Let mothers bring up their children in a Christian manner, for the time of tribulation is not over. If I were to tell you the number and the qualities of these tribulations you would be dazed, but I do not want to frighten you. Trust in God who loves you and loves all. Let us pray, let us pray! And the sweet, good and tender Mary will always be with us. Prayer disarms God's anger; prayer is the key to paradise. Let us pray for our poor soldiers; let us pray for all the mothers who are mourning the loss of their sons, and let us consecrate ourselves to our Blessed Mother in heaven. Let us pray, let us pray for those blind people who do not see that it is the hand of God that is pursuing France at this time. Let us pray much and do penance. I recommend that you be attached to the Blessed Virgin and to our Holy Father the Pope, who is the visible Head of the Church of Jesus Christ on earth. In your processions, in your penances, pray much, especially for him. Finally, everyone be at peace. Love one another as brothers. Do not get entangled in the politics of the Republic. Ask God for a Christian king and promise God to keep his commandments. Keep them exactly, in holiness. Then I hope that by the mercy of God you will be happy, and that you will make a good and holy death, which I wish for all of you by placing you under the protection of the august and holy Mary. I leave you, my dear mother, in the Sacred Hearts of Jesus and Mary, and I embrace you tenderly.

Mary of the Cross, Victim of Jesus

My salvation is in the Cross!
The eye of God is watching over me!

7. "HOW I PERCEIVED THE SECRETS" LETTERS FROM MELANIE TO FATHER FELICIEN BLIARD[21]

Melanie confides to Father Emile Millon, chaplain and historian of LaSalette, how she perceived Mary's message on the mountain on September 19, 1846. Millon remarked: "This letter and the subsequent ones are remarkable: they would not be surpassed by the most consummate of mystics, both in substance and in form."[22]

> The Blessed Virgin pronounced all the words, either of the Secret or the Rule, but I could have guessed or penetrated the rest of what She was saying: As She pronounced all the words, a great veil was lifted: Events were uncovered before my eyes and in my imagination, and a great space opened up before me. I saw the events, the changes in the works of the earth, and God immutable in his glory, looking upon the Virgin who stooped down to speak to two shepherds.

> There are people who would prefer that the Blessed Virgin had not spoken so much. It is a pity that they want to limit a poor shepherdess who wishes with all her heart that the whole world would have seen and heard everything that she saw and heard during half an hour, because everybody would have been

converted. And these people who say that Our Lady doesn't speak so much, would have understood well and better than what books teach, if there are any who teach it, that the words of heaven are not only words: that is to say that the person who listens does not stop at the letter, at the word. Rather each word develops, and the future action takes place in the moment, and one sees a thousand and a thousand times more things than what the ears hear. One rises to a height, not to heaven, and perhaps one does not even rise above the earth, but one sees and hears everything, understands without words being said, while completely unaware of oneself. And, without wanting to, one enters into the spirit of the scenes being displayed: That is, if it is a sad scene, you are sad; if it is joyful, you feel joy.[23] We see plots being made. We see the kings of the earth, each of whom having several guardian angels. We see them stirring, doing, undoing. We see the jealousy of some, the ambition of others, etc. All this comes in a single word, uttered by the lips of the one who makes hell tremble, the Virgin Mary. Yes, if these people had once seen someone from heaven, they would no longer say that the spirit who spoke to them could not say so many things. However, they would rather say that it is impossible for them to express everything they know. I am a great ignoramus. But if I were a most learned scholar, I could not write everything from above, because the expressions of the greatest scholars are a mere shadow of the full truth conveyed by the expressions that are used up above to communicate with one another. The language from above is a movement of the soul, of the desires of the soul, of the impulses of the soul. The bright eyes of souls communicate with one another.

So, I think that even if we wanted to explain all this, we couldn't do it. I, poor vile dust, am as one not yet born to talk about these things. Let us love the good Lord with all our heart: Oh, this is our knowledge and our treasure, that we must be mad with for love of Him who was the first to be madly in love with us [...]

I find it very difficult to explain something for which there is no comparison. If, for example, I wanted to explain how I saw the Blessed Virgin, how I heard her words, how I beheld what She was saying carried out in action, how I saw the whole world, how I saw the eye of the Lord - it was a picture in action. I saw the blood of those who were put to death, and the blood of the martyrs. But the love of this sweet Virgin was spread over me. It took the place of everything else. It melted me. I no longer thought. I had no power to reflect. I was well taught. Then I spoke, but I did not speak with words. When the sweet Virgin walked, She did not need to tell me to follow her, certainly not. I did not know that I was alive. I did not think that I had feet to walk. I was attracted. I simply adhered to this ravishing beauty, Mary! I say again, if I wanted to explain all this, I would never, never be able to express the truth.

8. LITANIES OF LOVE OF THE BLESSED VIRGIN MARY[24] COMPOSED BY MELANIE

O dear Lord, have mercy on us!
Jesus Christ,
Oh, dear Lord,
God the Father, ocean of love,
God the Son, victim of peace,
God the Holy Spirit, source of light,
Mary, Mother and Virgin, I love you!
Mary my dear Mother,
Mary, Queen of the Virgins,
Mary, my tenderness,
Mary, my sovereign,
Mary, my guide[25],
Mary, my hope,
Because you are the masterpiece of the Holy Trinity,
Because you were conceived without sin,
Because you are the bride of the Holy Spirit,

Because you are the Mother of the poor,
Because you will take care of my needs,
Because you will take care of my parents,
Because you will reward my benefactors,
Because you will obtain mercy,
Because you are full of graces,
Because you are my faithful friend,
Because you love me,
Because you will protect me,
Because you pray to your Son for me.
Because I take you for all my possessions,
Because I gave you everything.
Because you will be present at my death.
Because you shared the sufferings of Jesus Christ,
Because your heart has been pierced for me,
Because you are the greatest after God,
Because you are the friend of those who do not have one,
Because you are merciful,
Because you protect the sick,
Because you comfort the afflicted,
Because you are with those who are persecuted,
Because you bring sinners back to God,
Because you are Heaven of Heaven,
Because you are a gold mine,
Because you are the glory of the Holy Trinity,
Because you will save France,

Pray for us, O holy Mother of God,
that we may all see you one day in heaven!

9. PRAYER TO OUR LORD JESUS CHRIST IN A TIME OF SORROW[26]

Most sweet and adorable Jesus, who are the only Savior of mankind, I beg You to look with mercy on the great Christian family in desolation, and in fear of your justice. Your mercy, Lord, has always conquered the ingratitude of men. Make it triumph over our hardness. Glorify your mercy, by forgiving us, by giving us true and sincere repentance for our sins, by delivering us from our tribulations and by placing us on the path of your holy law.

Hear me, Lord, by the thirst that You suffered for us on the Cross. You who are the fountain of living water, can You bear to see your creatures, redeemed by your Precious Blood, reduced by so many afflictions? If our hearts are hard as stone, You can soften them, You, O my Jesus, to whom nothing is impossible! If the magnet attracts iron to itself, how would your mercy not attract our hearts to You, and to the observance of your Law? Hurry, Lord, to dry our tears. I ask this of You through your five open wounds, which, like five powerful voices, ask for mercy for mankind. For us they are like the rainbow of the New Testament, and the object of our hope. Amen![27]

JACQUES MARITAIN

This philosopher, above all a spiritual person, perceived and analysed with the means at hand, the deep value of Melanie. She was an important axis of his life.

1. LETTER TO DOM PAUL DELATTE, ABBOT OF SOLESMES (1890-1921) IN RESPONSE TO A COMMENT ABOUT MELANIE[28]

Versailles, 16 rue de l'Orangerie
Tuesday, March 2, 1912

Dear Reverend Father,

Please allow me to reply to your letter which has caused me very deep pain. However, I thank you for writing to me what you think and for showing me, once again, your paternal affection. For me I am only a layman, a poor and ignorant philosopher. It seems to me, however, that I must explain to you the reasons for my veneration of Melanie, not out of a spirit of obstinacy but out of love for the truth. I beg you to see in this letter only a humble testimony of my trusting affection. If I sound pedantic or presumptuous, forgive me in advance. I cannot help but submit to you, as they stand, the arguments by which I prove to myself my conviction.

I can't imagine for a moment that Melanie invented what she wrote:

1. Because she writes out of obedience and under the seal of confession.

2. Because the characteristic note of her story, the disposition of mind which manifests itself in every line, is an exclusive passion for truth, a virtual incapacity to conceive of lies and cunning (see. p.59, p.91, p.93-94 etc.) This cannot be a pretense. Sincerity has an accent that never deceives. Besides, if I study Melanie's story, I always and everywhere find a horror of lying. All her actions bear the mark of the sincerity of naiveté itself. Thus, for example, when Bishop Fava offered her in Rome to tempt her, a 100-franc note "for her small pleasures," she retained this proposal as an awful memory without suspecting for a moment that it might have merely been a test. As for her childhood years, nothing could be more decisive than her relationship with Miss DesBrulais. Also, isn't her whole life the best testimony? Do we expose ourselves, for the pleasure of supporting a lie, to abandonment, to exile, to the most atrocious slanders, to the worst sufferings? *Filii matris mea pugnaverunt contra me* [Song 1:5] [My mother's sons fought against me.] Such was her lot until death. Our Lord, by letting her participate in her dereliction, she signed away her life to Him. This mark is infallible. All those who knew her, her enemies themselves...eet some of them in LaSalette - noted her fidelity to Our Lady and her invincible faith in her mission. This is obvious, for anyone who goes to the trouble of studying the matter.

3. Because the veracity of Melanie is guaranteed to me by the Blessed Virgin and by the Church. At the age of 69, at the request of her confessor [Father Annibale DiFrancia], she wrote down the story of her childhood. She had already indicated the main features of it in a biography written in 1852, when she was twenty-one (at the request of Father Sibillat). If all this is wrong, she is a shameless actress, capable of maintaining the same hoax for fifty years. Would Our Lady have chosen such an actress, a child of lies, to send her people a solemn message, on September 19, 1846? On this point, in fact, the Church has pronounced itself. Am I expected to believe with the Church that Melanie was telling the truth regarding the Apparition of LaSalette on Sept. 19th, but after that time she was a liar all the remaining days of her life, a liar before God, a liar in the sacrament of Confession? Is it in accordance with divine convention, to choose a liar to receive a message, or to ask us to put faith in the testimony of an apostate? Does the Holy One choose wrongly, or does not know if the chosen one would preserve the message, or does God no longer have any knowledge of the predestination of souls? The honor of Our Lady is at stake. That's enough for me.

And afterwards, who will pass judgement on this soul? Who will declare her to be a deceiver or virtuous? Will it be myself, or the priests who have directed that soul? But all have paid homage to Melanie's holiness: the French priest (Sibillat) who sent this biography to Leon Bloy; Bishop Zola of Lecce, who gave his Imprimatur to the Secret; Archbishop Cecchini of Taranto, who had her as a penitent during her last years and who had her body exhumed, which was found intact; Canon DiFrancia, who on the anniversary day of her funeral delivered a eulogy in the cathedral of Messina.

If Melanie is not lying, how is it that she be accused by persons who openly raise a platform and are comfortable inventing "*quidquid site in mentem venerit*" [whatever thought comes to mind]?

If Melanie is insane (consistently for over fifty years!) I cannot believe this:

1. Because of her biography, which obviously denotes an author in full possession of her reason
2. Because of all the rest of her life, where there is no trace of imbalance, and where the virtues and the spirit of prayer shine forth
3. Because of the testimony of her confessors
4. Because of the honor of Our Lady

And, finally if all the facts are true but of diabolical origin, I can't believe it:

1. Because of the facts themselves, where everything leads to God and removes evil
2. Because of Melanie's holy life, because of prayer and penance, which the demon cannot promote, except by distorting them (yet Melanie was always discreet and submissive to her confessor)
3. Because of the honor of Our Lady

And then, there are signs that are perhaps more striking than all of this:

1. First, the extraordinarily theological and doctrinal character of her visions. I only have to reread her childhood biography to be convinced of this. Our Lord constantly gave her a theological and doctrinal instruction, sometimes even philosophical. She is so filled with the truths of the Faith that as soon as she starts talking about it, she tends to preach, and only stops with "etc, etc." She is better educated than many modern apologists on the Faith and on its formal motive. She has a precise and developed theological instruction on the mysteries of the Holy Trinity, on the attributes of God, on the Incarnation, on the Redemption! As for the topic

of grace, she speaks as a Thomist. And she feasts on these truths. They are her joy. They are also the mainspring of her spiritual life.

Oh no, this is not a mere note of piety! It is the mark of Catholicism, the note of intellectual light, that neither caprice, nor imagination, nor the demon are able to imitate. In vain do I try to ignore so many things. It seems to me that among the saints who are most elevated in grace, the very character of their holiness is that they live by the Truth, and the Truth is their joy. It seems to me that an exalted imagination, unconscious reactions of nature, a pious fantasy cannot give that. They can nourish the soul with images, but never with doctrine. Caprice has never been able to produce order. By abandoning myself to anything that passes through my mind, will I invent the creed of Saint Athanasius? Even if I am literate, more or less "subconscious" reminiscences will always be subject to rambling of the dream, and errors will inevitably seep in, unless my "subconscious" is crystallized in theology! And in any case, it would remain on the surface of my mind. I would not necessarily live by it. If someone, using sheer inventions, causes others to believe truth and doctrine, while lying, consciously and voluntarily, then this impostor must be a very learned doctor, of rare intelligence. And would that even be enough? Are not theological truths so delicate that in order to speak properly about them, the assistance of grace is necessary? Either way, Melanie was absolutely ignorant, absolutely uneducated. There is no better noted historical fact. But all her spiritual life breathes doctrine, supernatural truth. Therefore, this life cannot be the fruit of illusion, of whim or of dreams. And not only should this ignorant poor woman, if she invented what she said, be a learned theologian, she should also be an extraordinary poet. It is true that here the criterion has something subjective. But for me I do not know. Apart from the liturgy and the revelations of other great contemplatives, there is nothing as beautiful as certain pages of this autobiography.

2. I am also struck by a second sign. It is the perfect conformity of her life with everything I know, regarding my limited experience of the mystical life and of the teachings of the saints on prayer. It is also the perfect conformity of the descriptions that Melanie makes of certain [earlier, childhood] visions with the description she gave of the Apparition of LaSalette, an Apparition recognized by the Church. If the first are invented, how will I believe in the second?

3. The third sign, finally, is essential in my eyes: if Melanie's life is a farce, then her mission would be an illusion, and therefore her perception of the Apparition of LaSalette would disappear. Did not Our Lady come to weep over France to remind Christians and especially priests of their lofty vocation, or to warn her children of the approach of times of desolation? In an era of so much debasement of truths, of a general oblivion of the demands of the supernatural life, an evil, caused above all by the mediocrity of the clergy - not only did God remain silent, but he also allowed Melanie's life and the Secret of LaSalette, this great testimony and this great claim of its sovereignty to be nothing more than an illusion and a deception? Illusion! But the very mission of Melanie was to suffer for the clergy and to recall them to the supernatural integrity demanded by Our Lord, and at the same time Melanie would manifest for the priestly character the most eminent esteem and an unswerving obedience. Illusion? Consider these words of Melanie:

> "I understood that in the clergy, the purity of the spirit is the guardian of the purity of the body, that there is no chastity of the body in the absence of constant purity of the spirit, and that the spirit and the senses will not keep their purity unless they are crucified with Jesus Christ."

Illusion? Consider these words of Our Lord to Melanie:

"My daughter, look at your Jesus, crucified again by his chosen friends, my ministers, those who are my paths to my people. Offer to my Eternal Father the great sacrifice of Jesus Christ, the Eternal Priest."

Illusion? Consider this call of Our Lady, in the Secret:

[30] *I address an urgent call to the earth;*

I call the true disciples of the living God who reigns in heaven;

I call the true imitators of Christ made Man, the only and true Savior of men;

I call my children, my true devotees, those who have offered themselves to me so that I may lead them to my divine Son, those whom I carry in my arms, so to speak, those who have lived by my spirit;

Finally, I call the Apostles of the Last Times, the faithful disciples of Jesus Christ, who have lived in contempt for the world and of themselves, in poverty and humility, in contempt and in silence, in prayer and in mortification, in chastity and in union with God, in suffering and unknown to the world.

Dear and Reverend Father, when a book shows me an admirable fidelity to the truths which are most dear to me, to the truths of Catholic doctrine such as the mystical life, or of what my eyes see in this world, how would my heart resist? Do I not have within me through the holy Baptism, a Truth, which recognizes itself in the truth that is presented to me, and which leaps to meet it?

Allow me, dear and reverend Father, to tell you all my thoughts. Melanie speaks of a protection or preservative which Our Lord gave to her, in the form of small thorns without root on the surface of her soul. In my opinion, these were some natural imperfections and a certain sourness of character which made her unpleasant to her neighbor, and which Our Lord left her so that she would always be treated with harshness and contempt. This protection was not only in her person, but also in the events of her life and in the circumstances of her mission. Hence, her supporters sometimes behaved with imprudence and sometimes with excesses. Thus, from one point of view the way in which Leon Bloy presents his biography of Melanie, and even the tone of its introduction, it can put off those who are unfamiliar with Bloy's style that earned him the epitaph, "the apostle of scoundrels"… But it's only the "preservative." It's the outer shell of the nut. If we read this biography quickly, we see only the shell. But, I believe with all my heart that there is something more! Otherwise, farewell to all moral certitude.

Assuredly, throughout this biography there is on display an extraordinary physiognomy. But I tell myself that God is quite free. He who does not need to follow common rules for our spiritual development, can shower profusely, very early as He pleases, an abundance of mystical phenomena. Undoubtedly, God has a way of humiliating our wisdom, a way that displays his freedom to "sweep aside" worldly wisdom to transmit his messages to us. In many lives of saints, recognized by the Church, especially in modern biographies, this freedom of God is evident. For this reason, I do not reject Blessed Margaret Mary Alacoque, nor Gerard Majella, nor Sister Catherine Labouré, nor so many others. And above all, I tell myself that in Melanie's biography, her mystical physiognomy is even more wonderfully evident because it is accompanied by the purest and highest graces of the fullness of the supernatural life, of contemplation, of peace, and an illumination that compels me to rank her among the greatest saints.

I've opened my heart to you, dear Reverend Father, and I could not help but do so. I hope I haven't said anything that doesn't suit my condition as a poor, ignorant, unworthy Christian. *Adolescentulus sum ego* [Solomon's plea to God "I am very young." 1Kg 3:7] I feel it in a very hard way. But what would I become if I did not sincerely say what I think, especially to you, dear and Reverend Father, to whom I owe so many goods? I ask Saint Benedict [†] to intercede for me, and to make you accept, with this letter, the expression of my most respectful and devoted affection.

Jacques Maritain.

[†Editor: The patronage of Saint Benedict is an allusion to the Benedictine community of Solesmes which shared his concern for the reputation of Melanie. The Abbey would later accept the responsibility of housing the collection of documents gathered during the course of fifty years by Father Paul Gouin to defend Melanie against her detractors. The Abbey was less than five miles from the town of Avoise where Father Gouin served as pastor for most of his priestly life.]

2. IS MELANIE'S SECRET INSPIRED?[29]

I had answered Benedict XV, in that audience of April 1918, that I believed that the words reported by Melanie were true *to the letter*.

Forty-six years later, as I write these pages [in 1965], I wonder. Would I honestly give the same answer now? It seems to me that my answer would be formulated a little differently because I would no longer speak exclusively of the Secret of LaSalette, but rather in general of any message whatsoever concerning chastisements or future events, as transmitted by a messenger from the world beyond.

Assuming (as is moreover the case if I was still being questioned about Melanie) that I believe in the absolute veracity of the witness - thus excluding the hypothesis of any exaggeration, even involuntary on her part...ould rather say, "I believe in the full authenticity of the words reported." However, this does not imply that everything that is said there must be taken "literally" according to the current meaning of a particular expression, with regard to common earthly usage. For forty-six years we have had time to reflect a little on the infinite transcendence of the perspective of heaven compared to the perspective of those on the earth. Not only is it in the perspective of eternity that the saints beheld the events of the earth, so that if they speak of future things to someone here below, it is not the succession of time (which is naturally of great interest to us) in which they are interested. The periods mentioned can in reality be very distant from each other, and be more or less telescoped in what is expressed, and thus the chronological order may not be respected. However, in a still more general way it is clear that in order to be understood a little by men, it is necessary that the heavenly messengers use human language, which cannot just mean purely and simply *"to the letter"* what is said. The literal meaning of what they tell us goes beyond human words and therefore remains essentially laden with mystery, while a kind of excess, such as "too much" (overstatement) or in "not enough" (understatement), is introduced into our language as they use it. The voices of Joan of Arc in her prison announced to her that she was going to be delivered. Did they mean what they said, "literally" that she was going to escape her enemies? Come now! It meant she was going up to the stake, and would in that manner be delivered from the English and their prelates, and also delivered from this perishable flesh, and delivered from evil, and free to see her God...

Even more, the term "language" does not refer only to the words that we use. It also covers everything that we use to make ourselves understood. Therefore, we use images, which are familiar to the people to whom we are speaking at a given moment in time and at such a place on earth. (Suppose we could make a phone call back in time to a contemporary of Julius Caesar, could we tell him about airplanes and electronic machines, about the British Parliament, or the Communist Party Presidiums? The interlocutor could not understand anything unless we made use of images familiar in his culture, such as his own words and syntax.

We can go further. We know that in heaven the blessed do not use words to converse with one another. On the other hand, we also know that God uses what is in the mind of the prophet as an instrument. A heavenly being, speaking to someone on earth does not emit, as we do, sounds passing physically through the air. The words heard by the witness here below, instead of being carried by sound waves, are created within him from a divine activation exercised on the faculties of his soul. To put it another way, a heavenly being who appears and who speaks, does not utter word-sound, but rather dictates, while moving the lips as we do, into the mind of the person chosen to act as messenger. At that very moment the words are produced by a divine action upon the human faculties of the messenger.[30] The messenger can think that the words coming from heaven are really heard, and authentically transmitted in the typical manner through the instrument of his mind, and in the "archetypical"[31] perspective presented to the subconscious of the messenger, without any alteration in the meaning *or the letter* from what was willed from on high.

When someone from heaven speaks to some poor child here on earth, we have only to accept the words *as they are*, but must understand them (understand their "literal meaning"), according to the intention of the one who makes us hear these words, and whose intention is not to tell fortunes or to inform us in the manner of a secret agent, but, as is the case for any revelation under the New Law, to draw our attention, by impressive signs, capable of stirring hearts everywhere, to things which are important for our action, and which, of ourselves, we see more or less badly. These may be failures, or expectations, or warnings, which when they are realized in the designs of God will doubtless appear very different from what we may have imagined. All this is designated in essentially mysterious terms which, even when the words were reported exactly as they were heard, *"to the letter,"* the general practical meaning is communicated, but not necessarily the particular mental perspectives, nor the particular imagery, nor the words taken according to human measure by means of which transcendent ideas are signified to us.

Reputation for holiness

Despite rigorous criticism of Melanie, her reputation for holiness is very much alive in Italy, even among the hierarchy, which is considering opening her cause for beatification.

1. Letter from the Reverend Father Garrigou-Lagrange [O.P.] to Mr. Fernand Corteville

+ *Carmel of Vienne Isère*
September 1, 1957

Dear Sir:

Arriving in Vienne where I am until September 8th, I found everything you sent me. I believe I recognized in *La vie de Sœur Marie de la Croix, Bergère de la Salette* [The Life of Sister Mary of the Cross, Shepherdess of LaSalette], what the pastor of Avoise, Father Paul Gouin, had already communicated to me.

I have read quite a few publications on this subject and I am inclined to think that Melanie kept her mission until her death. I knew very well a Dominican lay brother who brought to her, her very frugal midday meal shortly before her death. This Brother was in the service of Bishop Cecchini, Dominican Bishop of Altamura where she died. She announced the day and hour of her death to this lay brother who verified this prediction.....]

Father Reg. Garrigou-Lagrange O.P.

2. Letter from His Eminence Bishop Paciello of Altamura (Italy) to the Postulator of Her Cause for Beatification, Father Ciro Quaranta

Melanie died in Altamura

[...] Father Michel Corteville spoke to me about the opportunity that you suggested to him, to constitute a *Standing Committee of the Friends of Melanie Calvat, Shepherdess of LaSalette*, with the aim of knowing, and making known through the research of documents, acts, testimonies, publications, the person and the work of Melanie Calvat, who died in Altamura after staying only six months in this city.

As far as I'm concerned, I see no difficulty in setting up this committee, and that my archivist, by becoming a member, can collaborate in his task.

I have only been in this diocese for a year, but I have had the impression of the great esteem of the faithful towards Melanie. If the committee is successful in its purpose, it will be able to provide the Church with material useful for its authorized judgment.

That's why I bless the initiative, and all who contribute to it.....]

Altamura, October 27, 1998
+ Mario Paciello, Bishop

3. LETTER FROM THE REVEREND FATHER GEORGES NALIN[32] SUPERIOR GENERAL OF THE ROGATIONISTS, TO FATHER MICHEL CORTEVILLE, AFTER READING DOCUMENTS COLLECTED FOR CORTEVILLE'S THESIS

Send, O Lord, holy Apostles to your Church!

July 27, 1999

Reverend Father:

I would like to thank you warmly for the collection of documents on Melanie Calvat that I read, with real pleasure, for my edification.

I was particularly struck by the second part relating to Melanie's relationship with our Blessed Founder [Annibale DiFrancia], which intensified during the year of her stay in Messina as a formator for our Sisters.

Her deeply spiritual and wise personality emerged clearly from the many letters she exchanged with Father Annibale. I had the subsequent confirmation of the deep esteem and veneration that Father A. cherished for the seer of LaSalette to the point of working, after her death, to recognize her extraordinarily spiritual life.

Father Georges Nalin

4. CIRCULAR OF FATHER CIRO QUARANTA, POSTULATOR TO THE SACRED CONGREGATION FOR THE CAUSES OF SAINTS

Rome, August 5, 1999

Dear Brother and Sister in Christ:

I am a priest of the Rogationist congregation. We were founded by Blessed Annibale Maria DiFrancia who invited Melanie to direct his foundation of Sisters. Later, he wished to introduce the cause of her beatification himself. In agreement with the Bishop of Altamura where the body of the Shepherdess of LaSalette rests, I am working today for this cause.

I know that you very much desire that the Church recognize the heroic virtues of Melanie. However, the numerous studies required by the Church are left to the charge of the faithful concerned. Therefore, in order to be able to undertake the first examination of the cause, I boldly call for your participation.

In the hope that your help will allow the prompt opening of the process of beatification of the Shepherdess of Our Lady of LaSalette, please accept the expression of my fraternal prayer, and my gratitude.

Father Ciro Quaranta.

P.S: You can send your testimony to:
   L'Association des Enfants de N.D. de LaSalette
   12 Avenue du Grain d'Or
   49600 Beaupréau, FRANCE
They will forward it to me.

[†Editor: See note below on ENS. The Association has been defunct since 2017, or earlier.]

5. PRAYER FOR THE BEATIFICATION OF MELANIE, APPROVED BY THE BISHOP OF ALTAMURA

O Holy Trinity, Father, Son and Holy Spirit, source of all holiness, we recognize and thank you for your immense love towards us, poor sinners, when in the Apparition of the Most Holy Virgin Mary on the mountain of LaSalette to Melanie and to Maximin, you called us to prayer and reparation, to cease offending your name with vile blasphemies, and to cease profaning the Lord's day.

We pray to you Lord, who chose Melanie, the shepherdess of LaSalette, to carry your message of conversion and reparation, and kept her worthy to contemplate the weeping face of the Mother of your Son, Jesus. If such is your plan, exalt her in your Church, as a model of faith and virtue. Amen!

Name a particular intention, pray three Glorias to the Most Holy Trinity and an Ave Maria to Our Lady of LaSalette, Reconciler of Sinners.

+ Bishop Agostino Superbo
Bishop of Altamura, Gravina and Acquaviva,
February 8, 1995

The prospect of the beatification of Melanie will encounter the necessity of a change of attitudes, because so much of the 19th century differs from the years that followed.

This challenge arose with the beatification of Pius IX. His Syllabus condemned those who wanted to "reconcile the Roman Pontiff with progress" as well as those who tried to do so, from a different perspective, namely John XXIII (beatified with Pius IX) and Vatican II. Faithful to the perspective of Pius IX, Melanie did not compromise.

What will be important is to discern what her holiness and her intrepid faith in the wake of Pius IX will bring to today's relativism. "The Devil's Advocate" will present objections and limitations, as is his duty. The Church will judge.

Italy Protected Melanie and the Secret

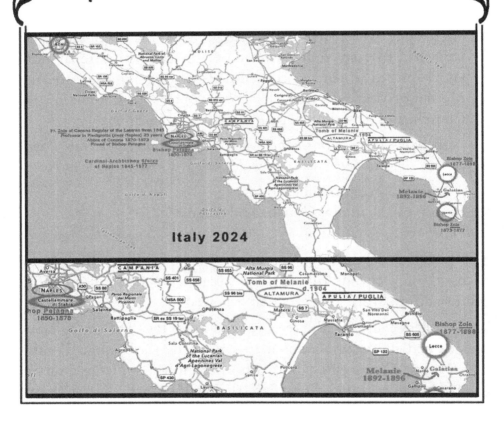

CHRONOLOGY

1818 February	Three sheets of prophetic warnings printed in Avignon are "seized" from a peddler. Similarities with the message of LaSalette will be noticed.[1]
1825 30 November	Civil wedding of Melanie's parents, Julie Barnaud and Pierre Calvat, nicknamed Mathieu (natural son of Anne Roulet), in Séchiliennes, Isère.
1827 11 January	Birth of Pierre Calvat, eldest brother of Melanie[2]
1828 28 January	Marriage (ecclesiastical) of Jean-Maximin Giraud and Anne-Marie Templar, parents of Maximin
1828 12 April	Birth of Henriette Rosalie Calvat, sister of Melanie, died in infancy
1829 3 May	Birth of Joseph Calvat, brother of Melanie
1829 13 November	Birth of Marie Angelique Giraud, Maximin's sister
1831 7 November	Birth of Melanie in Corps
1831 13 November	Birth of Marguerite Giraud, sister of Maximin
1834 3 February	Ecclesiastical marriage of Melanie's parents, Julie Barnaud and Pierre Calvat
1834 27 July	Birth of Henri Joseph Calvat, brother of Melanie

towards 1834	Melanie's father shows her a crucifix and tells her about the love of Jesus. Brought to parties and festivals, she screams and ultimately exasperates her mother. Melanie chooses to take refuge in silence in a corner of the house, contemplating the crucifix. Put out of the house one day, she gets lost and wanders in the woods. A child who says he is her Little Brother appears to her, consoles her, instructs her spiritually and finally helps her find the road to her house. Melanie falls gravely ill for 5 or 6 months.
towards 1835	Recovered, she is chased out again by her mother and falls asleep in a cart that takes her away. The driver discovers her identity at the crossing of the Drac [a river] and abandons her. "Brother" appears to her. She asks to be allowed to suffer like the Christ on the Cross, and then she feels intense pain. "Brother" brings her back; her aunt takes her in at her home for 2 or 3 years. (from her short biography written for her spiritual director, on September 3, 1852, and Italian and French autobiographies for her last directors, Saint Annibale DiFrancia and Father Émile Combes, 1897-1900). The stigmatization of Melanie began around the age of 4, according to her statement to her confessor, St. Annibale DiFrancia, who comments: "A stigmatization at such a tender age is a very rare thing and worthy of great admiration" (*Brèves nouvelles... sur Mélanie..., écrits du fondateur des Rogationnistes* - Brief news...on Melanie..., writings of the founder of the Rogationist Fathers, vol. 59, p.38)
1835 *27 August*	Birth of Maximin in Corps
1836 *16 October*	Birth of Eugène Joseph Calvat, brother of Melanie

1836-1837	Melanie, now about six years old, is sent by her Aunt Barnaud to school
1837 *11 January*	Death of Anne-Marie Templier, mother of Maximin
Lent 1837	Henriette Deluy-Fabry (b. 1828) has a vision at the age of 9: "You will found and be a co-operator of a religious Order" (The Sisters of Reparation of Our Lady of LaSalette).
1837 *12 April*	The marriage of Jean-Maximin Giraud, father of Maximin, with his second wife, Marie-Madeleine Court
1838	At the age of seven, Melanie is hired out. "My parents were poor. My mother put me in a family to take care of a little child." (Melanie's *Curriculum Vitae*, April 26, 1899)
1838 *9 June*	Birth of Jean-Francois Giraud, half-brother of Maximin
1838 *24 December*	The priest of Corps, Father Viollet, is served an interdict. A pro-curate assumes his charge.
1839 *28 May*	Birth and baptism of Marie Marguerite Calvat
1840	In the spring, Melanie begins to keep the sheep for the same employers. In the snowy season, she returns home. It was that year that the school-mistress arranged her hair more softly, but her mother cut it back with vengeance. Her father threatens to leave his wife.

1841 - 1842	Melanie is placed by her mother in the service of a family that lives in an isolated house in the mountains in the Commune of Saint-Jean-des-Vertus [Saint John of the Virtues]
1841 20 December	Birth of Barthelemy Auguste Mathieu, eighth child of Calvat, baptized the next day
End of December 1841	Rage of Pierre Calvat against his wife over shirts with missing buttons; Melanie intervenes.
1842	"One day I had the idea of making a belt of nails; I wore it about fourteen years." (Italian Autobiography, 1898) Melanie is about 10 or 11 years old.
End 1842	Pierre Calvat expels his wife. Melanie brings her mother some provisions and is rewarded with a heavy slap. In 1903, people try to make Melanie talk about the mistreatment of her mother. She answers only: "It's because I had a sour temper. My mother was so high-spirited that she danced the year she died at age 90." (JAC p.169) Melanie is placed in service in Ste-Luce.
1844	Thanks to the zeal of the pastor of Corps, Father Pierre Melin, her parents take up their religious duties again; Melanie returns to catechism; she has no skill for memorization. Her mother buys her blue leather shoes so that she can accompany her to the ball.
1844 1 April	Birth of Julie Calvat, sister of Melanie

1844 *2 June*	Melanie has a vision; she receives a mystical ring of espousal. Jesus told her: "Today we are united; you will love what I love, you will experience what I have experienced." (French autobiography)
1845	"I was placed in service at Quet-en-Beaumont," with the terrible "Moine" where she was mistreated. [Gouin: The Moines were a family of brigands.]
1846	"I was put into service with Baptist Pra in the village of Les Ablandins, Commune of LaSalette." (*Mémorandum*, 1893) Her mother sends her out to fetch wood even on catechism days. She misses so much instruction that she cannot receive her First Communion (French autobiography).
Beginning of September	A mysterious light guides Melanie in the night, from the St. Sebastien chapel to the house of her employers in Les Ablandins. This event, noted on April 13 1847, will be discussed by the commission of Inquiry.
1846 *17 September*	Maximin comes to Les Ablandins to replace a sick shepherd for eight days. Maximin guards a goat and four cows in the Babou field. In the evening (Thursday), he sees Melanie.
Friday *18 September*	Maximin obtains permission for them to keep their eight cows together, on the southern slope of Planeau, in the meadows of their employers and at Mont Sous-les-Baisses.

Saturday 19 September	The unique Apparition takes place in the valley of Sezia, at Mont Sous-les-Baisses, dominating the valley of LaSalette; they tell the story to their respective employers, Baptiste Pra and Pierre Selme; the same day (or the following day), Melanie breaks her staff and makes a Cross that she plants on the spot where the Virgin rose into the sky.
1846 21 September	Interrogation of Maximin in Corps by Pierre Peytard, Mayor of LaSalette; this will be followed by numerous others.
1846 5 October	Philibert DeBruillard, the Bishop of Grenoble (81 years old) is informed about the Apparition by a letter from the Archpriest of Corps, Father Pierre Melin.
1846 9 October	The Bishop cautions his priests not to speak from the pulpit about the presumed Apparition; he keeps himself informed of its potential reverberations.
1846 22 October	Discovery of a "Holy Face" on a spot on the stone where the Virgin had been seated
1846 8 November	The father of Maximin is converted; he receives Holy Communion.
1846 24 November	Procession of the parish of Corps to the place of the Apparition with Maximin and Melanie
1846 End of November	Maximin is admitted as a non-boarding student to the school of the Sisters of Providence in Corps. So eager to learn, he pushed in the door of Mother Superior Saint-Thecla, a primer in hand, to beg her to teach him to read *immediately*. His thirst for learning would never wane.

1846 2 December	The two shepherds are admitted to the boarding school of the Sisters of Providence in Corps. Maximin adopts as his "aunts," the inflexible Mother Superior Saint-Thecla and the young Sister Saint-Valerie.
1847	The first fulfillment of the prophecies of the public message of the Apparition: sick children, crop failure
1847 February	First brochure on the Apparition, published in Paris. The seers are interviewed by Father François Lagier, who speaks their patois very well. The impact of the Apparition spreads.
1847 24 February[3]	Maximin loses his half-brother, François, "the one who gave me bread when my stepmother did not give me any."
1847 1 March	Maximin states, before the priest of Corps: "I never told Melanie my Secret."
1847 March-April	Maximin is suffering from smallpox; people fear for his life. "He will not die of this disease," declares Melanie without seeing him.
1847 16 April	First recognized cure: Sister Saint-Charles of Avignon
1847 22 May	The Grenoble Prosecutor has the children interrogated.
1847 29 May	Father Lambert DeBeaucaire interrogates the two seers separately in front of six witnesses; he receives matching answers.

1847 *31 May*	5000 pilgrims gather on the Mountain. They erect a "Via Crucis" on the path of the Apparition.
1847 *26 June*	The inauguration of the "Confraternity of Reparation for Blasphemy and the Profanation of Sunday" at the town (or parish?) of St-Dizier, inspired by the message of LaSalette, is approved by Bishop Parisis of Langres, which is approx 250 miles north of LaSalette. St. Desiderius was an 8th c. abbot of Fontanelle.
1847 *15 July*	Bishop DeBruillard appoints two priests - Canon Jacques Philippe Orcel, superior of the major seminary, and Canon Pierre-Joseph Rousselot, one of the professors - to analyze the Apparition.
1847 *22 July*	Bishop Clement Villecourt, Bishop of La Rochelle, travels to Corps as a pilgrim. He insists on climbing the mountain LaSalette on foot. He puts the seers on an animal that has been prepared for the ascent. Maximin kisses his pectoral cross many times and puts on his ring. On the way back, Maximin climbs the bell tower of LaSalette with a small stone to strike the bell, but the bellringer grabs the rope; Maximin jumps astride the bell so as not to be thrown down.
1847 *15 August*	The cure of Melanie Gamon, the second recognized miracle
1847 *towards* *3 September*	Maximin, impressed by a representation of the Passion at Corps, affirms having seen there "something of his Secret."

1847 19 September	Despite the bad weather, over 50,000 pilgrims ascend the mountain of the Apparition for the first anniversary.
1847 4 November	A formal report is submitted to a commission of 16 priests in Grenoble: after 8 sessions, at least 12 priests were favorable.
1847 End of November	Cardinal DeBonald objects, so the Bishop of Grenoble suspends the judgment he had promised to give after the inquiry.
1848 24 January[4]	Death of Marie-Madeleine Court, stepmother of Maximin (Pierre Giraud's second wife)
1848 4 May	Blessing of the "second" sanctuary of LaSalette in Morlaix, under the title of "Our Lady of Reparation"
1848 7 May	First Communion of Melanie, age 17, and Maximin, age 13 [3rd Sunday of Eastertide. May 7th, 351 When St. Cyril was bishop, a luminous Cross was seen over Jerusalem, stretching about 5 miles. This apparition contributed to the conversion of many, including schismatic Arians.]
1848 10 May	Bishop DeBruillard approves the Confraternity of Maria Reconciliatrix, based at LaSalette started by Fathers Louis and Michael Perrin. These two brothers succeeded Father Jacques Perrin as pastor of LaSalette but neither joined the Missionary Fathers of LaSalette. Their nephew, Father Joseph Perrin, MS would become Superior General of that congregation.]

1848 *26 June*	Birth of Casimir, 10th and last child of the Calvat family
1848 *August*	Publication of the report of the Episcopal Commission by Canon Pierre-Joseph Rousselot: *La vérité sur l'événement de La Salette* [The Truth about the Event of LaSalette]
1849 *23 February*	Death of Maximin's father, Jean-Maximin Giraud. His maternal uncle, Louis Templar, becomes his guardian.
1849 *18 March*	Death of little Casimir Calvat
1849 *23-27 October*	The seers visit the Grande Chartreuse. Upon return, Melanie speaks to Benjamin Dausse about the 'ruin' of Paris. [He said:] "We were all three alone. I told them that I was soon going to return to Paris, where duty called me. At once Melanie […] took on an air and a tone of extraordinary authority to prevent me from going there: 'No, do not go there, I beg of you, because great misfortunes will happen in Paris.' Maximin then said: 'Oh!, here is Melanie revealing her Secret.'" (Father Antoine Bossan, *Notes sur l'histoire de la Salette*, 1871, No. 244 12°, MSG A 36) Bishop DeBruillard purchases the land of the Apparition.

1849 *30 November*	In the spirit of the message, Father Marche founds the Sisters of Reparation of Saint-Dizier, the first Sisters to serve the pilgrims to LaSalette. [see note above for June 26, 1847]
1850 *31 May*	Melanie explains her choice of a state of life: "Staying in the world is exposing oneself to losing oneself, however I would have more merit in the world! [...] I have to take the safest path. At my parents' home, there is not this tranquility, this peace that is so beautiful. [...] Finally, it is agreed that I want to be a religious, but now there are several congregations of religious, which will I choose? [...] an Order of cloistered nuns? I would like that [...] But! Will the mission I was given be accomplished? Alas no!... [...] finally I renounce this [contemplative] Order. I will not care for the sick, because often I would find myself alone with a demented sick person and I would feel afraid, so I renounce this also. Regarding the Congregation of Providence. I would like it a little [...] if God wanted to give me courage, [...] I will devote myself to it [...] I believe, this is the congregation that would please me the most! To go to a foreign land! To convert the infidels! To baptize the children! And even grown-ups, to help them know God and the Blessed Virgin." (*Réflexions de Melanie avant que de se faire religieuse*, 1850, EG 70: *Orthographe Revue*)
1850 *25 June*	Confirmation of the two seers, by Bishop Jean-Iréné Depéry [also spelled Déperry] of Gap (†1861) [25th is Tuesday, St. William Abbot]

1850 *12 August*	Melanie confides in her mother that she wants to be a missionary: - "But you will be eaten by savages or suffer outrages?" - "If I suffer [that], it is God's will." - "Then you do not love us?" - "God knows how much I love you." - "Those who go abroad [are sent by their] superiors for punishment. There they are made to suffer martyrdom, or are cut into pieces." - "The more you say 'They are made to suffer,' the more I want to go there. What a great thing it would be if I could suffer martyrdom!" - "And if there is no heaven, you would be well caught, ah! Beware and forewarned!" - "And you, mother, would you not be more caught than me, if there was a hell and you had not lived well? The good Lord who is just, will know how to place us all." Her father becomes angrier; he locks up his daughter at home. She looks for "a favorable moment to take flight, but her father, with rifle at hand, kept watch," even at the risk of killing her (Additional note by religious/nuns of Corenc). A creditor of Pierre Calvat, Mr. Brayer, "negotiates" Melanie's freedom.
1850 *1 September*	Father Pierre Melin of Corps censures the "reprehensible behavior" of Melanie's parents.

1850 25 September	Maximin is led by pilgrims to St. John Vianney, the Curé of Ars. Their difference of dialects causes them to misunderstand each other. The Saint interprets Maximin's "sharp" answers as a retraction. Father Raymond, his vicar, publicizes the retraction of the Curé. The controversy is relaunched.
1850 27 September	In Lyon, Maximin greets [exposes] the "Baron of Richemont," who was pretending to be Louis XVII. He is then taken to the Marists of Ecully, where their founder welcomes him.
1850 10 October	Melanie is admitted as postulant of the Congregation of Providence in Corenc [Thursday, feast of the Jesuit St. Francis Borgia].
1850 23 October	Recommended by Bishop DeBruillard, as "the child of Mary," Maximin enters the Rondeau seminary; the following year, he will continue at La Côte St André.
1850 5 December	The Curé of Ars writes to Bishop DeBruillard: "If this event is the work of God, man will not destroy it."
1850 16 December	Father Raymond, Vicar of Ars, communicates the so-called retraction of Maximin to Cardinal DeBonald, who announces it in the cathedral of Lyon.
1851 23 March	Father Auvergne questions the children: Will they write their Secret for the Pope? Maximin says yes, Melanie does not want to answer, in spite of her fear of being "separated from the Church" [i.e., excommunicated]

1851 *27 March*	Melanie, suddenly pacified, announces to Canon Rousselot that she will write her Secret.
1851 *20 June*	Cardinal DeBonald begs Bishop DeBruillard to ask the seers for the Secrets for which he has a mission to transmit them to the Pope.
1851 *3 July*	Melanie writes her Secret in the presence of the Sisters of Corenc and seals the document at 10:00 a.m. She refused to allow it to be communicated to Cardinal DeBonald. Maximin writes his Secret at the Bishop's palace; Bishop DeBruillard reads Maximin's Secret before sealing it at 5:00 p.m.
1851 *6 July*	Melanie rewrote her Secret "because she had assigned only one date for what must happen in two cities, so two different dates are needed" (notes of Benjamin Dausse). The Bishop reads it: he weeps. The first version was undoubtedly destroyed. At 10:00 a.m., Canons Gerin and Rousselot depart for Rome. They carry the two folded documents, sealed, in countersigned envelopes. Note the care and the haste.
1851 *7 July*	The two seers "communicate at length" about their Secrets.[4]
1851 *12 July*	Maximin orally communicates his Secret to Benjamin Dausse.
1851 *14 July*	Cardinal DeBonald interrogates the seers separately, without obtaining the Secrets.
1851 *18 July*	Pius IX reads the two texts of the Secrets in the presence of the envoys of Bishop DeBruillard and expresses emotion. The Pope sends the texts to the Prefect of Rites.

1851 11 August	Cardinal DeBonald writes to Pius IX (through the nuncio) to warn him against the Secret, suggesting that it would only be the ranting of a royalist political group welcomed eagerly by an 86-year-old Bishop. Maximin writes his Secret for his friend Benjamin Dausse. He then spends the night in the Chartreuse.
1851 19 September	Official date of the mandate in which Bishop DeBruillard declares: the Apparition "bears in itself all the characteristics of truth; it is indubitable and certain."
1851 6 October	Interrogation of Maximin by two Bishops and the Abbot of the Grand Chartreuse.
1851 7 October	Cardinal Lambruschini, Prefect of the Sacred Congregation of Rites approves "the inspiring and commendable rigor" of the pastoral letter of Bishop DeBruillard in recognizing the Apparition.
1851 9 October	Melanie enters the novitiate, and takes the habit of the Sisters of Providence under the name of Sister Mary of the Cross, in the presence of Maximin. "[God] allowed me never to be kissed or caressed by my mother. The first time I received a kiss from her was when I put on the religious habit." (Italian Autobiography, 1898).
1851 9 November	About a month later, Melanie began to experience communication problems (deafness, muteness); those closest to her attest its preternatural origin. Bishop DeBruillard has his decree read in all the churches of Grenoble...
1851 16 November	... and in the other churches of the diocese.

1851 *2 December*	Coup d'état of Charles Louis Napoléon Bonaparte
1852	Napoleon's visit to Grenoble. In Corenc, Melanie protests: "Oh! that ungrateful one, oh! that traitor, oh! that persecutor of religion!"
1852 *March*	Melanie predicts misfortunes and speaks of the origin of the Antichrist. According to Father Antoine Bossan who is responsible for the pilgrimages, people are beginning to talk about Melanie's stigmata in their correspondence.
1852 *1 May*	The Bishop announces the construction of the sanctuary.
1852 *2 May*	A grace for the month of Mary: Father Viollet, pastor of Corps [who had baptized the seers and married their parents], banned for fifteen years, submits to the pro-pastor Father Melin.
1852 *25 May*	Bishop DeBruillard lays the first stone and establishes the Missionaries of LaSalette to exercise there the ministry of reconciliation, to serve the purpose of the Apparition.
1852 *16 June*	Father Viollet, absolved from the sanctions, again celebrates the Eucharist.
1852 *2 July*	Bishop DeBruillard, age 87, submits his resignation to Pietro Garibaldi, the Apostolic Nuncio.
1852 *3 September*	Abridged Life of Melanie *(Abrégé de la Vie de Mélanie)*: the first autobiography of the seer is written for her confessor, Father François Sibillat, but not generally published at this time.

1852 October	Because of too many visitors, the novitiate of Melanie is extended one year. [The regulations for the canonical year of novitiate are still quite strict. If a few days are lacking, the canonical year is invalid.]
1852 21 December	Achilles Ginoulhiac is named Bishop of Grenoble. Bishop DeBruillard recommended him as his successor, after making certain that he would continue LaSalette.
1853 7 May	Enthronement of Bishop Ginoulhiac
1853 towards June	As an extension of the Secret, Melanie, has another vision of priests badly celebrating the Eucharist. "I recognized a dozen of them."6
1853 26 June	Detailed description of the Apparition, written by Melanie in Corenc (published by Andre Limoisin, Father Louis Gobert, Bishop William Ullathorne...)
1853 5 August	On the orders of Bishop Ginoulhiac, Maximin again writes the Secret. Father Champon, who becomes his guardian, welcomes him to the presbytery of Seyssins.
1853 12 August	Melanie yields in turn and rewrites her Secret.
1853 14 August	She writes it again with a few variations.
1853 October	Unanimously elected by the community to pronounce her vows, Melanie is rejected by Bishop Ginoulhiac. While her Sisters pronounce their vows, they send Melanie to the Grande Chartreuse.

1853 *30 November*	After the pupils leave the classroom, Melanie has a vision of a mysterious poor boy (the Child Jesus?) (manuscript of Mother Therese DeMaximy)
1853 *Christmas*	Father Sibillat observes her stigmata.
1854 *January*	Melanie, battered by the devil (as happens during this period), is sent by Bishop Ginoulhiac to the Daughters of Charity of Vienne France. She perceives that they want to remove her from Corenc, so she refuses to dress in the habit of this congregation. She feels desperate. Her most troubling reactions are regarded as whims. She calls for help and throws a note out the window asking for her freedom. The note is carried to the local parish priest.
1854 *February*	Sent to the Providence in Corps, she is welcomed at the Sanctuary of LaSalette.
1854 *11 March*	Letter to her spiritual director, Father Sibillat: "I have almost ceased to be tormented by the *gentlemen, my workers* [the demons]. It seems they are resting, but I do not imitate them. I try to make provision for when the French revolution will come. My laborers behave like the Prussians. They covet land that does not belong to them. I will do as the French, I will call the citizens of the kingdom of heaven [angels], and we will have victory." (EG 5)
1854 *May*	In Paris, the Brothers of St. Vincent de Paul relocate their orphanage to the upper Vaugirard district. The third cure obtained by Our Lady of LaSalette leads to the construction of the sanctuary on Rue de Danzig. Father Jean Pierre Cartellier, a priest of St. Joseph in Grenoble, begins writing a text against LaSalette Melanie goes down to the Providence convent in

	Corps.

Maximin is dismissed from the minor seminary by Bishop Ginoulhiac, charged with *"willful lies,"* discredited as having a dreamy mind and "telling tales." |
1854 *9 May*	Report of Bishop Ginoulhiac to the French Minister of Religion on the inanity of the Secrets of LaSalette.
1854 *1 June*	Countess Pauline DeNicolay agrees with Bishop Ginoulhiac and convinces the Superior of LaSalette of the "illusion" of Melanie. *"Her mission finished when yours began."*
1854 *6 July*	Father Antoine Cartellier gives Cardinal DeBonald a copy of his text [against LaSalette], bearing the signatures of fifty priests. At the Cardinal's request, Cartellier informs Bishop Ginoulhiac. With his agreement, Cardinal DeBonald transmits the text to the Pope.
1854 *7 August*	The memoire is published without authorization. Bishop Ginoulhiac denounces to Pius IX the abuses of the author and defends the Apparition.
1854 *11 August*	Bishop DeBruillard supports Bishop Ginoulhiac to reassure the Pope about the latest fruits of the Apparition.
1854 *30 August*	Pius IX invites Bishop Ginoulhiac to condemn the author's publication, and affirm the judgment of his predecessor.
1854 *20 September*	Bishop Ginoulhiac, assisted by Father Burnoud, "gives permission" for Melanie's absence from the convent that would extend until *sine die [without a date!]* contrary to his word. ("He told me that I would only go to England for a limited time and

	that he would call me back soon.")[7] She becomes the guest of the Carmel and their chaplain. Some English people want to found a community to observe the Rule which she received.
1854 September	Mr. Louis-Marie-Urbain Similien takes Maximin to Rome. The Diocese of Grenoble regrets this trip and warns Pius IX.
1854 3 November	Benjamin Dausse made and retained a copy of the Rule revealed by Melanie in 1853 after she was examined at the Chartreuse.
1854 4 November	A "Pastoral Letter" of Bishop Ginoulhiac to his clergy confirms the devotion to Our Lady of LaSalette and condemns, by mandate, the book of Father Jean Pierre Cartellier. But the Bishop also denounces the indiscretion and "conceit" of Maximin, his "attachment to his own ideas," and the "singularities" of Melanie, now in England.
1854 5 November	Canon Auvergne, former secretary to Bishop DeBruillard, sends Bishop Ginoulhiac the first letter from Melanie that he has intercepted: "I enclose this very letter from Melanie which we did not permit to arrive at its address, and, if it speaks truth, it indicates that this girl is more ambitious than ever [because she is preparing a foundation in England]. Perhaps it would be useful, my Lord, for you to be made aware of this situation before you left Rome where you will encounter certain prelates." (EG 7)
1854 8 December	Pius IX proclaims the dogma of the Immaculate Conception: "Mary was preserved from original sin in anticipation of the merits of Christ."

1855 *9 February*	Father Antoine Cartellier submits, but not in his thoughts
1855 *23 February*	Melanie receives the Carmelite habit in Darlington. Her stigmata have reappeared and are bleeding.
1855 *2 May*	The complaint of Miss de la Merlière against Fathers Cartellier and Déléon is dismissed.
1855 *May 23*	Cardinal Donnet crowns Our Lady of Laus, while the preacher deliberately omits to mention LaSalette among the Marian shrines. Bishop Ginoulhiac confides to the Cardinal that he does not believe in LaSalette, but is unable to disown Bishop DeBruillard. The cardinal repeats this on his return to Bordeaux. Bishop Ginoulhiac finally denies the rumor, which implicates him.
1855 *towards July*	Bishop Ginoulhiac orders Father Faure, former confessor of Melanie, under pain of prohibition, to give him the letters of the seer.[8]
1855 *5 July*	"The Superior of the Carmelites at Darlington wrote a few days ago, to a priest in Le Mans, that Melanie most certainly has the stigmata, and she really was cured of her blindness by the touch of the hand of an excellent Brigittine nun who had recently died." (Letter from Canon Sebaux, of the Diocese of Le Mans.)
1855 *19 September*	At LaSalette, Bishop Ginoulhiac preaches to the crowd: "The mission of the shepherds is over, that of the Church begins."

1856	Melanie's parents admit to Mr. Amédée Nicolas the ill-treatment they inflicted on her during her childhood. Pierre Calvat exclaims to his wife: "You think people are unaware of these things? Rest assured that they are known!"9
1856 24 February	Melanie makes her profession of vows at the Darlington Carmel, with a mental reservation regarding the enclosure, because she wants to remain available for the time when Mary would have her reveal the whole Secret (the long version).
1856 End of March	Maximin enters the Major Seminary in Dax where the brother of the Jesuit Father Champon is a professor.
1856 November	The Seminary of Dax is transferred to Aire-sur-Adour.
1857 6 May	A decision at the Imperial Court of Grenoble confirms the unsuccessful appeal of Miss de LaMerlière regarding her complaint against the Fathers Cartellier and Deléon (who accused her of having invented the Apparition). In this matter the opponents of LaSalette triumph.
1858 11 Feb to 16 July	Apparitions in Lourdes
1858 Summer	On the advice of his professors, Maximin leaves the Seminary in Dax. He passes through La Tronche, the home of his guardian, Father Champon.

1858 3 September	Melanie sends her full version of the Secret to Pius IX, through Bishop Hogarth [Exham], who writes: "Sister Mary of the Cross has informed me that part of the Secret given to her by Our Lady in LaSalette was to be reserved until the present year." She therefore wrote a letter to His Holiness conveying to him the rest of the Secret." This document has not been found.
1858 12 October	The Curé of Ars affirms his faith in the Apparition. Cardinal DeBonald ceases his opposition.
1859	Maximin is living in Paris, homeless, and in bad weather. In distress, he is rescued at St. Sulpice, at the foot of the statue of St. Joseph. The first Sanctuary of Our Lady of LaSalette is built outside of Europe, in St. Leu (Island of Réunion).
1859 25 August	Maximin is employed at the Hospice of the Vésinet.
1860 March	Maximin enrolls, for a year, at school in Tonnerre.
1860 July	Marie, one of Melanie's sisters, visits her in Darlington. She informs Melanie of the separation of their parents.
1860 18 September	Defeat of the pontifical army at Castelfidardo

1860 19 September	Melanie, called by her mission [to promulgate the Secret], is ready to leave Carmel but is held against her will. After tossing notes over the cloister wall to ask her freedom, she finally obtains permission from the Bishop of Exham to leave England and return to France, to Marseille. After staying eight days as a guest of the Geille family, who had taken in Melanie's mother, she is received by Father Barthes and his Sisters of the Compassion, thanks to the recommendation of Father Calage.
1860 October	Melanie meets the Italian Bishop Petagna, exiled from his diocese of Castelammare-di-Stabia, who becomes her spiritual director. At LaSalette, the Eucharist is celebrated in the new Sanctuary. Bishop DeBruillard dies on December 15, 1860 at 95 years of age. [Melanie will also die on Dec. 15th.]
1861	Melanie rewrites the Secret for certain superiors (see the draft of 5 pages, photographed by Father Paul Gouin: version 7).
1861 End of September	Maximin, returning from Le Havre, arrives ill in Paris. Treated at the St. Louis Hospital, he acquires an interest in medicine and begins studies, taking exams in 1861 and 1862. But a teacher steers him away: "Your patients will not approach you as a doctor, but as a visionary-healer." Maximin is adopted by the Jourdain couple.
1861 21 November	Accompanied by Mother Presentation, the Assistant of the Community of the Compassion, Melanie is sent to the island of Kefalonia (Greece) to restore order to an orphanage

1863 28 July	Melanie returns to Marseilles. She stays a few [ten] months with the Marseilles [extern] Carmelites, then rejoins the Compassion.
1865 Spring	Maximin visits Count DeChambord in Froshdorff, Austria, and dissuades him from aspiring to be King of France
1865 24 April	Maximin joins the Pontifical Zouaves to defend the Pope against Garibaldi.
1865 11 May	A Zouave named LeChauff of Kerguenec, discovers Maximin's identity in the registration directory.
1865 23 October	After 6 months of service, Maximin does not renew his enlistment. The troops are only being occupied pursuing robbers, in an atmosphere that does not suit him.
1866	Maximin publishes his account of the Apparition, followed by his answers to the main objections and official documents, under the title *Ma profession de foi sur l'apparition de N.-D. de La Salette, - ou - réponse aux attaques dirigées contre la croyance des témoins* [My profession of faith in the Apparition of Our Lady of LaSalette, - or–Response to the Attacks directed against the Belief of Witnesses.] Paris, Charpentier, 1866. (Excerpts above: Ch 1, Sec II)
1866 22 July	Pius IX encourages the project of Henriette Deluy-Fabry, to found the Sisters of Reparation of Our Lady of LaSalette [at LaSalette].
1867 13 April	Accompanied by Mother Presentation, Melanie leaves the convent of the Compassion to go to Grenoble and LaSalette

1867 *16 April*	At LaSalette, Mother Presentation reveals to the Fathers the mystical life of Melanie: demonic harassment, ecstasies and stigmata "which she has seen regularly for seven years, on the hands, the feet, the head." (Refer to Additional Testimonies: Sec. D. Marseille) They are welcomed for a month at the Visitation Convent of Voiron.
1867 *21 May*	Melanie and Mother Presentation leave France for Naples, then Castellammare-di-Stabia, where Bishop Petagna, the local ordinary, welcomes them. The seer stays there for 17 years. [This city with its 9th century castle is not far from Naples, Pompeii and the ocean.]
1867 *27 May*[10]	Pierre Calvat, Melanie's father, dies in Corps.
1868	Pius IX confirms to Bishop Petagna the exclaustration of the seer. The latter appoints Abbot Zola, future Bishop of Lecce, as her extraordinary confessor. Melanie and her "superior" [Mother Presentation] open a school in Castellammare.
1868 *4 December*	Maximin is received in audience by Archbishop Georges Darboy of Paris and predicts that he will be shot.[11] [The prelate was abusive to Maximin: "The words of your beautiful Lady contain stupidity, and stupid will be your Secret."]
1869 *3 May*	Father Orcel, now Vicar General, blesses the chapel of the companions of Henrietta Deluy-Fabry, future Sisters of Reparation of LaSalette.
1869 *August*	Maximin returns to LaSalette.

1870 End January	In Castellammare, Melanie reveals to Father Felicien Bliard the long version of the Secret. She copies, at his request, the Marseilles sheet, written in 1861.
1870 21 May	At the First Vatican Council, Bishop Petagna defends the proclamation of papal infallibility, contrary to Bishop Ginoulhiac.
1870 19 July	Napoleon III declares war on Prussia.
1870 28 August	Melanie sends the long version of the Secret to Father Sylvain Marie Giraud, M.S., Superior of LaSalette.
1870 6 September	Bishop Paulinier, successor of Bishop Ginoulhiac promoted to the see of Lyon, is enthroned.
1870 19 September	24th anniversary of the Apparition. Beginning of the siege of Paris; the house of Maximin and the Jourdains at Petit Jouy-en-Josas near Versailles, is ransacked. As refugees in Corps, the adoptive parents of the seer find themselves short of resources. Pius IX creates in Rome the archconfraternity of Our Lady of LaSalette.
1870 20 September	The Pope capitulates to the Piedmontese.
1870 3 October	Maximin is mobilized in the National Guard. He is denied the position of nurse.
1870 End of the year	First versions of Melanie's Secret are published by Victor DeStenay [pen-name of Father Collin LaHerte], and Father Jean-Marie Curicque.
1871 18 March	Beginning of the Commune uprising in Paris

1871 21 April	Maximin attests: "I firmly believe, even at the cost of my blood, in the heavenly Apparition of the Blessed Virgin on the mountain of LaSalette, September 19th 1846 Apparition, which I defended with words, by writings, and sufferings."
1871 24 May	Archbishop Darboy of Paris is shot by the Commune in retaliation. [Pius IX had refused this proud man the cardinal's hat for his liberalism, but Darboy humbly declared Maximin's prophecy, and died in an attitude of blessing and forgiveness.]
1871 - 1874	Canon Regis Girard was canon lawyer and editor of *Oeuvre d'Orient* ["Apostolate of the East"] a magazine published in Grenoble to promote interest among French Catholics in missionary work in the east. He published a similar journal, *"La Terre Sainte"* [The Holy Land]. Father Girard also served as official censor for the Procurator General of the Oriental Rites-in-union-with-Rome and had received an autographed blessing from Pius IX for his efforts. Around 1870, Father Felician Bliard sent Father Girard the long version of the Secret [Version 7]. With the knowledge and blessing of Pius IX, Father Girard devoted five issues to this topic, accompanied with commentary by Father Antoine Bossan (former M.S. Father and first LaSalette historian).
1872 June	Bishop Ginoulhiac refuses to help Maximin. To escape poverty, he associates with Alfred Vivier, a distiller in Varces (Isère), to sell an elixir made from plants. The Fathers at the Sanctuary criticize this initiative. Maximin's partner betrays him.
1872 15 July	Melanie is invited to Naples by the foundress of the Sisters of Stella Matutina: Mother Louise of Jesus.

1872 *15 August*	First National Pilgrimage to LaSalette
1874 *4 September*	Maximin makes his final pilgrimage to LaSalette.
1874 *November*	Father Sylvain Marie Giraud visits Melanie.
1875 *1 March*	Maximin dies piously at Corps, in misery. His heart is extracted by a surgeon to be sealed in a wall in the Sanctuary Basilica, as was done for Bishop DeBruillard. [The heart was interred hastily before Bishop Ginoulhiac returns from a journey and could oppose Maximin's desire.]
1875 *3 March*	Maximin's funeral at Corps
1875 *23 September*	Armand Joseph Fava is appointed Bishop of Grenoble.
1875 *18 November*	Armand Joseph Fava is consecrated Bishop of Grenoble
1876 *26 November*	Melanie communicates her "Sight" of Apostles of the Last Times to Father Felician Bliard, answering his questions. The Rule given by Our Lady of LaSalette, studied by two bishops and two theologians, is "recognized as worthy of the [heavenly] origin attributed to it"[12] Melanie commences a foundation at Castellammare with Father Alfonso Fusco, [and a few others whose names are lost. Canon DeBrandt in Amiens is the superior, but he never makes a firm decision to move to Italy and lead the community in Italy.]

1878 *2 February*	Death of Pope Pius IX, the longest papal reign in recorded history (31 years, 7 months, 17 days)
1878 *3 March*	Leo XIII is elected pope.
1878 *21 November*	Melanie finishes writing her complete account of the Apparition.
1878 *24 November*	Bishop Fava and Father Henri Berthier visit Melanie.
1878 *End of November*	Cardinal Ferrieri, prefect of the Sacred Congregation of Bishops and Regulars, proposes to Bishop Fava [for his community] the Rule of Melanie, but without success.
1878 *3 December*	Leo XIII receives Melanie in private audience. He asks her to go to Grenoble and to implement there, the Rule she had received. Melanie explains to the Pope the opposition of Bishop Fava. The letter, in which the Dominican Cardinal Guidi explains [Fava's opposition], is misappropriated. The Pope blesses Father Alfonso Fusco and Mother Presentation.
1878 *4 December*	Melanie stays in Rome, at the Visitandines, to draft the Constitutions of the Order of the Mother of God which she is asked to found. [Bishop Petagna dies of leukemia, December 18, 1878 in absolute poverty. On December 20, 2012, Pope Benedict XVI published a decree recognizing his heroic virtues, granting him the title of venerable.]

1879 4 January	Melanie is to "remain quiet in a convent of the eternal city." (Letter from Father Carra, secretary to the Diocese of Grenoble)
1879 5 January	Melanie completes her writings, namely, her draft of Constitutions for the male branch of the Order as Pope Leo had asked.
1879 8 March	Melanie writes about the death of the Dominican Cardinal Filippo Maria Guidi, [Feb. 27]. He had been the first to read the Constitutions.
1879 5 May	Melanie, who is wasting away, must, in spite of everything, leave the Visitation Convent in Rome to recover in Castellammare. But a mysterious letter will forbid her from leaving that diocese for more than 8 days, and from going to France.
1879 27 May	Father Daum of the French seminary completes his report on the Constitutions of Melanie and those presented by the Bishop of Grenoble. To the Ordinaries concerned, he recommends a time of testing for the first, and the "decree of praise" for the second, on condition that any mention of the Apparition is removed from the latter. Father Daum suggests that Bishop Fava should incorporate elements of Melanie's Rule. His conclusions are approved by the Sacred Congregation of Bishops and Regulars.

1879 *16 June*	Melanie sends to Leo XIII a copy of the documents given to Cardinal Ferrieri "I had no other thought and no other purpose, in handing to Your Holiness, the Rule given me by the Virgin Mary on September 19, 1846 on the mountain of LaSalette, and what She showed me in her pure mercy in relation to this Order, than of contributing to the desires and designs of God [...] so that Your Holiness, if he thinks it opportune, would have the said Rule begun to be observed by men of good will. Moreover, the vision of the very sad events, of the chastisements and the plagues that are developing, and will develop everywhere, have been the second reason. For these apostolic men, called to be part of this new Order that the Virgin Mary wants in the Church of her Son, will be armed with very lively faith, zeal and charity, ready to fight the battles of the Lord, under the banner of the Mother of God, even at the cost of their own lives, to calm the just indignation of God." (EG 105) The Pope retains the documents at the Vatican for two years.
1879 *20-21 August*	Consecration of the Basilica of Our Lady of LaSalette, and the crowning (of a plaster model) of the new statue.
1879 *15 November*	Melanie publishes, the complete account of the Apparition, including the Secret, with the imprimatur of the Diocesan Curia of Bishop Zola of Lecce.
1880 *29 January*	The Commissioner of the Holy Office writes to the Patriarch of Venice regarding the Italian translation of the [original French] Lecce pamphlet: "*Your Excellency may have the pamphlet examined by a prudent ecclesiastic, or write to the Bishop of Grenoble to know the truth of its content.*"

1880
February

Melanie is seriously ill.

Bishop Cortet of Troyes, was making every effort to have the Secret put on the Index on the pretext that it "was causing trouble in France." When his request continued to meet with refusal by the Vatican's Holy Office, he threatened its Secretary, Cardinal Prospero Caterini, with the withdrawal of Peter's Pence "if something was not done in his favor." With the suppression of income from the Papal States, financial assistance from French Catholics was critical. Under duress The cardinal-priest, only the Secretary and not the Prefect, wrote a private letter to the Superior of the LaSalette Fathers dated August 8, 1880, in which he stated that the work in question had been remitted to the Inquisitors, who found it proper to reply that "it was not pleasing to the Holy See that the said work be delivered to the public," and expressed the desire that "wherever copies have been distributed, they be removed, insofar as possible, from the hands of the faithful.......... . ." When the authentic Latin text of the letter was published seventeen years later [1897] in *Ami du Clergé*, the last sentence terminated in an extended series of dots, which indicated missing words. Eventually Father Isidore Roubaud learned that the dots stood for a phrase laying down the condition - "if as the Bishop affirms, the Secret was causing trouble in France." This qualification had been expurgated wholesale, along with the rest of the sentence, which had instructed the authorities to "leave it in the hands of the clergy, so they may profit by it." [PS]

1880 *26 February*	On the intervention of Cardinal Bartolini, the Holy Office orders Bishop Zola to withdraw Melanie's pamphlet, and asks him to give an account of his authorization. In a letter to Bishop Sarnelli [Petagna's successor], Cardinal Caterini, Secretary to the Holy Office, prohibits Melanie from commenting on her Secret.
1880 *9 March*	Father Semenenko, Superior of the Polish seminary, Consultant to the Holy Office, is an "expert" on the Secret; "I hold it to be true in substance." He takes into account the exaggerations of the literary genre. His opinion, and that of Bishop Zola, will be the accepted opinion in Rome until 1922 when a fraudulant edition of "the Lepidi brochure" appears in the last year of Benedict XV.
1880 *10 March*	The cardinal inquisitors beg Pope Leo XIII to communicate to them the manuscript of the Secret that he had received from Cardinal Domenico Consolini, Prefect of the Propaganda Fidei, to compare it with the pamphlet and examine the truth.
1880 *28 March*	Cardinal Mieczysław Ledochowski, who had reviewed the Secret before publication, calls to Rome at the behest of Leo XIII, the attorney Amédée Nicolas at the Vatican and asks him "to draft a brochure explaining the whole Secret so that the general public can understand it properly." Mr. Nicolas will prove to be an enthusiastic promoter of the Lecce pamphlet, and win the trust of Melanie. This popular commentary was printed with the Imprimatur of the Dominican Alberto Lepidi, chair of theology in France, then Rome, then Master of the Sacred Palace.

1880 30 May	Bishop Sarnelli [Petagna's successor] writes to Cardinal Caterini; "Strong and painful complaints reach me from France about [...] the little book of Sister Mary of the Cross, that has filled with alarm and fear the nation's clergy, already so tried"[13]
1880 13 June	Questioned by the Bishop of Troyes about the brochure of Lecce, the Sacred Congregation of the Index declares itself incompetent to assist the Holy Office: "It is a question of fact [and not of doctrine] to know whether or not the clergy and religious Orders are so corrupt." Melanie remains five days in Palermo with the Congregation founded by Blessed Giagomo [Jacques, James] Cusmano.
1880 July	Report of two consultants on the Secret: Father Bernard Smith, Consultor to the Sacred Congregation of the Index pronounces against its orthodoxy; the Dean of the Rota, Msgr. Giovanni DelMagno, in favor.
1880 14 August	There were, in fact, several "private letters" from Cardinal Caterini, two commonly cited: the first of August 8th, 1880 mentioned earlier in this chronology; the other a week later to Bishop Cortet of Troyes, dated August 14th

1881 28 February	Melanie is threatened with excommunication by the Holy Office if she speaks about the Secret. Bishop Sarnelli expresses the seer's doubt that Pope Leo has assented to this threat. From Italy Melanie writes Fr. Roubaud, "Don't worry about what the devil does by means of men; the good Lord permits it to strengthen the faith of the true believers. One of the persons I addressed in Rome belongs to the Congregation of the Index and the other to that of the Holy Office, or the Inquisition, which is the same thing. Neither one, nor the other, knew anything about Cardinal Caterini's letter. That's why they said it was a party acting independently of the Pope and even of the Congregations of the Index and the Inquisition." The two persons whom Melanie refers to are Cardinals, one of whom was Cardinal Ferrieri. Mgr. Pennachi, Consultor to the Index, on being questioned by Melanie, told her the same thing as the two Cardinals. But because poor Melanie was unable to prove beyond a shadow of doubt that the letter had indeed been sent without the Pope's knowledge, she believed herself bound to comply with its strictures to the end of her life. [PS]
1881 12 September	Cardinal Ferrieri consults Bishop Fava about the request of Melanie (16 June 1879) concerning the foundation related to the Apparition.
1882	After the death of Cardinal Caterini, October 28, 1881 at the age of 86, there are new appointments to the Holy Office, including Cardinal Mieczysław Ledochowski [always favorable to the Secret]

1882 28 June	Bishop Vincenzo Sarnelli brings up the favorable decision of the Congress of Cardinals convened in November 1878 by the Pope concerning Melanie. [Bishop Petagna's coadjutor and successor, Sarnelli, was a holy bishop, a tertiary of the Servite Order, devoted to Our Lady's Sorrows. Soon after his death on Jan 2, 1898, he was declared "Servant of God." A century later in 1999, the Compassionist nuns, founded by Bishop Petagna, urged the Holy See to authorize the opening of his cause for beatification.]
1882 26 July	Bishop Vincenzo Sarnelli of Castellammare alludes to the apologies made by the Supreme Congregation to Bishop Zola. Cardinal Caterini, by an ordinary private letter, had FALSELY implicated his colleagues in the Holy Office, and even the Holy See, for which the Cardinal's secretary, who had drafted it, apologized to Bishop Zola, adding that his hand had been forced. Sarnelli no longer wishes to appear to be the enemy of the Blessed Virgin by restricting the freedom of Melanie.
1884 21 August	With the agreement of the Pope, Melanie returns to France to care for her mother. Both settle in Cannes, then in Le Cannet.
1888 1 January	Bishop Bernard, Apostolic Prefect Emeritus of Norway, visits Melanie; he wants the Missionaries of LaSalette (of whom he is one) to adopt the Rule of Our Lady of LaSalette.
1888 14 March	Death of Blessed Giagomo [Jacques, James] Cusmano, Melanie's confrere, founder in Sicily.
1889 1 December	Death of Melanie's mother, Julie Calvat (born Barnaud on 29 August 1803). Melanie settles in Marseille in her sister's house.

1890 5 July	Henriette Deluy (Mother Saint-Joseph) with Mother Saint-John (first Superior at the LaSalette Sanctuary) leaves her foundation of the Sisters of Reparation of Our Lady of LaSalette to begin a new foundation with the Rule received by Melanie.
1892 22 August	The Bishop of Marseilles threatens Melanie with banishment if she does not hand over the inheritance of Father Ronjon to the Ordinary of Autun, namely, Bishop Perraud, which had been designated very specifically for a foundation of the Order of the Mother of God.
1892 12 September	Invited by Bishop Zola, Melanie returns to Italy, and settles in Galatina, in the Lecce Diocese.
1893 May to July	Melanie accepts the keys to the Citadel of Châlons-sur-Saône, the property bequeathed by Father Ronjon. The Bishop of Autun excommunicates her from his diocese.
1893 9 June	A copy of the Secret of Melanie with commentary, is referred to the Inquisition, and personally kept by Pope Leo XIII. Publication is not prohibitted.[14]
1895 May	Melanie, threatened with excommunication as far as Galatina, wins her appeal to Rome and is no longer disturbed. But she loses her appeal to the executors of the will of Father Ronjon, against Bishop Perraud.
1895 20 August to 3 September	The doctor sends Melanie to Gallipoli for a water cure in the ocean.
1895 27 September	Father Jean Baptiste Berthier leaves the LaSalette Fathers to found, in Holland, the Missionaries of the Holy Family. [1000 members in 2022]

1896 *19 May*	Melanie makes a pilgrimage to LaSalette with three priests. "This unhappy letter (Caterini) has finished, you might say poisoned, my existence, and has evaporated my trembling hope that by Christianity's return to its God the long and great scourges which our prevarications deserve might be much mitigated." (Letter to Mr. A. M. Schmid, editor of the periodical *Légitimité*, July 25, 1896).
1897 *18 August*	At the request of [Saint] Annibale Di Francia, Melanie takes charge of the community of the Daughters of the Divine Zeal, and their orphanage in Messina (Sicily). She remains one year and will be regarded as co-foundress of the Congregation. Father Annibale orders her to write her autobiography; she writes it in Italian. During this year at Messina, Bishop Zola dies. She never returns to the Lecce Diocese.
1898 *2 October*	Father Gilbert-Joseph-Émile Combes, parish priest of Diou, invites Melanie to visit France. She makes a stop at Moncalieri, near Turin.
1899 *20 May*	Melanie resumes her journey and meets Father Émile Combe.
1899 *June*	Melanie settles in Saint-Pourçain, near Diou.
1900 *11 June*	Melanie moves to Diou, and translates into French her Italian autobiography, at the behest of the young priest, Father Combe.

1902 *19 September*	The secular chaplains of LaSalette welcome Melanie with enthusiasm. She tells her story on the very location of the Apparition. Extracts of the Secret are read aloud. In private, she tells these priests about the Rule, then visits Father Hector Rigaux [a friend of Father Combe] the parish priest of Argœuves, near Amiens.
1903 *24 February*	Melanie, who lives alone, is recovering from a serious malady. Marie Janin says to her: - "Do you not see that you could die and no one would even know it? Not seeing you any more, someone could push your door open and find you dead!"
1903 *20 July*	Death of Leo XIII, after 25 years as Pope
1903 *28 July*	Melanie makes a fresh pilgrimage to LaSalette then moves to Cusset, France - "That's how I'll die: they'll find me dead, but not here. Father [Combe] believes that I will die here. I will not die here. I will die in Italy, in a vicinity I do not know, where I do not know anyone, a country almost wild, but where people don't swear, and where they love the good Lord. I will be alone. One morning people will see my shutters closed. The door will be opened by force and I will be found dead." (JAC p.168)

1904 13 June	Melanie, wishing to die in Italy, Father Fusco reaches out to a confessor of her latter years, the Dominican Father Carlo Cecchini, newly appointed Bishop of Altamura. Melanie departs alone for his cathedral city of Altamura, near Bari. Arriving there, but not finding the Bishop, she stays in a house of ill repute near the railroad station. Finally, someone finds her a place to rent. Cecchini will be appointed Archbishop of Taranto in 1908. It is he who will order the exhumation of Melanie's body. - St. Pius X is elected pope Aug 4, 1903.
1904 18 October	Melanie writes to Mr. de la Rive: "I am very grateful that, in these days of dead faith, you have dared to publish the Secret in *La France Chrétienne* [a periodical], as I had published it in 1879 with the imprimatur of Bishop Zola, of Lecce (Italy) and had it reprinted [in French] this year in Lyon before leaving France. I strongly protest against any changes to the text which anyone might dare to publish after my death. I strongly protest against the very false statements of all those who have dared to say and write: 1st) that I embellished the Secret, and 2nd) against those who claim that the Queen of Wisdom did not say "make known the Secret to all her people."
1904 14 to 15 December	Death of Melanie, 72 years old. Although she lived alone, neighbors heard singing in harmony that evening. The next day, they do not see her at the morning Mass, which she never missed. Someone forces her door open and she is found lying on the floor, as she had prophesied on February 24th, 1903.

1904 *16 December*	Solemn funeral of Melanie at the Cathedral, presided over by Bishop Carlo Cecchini O.P.
1905 *June*	Melanie's body is discovered intact by workers in the cellar of the Gianuzzi family where it had been interred.
1905 *14 December*	Anniversary service at the Altamura Cathedral. [Saint] Annibale DiFrancia delivers a eulogy of Melanie.
1908 *5 May*	Bishop Cecchini asks for donations to build a monastery and church where the remains of Melanie will rest in this neighborhood of Mount Calvary. Leon Bloy publishes *Celle qui pleure* [She Who Weeps].
1912	Bloy publishes Melanie's later autobiography, which she had composed in Italian in Messina, for Father Annibale DiFrancia, and then translated into French in Diou for Father Combe.
1915 *21 December*	A decree is promulgated on December 21, 1915 which ordered "the faithful of all countries to abstain from treating or discussing this said question under whatsoever pretext or form, either in books, pamphlets or articles signed or anonymous, or in any other way." Although the action is duly recorded in the *Acta Apostolicae Sedis* for December 31 of that year, certain irregularities were soon noted in its regard. To begin with, it carries signatures of no Cardinals or members of the Sacred Congregation, but only that of its notary, Luigi Castellano. There is moreover no mention of the date on which the Holy Office presumably met to vote on this piece

	of legislation, nor any reference to its ever having been submitted to Pope Benedict XV for final approval. Although the decree forbade all discussion of the Secret and specifies penalties to be imposed on transgressors, no censure whatever is attached to the text of the Secret itself, as would be expected in the circumstances. There is not even a prohibition against possessing, reading or distributing it. [PS]
1916 *17 December*	Death of Bishop Carlo Guiseppe Cecchini, who had become Archbishop of Tarento.
1918 *2 April*	Benedict XV receives the Maritain couple [Jacques and Raïssa] in a private audience, to discuss LaSalette and the Secret of Melanie.
1918 *19 September*	In Altamura, 12 religious, the Daughters of the Divine Zeal of the Heart of Jesus, carry Melanie's coffin from the cemetery to the chapel of their new orphanage in the Mount Calvary neighborhood. Canonical recognition of the remains, and temporary burial.
1919 *4 February*	In Sicily, Sister Paolina Bianchi, a Daughter of Divine Zeal, declares her cure at the brink of death, through an apparition of Melanie. Her deposition and those of the Sisters, collected by Canon DiFrancia (about 20 pages) is accompanied by medical certificates.
1919 *5 September*	Opening of the temporary tomb, the cleaning and restructuring of Melanie's skeleton. The bones appear to be saturated with blood, which is collected on cotton wool.

1919 *2 October*	The remains of Melanie, dressed in the habit of a Daughter of the Divine Zeal, is solemnly buried in their chapel, in a marble monument surmounted by an image of Melanie and the Virgin. Sixty years later, during the 1980 renovation of the building, the tomb was transferred to a side oratory.
1922 *6 June*	A Prayer to the Most Holy Trinity for the beatification of his humble servant Melanie Calvat, shepherdess of LaSalette, was approved by the Vatican. The 1880 brochure of Amédée Nicolas explaining the whole Secret so that the general public could understand it properly is reprinted under Fr. Lepidi's Imprimatur. An extant letter of ten years previous from Fr. Alberto Lepidi, O.P., Master of the Sacred Palace, dated December 16, 1912 to Cardinal Luçon, stated officially, that the Secret of LaSalette had never been condemned by the Index nor by the Holy Office. Unfortunately, Dr. Grémillon of Montpellier, took it upon himself to distribute a thousand copies of the 1880 brochure in 1922, to all ranks of clergy with the insertion of a 12-page letter (all falsely under the Lepidi Imprimatur). Among other things, he labeled all priests as "cesspools," taxed St. Thomas Aquinas with "obscurantism" and declared that the Pope should impose the Secret of La Salette on the faithful as an article of faith. The copies were expedited in wrappers proclaiming, "Great News! A voice from heaven! A message from the Blessed Virgin is declared authentic by the Vatican." Reaction on the part of the Holy Office was swift. On May 10, 1923 a decree was issued proscribing and condemning the brochure, designated by the title *The Apparition of the Most Holy Virgin on the Mountain of La Salette on Saturday, September 19, 1845.*" That the Apparition took place in 1846

	and not in 1845 would alone serve to invalidate the decree, besides the fact that for over 43 years Melanie's account of the happening had incurred no condemnation whatsoever from any authorized quarter. To make matters worse, the Holy Office took its fateful action in a session when Fr. Lepidi was on his death-bed and unable to defend the Imprimatur he had accorded the original publication, or to repudiate the unauthorized letter which had been attached to it. [PS]
1923 June	[Saint] Annibale, as postulator, asks Bishop Verrienti of Altamura, for "permission to open the informative process" for the cause of the beatification of Melanie, his "true companion in the foundation,...... he co-foundress of the Daughters of the Divine Zeal of the Heart of Jesus."
1927 30 May	[Saint] Annibale DiFrancia has a vision of the Virgin Mary.
1927 1 June	Death of Annibale DiFrancia.
1944 26 January	Arrest of Marguerite Aron by the Gestapo at the Solesmes Abbey, at the end of Mass. Marguerite was the co-author of a biography of Melanie completed by Father Gouin in 1954, *Sister Mary of the Cross: Shepherdess of LaSalette,* published posthumously in 1970. Dom Germain Cozien, Abbot of Solesmes (1921-1959), tried to have Marguerite freed in Drancy. She was killed in Auschwitz soon after her arrival there, approximately February 13, 1944.

1946 *15 August*	Angelo Roncalli, the future John XXIII, presides at the feast of the Assumption at the sanctuary of LaSalette to celebrate the centenary year of the Apparition.
1946 *26 August*	Maritain, ambassador to the Holy See, warns Bishop Montini (the future Paul VI) against a book by Father Jean Jaouen, Missionary of LaSalette, published for the centenary: *The Grace of LaSalette*. In declaring Melanie "hysterical," the author relaunches the controversy over the Secret.
1946 *2 to 8 September*	Marian Congress in Grenoble
1947 *26 January*	Informed that Pius XII is aware of the doubts raised against LaSalette, Maritain sends to Bishop Montini a note defending Melanie and the Apparition, and makes available to the Pope his 1918 essay which is forwarded to the Holy Office.
1954 *15 December*	Fiftieth anniversary of Melanie's death. At the request of Maritain, Monsignor Baron, rector of Saint-Louis-of-France [Rome], fulfills the "sweet mission" of celebrating a Mass near her grave in the Diocese of Altamura. "Melanie's time will come when the Virgin wishes," concludes the Diocese of Altamura.
1996 *19 September*	John Paul II, during a visit in France to the grave of St. Louis-Marie DeMontfort at the Basilica of St-Laurent-sur-Sèvre, recalls the Apparition of LaSalette on its one hundred-fiftieth anniversary.

1999 *2 October*	The "discovery" of the Secrets in the archives of the Sacred Congregation for the Doctrine of the Faith. First Saturday of the month of the Holy Rosary, Feast of the Guardian Angels. [cf Chapter 2 above]

Most Accurate LaSalette Sketch
attested by both children

BIBLIOGRAPHY

Stern, Father Jean, MS: *Documents authentiques sur la Salette* [Authentic Documents of LaSalette], September 1846 - Beginning of March 1847, DDB, 1980. (3 volumes, the first in the collection *Sanctuaries-pilgrimages-Apparitions* at DDB, the two others at Cerf) has published an exhaustive bibliography on the Apparition:

Stern, Father Jean, MS: *La Salette, bibliographie*, Marian Studies Library, A, new series, vol. 7, Dayton University, Ohio, USA, 1975.

Suffice it to mention the foremost French publications after 1975:

Calvat, Melanie:

- *Pour servir à l'histoire réelle de La Salette,* [To Serve the Real History of LaSalette], Documents, IV: *Letters of Melanie to Canon DeBrandt,* Montsurs, Resiac, 1978. [†Editor: Our English translation is in preparation now]

- *Témoignages historiques sur Mélanie Calvat, Bergère de La Salette, présentés par l'Association des Enfants de N. D de La Salette et de Saint Louis-Marie Grignion de Montfort,* [Historical Testimonies on Melanie Calvat, Shepherdess of LaSalette, presented by The Association of the Children of Our Lady of LaSalette and Saint Grignion DeMontfort], Paris, ŒIL, 1993 49600 Beaupréau.)

Angolier, F.: *La Salette, Apocalypse, pèlerinage et littérature, textes réunis* [Apocalypse, Pilgrimage and Literature, texts brought together] by F. Angolier and C. Langlois, Grenoble, Editions Jérôme Millon, 2000.

Chrétiens Magazine: N° Special issue of March 15, 2001, pages 10-20 (1st report on the Secrets, published to assure Corteville the right to his discovery).

Corteville, Mr. Fernand:

- *La Bergère de La Salette et le Serviteur de Dieu Mgr Zola* [The Shepherdess of LaSalette and the Servant of God, Bishop Zola], Montsûrs, Resiac, 1978.

- *Pie IX: Le Père Sémenenko et les défenseurs du message de N. D. de La Salette* [Pope Pius IX: The Servant of God, Father Semenenko, and the Defenders of the Message of LaSalette], Paris, Téqui 1987.

Corteville, Father Michel:

- *La "grande nouvelle" des Bergers de La Salette: Vol I. Les Secrets, (pars Dissertatio ad Lauream Faculatis S. Theologiae apud Pontificiam Universitatem S. Thomae de Urbe,* Roma, 2000) Paris, Téqui, 2001

[The Great News of the Shepherds of LaSalette: Vol I. The Secrets, Dissertation defended at the Angelicum in Rome.]

- *La "grande nouvelle" des Bergers de La Salette Vol II. Mélanie et l'appel des Apôtres des derniers temps.* Paris, Téqui, 2009

[The Great News... Vol II. Melanie and the Call of the Apostles of the Last Times]

Dion, Henri:

- *Mélanie Calvat Bergère de La Salette, Etapes Humaines et Mystiques* [Melanie Calvat Shepherdess of LaSalette, Human and Mystical Development], Paris, Téqui 1984.

- *Maximin Giraud, Berger de La Salette - ou - La Fidélité Dans L'Epreuve* [Shepherd of LaSalette - or - Fidelity to the Event], Montsurs, Résiac 1988.

Galli, Monsignor Antonio: (1908-still active in 2010) Author of various historical works including:

- *La Pastorella de la Salette,* 1994, 1996, p.40.

- *Scoperti in Vaticano: I Segreti de la Salette, l'apparizione, le polemiche, le profezie apocalittiche* 1997

Société: *Bulletin de la Société des Etudes Bloyennes* [Bulletin of the Society of the Studies of Leon Bloy] N° 7-8, Paris, Nizet 1990

Schlewer, M.: *Choisissez donc la vie* [So, Choose Life], Siloe, 1996.

ABBREVIATED REFERENCES

References are usually followed by file, exhibit, or page numbers.

ACDF	Archives of the Sacred Congregation for the Doctrine of the Faith
ACDF, LS	LaSalette Dossier (Censura Librorum, 1879-1888, P. II, 19)
ASV	*Archives secretes Vaticanes, S.C[ongregatio] Ep[iscoporum] et Reg[ularium], A[chivium] S[ecretum], Ep[iscopi]*, 1881, Castellammare (part of the dossier on Melanie and her writings for religious life).
BMG	Municipal Library of Grenoble (and n° of the repository, in the history room: the dauphinoise).
EG	*Archives de l'Evêché [Diocese] de Grenoble,* LaSalette dossier (and bundle number).
ENF	*L'enfance de Mélanie Calvat, bergère de la Salette* [Autobiography of the childhood of Melanie Calvat, Bergère de LaSalette], Saint Céneré [France], published by Éditiones St-Michel, 1966, (then Téqui).
ENS	Archives of *l'Association des Enfants de N. D de La Salette et de Saint Louis-Marie Grignion de Montfort,* [The Association of the Children of Our Lady of LaSalette and Saint Louise-Marie Grignion DeMontfort] Beaupréau, France. [†Editor: The Association never had a formal headquarters. 12 Avenue du Grain d'Or, Beaupréau-en-Mauges was the family home of Fernand Corteville (1917-2012) until the death of the wife Andrée (1917-2019). *L'Impartial* was the organ of

L'Impartial was the organ of the Association and the management was inherited by Fernand's youngest son, A. [Abbé Michel] Corteville who lived there only temporarily, having been ordained for the mission of Ivory Coast in Africa. Many issues bore the subtitle "*Journal de Marie,* blessed by His Holiness Pope Pius XII, April 13, 1958. There is some evidence that the periodical lasted until 1983 or beyond? The Association is no longer active. Digital copies don't seem to be available. Father Gouin's *Shepherdess of LaSalette* was issued as a supplement to the Mar-April 1970 edition.]

JAC · *Journal de l'Abbé [Gilbert-Joseph] Émile Combe, Dernières années de Sœur Marie de la Croix, Bergère de LaSalette,* Éditiones St-Michel, (Téqui) 1967, presented by *l'Association des Enfants de N. D de La Salette et de Saint Louis-Marie Grignion de Montfort* [The Association of the Children of Our Lady of LaSalette and Saint Louise-Marie Grignion DeMontfort]. Marie des Brulais, *L'écho de la Sainte Montagne* [†Editor: The *Echo of the Holy Mountain* was Melanie's favorite account] Nantes, Charpentier, 1852.

JS · I-III. Father Jean Stern, *LaSalette, authentic documents,* 3 volumes:
I. September 1846 - early March 1847, DDB, 1980.
II. Late March 1847 - early April 1849, Cerf, 1984.
III. 1 May 1849...ovember 1854, Cerf, 1991.

MC	Michel Corteville:
	- *La "grande nouvelle" des Bergers de La Salette:* Vol I. Les Secrets, (*pars Dissertatio ad Lauream Faculatis S. Theologiae apud Pontificiam Universitatem S. Thomae de Urbe,* Roma, 2000) Paris, Téqui, 2001
	[The Great News of the Shepherds of LaSalette: Vol I. The Secrets, Dissertation defended at the Angelicum in Rome.]
	- *La "grande nouvelle" des Bergers de La Salette* Vol II. *Mélanie et l'appel des Apôtres des derniers temps.* Paris, Téqui, 2009
	[The Great News…: Vol II. Melanie and the Call of the Apostles of the Last Times]
MIL I-VIII	*The Secrets of LaSalette*, by Canon Emile Millon, 1938, parts I to X, manuscript, 6 typed volumes (EG and MSG.) [(OSB?) LaSalette historian, chaplain of the Pilgrimage in the 1840s, later on he served as chaplain of the Ursulines of St-Jean-de-Bournay, Isère in the 1930s, died 1944]
MSG	Archives of the Curia of the Missionaries of Our Lady of LaSalette, in Rome.
OMD	Father Paul Gouin: *L'Ordre de la Mère de Dieu, pro manuscripto,* Sablé [France], published by Coconnier, 1941.
PS I-IV	*Pour servir à l'histoire réelle de LaSalette* [To Serve the True History of LaSalette] texts presented by *l'Association des Enfants de N.D. de LaSalette et de Saint Grignion de Montfort* [The Association of the Children of Our Lady of LaSalette and Saint Louise-Marie Grignion DeMontfort], 4 volumes:

I: Documents, I, Paris, Nouvelles Éditiones Latines, 1963

II: Documents, II, Paris, Nouvelles Éditiones Latines, 1965

* III: Documents, III, Paris, Nouvelles Éditiones Latines, 1966

* IV: Documents IV, Montsûrs [France], Résiac, 1978

[*Collections of Melanie's letters. An English translation is in preparation]

TEM — *Témoignages historiques sur Mélanie Calvat, Bergère de La Salette* [Historical Testimonies of Melanie Calvat, Shepherdess of LaSalette], Paris, published by ŒIL, 1993.

The Theotokos Weeps as She Speaks

ENDNOTES

CHAPTER 1

1. Pra Baptiste, J. Moussier, Selme Pierre. (JS p.47-48), Mr. Pra and Mr. Selme translated into French the second part of the message which was received in patois by the children.

2. Maximin Giraud, *Ma profession de foi sur l'apparition de N.-D. de La Salette--ou--réponse aux attaques dirigées contre la croyance des témoins* [My Profession of Faith in the Apparition of Our Lady of LaSalette--or--Response to Attacks against Belief in the Witness] Paris, Charpentier, 1866, p.4, 17-32.

CHAPTER 2

1. LaSalette examined by Rome, the story by Canon Pierre-Joseph Rousselot, according to L. Bassette: *Le fait de La Salette* [The fact of LaSalette], Cerf, 1955, p.205.

CHAPTER 3

1. JS III p.253
2. JS I p.383-392
3. JS I p.389-390
4. Relation Pra, J....47
5. no 1, JS I p.385
6. JS I p.28, 34, cf. 281
7. JS I p.47
8. JS I p.382
9. The symbols of the Apparition--mountains, fire, chains--are very common in spirituality: "O my God, what happiness and what glory to be bound to you by the chains of love, and to burn in the same fire of love and the same furnace as yourself! When will we have hearts consumed in your love?... .] what woul...sk God other than the pure and holy love of my Savior?" (Saint Francis DeSales, *Traité de l'amour de Dieu* [Treatise on the Love of God])

CHAPTER 4

1. MC p.109
2. MC p.175-177, 203-205
3. MC p.152 The two Secrets are produced line by line.

4	Maximin repeats his signature at the bottom of the page.
5	She: the Lady. Maximin testifies bluntly to instructions received from the Virgin shortly before writing this Secret. Melanie, without wanting to admit it, will imply this intervention.
6	MC p.153-154
7	prophetic anthropomorphism... theologically: God will stop protecting, etc...
8	JS III p.190
9	Addition in the margin
10	Engineer Dausse learned in 1851 that Maximin thought he was living in the 18th century. This explains why Maximin adjusted the dates, a sign of his educational development.
11	MC p.178
12	MC p.186
13	The Emperor's police had learned that the seers had criticized Napoleon III. Bishop Ginoulhiac, informed of Maximin's remarks by the Archbishop of Lyon, and then questioned by the Prefect of Isère, replied directly to the Minister of Worship on May 8, 1854. To satisfy him, Ginoulhiac blames Maximin for "prophetic fantasies" and "lies." "I kicked him out of the seminary," he concludes. (JS III p.229) As for Melanie, although she "seems to be less forward" than her companion, the bishop "has placed her under severe surveillance" and has threatened her with dismissal from her religious community. It is by way of rigorous sanctions, and by dissociating the young seers from the Apparition (which he is obliged to defend), that Bishop Ginoulhiac will be able to satisfy both the Pope and the Emperor. Thanks to this dissociation, progressively actualized in practice and finally vocalized firmly, as it were, in stone, Bishop Ginoulhiac maintained the continuation of the Pilgrimage, an...avorable judgment of the Apparition. The stages of this humanly coherent policy are brought together in Chronology, 1853-1855.
14	JS III p.319
15	A Pencil correction in book indicate...ypographical error: 1853 instead of 1846
16	Mathieu was the surname of her father, who was called Calvat after his mother, of whom he a "child of nature," a euphenism for illegitimate. (Henri Dion, *Mélanie... étapes mystiques et humaines* [Melanie Calvat, Human and Mystical Development] Téqui, 1984, p.50.) It was under the paternal surname Mathieu that Melanie was inscribed in civil and baptismal registers. (cf. J....20.)
17	On the 14th she formulated this a bit differently: "The people will forget about their religious duties; those consecrated to God will fall into a relaxation and almost a forgetfulness of God altogether, and some of them will commit great crimes."

18 The signature follows in large letters and poor handwriting. Melanie seems to be suffering.
19 The two citations: MC 1 p.207
20 Lyon, Library of the Sacred Heart, and Paris, Vic and Amat.
21 JS III p.128-129
22 In his collection of *Les plus beaux textes sur la Vierge Marie* [The Most Beautiful Texts of the Virgin Mary] (La Colombe, 1946), Father Régamey inserts Melanie's description of the Virgin.
23 Tipo-Litografia Editrice Salentina, Lecce, 1879. On the cover, the title is accompanied by the words of the Apparition: "Well, my children, you will make this known to all my people."
24 From the Virgin's speech in patois (as reproduced in Maximin's account)
25 This is from a letter of an unnamed clergyman of June 20, 1872: MI....44 note 27.
26 Father Felician Bliard, *Lettres à un ami sur le secret de La Salette* [Letters t...riend about the Secret of LaSalette], Ancoa, Naples, 1873, p.32
27 Gilbert-Joseph-Émile Combe, Le Secret de Melanie et la crise actuelle, Jonquières et Dati, Rome 1906, p.138-139.
28 Question of Father Combe (JAC p.29): "The resurrected, whom you mention, can they have children? Why not?" This point seemed crucial to me, but she did not want to talk about it again. Is it a yes?"
29 We have seen the Secrets of LaSalette being revealed, little by little, by their bearers. That was their destiny. This new information from Melanie brings to completion the last lines of the Secret, published in 1879: "The time is at hand! The abyss has opened, until God will be served and glorified."

CHAPTER 5

1 The Vicar General, Canon Pierre-Joseph Rousselot MIL V p.138
2 JAC p.157
3 Letter from Sister Valerie to Father Émile LeBaillif on the 4th of September 1879, ENS.
4 Letter copied by Father Émile LeBaillif, ENS
5 Note: Great authors have marveled at Melanie. She She had a style inspired by her experiences. She was a tireless correspondent to "pass on" Mary's message. During her lifetime she read some of her own letters published by Saint Don Bosco. Pierre Arrou gave an enthusiastic literary review of her autobiography:

In this era in which the supernatural apparently makes us sulky, or at least, unable to perceive it, what refreshment is derived from the story of the shepherdess of LaSalette, recounting her marvelous childhood!... This book plunges the reader into an amazing world. And yet, these are simple, naïve--even delightful--memories of an old nun (referring to Melanie), ignorant about literary techniques and even, at certain moments, of the vocabulary needed to express her feelings. Consider how she wrote about her dismay at Christ appearing to her: "Seeing his inestimable majesty...etreated into my nothingness."

Leon Bloy explains: In Melanie Calvat's narrative, anecdotes are mingled with edification. Daily tasks unravel into miracles. Celestial visions refract or illuminate the winter nights of the mountain pastures. Reading her, one thinks of the Fioretti, of the Golden Legend. One also thinks--and this is its unexpected charm--of some ancient and pious collection of peasant stories, or of some obsolete chapter of a popular country novel. But, above all this, or rather, in the weft of this rough cloth, there is a blue thread woven through [...] the angelic spirit of the narrator. [...] Consumed by love, overwhelmingly candid, familiar with the Invisible, she must struggle Constantly [...] But no, she does not struggle--she abandons herself. She suffers with rapture. She asks to be even more rejected, hated, and beaten for the glory of Jesus.... To reintegrate with the world of the living, that is, of the blind, she must shake off this luminous dust of the supernatural, into which the seer of LaSalette had been immersed as a golden mist. (Ecclesia N° 85, April 1956, p.31-32)

This may explain the passionate allegiance of writers who have recognized in her a sister of genius, averse to vain conventions. Above all, they admired the spiritual inspiration, without which there can be no literature, and which is sometime the cause of the style to burst forth from the pen of the poor.

6 ACDF, LS 111
7 ACDF, LS 111
8 Reflections of May 31, 1850. See Chronology 31 May 1850
9 The discipline is a small whip made of cords. It is not corporal penitence that frightens Melanie, but rather the special [communal] manner in which Carmelites take it. In Corenc, Melanie also criticized the custom of "confession," an expected account of conscience to their superiors (which has been abolished in all the congregations since 1890).
10 Melanie, letter to several Sisters of Corenc, February 13, 1855, EG 7
11 Copy: MSG 15-C-3
12 Note the euphemism.
13 Notes of Father Louis Beaup, MSG 16-C-4
14 Notes from Father Louis Beaup, MSG 16-C-4.
15 Letter to Cardinal Guidi of December 3, 1878
16 Reproduced by G.C. *Parascandalo: Governo Ecclesiastico di Mons. F.S. [Francis Xavier] Petagna, Religiose S. Cuori*, Castellammare, 1992, II, p.46-47
17 ACDF, LS 2
18 Sister Valerie to Father Émile LeBaillif, letter of September 4, 1879, ENS
19 *La Grace de la Salette*, Cerf 1946

20   The testimonies about the humility of Melanie at that time (and any other time for that matter) are very numerous. But we also know that Melanie did not agree with the Sisters who administered corporal punishment on the children. Was that a fault? The superior exempted Maximin from all criticism: nevertheless Bishop Ginoulhiac (*Instruction Pastorale* of November 4th, 1854) claims that Maximin let himself "be very much infatuated with his importance." Who should we believe?

21   no 7, 1946, p.17-33

22   Cerf, 1964

23   This affirmation has been repeated by H. Engelmann in his book: Pelerins [Pilgrims] de la Salette (Cerf 1987, p.79): "From 1885 onward, the time when Melanie started living alone with her mother in Cannes, until her lonely death in 1904 in Altamura, it was in the realm of a pure and simple psychiatric case, which clearly reveals the role that the "visionary" had assigned herself."

24   JS III p.130-131

25   JS III p.129

26   Julien Green, Journal, Paris, 1946 p.210

27   JS III p.128

28   JS III p.125

29   A. Avitabile and G.M. Roggio, *LaSalette*, ed. Paoline, Rome, 1996, p.22

30   BOS III, v. 2 p.67, no 827

31   MIL VII p.11

32   "The law of charity makes everything turn out for the best. The Blessed Virgin wants much love and not many practices," she wrote to Canon Alexander DeBrandt on March 23rd, 1877, concerning the Rule that was given to her (PS IV p.17.)

33   Note from Melanie, copy MSG 16-C-2

34   Notes of [Saint] Annibale DiFrancia on April 14. 1925, copy MSG 15-C-1

35   *Marie, l'Eglise et le Sacerdoce* [Mary, the Church and the Priesthood], 1952, p.436-442

36   *Note complémentaire par les religieuses de Corenc,* published in ENF p.167. It is true that later on in LaSalette, Mother Therese seems to have believed in a pseudo-mystic who imitated Melanie and claimed to have received a rule given by the Virgin, so as to win, in the manner, the esteem of the Fathers of the Sanctuary. It is not always easy to navigate one's judgment of mystical phenomena between naïve credulity and a demonizing witch-hunt. Some superiors have regarded the unnatural struggles of [the Carmelite Saint] Mariam of Bethlehem, of [Saint] Padre Pio, and of Marie-Therèse Noblet as simulations.

37   Letter of Bishop Ullathorne on April 3rd, 1855 to Bishop Hogarth, copy: MSG 15-C-5

38   Saint Annibale DiFrancia, director of Melanie in Messina, notes laconically in 1898 on the subject of her direction: "Ten years of mystical hell." To the Grande

	Chartreuse: "God does not exist" (notes of April 14th, 1925, copy: MSG 15-C-1) Note the conformity of the two sources, fifty years apart from each other.
39	Note from April 18, 1867
40	Letter of Melanie to Father Sibillat, March 16th, 1854, EG 5.) The fact that she did not like to take the "discipline" at Carmel (refer to Ch 5 Sec II) was because she had to undress for the self-flagellation.
41	A. Bossan (Fr. Antoine Bossan, sometimes J-A. in Polish manuscripts for *Jegomosc* "Reverend Father,") *Notes pour l'histoire de la Salette*, 1863, p.39-40, no 58, MSG A-36
42	Letter of January 23rd, 1997 to Monsignor Antonio Galli
43	Father René Laurentin, *Les Stigmates de Mere Yvonne Aimee*, Paris 1988, with a chronological list of stigmatized persons (p.19 sq.) and bibliography (p.163 sq.)
44	Vol. II, Palme, Paris, 1873...12
45	January 12, 1901, JAC p.56
46	*L'A(brege) D(e) L(a) V(ie) D(e) M(elanie,)* from the 3rd of September 1852, consists of 11 pages, and is unfinished (copy in Solesmes, *fund P. Gouin*, [the Collection bestowed by Father Paul Gouini], MYC 1-40.) There is another manuscript of Melanie, written for Dom Mortaise, Prior of the Chartreuse, copied by Benjamin Dausse on the 3rd of November 1854: BMG R 9670,, 68. Yet another copy: BM...716. (Mother Thérèse DeMaximy, mistress of novices of Corenc, has reworked this writing of Melanie under the title of *Au bon Père Sibillat*, mes souvenirs [To the Good Father Sibillat, My Memories], and had supplementary notes appended to it.)
47	A third objection, of plagiarism, had been presented by others. Father Emile Millon has refuted these in his research on Melanie at Corenc (see below).
48	This is not normal. One has to admit that something (voluntary or not) made it impossible for Melanie to memorize this simple thing to recite "by heart." At this rate, even a parrot would have learned its catechism. [†Editor: Melanie suffered severe psychological abuse from infancy, and never received anything remotely resembling modern counseling. In fact, she received the opposite, continual humiliations from "well-meaning" Catholics who wanted to guard her from any temptation to pride in the privilege of the Apparition. Memorization requires a baseline of certainty in one's ability to objectively assimilate information. Without special coaching, such self-certainty is virtually impossible for persons who were prevented from developing a natural sense of self-confidence in those critically important toddler years.]
49	Letter to Bishop Hogarth, April 3rd, 1855, copy: MSG 15-C-5
50	Sister Lucia asked a child,, who just arrived, to pray, and He revealed Himself as Jesus (cf J.M. Alonso, *Le message de Fatima a Pontevedra*, Tequi, 1974, p.14.)
51	[Saint] Annibale DiFrancia, *Notes sur l'autobiographie de Messine*, copy: MSG 15-C-1
52	Melanie to Father Sylvain Giraud, M.S., April 18, 1877, copy: MSG 16-C-2

53   Melanie to Father Sylvain Giraud, M.S., April 18, 1877, copy: MSG 16-C-2

54   Rev. Pierre-Joseph Rousselot, *La vérité sur l'événement de La Salette* [The Truth of the Event of LaSalette], Grenoble 1848, p.26

55   Melanie to Father Sibillat, March 16th, 1854, EG 5

56   Copy: MSG 15-C-1

57   Saint Louis-Marie DeMontfort, well-balanced by his obedience and perfect cheerfulness, used all kinds of penitential instruments; he even dragge...ymbolic ball of iron tied wit...hain to his ankle, when, after he had stopped usin...orse, he walked from one place to another. His penances shortened his life, however, without altering his literary, poetic or oral creativity, nor his missionary and musical enthusiasm during his exhausting and always well-organized missions. [†Editor: Father Doherty relates that evidence has come to light which suggests that the saint died of poisoning in the city of La Rochelle:

How was he going to handle the Calvinist and Huguenot heretics of La Rochelle, especially the educated ones, the *intelligentsia*.... It was shortly after he brought Madame DeMailly into the Church that someone sneaked into the kitchen of the house in which he dwelled, and placed a powerful dose of poison in the soup that was meant for him. Madame DeMailly, had been "a staunch and most intelligent Hugueno.... who was endeared to her sect not only by the brilliant qualities of her mind, but also by her high birth, and her firm attachment to her faith." If he had swallowed the poison, he would not have regretted that he died for Madame DeBenigne Pagé, or, for Madame DeMailly. But he swallowed only a little of it. He spat most of it out of his mouth, then took an emetic. That saved his life, but his health was shattered. "Never again," says a biographer, "would he have those giant reserves of strength to call upon in time of stress. And his early death must undoubtedly be attributed, in part, to the poisoned broth of La Rochelle." [*Wisdom's Fool* by Father Ed Ed Doherty, Montfort Publications, 1975 p.172-178 passim]

58   PS II p.80

59   June 26, 1896, copy: ENS

60   JAC p.116

61   Letter to Canon Alexander DeBrandt, November 8, 1890, PS IV

62   PS II p.65

63   PS IV p.178

64   PS IV p.67

65   Letter to Father Joseph DeBrandt, October 10, 1888, PS IV

66   "Nothing [...] is better proof of the authenticity [of revelation] than a profound humility. All experts insist on this virtue. [...] This is very common knowledge, as the words of Our Lord tell us: "He who speaks on his own authority seeks his own glory; but he who seeks the glory of him who sent him is true, and in him there is no falsehood." [Jn 7:18] (L. Volken, *Les Revelations dans l'Eglise*, Salvator,

Mulhouse, 1961, p.167)

67 Father Antoine Bossan: *La Sainte Apparition de Notre-Dame de LaSalette et ses suites* [The Holy Apparition of Our Lady of LaSalette and its Consequences], Solesmes, fund P. Gouin, [the Collection bestowed to Solesmes by Father Paul Gouin], MYC 1-75...14, no 290

68 Father Antoine Bossan: *La Sainte Apparition de Notre-Dame de LaSalette et ses suites,* Solesmes, fund P. Gouin, [the Collection bestowed to Solesmes by Father Paul Gouin], MYC 1-75 p.115, no. 292

69 Episode of September 11, 1849, MB p.142.

70 Louis-Marie-Urbain Similien, *Le Pèlerinage de LaSalette,* Barasse, Angers, 1853 p.205-206

71 Conversation on September 9, 1847, MB p.15-16

72 JAC p.10-11

73 Letter of Sister Mathilde Cagiati of April 3, 1879, ENS

74 This Manuscript can be consulted at *Cercles d'etudes J. et R. Maritain* [Study Group of Jacques and Raissa Maritain] at Kolbsheim (II, chap.3 p.10...

75 Letter of Blessed Giagomo [Jacques, James] Cusmano, March 14, 1887: *Cuaderni di Spiritualita Cusmaniana 6,* Palermo, 1976, p.173)

76 As reported by Father Hector Rigaux: Letter of February 11th, 1909 to M. Laine, ENS.

77 Letter of November 5th, 1923 to Joseph Molière, ENS

78 The account of this healing in *articulo mortis,* together with certified medical reports on the matter, was properly arranged by [Saint] Annibale DiFrancia (copy: MSG 15-C-1).

79 JAC p.148-149

80 JAC p.148-149

81 Letter of Bishop Ginoulhiac, May 9th, 1854: JS III p.228. In reality, it was his overflowing imagination that made him exaggerate, not lie.

82 Claude-Joseph DeLeon, *Dernier mot sur LaSalette* [Last Word on LaSalette], Grenoble, 1873, p.334-335

83 Letter to Father Émile LeBaillif, ENS, doc. 15 Vale

84 Henry Dion, *Maximin Giraud --ou-- La Fidelite Dans L'epreuve* [-or- Fidelity on Trial] Montsûrs, Resiac, 1988, p.234-236)

85 *op. cit.,* p.236

86 Letter of Bishop Zola to Amédée Nicolas, December 1, 1878, EG 39

87 Abbot Zola (January 29, 1872) and Bishop Petagna (March 5, 1872) had written to Bishop Baillès, begging him to reassure the Pope.

88 R. Masson, *La Salette --ou- Les Larmes de Marie* [LaSalette or The Tears of Mary], ed. SOS, Paris, 1974

89 *Ecclesia,* August 1956, p.71

90 Letter of Canon Rossero, Secretary of the Bishop, to H. Guilhot on April 12 1976).

91 Letter of Melanie to Canon Alexander DeBrandt of October 10, 1901, PSIV p.414-415)

92 JAC p.150-153

93 (A. Veillard M.S., *La grâce fait...aximin and Melanie in Notre-Dame de la Salette.* [The Grace bestowed on Maximin and Melanie ...] Etudes d'histoire religieuse et de theologie, Tournai, 1935, vol. III p.113)

94 *Abrégé de la vie de Mélanie, écrit en 1852* [Brief Autobiography of Melanie's Childhood, published by Leon Bloy]

95 *Abrégé de la vie de Mélanie, écrit en 1852* [Brief Autobiography of Melanie's Childhood, published by Leon Bloy] p.165

96 *Vie de Mélanie Calvat, Bergère de la Salette, écrite par elle-même en 1900* [Melanie's later autobiography written in Italian for Fr. Annibale DiFrancia, then translated into French for Father Diou, ENS, was published by Leon Bloy in 1912]

97 Father Antoine Bossan, *Notes sur l'histoire de la Salette,* 1863, p.39-40, no 58)

98 *Un Parfum de la Salette,* PS II p.148)

99 JAC p.56

100 JS III p.227

101 Father Antoine Bossan, *Notes sur l'histoire de la Salette,* 1863, p.14, no 185., no 20, MSG

102 Father Antoine Bossan, *Notes sur l'histoire de la Salette,* 1871, p.14, no 185, 22o, MSG.

103 JS III p.373, no 1207

104 Father Antoine Bossan, *Notes sur l'histoire de la Salette,* 1863, p.39-40, no 58, 3o

105 Louis-Marie-Urbain Similien, *Importance des procès* [Important items in the Process], 1869, p.134

106 Letter of March 9, 1855, EG 7

107 MIL VII p.13

108 EG 70

109 Notes: Father Louis Beaup, MSG 16-C-4

110 Letter to Canon Regis Girard, MIL V p.25-26, note 5

111 TEM p.86

112 Letter to Father Paul Gouin, TEM p.125

113 Henri Dion, Mélanie... étapes mystiques et humaines [Melanie Calvat, Human and Mystical Development] Téqui, 1984, p.106)

114 PS III, p.23

115 Letter of July 10, 1905 to Father Ernet Rigaud. Copy kept in the Rogationist Archives.
116 Rogationistic Archives Recollections [or Collections] by G. Leo
117 *Vie de Mélanie Calvat, Bergère de la Salette, écrite par elle-même en 1900* [Melanie's later autobiography written in Italian for Fr. Annibale DiFrancia, then translated into French for Father Diou, ENS (archives of Fr. Paul Gouin), was published by Leon Bloy in 1912]
118 JAC p.51, 55-57
119 Archives ENS
120 Letter of August 8, 1912, copy: ENS
121 Letter of July 9, 1854, EG 79
122 Father Jean Stern, M.S. entitles one of his chapters: *Les "Secrets" après 1851 --ou-- LaSalette numéro deux* [The "Secrets" after 1851 --or-- LaSalette Number Two] (JS III p.109). His criticism encompasses the Secret of 1851.
123 Letter to Catherine Buis on the 14th of November 1950, ENS
124 Letter of the 3rd of February 1854, of Sister Butruille to Bishop Ginoulhiac, EG 7

CHAPTER 6

1 Victor Hostachy, M.S., Historian for the LaSalette Fathers, *LaSalette dans les lettres françaises,* Grenoble, Revue des Alpes, 1945
2 Victor Hostachy, M.S., op.cit., p.83-84
3 Là Haut, Castermann 1965, p.154
4 Letter to Pierre Termier of December 12, 1906 (L'invendable), o.c.t. XII p.330
5 Letter to Pierre Termier, December 21, 1906 op.cit.
6 Leon Bloy, in *The Symbolism of the Apparition* (Imprimeries Lemercier & Cie, Paris, 1925 p.101-105
7 Carnet de notes, DDB, 1965, p.116
8 He does not take into account the 'secret' Apparitions of Catherine Labouré (1830)
9 Report of Jacques Maritain on LaSalette on January 28, 1947; fingerprinted version--on embassy paper--in the Maritain archives. *Cercles d'etudes J. et R. Maritain* [Study Group of Jacques and Raissa Maritain], Kolbsheim.
10 M. Malicet, Claude-Massignon, DDB, 1973, p.153
11 Even Renan (1823--1893) was impressed by LaSalette. In his foreword on *The Life of Jesus,* edited in 1864--a disastrous year for Melanie's Secret--he recognized: "LaSalette is one of the biggest spiritual events of our century." However just as for Jesus whom he admired as [...] a non-believer, his radical skepticism makes him emphasize "the disproportion between the fire and its cause." [Back]

12   Letter to Paul Claudel, *op.cit.*, p.143
13   *op.cit.*, p.145
14   *Le Symbolisme de LaSalette,* Gallimard, 1952, p.28
15   *Révélations de LaSalette,* La Table Ronde, 1946, p.1-2
16   Father Sylvain Marie Giraud, M.S. (1830–1885) wrote:

La pratique de la dévotion à N.-D. de LaSalette [The Practice of Devotion to Our Lady of LaSalette] (1863)

De l'union à N.-S. J.C. dans sa vie de victime [On Union with Our Lord Jesus Christ as Victim] (1870)

J.-C. prêtre et victime, méditations sur les mystères de N.-S. [Jesus Christ Priest and Victim, Meditations on the Mysteries of Our Lord] (1873)

J.-C. considéré au point de vue de son sacerdoce et de son état de victime [Jesus Christ Regarded in his Priesthood and his State a...ictim] (1873)

De l'esprit et de la vie de sacrifice dans l'état religieux [On the Spirit and Life of Sacrifice in the religious state] (1873)

Immolation et charité dans le gouvernement des âmes [Immolation and Charity in Guiding Souls] (1875)

Prêtres et Hostie. N.-S. J.-C. et son prêtre considérés dans l'éminente dignité du sacerdoce et les saintes dispositions de l'état d'hostie [The Priest and the Blessed Sacrament. Our Lord Jesus Christ and his Priest Considered in the Eminent Dignity of the Priesthood and the Holy Dispositions of the State of Victimhood] (1883).

17   Note 2: In Le Père Giraud, from M. A.Valentin, Editions Saint-Augustin, 1945, p.216
18   LaSalette, témoignages, Bloud et Gay, 1946, p.159-160
19   L. Carlier, Histoire de l'Apparition (History of the Apparition) Tournai 1914, p.130
20   *Apparizione della Beata Vergine sulla montagna di LaSalette, con altri fatti prodigiosi raccolti JS pubblici documenti per Sacerdote Giovanni Bosco terza edizione, Tipografi...ibreria dell'Oratorio di S. Francesco di Sales,* Turin, 1875. In this book Don Bosco translates the lively letter of Melanie of September 11, 1870, [see DOCUMENTS II. Melanie: 6. Letter to her Mother and the Inhabitants of Corps.
21   E. Picard, LaSalette, *précis historique Grenoble*, 1946, p.224
22   Letter to Father Daniel Bassano, confessor of H.H. Leo XIII, of May 19, 1882: Blessed Giagomo [Jacques, James] Cusmano, *Lettres choisie...* (corrected translation), la Carità, Palermo, 1992
23   He was beatified on October 7, 1990, during the Synod of sacerdotal formation
24   Letter in Italian to the director of the Annals of Our Lady of LaSalette, ACDF, IS 119
25   C. Villecourt, *Nouveau Récit de l'Apparition de la Sainte Vierge sur les montagnes des Alpe...*, Lecoffre, Paris, 1847, p.52

26	Letter of December 14, 1855: Father Antoine Bossan: *Lettres édifiantes,* no 431 MSG
27	Cardinal Martini, *Mary still suffers,* Saint-Paul, Paris, 1998, p.70--72
28	*LaSalette examined by Rome,* The story by Canon Pierre-Joseph Rousselot, according to L. Bassette, *The fact of LaSalette,* Cerf, 1955, p.227
29	According to a letter of Father Hector Rigaux on January 4, 1911, ENS
30	Jacques Maritain, *Carnet de notes* (edition DDB, 1965, p.130-131)

CHAPTER 7

1	He did not receive the *Rule* of religious life intended for Melanie. However just like Melanie, Bernadette, Catherine Labouré and the children of Beauraing, Maximin, in addition to the Secret, did receive personal, thus unpublishable "advice." Father Michel Perrin, the new parish priest of LaSalette, made reference to these counsels on October 16, 1846 (JS I p.75): "After that, the Lady gave wise and sound advice to each of the children individually, and when she was talking to one, the other saw her talking but did not understand her, and vice versa. The Lady recommended to never ever say to anyone what only was meant for themselves. Foremost little Melanie said she remembered very well those Secret things the Lady told her specifically, and that she would never divulge them."
2	PS II p.64
3	JS III p.129
4	JS III p.139
5	MC p.1721
6	Biography, t.I, p.225-227
7	JAC p.131
8	*La Sainte Apparition de Notre-Dame de LaSalette et ses suites,* by Father Antoine Bossan, p.16, no 189. (Solesmes, fund P. Gouin, [the Collection bestowed by Father Paul Gouin] MYC 1-75)
9	Rev. Father Labat, SJ, professor at the seminary of Aire-sur-Adour, reported these words (not confirmed by others) to Father Émile LeBaillif, in his letter of October 12, 1878 ENS.
10	Letter of Father Brissaud to Father Blanchet on July 24, 1899: MIL III p.36. The episode is situated between 1865 and 1873. The entourage of the count of Chambord has confirmed this meeting.
11	PS IV p.231
12	MB p.256
13	Pope John XXIII, *Journal of a Soul,* Cerf, 1964, p.175-176
14	Letter from Melanie to Miss Vernet on the 20th of July 1894 ENS. Many do place the Antichrist immediately after the return of Christ (or Parousia) basing this thought on the words of Saint Paul: "The coming of the lawless one

is by the activity of Satan with all power and false signs and wonders" (2Thes 2:9). However, is this text to be taken literally? The Scriptures are as evasive as the Secrets of LaSalette about this mystery. In the footsteps of Dn 12:1, Apoc 12:7; 19:20, 20:1-3, Melanie attributes to the Archangel Saint Michael or one of his helpers, the victory against the dragon and false prophet, identifiable as the Antichrist. This is well illustrated by a fresco of Signorelli in the cathedral of Orvieto, Italy.

15   Synopsis of Maximin's confidences in MC p.204. The collective Antichrist whom he mentions is in concordance with 1Jn 2:18-22; 2Jn 7

CHAPTER 8

1. Letter from December 22, 1851 to Bishop DeBruillard, EG 112
2. Document of March 5, 1852, EG 79
3. Letter of September 18, 1855 to Bishop Ginoulhiac, EG 79
4. Letter of Father Berlioz to Bishop Ginoulhiac from March 1, 1856, EG 67b
5. Letter of Miss Sidonie Petitjean to Canon Rousselot on March 8, 1860, EG 67B
6. On this apostolic and Marian current, cf. MC p.41
7. "It's to the children of LaSalette that the Beautiful Lady, She who is weeping, announces the wrath (chastisements) of her Son which looms over the lands of the Occident. This includes the crisis of the Christian faith and the mission of the *Apostles of the Last Times [...]* those by whom the Holy Spirit will re-establish the Church regenerated by sufferings," specifies Orthodox theologian Vladimir Lossky *(The Spiritual Life, from Nov-Dec 1987, p.642)*. Did the Apparition of Pontmain also announce, by an image, these new apostles? Mary was holding the crucifix in her hands, and at the end of that Apparition, two additional white crosses were resting on her shoulders. "What could be the significance? Until now writers and seers had very little to explain it. The fact is that the original true and victorious interpretation were not obvious. The two white crosses of Pontmain were resting on the shoulders of the Holy Virgin as though carried by her. Is it not thus that, at times, in the style of women of the east, she carried her Son Jesus? Wouldn't it be thus that she would carry once again, mystically, the souls of her regenerated children, purified and transformed by Eucharistic graces, each becoming truly as another Jesus Christ?" (J. Grimault, *The Message of Pontmain historical context*, Tequi, 1971, p.86)
8. French translation of the funeral oration for Sister Mary of the Cross in: *La Bergère de Notre-Dame de la Salette* ["The Shepherdess of Our Lady of LaSalette] by Monsignor Antonio Galli, Tequi, 1997, p.160-161
9. Rather 1853, since Bishop Ginoulhiac arrives in this year
10. Respons...o Father Felicien Bliard, from October 4, 1876. JAC p.148
11. According to the letter from Bishop Ullathorne from April 3, 1855: "When it had been a question of having some Sisters at LaSalette, Melanie had told him

for the first time, that she had had a revelation during the Apparition about these religious, and that a Rule and a habit had been revealed to her. The present Bishop [Ginoulhiac] was inclined to call into question this fact. He hesitated especially on the article in the Rule regarding daily Communion, which was stipulated." (Copy: MSG 15-C-5)

12   She wrote *"je reçoive,"* Anglicism from "receive"
13   Maximin and Melanie shared this expression
14   Letter from November 8, 1854, EG7
15   The process was not to the honor of Bishop Ginoulhiac, who relapses into having returned, under pain of secrecy, Melanie's letters to her former confessor. The severity of historians toward Melanie are often accompanied by leniency to this Bishop.
16   Father Felicien Bliard, *Lettres à un ami sur le secret de La Salette*, [Letters to a Friend about the Secret of LaSalette], Ancoa, Naples, 1873, p.20
17   Melanie responded to Father Felicien Bliard in Letter #17, published later by Father Gilbert-Joseph-Émile Combe, JAC p.144-149
18   The description could not be more true than it is today.
19   *La vue du costume et des œuvres des fils et filles de l'Ordre de la Mère de Dieu* [The Sight of the Habit and the Apostolates of the Sons and Daughters of the Order of the Mother of God," published by Father Paul Gouin *L'Ordre de la Mère de Dieu, pro manuscripto: Règle, vue, constitutions,* [Rule, Sight, Constitutions] OMD p.9-13 [†Editor: This document is out of print and difficult to obtain. The Sight was also reproduced in Gouin's life of Melanie, posthumously published in 1970: *Sœur Marie de la Croix, Bergère de La Salette* [Sister Marie of the Cross, Shepherdess of LaSalette]
20   Letter to Father Émile LeBaillif from January 3, 1880. PS I p.112
21   Pastoral Letter of Bishop Fava, of Grenoble, on Our Lady of LaSalette, for the 30th anniversary of the Apparition, from September 1st, 1876, Grenoble, Baratier, 1876, p.1-9
22   The promise to study the Rule of Melanie and to be inspired by it for the Constitutions of the religious of LaSalette, can only be interpreted as a concession. Fava witnessed the positive opinion of the Holy See, the Prefect of the Sacred Congregation and of the Pope, toward the Rule of the seer of LaSalette, on the eve of Melanie's Pontifical audience. Would the Pope officially meet with her, one-on-one, if she was the bearer of a revelation held to be false? Leo XIII had summoned Melanie to meet with him personally but the Pope had *not* asked to speak with Bishop Fava. The subsequent examination of Constitutions which the Pope asked from the seer hardly contradicts this starting point.
23   Letter from Bishop Fava to Monsignor Bianchi, November 26, 1878, ASV. The Bishop of Grenoble with his many supporters, will have no difficulty in compromising Castellammare, having gained experience in opposing the seer in Rome.

24	Retold by Melanie to Canon Hector Rigaux, Pastor of Argoeuves (near Amien), and published under the title of *Leo XIII and the Shepherdess of LaSalette*, Chartres, Garnier, 1904, p.16-19.
25	Letter from Father Carra to Father Émile LeBaillif from January 4, 1879, ENS.
26	From a letter of Father Bernard to Father Louis Beaup from January 30, 1895, MSG
27	*La Voice du Désert et la Réparation*, [The Voice of the Desert and Reparation], Lyon, 1895 p.28... .)
28	(From the "Rule of Melanie" there exists in the Archives there exists in the Archives of the Servants of the Poor, an autograph of Father Cusmano [...] there exists in the Archives preceded by the following introduction: "Rule of the Order of the Mother of God" by which She deigned to welcome as her very special Sons, the Missionary Priests, the Brothers and the Sisters united in distinct congregations under the title Servants of the Poor, and the filial congregation... ... which wanted to cooperate in the work of the Feeding of the Poor." Is this "Rule" really that "dictated to Melanie" by the Most Holy Virgin? [...] Is it the Rule spoken of so often by Blessed Giagomo Cusmano in his letters? [...] One discovers in them more resemblance with the "Cusmanian" spirit; a strong Marian fingerprint, an absolute centrality of Christ Crucified and Eucharistic, a spirit of "charity without limit," a union of contemplation and activity, an exhortation accentuated by humility and obedience, by an abandonment extending to the offering of oneself as a victim Jesus Crucified, the salvation "that Jesus be loved by all hearts," and zeal for the spread of the Gospel ..." (M.T. Falzone, *Cuaderni di spiritualita cusmaniana*, 6, Palermo 1976, p.19-20)
29	Letter from Annibale to Father Radiguet, Curé de Esquay Notre Dame, from October 17, 1905, ENS.
30	Letter from Father P. Laurent to Mr. Champion, July 8, 1943, (TEM p.146)
31	Response to Father Felicien Bliard, cited in the preceding chapter (JAC p.145 n. 2)
32	Annibale DiFrancia, anniversary funeral eulogy for Melanie printed in Monsignor Antonio Galli's book, *Scoperti in Vaticano: I Segreti de la Salette*, 1997, p.160).
33	1Jn 4:2: every spirit that confesses Jesus Christ come in the flesh is of God
34	Leon Bloy, in *The Symbolism of the Apparition* (Imprimeries Lemercier & Cie, Paris, 1925 p.41-42) asks: Is LaSalette evocative of Carmel? Then he cites Saint John of the Cross, Ascent of Mount Carmel, Book 1, ch. 5, par 7:

"It is given (to the soul) to understand, that she who wishes to climb this mountain to make of herself an altar on which to offer God a sacrifice of pure love, praise and pure reverence, before climbing to the heights of this mountain, must have perfectly accomplished these three things." [cf Gn 35:2 "First, that they should cast away from them all strange gods; the second, that they should purify themselves; the third, that they should change their garments." discussed par. 6 in the same chapter of the *Ascent*.

35   *Tractatus de Vita Spirituali* [Treatise on the Spiritual Life], Saint Vincent Ferrer, ch. 21

36   Father Paul Gouin, OMD p.136

37   [Mt 22:36-40; Mk 12:28-34; Lk 10, 25-28; Jn 13:34; 15:12; 15:19; 17:23; 1Jn 4:8,16; Dt 6:5; Lv 19:18 ...]

- "The love of God is the first commanded, love of neighbor is the first practiced." (Augustine, Treatise 17 on the Gospel of John)

- "The smallest act of pure love is more useful to the entire Church than all the greatest works without love put together." (Thérèse of Lisieux, interpreting John of the Cross)

- "This Mother of loving kindness will remove from your heart all scruples and disturbing servile fear; she will open and enlarge it to run in the commandments of her son, with the holy freedom of the children of God, and to introduce to them the pure love, of which she is filled." (Saint Louis-Marie Grignion DeMontfort, *Treatise on True Devotion,* No. 215)

38   [Gal. 2:20, Ph 1:20; Rm 8:9]

"It will suffice for you, it seems to me, to explain that the *Apostles of the Last Times* will not have greater obligations, no greater perfection than that of the Apostles of the primitive Church, after the descent of the Holy Spirit. The spirit is the spirit of Jesus Christ in oneself and for souls. True charity is the soul of this religious body. Total poverty is its wings, and all this, not in words but in deeds." (Melanie, Letter to Canon DeBrandt October 22, 1881; PS IV p.70).

- "Wanting to be for Jesus Christ, we must remain in Him ... that is to say, to live in his spirit (...) to walk as Jesus Christ walked himself, to live as He lived on the earth, to think and to act like Him" (Jean Baptiste Delaveyne, Rule of life of the Sisters of Charity of Nevers, Nevers, 1992, p.1, 11.)

39   [Jn 15:5; 1Cor 1; Phil 3:8; Jn 3:20]

- Vatican II, Constitution "Dei Verbum" No. 25; " ... the holy Council insistently exhorts especially all Christians, and notably the members of religious Orders, to learn, by the frequent reading of the Sacred Scriptures, "the eminent science of Jesus Christ" (Phil 3:8).

- The humility of the knowledge of self is inseparable from that of God; "That I may know You, that I may know myself!" Augustine, Let me know you Lord, then I shall know myself. ("Soliloquies" Book 2, ch. 1)

- "I felt that the singular thing necessary was to unite myself more and more to Jesus and that the rest would be given to me as extra. (...) At first glance it seems easy to do good for souls, to make them love God more, by forming them according to one's vision and personal thoughts. Up close, on the contrary, the illusion disappeared ... one feels that to do good, it's something as impossible, without the rescue of the good God, as to make the sun shine at night ... " (Thérèse of the Child Jesus, Autobiographical Manuscripts, Lisieux, 1957, p.275-276.)

40   [Ph 2:8]

- In any domain where, with charity, one may extend obedience, we must be attentive to its voice as to that of Christ Our Lord. In fact we put ourselves in his place, for love and reverence; and we must leave incomplete any syllable (iota) or thing that we have started, directing all our intention and all our strength to the Lord of all, so that holy obedience will be always perfect in everything." (Ignatius of Loyola, Constitutions, no 547).

41   [Jn 14:23]

- "I understand that, among the consecrated, the purity of spirit is the guardian of purity of the body, and that there is no chastity of body in the absence of constant purity of spirit, and that the spirit and the senses will not keep their purity if they are not crucified with Jesus Christ." (*Childhood of Melanie*, ENF p.61

42   [Jn 17:11; 21-22; Ph 2:2 and Acts 4:32]

- "The first thing for which you are united is to live unanimously in the house of God, and to have one single heart and one single soul extending toward God." (Augustine, Rule, ch. 2)

- "The principal reciprocal link for the unity of the members, among themselves and their superior, is the love of God Our Lord." (*Ignatius of Loyola, Constitutions*, no 671)

43   [Acts 4:32, Mt 6:25-26; cf Mt 8:20.]

- "You will not say that something is your own because, if you have the imperishable goods in common, how much more the perishable goods." (Letter from pseudo-Barnabas, 19, 8)

44   [Jer 11:19; Mt 5:38-48; 1Cor 13:7]

- "The measure of love is to love without measure," says Saint Bernard.

45   [2Cor 2:9; 1Pt 1:14; Lk 10:16; Sir 2:15]

46   [Mt 20: 35-38; Mk 9: 33-35; Jn 13:13-16; Jam 5:19]

- The true Superior is Our Lady, who gives the Rule and says little before "I want." (art. 6) "The one who presides over you does not esteem himself happy because he dominates with power, but rather serves by charity. He may be honored by you, but he prostrates himself at your feet in the fear of God." (Augustine, Rule ch. 7)

- It's in prayer and in union with God that Sister Thérèse drew this wisdom and this discernment of souls (...) I thought she had the gift to read my soul. I made this remark to her and she responded "I do not at all have this gift. But behold my Secret, that I never make an observation without invoking the Holy Virgin. I ask her to inspire me to do for you the greatest good." (Sr. Marie of the Trinity, Apostolic Process of Thérèse Martin, 2347)

47   [Mt 26:26-28; 1Cor 11:23-26; Act 4; 1P 1:8-9]

- Directory for the Ministry and the life of Priests, No 50; from Loyola, Constitutions, no 671) "The centrality of the Eucharist must appear not only in the living celebration worthy of the holy Sacrifice of the Mass, but also in frequent Adoration of the Blessed Sacrament."

- The three months indicated for Perpetual Adoration are linked to Mary and her Apparitions (February 11, first Apparition of Lourdes, soon after the Feast of the Presentation; May 13, first Apparition of Fatima, in the Marian month of the Visitation; September 19, LaSalette, after the Nativity of the Virgin, and after Our Lady of Sorrows).

- "It is not leaving God, but to leave God for God, that is to say one work of God for another, or of greater obligation or merit. You leave prayer or reading, or you break the silence to assist a poor soul; Oh! Know, My daughters, that doing all this is to serve Him ... Charity is at the top of all the rules and it is necessary that all be related to this." (Vincent de Paul, Office of September 27).

48 [1Cor 2:2; 1Jn 2:2; 4:10; Rm 12:1]

- "In order to live in one single act of perfect Love, I offer myself as a victim of holocaust to your merciful love, asking You to consume me incessantly, allowing the waves of infinite tenderness shut up within You to overflow into my soul, and that thus I may become a martyr of your Love, O my God! ... " (Thérèse of Lisieux, 643193578 Act of offering of June 9, 1895.)

49 [Jn 6:35-51; 1Cor 11:27]

[†Editor: Daily Communion was almost unheard of in the century before Pope Pius X. St. Therese of Lisieux suffered very much on this point.]

- John Paul II, *Redemptor Hominis* encyclical, no 20: "The essential commitment and above all, the visible grace and source of supernatural strength for the Church as the People of God, is to persevere and advance constantly in Eucharistic life ... " "A Communion with the Body of Jesus Christ must be joined to love and the practice of the life according to the true sense of the words of Our Lord: "Do this in memory of Me," that which is not a simple memento of a sterile thought ... but a remembrance of action and a conformity of morals, of inclination and of will with Him" (Jean Baptiste Delaveyne, Rule ... p.17)

- "It is very painful for me to see the souls of religious approach the Sacrament of love solely out of habit (...) It would be better for them not to receive Me." (Saint Faustina Kowalska, Little Journal ... p.423)

- In Melanie's time, daily Communion was unusual. The last text of the Rule, written by Melanie on November 3, 1904, omitted the part of the article in parentheses.

50 [Mk 9:29; Ac 13:2-3; 14:23]

- The religious Orders have their own fast, from All Saints to Christmas and from Epiphany to Easter among the Franciscans). Formerly, one fasted three days to "Four Stroke," among others for the intention of the ordinaries. The mortifications are no longer in common use, but one finds them practiced by the children of Fatima, as a lesson for the adults.

51 [Jn 15:13]

- It must be known how good it is to convert a sinner or to deliver a soul from Purgatory; infinitely good, greater than to create the heavens or the earth, since one gives to a soul the possession of God. It must be noted that our good works, passing through the hands of Mary, receive an augmentation in purity, and consequently in merit and in value to make satisfaction and intercession; it's why they become much more capable to console souls and to convert sinners." (Saint Louis-Marie de Montfort, *Treatise on True Devotion* no 172. Cf. Saint Augustine, *Treatise 72* on the Gospel of John)

52   [Mt 25:35; Lk 15:1; Rm 15:7; Mt 11:29]

- It's a ministry of the monastic life (Cf. Benedict, Rule ch.23; the welcoming of guests). The Constitutions of Melanie speak of the "monasteries" of the Order, that which highlights the semi-contemplative character. The seculars are the priests and laity of the age.

53   [Act 4:32, cf. Mk 14:36]

- "The will which has died to self to live in the Will of God, is without any particular desire, lives not just conformed and subject, but completely annihilated in herself and converted to that of God; as one says of a little child who has no need of his own will, to desire or to love anything but the breast and face of his mother." (Saint Francis de Sales, *Treatise on the Love of God*, Bk. IX, Ch. XIII)

- "Beginning today, my own will no longer exists (...) I accomplish the Will of God, everywhere, always, in everything." (Sr. Faustina, Diary p.168)

54   [Mk 12:25]

"That which regards the vow of chastity has no need to be explained, since the perfect means of observing it is self-evident, to know how to strive to imitate in this way an angelic purity, by the chastity of the body and of the soul ... " (Ignatius of Loyola, Constitutions, VI, 1.) In your walk, in your attitude, in your attire (...) that all emanates fitting decency and the holiness of your state in life. (Augustine, Letter 211, No 10-11).

55   [Lk 2:19 and 51]

- "One calls them "monks" (from the Greek "monos") because they unify themselves with each other by a holy recollection that excludes all division in a way that strives toward the perfection of divine love.

- (S.T, II-II Q. 184 a. 5 ad. 1) "For the rest of the time, while the silence is not to be as rigorously guarded, you will nevertheless avoid with great care to speak too much ... " (Rule of Carmel, ch. 16)

56   [Jn 15:13; Lk 9:23-24; Act 20:35]

- There are, My daughter, those who put all their effort into stirring up in themselves this gentle fire of love for this obedience, at the same time as a hatred of their own sensuality ... Love and hate grew to this point that (...) they want as well to impose on themselves a particular obedience which brings them straight to perfection." (Catherine of Siena, Dialogue, ch. 157)

57 [Is. 53; Lk 14:26; Jn 1:29,36]

- The religious vocation is comprised of two distinct elements; the anterior divine vocation to the call of the superior, and the canonical call. The first consists in an ensemble of interior or exterior graces that suggest to the person to direct themselves to the religious life; it is accomplished by the call from the superior of the institute" (Father Paul Gouin, OMD p.156). The salvation of souls is the first goal of the Church: Code of Canon Law, c. 1752

58 [Mt 28:18-20; Act 1:8; cf Mk 16:15-20]

- The missionary spirit must absolutely be conserved in the religious institutions (...) so that the Gospel will be preached efficaciously among all the people (...) So that all the religious (...) spread the Good News of Christ in the whole universe." Vatican II, decree "Perfectae Caritatis" no 20 and 25. "These will be the true *Apostles of the Last Times* (...) teaching the straight way of God in the pure truth, according to the Holy Gospel, and not according to the maxims of the world, without putting themselves in pain about things or accepting persons." (Saint Louis-Marie Grignion DeMontfort, *Treatise on True Devotion*, no 58-59).

59 [Mt 3:2; Mk 16:16; Mk 13:22]

- Francis of Assisi also included in his Rule, (ch. 21) the principle exhortations that his brothers would give in their missions.

60 [270] [Mt 16:24]

- "I find the same simple requirements of God; gentleness, humility, charity, interior simplicity; one demands of me nothing else (...) by these the heart becomes habitable to God and to neighbor in an intimate and permanent manner. They make an agreeable cell. Hardness and pride hurt; complexity causes worry. But humility and gentleness welcome, and simplicity reassures. These "passive" virtues have an eminently social character." (Raissa Maritain, Journal, p.65)

61 [Lk 14:28; 1 Tm 6:12]

- One will not specify the subdivisions of the years of formation, "novitiate" in the large sense. All Christians are confirmed as "soldiers of Christ" (not only with Ignatius of Loyola in his "Society" of Jesus, or Saint Grignion DeMontfort and his "Society" of Mary).

62 [Act 1:14; 2:42; 3:1]

- "Pray at the indicated times." (Augustine, Rule, ch. 1) Directory for the Ministry and the Life of Priests, No 50: "The faith and love for the Eucharist cannot allow the presence of Christ in the tabernacle to remain alone." (cf. Catechism of the Catholic Church, No 1379-1380.)

63 [cf Mt 4:4]

- "However you take the food you will have been given in the common refectory, listening together the reading of some passage from the Holy Scriptures, while this may be done conveniently" (Rule of Carmel, ch. 4).

64 [Mt 25:36]

65 [Mt 5:23-24]

- " Before and above all, one takes care of the sick, and one serves them as if they were Christ in person." (Rule of Saint Benedict, ch. 36)

- "When a Sister will have offended another by injury, by backbiting or by a false accusation, she must, as promptly as possible, seek to make amends." (Augustine, Rule ch. 6).

66 [Mt 2:11; 4:10]

- "A pause of true adoration has more value and spiritual fruitfulness than the most intense apostolic activity." (John Paul II, Address of November 24, 1978)

67 [Jn 17:21-22; cf Col 3:15-17]

- Melanie introduced her letters by this formula. Saint Grignion DeMontfort began his formula with "The pure love of God reign in our hearts!" "The pure Love of God" appears at the beginning of the Rule, and the salutation at the end is an aspiration that this reign spreads to everyone.

68 [1 Thes 5:17]

- Vatican II, Constitution Sancrosanctum Concilium, no 85: "All those who ensure this task of accomplishing the Office of the Church, and at the same time, participate in the supreme honor of the Spouse of Christ, because in offering the divine praises, they place themselves before the throne of God in the name of Mother Church." In an Italian version of the Rule, Melanie wrote that which seemed to her the most important: "the Sisters will say the Office of the Holy Virgin, and will say their confession once a week." The Rule, primarily 69 is attached to Rule #33, but the note is not given here. It represents the practices current in that era.

CONCLUSION

1 [Jn 19:25; Lk 14:27]

- To remind oneself that her own exaltation came at the cost of the abasement of a God (...) a sorrowful thought for the Mother of God." [Father Dominic Chardon DuRanquet, a Jesuit missionary who spent 66 years serving the remote residents of Northern Ontario. He died at 86 in 1900.]

- " ... The love of the Most Holy Virgin is thus full of sorrows, as her sorrows were full of love (...) Her crucified union is the model of ours. Do not be surprised that she tells us: "All the members will wear a cross like mine." (Father Paul Gouin, OMD p.162)

Letter of June 1, 1854, EG9

(October 19, 1869) (ACDF, St. St. C, 4-0, no 43: *"De Falsa Sanctitate Comitissam Paulinam Nicolay."* [Report on the False Sanctity of the Countess Pauline DeNicolay

DOCUMENTS

1. ACDF, LS 100
2. F. LeChauf de Kerguénec, *Souvenirs des Zouaves pontificaux*, 1864, 1865, 1866, [Memories of the Pontifical Zouaves Collected by a Former Papal Zouave], Paris, Oudin et Leday, 1891, p.251-254.
3. *Recueil de lettres photographiées* [Collection of photocopied letters] Solesmes, *fund P. Gouin*, [the Collection bestowed by Father Paul Gouin]
4. What seems to be greed conceals the poverty of the seer and his adoptive parents.
5. Published by Father Émile LeBaillif in *Triomphe de N.D. de la Salette dans l'un de ses témoins, Maximin peint par lui-même* [Maximin: Self-Portrait] Nîmes, Clavel-Ballivet, 1881, p 10, 44-45, 55-74, 84-86. (Do not confuse these Memoirs with the unpublished *Histoire monumentale* of Father Champon--Archives MSG--which was inspired by the memories of Maximin.)

   Father LeBailiff begins his book by interspersing his remarks with Maximim's Memoirs: two notebooks written in 1863 in Paris, then continued in Rome at the Camaldolese monastery during his service as a Papal Zouave in 1865. The original notebooks were lost. We reproduce the first part, regretting to omit many other picturesque episodes. Let us note that Maximin (or Father Émile LeBaillif) reformulates in good French, and in an elegant style, the memories of his childhood, or the Memoirs already reported in the books.
6. *Maximin Peint par lui-même* [Maximin: Self-Portrait] p.466-468 ENS, manuscript from Father Émile LeBaillif *folio* 93-94
7. ms f 95: text crossed out and not printed.
8. Louis-Marie-Urbain Similien, *Le pèlerinage de LaSalette*, Angers, Barassé, 1853 (en fait, 1854).p.312-314. This is the patron saint of Melanie aux Ablandins, wife of Baptiste Pra.
9. BMG R 9670, 61. Slightly revised spelling.
10. That is to say, contrary to the "pure love" of which the Rule of Mary will speak. Melanie wants to say that true love does not abide: whatever one has already done, one cannot manage to satisfy it.
11. Copy retained: BMG R. 9670, 60.
12. Or is the message about enmities? Towards the beginning of the Secret that she will publish (1879) we read: God will allow the old serpent to put divisions [. . .] in all families.
13. Enumeration present in the Rule for the *Apostles of the Last Times*.
14. This was indeed accomplished, partly by Melanie, partly by Maximin.
15. Published by Father Louis Gobert: *Un pèlerinage à LaSalette*, Lille, Lefort, 1854, p.104.

16 Melanie and Maximin mention these three colors ... seen, by Catherine Labouré, attributed to the ordeal that would occur in Paris. (cf. René Laurentin - C. Roche, *Catherine Labouré et la Médaille Miraculeuse*, Paris, Lethielleux 1976) The colors of Mexico (green, white, orange) are found on the wings of the angel of the Virgin of Guadalupe.

17 Melanie adopted this simplified letterhead on May 28, 1854.

18 EG 70.

19 The expression "good Father" undoubtedly refers to Melanie's spiritual director (Father Sibillat) because she uses it elsewhere to refer to him.

20 *Le nouveau Sinaï: Menaces et promesses de N. D. de la Salette*, [The New Sinai: Threats and Promises of LaSalette] by Frédéric Delbreil (Paris, Victor Palmé Libraire-Éditeur, 1873. p.214.) This was translated into Italian and widely distributed by Don Bosco.

21 Extracts from a letter of December 26, 1870 and a subsequent letter, published by Father Felicien Bliard in *Lettres à un ami sur le secret de La Salette*, [Letters to a Friend about the Secret of LaSalette], Ancoa, Naples, 1873, p.34-37.

22 MIL V p.35.

23 The prophetic vision seems to transport the seer into the scene. Regarding her vision of the cataclysms in Martinique, Father Combe asked her: "Did you see the eruption? Speak then! – "Ah! my Father, I was in the midst of it!" (JAC p.131).

24 Published by Father Radiguet (Timothée Philalèthe): *Notre Dame de La Salette et ses deux élus, Mélanie Calvat peinte par elle-même en 160 lettres*. [Our Lady of LaSalette and her two chosen representatives, Melanie Calvat, autobiography in 160 letters] ... Caen, Imp. Domain, 1906, p.348

25 Melanie put "my governess." This is also the title of a Russian icon.

26 One of the six prayers sent by Melanie to Canon Alexander DeBrandt on May 1, 1884 (PS IV p.103).

27 This passage is evocative of the declaration of Christ to Sister Faustina of Mercy: "Before coming as just Judge, I come as King of Mercy. Before the day of justice comes, men will be given this sign in heaven: all light will be extinguished in the heavens, and there will be great darkness over all the earth. Then the sign of the Cross will appear in heaven. From the holes where the hands and feet of the Savior were nailed, great rays will emerge which will illuminate the earth for a while. This will happen shortly before the last day. " (Faustine Kovalska, PETIT JOURNAL, Marquain, Hovine, 1985 p.65.) '

28 Manuscript in the Solesmes archives. J. L. Barré published an extract in *Jacques et Raïssa Maritain, Les Mendiants du Ciel* [Heavenly Beggars], Stock, 1995, p.179-180.

29 Jacques Maritain, *Carnet de notes*, DDB, 1965, p.126-129. It is we who give this title to the extract.

30 So, she seems to speak like us - really she speaks, but not like us.

31 I don't believe, as Jung seems to, in a psychological heredity through which archetypal representations are transmitted to our unconscious. I do not believe either in a collective Unconscious as a supra-individual entity in which everyone would participate. I rather think that each of us, throughout our life but more particularly during our childhood, undergo the influence or the "contagion," in what I call the unconscious of the spirit, of what consciously or unconsciously forms the mentality of his contemporaries, and which is expressed by signs whose impact can moreover be quite fleeting and imperceptible [. . .]

32 Letter translated from Italian. This Rogationist Father General gives his opinion on a new exhaustive (and unpublished) collection of the Italian writings of Melanie.

NOTES IN THE CHRONOLOGICAL TABLE

1 Cf. JS I p.385-388.
2 We only report dates of birth, not those of death
3 Date of death according to "Dictionary of LaSalette," unpublished (6 March according to JS I p.354).
4 According to JS II p.240; Date from Henri Dion: February 1848
5 According to Maximin's confidences to B. Dausse, Cf. JS III p.188.
6 Letter of June 16, 1855 to Father Faure (former confessor of Melanie), EG 5
7 Letter from Melanie to Father Mélin of October 4, 1854 MIL V p.16
8 "The four letters that I had received from Melanie were requested from me by the Bishop under threat of interdiction; he came up to LaSalette himself expressly for that purpose. Melanie did not speak well of him when she revealed her Secret." (Letter from Father Faure, former confessor of Melanie, to Canon Regis Girard on Feb 6, 1873, EG.)
9 Letter of Amédée Nicolas to Father Émile LeBaillif of May 20, 1880, ENS.
10 Or 21 May?
11 Maximin told about this interview (cf. MIL III p.30 . . .). His story is supported by the testimonies of Amédée Nicolas and Father Déprimoz.
12 Letter from Bishop Fava to Monsignor Bianchi, dated November 26, 1878, ASV
13 ACDF, LS 22
14 Message of God to men . . . comment of a friend of the truth », Galatina, Tip. Mariano, 1893. (MC p.289)

TABLE OF CHARACTERS

Many personalities passed through the lives of Maximin and Melanie in their efforts to obey the beautiful Lady of LaSalette: "Make this known to all my people." An ongoing effort is being made to gather and collate information regarding names mentioned in their letters, biographies and pertinent documents.

Please find information at the website of the Theotokans who are presently starting the Order of the Mother of God (Ordo Matris Dei), according to the Rule that She dictated to Melanie, in a diocese in the United States.

https://houseofmaryomd.org/

The website features 12 doors, and each opens into many categories. The "Table of Characters: Persons of Interest in the Saga of the LaSalette Apparition" will be found at the second door "Convert" in the section of "Approved Apparitions", in the subsection "Mary Speaks to the World"

https://houseofmaryomd.org/wp-content/uploads/02-convert/02a-approved/02aa-mary-speaks-to-the-world/02aa-mary-speaks-to-the-world

They invite you to contact them or subscribe to their newsletter.

https://houseofmaryomd.org/welcome/contact-subscribe/

ABOUT THE PUBLISHER

SCOTT L. SMITH, JR., *J.D., M.T.S.*

Scott L. Smith, Jr. is a Catholic author, attorney, theologian, publisher, and 13th generation Pointe Coupeean. He and his wife Ashton are the parents of six wild-eyed children and live in their hometown of New Roads, Louisiana.

Smith is the Grand Knight of his local Knights of Columbus council, co-host of the Catholic Nerds Podcast, and on the board of the Men of the Immaculata. Smith's far-ranging experiences include prison minister at Angola, Louisiana's notorious maximum-security prison, teacher in the slums of Kenya, and Jesuit novice, having completed the 30-day silent retreat.

Smith's books include *Consecration to St. Joseph for Children & Families*, which he co-authored with Fr. Donald Calloway, *Pray the Rosary with St. Pope John Paul II*, *The Catholic ManBook*, *Lord of the Rings & the Eucharist*, among other titles. His fiction includes *The Seventh Word* and the *Cajun Zombie Chronicles*, horror novels set in New Roads, Louisiana.

Scott regularly contributes to his blog, "The Scott Smith Blog" at www.thescottsmithblog.com, winner of the Fisher's Net Award for Best Catholic Blog. Scott's other books can be found at the Holy Water Books website, holywaterbooks.com, as well as on Amazon.

Catholic Prayer Journals from Holy Water Books

Holy Water Books has published a series of prayer journals, including *The Pray, Hope, & Don't Worry* Prayer Journal to Overcome Stress and Anxiety.

Pray, Hope, & Don't Worry: Catholic Prayer Journal for Women

Daily Bible verses and quotes from the Saints to reflect on. Use the prayer journal either as a 52-day or 52-week retreat to overcome stress and worry. There is also a separate edition for women of other Christian faiths: *Pray, Hope, & Don't Worry Women's Prayer Journal For Overcoming Anxiety: A 52-week Guided Devotional of Prayers & Bible Verses to Conquer Stress & Fear.*

Prayer Journal for Catholic Moms:

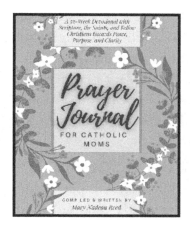

A praying woman finds her strength in Almighty God and the wisdom of His Saints. This Prayer Journal for Catholic Women is a 52-week guided devotional through Scripture and the Saints. The journal includes Bible verses and quotes from the Saints to help you achieve peace, purpose, and clarity.

PRAYER JOURNAL FOR CATHOLIC HOMESCHOOLING MOMS:

A 52-week Guided Devotional with Scripture, the Saints, and fellow Christians towards Peace, Purpose, & Clarity

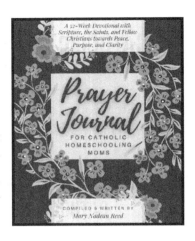

Using a similar 52-day or 52-week format as the *Pray, Hope, and Don't Worry* Prayer Journal above, this journal was created by Mary Nadeau Reed specifically for Catholic homeschooling moms.

ROSARY DEVOTIONALS:
PRAY THE ROSARY WITH ST. JOHN PAUL II

St. John Paul II said "the Rosary is my favorite prayer." So what could possibly make praying the Rosary even better? Praying the Rosary with St. John Paul II!

This book includes a reflection from John Paul II for every mystery of the Rosary. You will find John Paul II's biblical reflections on the twenty mysteries of the Rosary that provide practical insights to help you not only understand the twenty mysteries but also live them.

St. John Paul II said "The Rosary is my favorite prayer. A marvelous prayer! Marvelous in its simplicity and its depth. In the prayer we repeat many times the words that the Virgin Mary heard from the Archangel, and from her kinswoman Elizabeth."

St. John Paul II said "the Rosary is the storehouse of countless blessings." In this new book, he will help you dig even deeper into the treasures contained within the Rosary.

You will also learn St. John Paul II's spirituality of the Rosary: "To pray the Rosary is to hand over our burdens to the merciful hearts of Christ and His mother." "The Rosary, though clearly Marian in character, is at heart a Christ-centered prayer. It has all the depth of the gospel message in its entirety. It is an echo of the prayer of Mary, her perennial Magnificat for the work of the redemptive Incarnation which began in her virginal womb." **Take the Rosary to a whole new level with St. John Paul the Great! St. John Paul II,** *pray for us!*

PRAY THE ROSARY WITH BLESSED ANNE CATHERINE EMMERICH

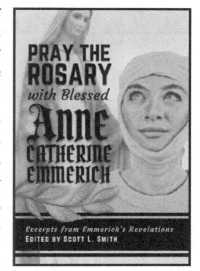

Pray the Rosary like never before! Enter into the mysteries of the Rosary through the eyes of the famous 19th-century Catholic mystic: Blessed Anne Catherine Emmerich.

Incredibly, God gave this nun the special privilege of beholding innumerable Biblical events from Creation to Christ's Passion and beyond. You may have already seen many of her visions, as depicted in the 2004 film The Passion of the Christ.

Never before have Emmerich's revelations been collected in a single volume to help you pray the Rosary. Emmerich was able to describe the events of the Rosary in intimate, exquisite detail. Adding depth and texture to the Gospel accounts, these passages will greatly enhance your experience of the meditations of the Rosary. Enjoy!

Classic Catholic Reprints & New Translations

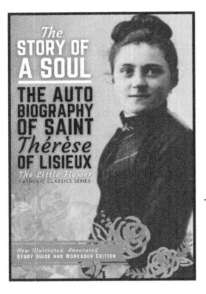

THE STORY OF A SOUL, THE AUTOBIOGRAPHY OF SAINT THERESE OF LISIEUX:
New Illustrated, Annotated Study Guide and Workbook Edition

One of the most popular biographies, not just saint biographies, of ALL TIME. Saint Thérèse, one of the most beautiful souls of modern times, also gave us the most beautiful spiritualities of modern times: the "Little Way" of the "little flower" of Jesus.

Read this with your Catholic book group. This edition features additional sections with study questions to help your group dig into the spiritual wisdom of the Little Flower.

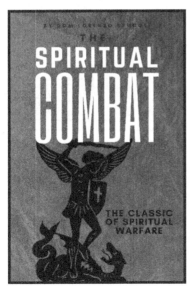

THE SPIRITUAL COMBAT:
The Classic Manual on Spiritual Warfare, by Dom Lorenzo Scupoli

St. Francis de Sales always carried this book in his pocket! The Spiritual Combat is the classic manual of spiritual warfare. Its wisdom has helped form the souls of the Church's greatest saints. Now this book can do the same thing for you. It's no longer fashionable to speak about the realities of the devil and demons, and so the world has become more vulnerable than ever before. The Christian life is a battle between God and the forces of darkness.

This is the *Art of War* for the Christian. Pick up your sword and fight! Here, Father Lorenzo Scupoli helps guide you through this spiritual battle, so that you can win - decisively - the war for your soul. Pick up the sword of prayer and conquer the evil which afflicts you, and through you, your family, your friends, and the world. Don't go into battle alone. Go with Christ and this classic combat manual.

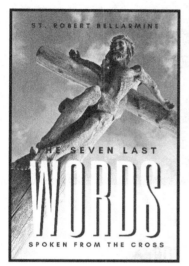

THE SEVEN LAST WORDS SPOKEN FROM THE CROSS BY ST. ROBERT BELLARMINE S.J.

Come, sit at the foot of the Cross!
These seven words were the "last sermon" of the Savior of the World. Jesus' words from the Cross contain everything that the prophets foretold about His preaching, suffering, and miracles.

The Seven Last Words Spoken from the Cross is a powerful reflection on the final words of Jesus Christ. The author, St. Robert Bellarmine, was a major figure in the Catholic Counter-Reformation and his insights are as profound now as ever, perhaps more than ever.

Deepen the Way of the Cross! Use Bellarmine's contemplations of Christ's words to enrich your Lenten journey to Good Friday and Easter. The Seven Last Words Spoken from the Cross is a wealth of insights for the whole of the Christian life, which points always to Christ, who was lifted up on the Cross so "that everyone who believes in Him may have eternal life."

ST. LOUIS DE MONTFORT'S TOTAL CONSECRATION TO JESUS THROUGH MARY:
New, Day-by-Day, Easier-to-Read Translation

Featured on HALLOW, the #1 Catholic Prayer App and narrated by Sister Miriam Heidland!

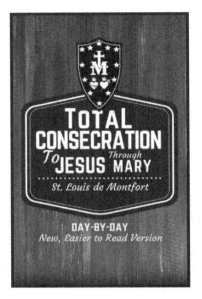

Popes and Saints have called this single greatest book of Marian spirituality ever written. In a newly translated day-by-day format, follow St. Louis de Montfort's classic work on the spiritual way to Jesus Christ though the Blessed Virgin Mary.

Beloved by countless souls, this book sums up, not just the majesty of the Blessed Mother, but the entire Christian life. St. Louis de Montfort calls this the "short, easy, secure, and perfect" path to Christ. It is the way chosen by Jesus, Himself.

PRAYER LIKE A WARRIOR:
Spiritual Combat & War Room Prayer Guide

Don't get caught unarmed! Develop your Prayer Room Strategy and Battle Plan.

An invisible war rages around you. Something or someone is attacking you, unseen, unheard, yet felt throughout every aspect of your life. An army of demons under the banner of Satan has a singular focus: your destruction and that of everyone you know and love.

You need to protect your soul, your heart,

your mind, your marriage, your children, your relationships, your resolve, your dreams, and your destiny.

Do you want to be a Prayer Warrior, but don't know where to start? The Devil's battle plan depends on catching you unarmed and unaware. If you're tired of being pushed around and wrecked by sin and distraction, this book is for you.

Do you feel uncomfortable speaking to God? Do you struggle with distractions in the presence of Almighty God? Praying to God may feel foreign, tedious, or like a ritual, and is He really listening? What if He never hears, never responds? This book will show you that God always listens and always answers.

In this book, you will learn how to prayer effectively no matter where you are mentally, what your needs are, or how you are feeling:
- Prayers when angry or your heart is troubled
- Prayers for fear, stress, and hopelessness
- Prayers to overcome pride, unforgiveness, and bitterness
- Prayers for rescue and shelter

Or are you looking to upgrade your prayer life? This book is for you, too. You already know that a prayer war room is a powerful weapon in spiritual warfare. Prepare for God to pour out blessings on your life.

Our broken world and broken souls need the prayers and direction found in this book. Don't waste time fumbling through your prayer life. Pray more strategically when you have a War Room Battle Plan. Jesus showed His disciples how to pray and He wants to show you how to pray, too.

MATERIALS FOR THE CATHOLIC NERD IN ALL OF US:

CATHOLIC NERDS PODCAST

As you might have noticed, Scott is well-credentialed as a nerd. Check out Scott's podcast: the Catholic Nerds Podcast on iTunes, Spotify, Google Play, and wherever good podcasts are found!

THE THEOLOGY OF SCI-FI:
The Christian's Companion to the Galaxy

NOW ALSO AN AUDIOBOOK! Fold space using the spice mélange and travel from "a long time ago in a galaxy far, far away" to the planet Krypton, from Trantor to Terminus, and back to the scorched skies of earth.

Did you know there is a Virgin Birth at the core of *Star Wars*? A Jewish Messiah of *Dune*? A Holy Family in *Superman*? A Jesus and Judas in *The Matrix*? And the Catholic Church is Asimov's *Foundation*?

This book covers a lot of territory. It spans galaxies and universes. Nevertheless, the great expanse of human imagination will forever be captivated by the events of the little town of Bethlehem.

There is a reason that all of mankind's stories overlap, coincide, correlate, and copy. Like it or not, all mankind bears the same indelible stamp, the mark of Christ. Why should there be a singular story binding us all? Unless we are truly all bound as one human family. At the core of the Monomyth is not another myth, a neat coincidence, but a reality—the reality of Jesus Christ.

At the heart of the Monomyth is a man, a very real man. The God-Man. The source and summit of all hero stories and myths ever told, both before and after those short 33 years in First Century Israel.

LORD OF THE RINGS & THE EUCHARIST
NOW AN AUDIOBOOK!

What is "the one great thing to love on earth", according to J. R. R. Tolkien, the author of The Lord of the Rings? The Eucharist! Tolkien made sure his one great love was woven throughout his books. It's easy to find if you know where to look. In Smith's new book, find Tolkien's hidden Eucharist!

The Lord of the Rings can't be fully understood without understanding its hidden Eucharistic significance. What's more, perhaps: J. R. R. Tolkien can't be fully understood apart from his Catholic identity and his devotion to the Eucharist. **Are you ready to read Lord of the Rings like you never have before?**

WHAT YOU NEED TO KNOW ABOUT MARY BUT WERE NEVER TAUGHT
NOW AN AUDIOBOOK!

Give a robust defense of the Blessed Mother using Scripture. Now, more than ever, every Catholic needs to learn how to defend their mother, the Blessed Mother. Because now, more than ever, the family is under attack and needs its Mother.

Discover the love story, hidden within the whole of Scripture, of the Father for his daughter, the Holy Spirit for his spouse, and the Son for his MOTHER.

This collection of essays and the All Saints University course made to accompany it will demonstrate through Scripture how the Immaculate Conception of Mary was prophesied in Genesis.

It will also show how the Virgin Mary is the New Eve, the New Ark, and the New Queen of Israel.

And For the Catholic Man ...
THE CATHOLIC MANBOOK

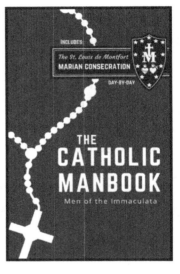

Do you want to reach Catholic Man LEVEL: EXPERT? *The Catholic ManBook* is your handbook to achieving Sainthood, manly Sainthood. Find the following resources inside, plus many others:

- Top Catholic Apps, Websites, and Blogs
- Everything you need to pray the Rosary
- The Most Effective Daily Prayers & Novenas, including the Emergency Novena
- Going to Confession and Eucharistic Adoration like a boss!
- Mastering the Catholic Liturgical Calendar

The Catholic ManBook contains the collective wisdom of The Men of the Immaculata, of saints, priests and laymen, fathers and sons, single and married. Holiness is at your fingertips. Get your copy today.

This edition also includes a revised and updated St. Louis de Montfort Marian consecration. Follow the prayers in a day-by-day format.

BLESSED IS HE WHO ...
Models of Catholic Manhood

BIOGRAPHIES OF CATHOLIC BLESSEDS

You are the average of the five people you spend the most time with, so spend more time with the Saints! Here are several men that you need to get to know whatever your age or station in life.

From Kings to computer nerds, old married couples to single teenagers, these men gave us extraordinary examples of holiness:

- Pier Giorgio Frassati & Carlo Acutis – Here are two extraordinary **young men**, an athlete and a computer nerd, living on either side of the 20th Century
- Two men of royal stock, Francesco II and Archduke Eu-gen, lived lives of holiness despite all the world conspiring against them.
- There's also the **simple husband and father**, Blessed Luigi. Though he wasn't a king, he can help all of us treat the women in our lives as queens.

Blessed Is He Who ... Models of Catholic Manhood explores the lives of six men who found their greatness in Christ and His Bride, the Church. In six succinct chapters, the authors, noted historian Brian J. Costello and theologian and attorney Scott L. Smith, share with you the uncommon lives of exceptional men who will one day be numbered among the Saints of Heaven, men who can bring all of us closer to sainthood.

EVER HEARD OF CATHOLIC HORROR NOVELS?

It's time to evangelize *all* readers …

THE SEVENTH WORD

The FIRST Pro-Life Horror Novel!

Pro-Life hero, Abby Johnson, called it "legit scary … I don't like reading this as night! … It was good, it was so good … it was terrifying, but good."

The First Word came with Cain, who killed the first child of man. The Third Word was Pharaoh's instruction to the midwives. The Fifth Word was carried from Herod to Bethlehem. One of the Lost Words dwelt among the Aztecs and hungered after their children.

Evil hides behind starched white masks. The ancient Aztec demon now conducts his affairs in the sterile environment of corporate medical abortion facilities. An insatiable hunger draws the demon to a sleepy Louisiana hamlet.

Monsignor, a mysterious priest of unknown age and origin, labors unseen to save the soul of a small town hidden deep within Louisiana's plantation country, nearly forgotten in a bend of the Mississippi River. *You'll be gripped from start to heart-stopping finish in this page-turning thriller.* With roots in Bram Stoker's Dracula, this horror novel reads like Stephen King's classic stories of towns being slowly devoured by an unseen evil and the people who unite against it. The book is set in southern Louisiana, an area the author brings to life with compelling detail based on his local knowledge.

THE CAJUN ZOMBIE CHRONICLES
The Catholic Zombie Apocalypse!

How does civilization survive the zombie apocalypse? There's only one institution on earth that hell cannot prevail against. The Church. When the Black Death ravaged Europe in the 14th century, the Church brought humanity back from the brink of extinction. Now again, the dead reign on earth, and we turn to the Church for survival.

NOW ALL AVAILABLE AS AUDIOBOOKS

THANKS FOR READING
Totus Tuus!

Made in the USA
Monee, IL
16 November 2024

70256632R00256